Soviet Defectors

Series Editors: Richard J. Aldrich, Rory Cormac, Michael S. Goodman and Hugh Wilford

This series explores the full spectrum of spying and secret warfare in a globalised world.

Intelligence has changed. Secret service is no longer just about spying or passively watching a target. Espionage chiefs now command secret armies and legions of cyber warriors who can quietly shape international relations itself. Intelligence actively supports diplomacy, peacekeeping and warfare: the entire spectrum of security activities. As traditional inter-state wars become more costly, covert action, black propaganda and other forms of secret interventionism become more important. This ranges from proxy warfare to covert action; from targeted killing to disruption activity. Meanwhile, surveillance permeates communications to the point where many feel there is little privacy. Intelligence, and the accelerating technology that surrounds it, have never been more important for the citizen and the state.

Titles in the *Intelligence, Surveillance and Secret Warfare* series include:

Published:

The Arab World and Western Intelligence: Analysing the Middle East, 1956–1981
Dina Rezk

The Twilight of the British Empire: British Intelligence and Counter-Subversion in the Middle East, 1948–63
Chikara Hashimoto

Chile, the CIA and the Cold War: A Transatlantic Perspective
James Lockhart

The Clandestine Lives of Colonel David Smiley: Code Name 'Grin'
Clive Jones

The Problem of Secret Intelligence
Kjetil Anders Hatlebrekke

Outsourcing US Intelligence: Private Contractors and Government Accountability
Damien Van Puyvelde

Forthcoming:

The Snowden Era on Screen: Signals Intelligence and Digital Surveillance
James Smith

The CIA and the Pursuit of Security: History, Documents and Contexts
Huw Dylan

https://edinburghuniversitypress.com/series-intelligence-surveillance-and-secret-warfare.html

Soviet Defectors

Revelations of Renegade Intelligence Officers, 1924–1954

Kevin P. Riehle

EDINBURGH
University Press

Edinburgh University Press is one of the leading
university presses in the UK. We publish academic
books and journals in our selected subject areas across
the humanities and social sciences, combining cutting-
edge scholarship with high editorial and production
values to produce academic works of lasting
importance. For more information visit our website:
edinburghuniversitypress.com

Edinburgh University Press Ltd
The Tun – Holyrood Road, 12(2f) Jackson's Entry,
Edinburgh EH8 8PJ

First published in hardback by Edinburgh University Press 2020

Typeset in 11/14 Sabon by
Servis Filmsetting Ltd, Stockport, Cheshire
and printed and bound by CPI Group (UK) Ltd,
Croydon, CR0 4YY

A CIP record for this book is available from the
British Library

ISBN 978 1 4744 6723 0 (hardback)
ISBN 978 1 4744 6724 7 (paperback)
ISBN 978 1 4744 6725 4 (webready PDF)
ISBN 978 1 4744 6726 1 (epub)

The views expressed in this book are those of the
author and do not reflect the official policy or position
of the Department of Defense or any US government
agency.

Contents

List of Figures and Tables   vi
Acknowledgements   vii

Introduction   1
1. Early Defectors, 1924–1930   11
2. *Yezhovshchina*-Era Defectors, 1937–1940   45
3. World War II-Era Defectors, 1941–1946   100
4. Early Cold War Defectors, 1947–1951   171
5. Post-Stalin Purge Defectors, 1953–1954   215
Conclusion   264

Appendix: Organisational Changes in Soviet Intelligence
     and State Security, 1918–1954   286
Bibliography   287
Index   320

Figures and Tables

Figures

1.1 Lives of Early Defectors, 1924–1930   15
1.2 Non-Returnees from the Soviet Union during the
     1920s   36
2.1 Origins of *Yezhovshchina*-Era Defectors, 1937–1940   48
2.2 Lives of *Yezhovshchina*-Era Defectors, 1937–1940   50
3.1 Lives of World War II Defectors, 1941–1945   109
4.1 Lives of Early Cold War Defectors, 1947–1951   178
5.1 Lives of Post-Stalin Purge Defectors, 1953–1954   220
5.2 Political Cartoon: 'After the Petrov Affair'   254
6.1 Average Ages of Defectors in Each Group   274

Tables

1.1 Early Defectors, 1924–1930   12
2.1 *Yezhovshchina*-Era Defectors, 1937–1940   46
3.1 World War II-Era Defectors, 1941–1946   101
4.1 Early Cold War Defectors, 1947–1951   172
5.1 Post-Stalin Purge Defectors, 1953–1954   216

Acknowledgements

Several people have been instrumental in completing this thoroughly enjoyable project. Mariah Loukou and Cecilia Notini Burch provided research assistance and access to materials I could not have gotten without their help. The Hoover Institution Archive offered research funding that allowed me to travel to Stanford University and obtain invaluable material in support of this research. Professor Michael Goodman gave expert and patient guidance along the whole path. Most importantly, my wife Crystal and children endured many months of seeing their husband and father working rather than spending time with them. I am grateful for their sacrifice.

Introduction

Defectors are a phenomenon that governments both fear and seek. They repudiate the system from which they came, and, if they held a position of trust, they reveal to the receiving side information about the inner workings of their former country. For the losing side, this can be catastrophic, while for the receiving side it can be a unique and valuable source of information. This book explores defectors from a closed political system – the Soviet Union of the 1920s to 1950s – determining the insights they gave into a notoriously opaque Soviet decision-making process.

For the purposes of this book, a defector is a person who renounces allegiance to one state or cause in exchange for allegiance to another, in a way that the losing side considers illegitimate. While the phenomenon of defection is not unique to states and may affect any organisation, such as a political party or a corporation, this book focuses on defectors from a state, especially a state with a closed political system. A closed political system is one that allows little or no transparency into the decision-making process that governs it. In a closed political system, the authority to change the system is reserved only for a ruling elite; the elite has power over the whole society, leaving no group immune from its control; and laws are constructed to satisfy the demands of the elite.[1] Typically, those outside the elite have little influence on or visibility into the elite's plans, which is accentuated for those outside the system entirely. The domestic and international goals and objectives of a closed political system are known only to a privileged few. Hence, when such a system interacts on the international stage, it obscures its strategies and plans that are focused largely on the interests and survival of the elite. This book examines how the compounded revelations of one category of the Soviet elite, intelligence officers, opened a window into Soviet national security decision-making.

When defectors leave their home and relocate to a new state, they take with them the information they possessed before defection and often communicate it to the receiving state. This is particularly true of intelligence officer defectors, who have privileged access to sensitive information that a government takes great care to keep secret. Intelligence services are an authoritarian leader's direct instrument for answering his highest-priority questions and for protecting the ruling elite. An aggregate analysis of a closed system's intelligence activities as revealed by knowledgeable defectors can uncover the leader's strategic priorities and concerns. Michael Warner stated that, in developing a framework for analysing intelligence systems, 'What the leadership is trying to accomplish or prevent dictates the targets and tempo of intelligence collection and operations.'[2] It is that leadership–intelligence nexus that this book derives from the information revealed by and the characteristics of intelligence officer defectors.

A Soviet intelligence officer enjoyed privileges, freedoms, and access to information that other professionals did not. During the Soviet era, a badge indicating affiliation with the People's Commissariat for Internal Security (*Народный Комиссариат Внутренних Дел*; NKVD) or later, Ministry of State Security (*Министерство Государственной Безопасности*; MGB), implied authority well beyond the superficial rank of the person carrying it. Both military and civilian intelligence officers profited from the advantage of travelling abroad and the freedom to operate in foreign environments unknown to even Soviet diplomats. Several intelligence officer defectors attested to the special access to both comfort items and information that they enjoyed.[3]

In the Soviet system, the relationship between Soviet leaders and their intelligence services existed in two contradictory dimensions. First, their activities reflected the priorities of the Party and the state and they acted as a direct instrument of domestic and foreign policies. Hence, Soviet leaders assigned them the most sensitive and important missions to further those policies. On the other hand, Soviet leaders feared the intelligence services and deterred them from becoming an independent force outside their direct control.[4] On both levels, Soviet leaders kept the intelligence services very close, ensuring that they applied their powerful capabilities only to missions that were in the direct interests of the ruling elite. While the intelligence services enjoyed some independence in their day-to-day operations, Stalin personally determined the general direction of their activities inside the USSR and abroad.[5] One defector, Samuel Gershovich Ginzberg (better known as Walter Germanovich Krivitsky; see Chapter 2), described the relationship between Stalin and his state security chief: 'Any question of policy [Nikolay Ivanovich Yezhov][6] took up with Stalin at once, and whatever the big boss said, he repeated word for word, and then translated into action.'[7] When defectors broke free from the intelligence services, they took with them knowledge of those interests and direction and often passed it on to the receiving country.

This book examines two types of data to show the aggregate insights Soviet intelligence officer defectors provided into the internal workings of the Soviet system. The first type of data consists of intelligence officer defectors' revelations, which they disclosed in a combination of three ways: through documents that they brought with them when they defected; in debriefings by the receiving government(s); and in books, magazine articles, interviews, or public testimony. This data is analysed against a series of questions that yield insights into Soviet strategic thinking:

- What were the intelligence service's operational priorities? What was the intelligence officer tasked with collecting?
- What types of people was the defector tasked with recruiting, influencing, harassing, or in some cases, assassinating?
- How was the defector's service organised and against what missions were its resources allocated?
- What liaison relationships did the defector report or participate in developing or exploiting? What did the service desire to receive from these relationships?
- What besides information about intelligence operations did the defector reveal?

The second type of data consists of meta-information about the defectors, including information about their backgrounds and personal characteristics, which reveals information about the circumstances inside the Soviet Union at the time of their defection. This data includes:

- Motivation for defection: Motivations for defection varied over time due to upheavals, purges, and other internal events, and these variations give some insight into the changing environment inside the Soviet Union.
- Recipient country: The country or organisation to which the defector offered cooperation reflected the defector's belief about what entity could most reliably provide shelter from Soviet retaliation and could use insider information effectively against the Soviet Union. These beliefs were formed from the officer's knowledge about Soviet relations with other countries and expose the mindset and threat calculation within the Soviet system at the time of defection.

In addition to these two primary comparison points, this study also compares demographic data about the defectors:

- Biographical information (ethnic background; age and rank at time of defection).
- Whether/when the defector joined the Communist Party.
- When and under what circumstances the defector joined a Soviet intelligence organisation. How long had the defector been an intelligence officer before defection?
- To what Soviet intelligence organisation did the defector belong? What was the defector's service status (civilian/military; specialisation/directorate; legal/illegal)?

These data show drivers for defection, which, when combined with the information that defectors revealed, gives a more complete picture of what the Soviet intelligence officer could offer and provides insight into the threat perceptions, priorities, and anxieties of the closed Soviet decision-making system.

The time scope of this book begins in 1924, when the first

known defection of a Soviet intelligence officer occurred, and ends with 1954, when purges within the Soviet state security system following Stalin's death and Lavrentiy Pavlovich Beriya's execution forced a surge of intelligence officers to flee. It focuses, therefore, primarily on the rule of Stalin, allowing defectors' information to show the evolution of Stalin's priorities over time.

Definition of Study Population

This study analyses a specific group of individuals who fit all the characteristics of the phrase *Soviet intelligence officer defector*, which is defined as a staff officer of a Soviet intelligence or state security service who detaches him- or herself from that service and physically separates from the Soviet government to take up residence in another country.

First, this study looks at employees of *Soviet* government organisations, and excludes defectors from other countries' intelligence services. While non-Soviet individuals often disclosed valuable information, they spoke from the perspective of someone outside Soviet thinking and culture, and outside the closed Soviet decision-making apparatus.

Second, it looks at *staff officers* of Soviet intelligence services. These include officers from the Soviet military intelligence service and a comparatively larger number of officers from the Soviet civilian intelligence and state security service (see Appendix A for a representation of the changes in Soviet civilian state security organisations up to 1954). This study combines the information from military and civilian officers because of the compounded insights they give into different aspects of Soviet decision-making and the benefit of analysing an intelligence system in its entirety. It focuses on officers within this definition whose defection was genuine and who were not under continued Soviet control. However, in cases where there is debate over a defector's bona fides, this study leans towards including him or her.

This research includes three broad officer duty types: (1) 'legal' cover abroad; (2) 'illegal' cover abroad; and (3) employment within Soviet-controlled territory. In Soviet intelligence jargon, 'legal' cover indicated overt affiliation with a Soviet government establishment abroad, such as at an embassy or trade representation or aboard a Soviet-flagged vessel. Although Soviet government connection was overt and was often accompanied by diplomatic immunity, legal officers' affiliation with the intelligence or security services remained clandestine. An 'illegal' intelligence officer, sometimes called a 'deep cover operative', was trained to work under non-official cover in a foreign environment, using a false identity with no visible ethnic, familial, or business connection to the Soviet Union or to any of its official, or 'legal', establishments. The third category came from within the vast state security apparatus inside the Soviet Union or in Soviet-occupied territory, and included officers who defected by crossing a Soviet-controlled border and those who defected from a Soviet military unit in combat. Individuals in these three categories gave different types of information, with the aggregate of all three presenting a detailed picture of Soviet intelligence and state security priorities and missions.

Finally, this study looks at *defectors*, meaning those who actually separated physically from the Soviet Union. This excludes individuals who were recruited as intelligence agents while remaining in their positions within the Soviet system, who in some cases established emergency escape plans for possible defection but never activated them. These are sometimes erroneously labelled 'defectors in place'.[8] This exclusion is not intended to downplay the importance of those individuals who remained in place and never defected, some of whom revealed substantial information about the Soviet system. However, several things change when an individual becomes a defector. First, the individual moves outside the control and security envelope of his home territory, affording the receiving country greater freedom to collect the defector's information and requiring less stringent security measures than if the individual is an intelligence penetration. As a result, defection offers more time to debrief the officer than is available in short, clandestine meetings.

On the other hand, the defector's information begins to lose currency from the moment of departure from the home country. Some of the defector's information is perishable, like cover positions and locations of fellow intelligence officers, the organisation and structure of work units, and the identities of recruited agents. Almost as soon as a Soviet intelligence service discovered a successful defection, it typically began to recall vulnerable officers and suspend contact with recruited agents until the full extent of the damage could be assessed. The information that has the most enduring lifespan is a defector's strategic insights, which changed more slowly and were not usually impacted by the departure of one individual. It is those broader insights that are the principal focus of this study.

By limiting this analysis to *Soviet intelligence officer defectors*, this study examines individuals who share all of the above characteristics. Even within those limitations, this encompasses a diverse group of one-hundred individuals – ninety-five men and five women – the greatest number ever compiled publicly, forty-two of which have never been previously mentioned in literature. However, as this study relies on open source and declassified data, it does not claim to represent a comprehensive list of all Soviet intelligence officer defectors, about whom much information remains classified.

Public sources in some cases exclude even the names of the defectors. Thus, some individuals in this book are identified by numbers rather than names. The numbers are derived from a KGB book titled *An Alphabetical List of Foreign Intelligence Agents, Traitors to the Homeland, Members of Anti-Soviet Organisations, Collaborators, and Other Wanted Criminals* (*Алфавитный Список Агентов Иностранных Разведок, Изменников Родины, Участников Антисоветских Организаций, Карателей, и Других Преступников, Подлежащих Розыску*). The book contains background information, circumstances of defection, last known location, and disposition in the Soviet legal system for nearly 600 Soviet citizens who defected up to the book's publication in 1969.[9] The book came to the West when Artush Sergeyevich Hovanesyan, an officer from the Armenian Republic KGB, brought a copy when he defected to Turkey in 1972. It became the basis for Vladislav Krasnov's 1985 book, *Soviet Defectors: The KGB Wanted List*,[10] in which Krasnov analysed 470 of the listed individuals whose defections occurred after World War II.

Although Krasnov published an alphabetical list of defectors' names in his book, he redacted the names in his research data (now located in the Hoover Institution Archive) and scrambled their order to prevent correlating names with descriptions. As a result, while some of the entries in the list can be correlated with a defector's name based on circumstantial indicators, others cannot. These are thus identified by the number Krasnov assigned to them in his redacted list.

The data in this book are presented in five chapters reflecting chronological groups of Soviet intelligence officer defectors in that timeframe. The same methodology of compiling and analysing information from and about intelligence officer defectors is applied to each group to allow for cross-comparison. The chronological groups are defined by time periods in Soviet history when intelligence officer defections occurred and the major events that prompted them:

- Early defectors, 1924–1930, beginning with the first case of a Soviet intelligence officer defector up to the enacting of government measures to prevent defection.
- *Yezhovshchina*-era defectors, 1937–1940, including those who fled the Soviet Union for fear of execution in the Great Purge.
- World War II defectors, 1941–1946, including those who were captured and cooperated with Nazi Germany, as well as others who approached Western powers during and immediately after the war.
- Early Cold War defectors, 1947–1951, including the first defectors who benefited from the post-war reversal of Western repatriation policies.
- Post-Stalin Purge defectors, 1953–1954, including those who fled the political upheaval that followed Stalin's and Beriya's deaths.

Each chapter begins with a chart listing the individuals analysed in that chapter, followed by four sections: defectors' personal backgrounds, motivations, receiving countries, and defectors' intelligence and operational targets. The seven-year gap separating the first and second chronological groups is explained at the end of the first chapter. The final chapter identifies three major themes across all five groups, including changing defector motivations over time, fluctuation in Soviet vetting standards for employees with sensitive access, and the evolution of Soviet threat calculations and development of the 'main enemy' concept. Each of these themes reveals aspects of Soviet national security decision-making. In the final analysis, Soviet intelligence officer defectors gave unique insights into the closed Soviet decision-making system regarding the threats it faced, both internal and external, at a time when few other sources were available.

Notes

1. R. J. Rummel, 'The State and Political System', in *Understanding Conflict and War: Volume 2, The Conflict Helix* (Hoboken, NJ: John Wiley & Sons, 1976), Chapter 31.
2. Michael Warner, 'Building a Theory of Intelligence Systems', in Gregory F. Trevorton and Wilhelm Agrell (eds), *National Intelligence Systems: Current Research and Future Prospects* (Cambridge: Cambridge University Press, 2009), 27.
3. See for example, A. I. Romanov (pseudonym of Boris Ivanovich Baklanov), *The Nights Are Longest There: A Memoir of the Soviet Security Services* (Boston: Little, Brown, 1972), 84–5, 145–6, etc.; Alexey Myagkov, *Inside the KGB: An Expose by an Officer of the Third Directorate* (Richmond, UK: Foreign Affairs Publishing, 1976), 64. Aleksandr Kaznacheyev, a co-opted Soviet diplomat who was employed full-time to support the KGB *rezidentura* in Burma, also highlighted the greater access he had to information as an intelligence worker than as a diplomat; see *Inside a Soviet Embassy: Experiences of a Russian Diplomat in Burma* (New York; Philadelphia: Lippincott, 1962), 196–8.
4. See V. P. Artemyev and G. S. Burlutsky, 'Structure and Condition of the Soviet Organs of State Security After World War II', in Simon Wolin and Robert M. Slusser (eds), *The Soviet Secret Police* (New York: Praeger, 1957), 153.
5. See Aleksey Vladimirovich Shavrov, Preface to 1992 edition of Georgiy Agabekov, *ЧК за Работой* (*Cheka at Work*) (Moscow: Отечественные Архивы [Patriotic Archives], 1992).
6. People's Commissar for State Security from 1936 to 1938.

7. W. G. Krivitsky, *I Was Stalin's Agent* (London: Hamish Hamilton, 1939), 38.
8. R. C. S. Trahair, *Encyclopedia of Cold War Espionage, Spies, and Secret Operations* (Westport, CT: Enigma Books, 2012), 462.
9. Hoover Institution Archives (HIA), Vladislav Krasnov Writings file.
10. Vladislav Krasnov, *Soviet Defectors: The KGB Wanted List* (Stanford, CA: Hoover Institution Press, 1986). The redacted list upon which Krasnov based his research, referred to hereafter as the 'KGB Wanted List', is located in HIA, Vladislav Krasnov Writings file.

1 Early Defectors, 1924–1930

The first group of Soviet intelligence officer defectors included sixteen men who broke with their intelligence or state security employer beginning in 1924, when Petr Mikhailovich Karpov became the first known Soviet intelligence officer defector. It extends to 1930, when defectors and their revelations became a vexing problem for the Soviet Union, prompting new laws that threatened stronger consequences for anyone who refused to return home. Eleven held positions in the civilian state security organisation. The remaining five were affiliated with the Intelligence Directorate of the Red Army Staff (Razvedupr), which was responsible for collecting intelligence about foreign military capabilities and exporting Soviet-style revolution in support of the Communist International (Comintern) International Relations Department (*Отделение Международных Связей*; OMS). The careers of these defectors cover the period beginning with the genesis of Soviet intelligence organisations in 1917 up to 1930.

At least half of these defectors had been affiliated with Soviet state security from the earliest years of the ChK. In December 1917, Lenin directed Feliks Edmundovich Dzerzhinsky to form an 'extraordinary commission' (*чрезвычайная комиссия*; ChK) to fight counterrevolutionary activities and to curb criminality that proliferated while the Bolshevik Party consolidated its power over the former Russian empire. The ChK, later called an All-Russian Extraordinary Commission (*Всероссийская чрезвычайная комиссия*; VChK) used a combination of mass arrests, intimidation, and military-style actions to root out anti-Bolshevik elements and to defeat tsarist forces during the Russian civil war that lasted until 1921. These actions laid the foundation on which

Table 1.1 Early Defectors, 1924–1930

Name	Best-Known Alias	Service	Became Intel Officer	Date of Defection	Location of Defection	Receiving Country
Petr Mikhailovich Karpov	Mikhail Georgiyevich Sumarokov	ChK/GPU/OGPU	1917	August 1924	Germany	Germany
Aleksandr Yanovich Sipelgas	Andrey Pavlovich Smirnov	Razvedupr	1920	Late 1924	Finland	France
Vladimir Stepanovich Nesterovich	Mieczyslaw Jaroslawsky	Razvedupr	1924	April 1925	Austria	France
Ignatiy Leonovich Dzevaltovskiy	Ignatiy Lvovich Yurin	Razvedupr	1925	December 1925	Poland	Poland
Stefens	Ivan Vasilyevich Gavrilchenko	ChK/GPU/OGPU	1920	1926	France	France
Unnamed Defector		ChK/GPU/OGPU	??	August 1926	Unknown	Unknown
Mikhail Hendler	Miguel Stein	ChK/GPU/OGPU	before 1922	May 1926	Cuba	United States
Yevgeniy Mikhailovich Kozhevnikov	Eugene Pik	ChK/GPU/OGPU	1918	May 1927	China	China/Japan
Ivan Nikitin		ChK/GPU/OGPU	1923	October 1927	Latvia	Latvia
Yevgeniy Vasilyevich Dumbadze		ChK/GPU/OGPU	1921	June 1928	Turkey	France
Unnamed Defector	Vasiliy Petrovich	OGPU	??	~1929	France	France
Eduard Miller	Peter Peterson	Razvedupr	1927?	March 1930	Latvia	Latvia
Fedor Pavlovich Drugov	Leonard Frantsovich Benar	ChK	1918 (resigned in 1918)	March 1930	Finland	France
Aleksandr Aleksandrovich Sobolev		Razvedupr	1925	April 1930	Sweden	Belgium
Georgiy Sergeyevich Arutyunov	Georgiy Sergeyevich Agabekov	ChK/GPU/OGPU	1920	June 1930	Turkey	France/Belgium
Nikolay Ignatyevich Kiselev	Nikolay Ignatyevich Karpov	ChK/GPU/OGPU	1920	June 1930	Finland	Germany/Czechoslovakia

Soviet state security and intelligence activities rested throughout the history of the Soviet Union. Even today, Russian intelligence and security services celebrate 'Chekists' Day, formally called Security Service Workers' Day, on 20 December each year to commemorate the 1917 founding of the ChK.

Soviet intelligence officer defectors up to 1930 represented a mix of mid-level functionaries and senior-level officers and reflected diversity of backgrounds, the countries to which they defected, targets they were assigned to pursue, and their motivations for defecting. However, despite this diversity, their revelations show some rough trends regarding Soviet priorities and internal struggles during the 1920s.

Personal Backgrounds

The diversity of early defectors' backgrounds was typical of the Soviet Union at the time. Bolshevik forces that took control of the Soviet government in 1917 represented only a small portion of the Russian population, necessitating alliances with other parties and groups to maintain their grip on power. These alliances resulted in a patchwork of backgrounds amongst the members of Soviet institutions, including intelligence and state security organisations. The fourteen defectors in this group for whom personal background information is available[1] represent four broad types: early Bolshevik adherents; former Imperial officers and soldiers; former Socialist Revolutionaries; and former anti-Bolsheviks who were coerced into cooperation.

Early Bolshevik Adherents

Six of the defectors in this group were early members of the Bolshevik Party who joined enthusiastically and initially perceived their service to the Soviet cause to be respectable and honourable. These included Arutyunov, Dumbadze, Dzevaltovskiy, Kozhevnikov, Nesterovich, and the unnamed OGPU officer who defected in August 1926. Nikitin, who may have served in the Red Army in the early 1920s, was possibly a seventh member of this category.[2] These defectors' eventual disenchantment with their Soviet intelligence employment was a particular shock to the Soviet system, especially in light of the trust and senior rank afforded to several of them. These defectors were all in their late teens or twenties when the revolution occurred, and their disenchantment is perhaps the most telling of the Bolshevik activities of the 1920s, which over the course of five to ten years transformed youthful enthusiasm into antagonism and defection.

Former Imperial Officers and Soldiers

In the early days of the Bolshevik regime, some tsarist Imperial military officers and soldiers willingly sided with the Bolsheviks, mostly out of devotion to Russia, not the party. Many of these were given positions of responsibility because of their skills and training, which the Bolsheviks desperately needed. The difference between these individuals and those noted above is that they never joined the Bolshevik Party, even while serving Soviet needs. They include two defectors in this group: Sobolev, who was an Imperial naval officer, and Miller, who was initially drafted into the Estonian Army but deserted and fled to the Soviet Union around 1927. They found themselves at odds with their Bolshevik supervisors.

Former Socialist Revolutionaries

Socialist Revolutionaries (SRs) actively opposed tsarist rule in the twenty years before the February 1917 revolution and held a prominent place in the regime of Aleksandr Fedorovich Kerensky. They competed with Bolsheviks for dominance in Russian politics before the October revolution. But when Bolsheviks took control of the government, the SRs allied with the Bolsheviks and were promised a role in ruling Russia. The promises were short-lived, however, and by the spring of 1918, SRs were exerting greater autonomy and diverging in their policies, while the Bolsheviks began to exclude them from governing positions and round them up as criminals.[3] Karpov and Drugov both began as SRs, and there is no indication they joined the Bolshevik Party.

Active Anti-Bolsheviks

The VChK/GPU cast a wide net in the early days of Bolshevik rule, catching not only those who willingly joined forces with them, but also oppositionists who required fear and threats of death in VChK interrogation 'cellars' to coerce cooperation. Three intelligence officer defectors up to 1930 – Sipelgas, Stefens, and Kiselev – were among these, and all three published highly emotionally charged exposés after their defection, revealing the horrors of their service to Soviet state security.

This diversity represented by these four groups of officers was a temporary phenomenon in Soviet history, and it narrowed significantly after 1930, due to periodic purges that culled out those whose backgrounds did not conform to the strict Bolshevik criteria. Purges ensured that only Komsomol or Communist Party members held a position in a sensitive organisation like intelligence and state security, as reflected in the second group of

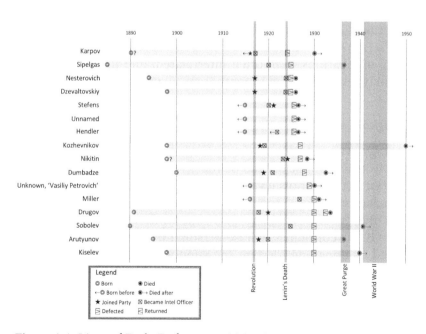

Figure 1.1 Lives of Early Defectors, 1924–1930

defectors (see Chapter 2). Although these purges were not directly related to the phenomenon of defectors, they did result in a cadre of more reliable officers who materially benefited from party membership, and for whom defection represented a higher risk to their livelihood. Even loyal party members were further culled later in the 1930s to root out old Bolsheviks and retain only those with pure Stalinist histories.

Motivations

These backgrounds often formed the basis for the defector's motivation to defect. Defector motivations during this early period showed several common themes:

- Dissonance with Bolshevik policies and ideologies
- Disagreements with Bolsheviks' behaviour
- Recruitment by a foreign intelligence service
- Personal illegal activities and desire for fame and fortune
- Recalls to Moscow

These motivations were often interrelated, and individual defectors may have exhibited more than one simultaneously.

Ideological Dissonance Leading to Personal Conflicts

Ideology was a factor in several intelligence officers' decisions to defect in the first decade of the Soviet Union, generated by a contrast between Bolshevik ideals and practices. Some defectors' disenchantment was founded in the Soviet state security missions they were ordered to perform, while others clashed with their OGPU colleagues, whose personal lives and behaviour they viewed as appalling, despite the supposed emergence of a 'new Soviet man'.[4] This dissonance was probably not rare; several defectors remarked in their writings that other intelligence personnel would similarly be inclined to defect if given the opportunity and the enticement.[5]

Ideological dissonance often grew from the defector's background. As noted above, Karpov and Drugov were SRs, and Karpov claimed to have held anti-Bolshevik views throughout his OGPU career. He stated that he had been considering defecting for several years and that he had arranged for an assignment abroad in 1923 to position himself for a break from the Soviet Union.[6] Drugov also became disenchanted when Bolsheviks began rounding up SRs in 1918, highlighting a fundamental divergence between his views and the VChK's actions. Drugov wrote a formal protest to Dzerzhinsky when he learned that the VChK planned to disarm anarchists.[7] His resignation came after serving on the VChK Collegium for less than five months, sparked by a VChK operation to 'cleanse' Moscow of anarchists, whom Dzerzhinsky blamed for criminal activities, including narcotics trafficking.[8] Drugov did not defect until over ten years after his resignation, but his views only became more antagonistic towards Bolsheviks' treatment of the Soviet people over that time. His experience with the VChK, which he equated with the hated tsarist Okhrana, intensified his ideological motive. After he defected in 1930, he appealed to the West to stop cooperating with the Soviet Union and stop purchasing Soviet goods, which he claimed legitimised a regime he labelled 'a bunch of criminals that has for thirteen years tormented the bodies and souls of a population of dozens of nations and 150,000,000 people on one fifth of the earth's surface'.[9]

Kiselev joined Drugov in claiming that as early as 1923 the Soviet Union earned hard currency for its economy by exporting products that were the result of forced labour.[10] Kiselev also wrote a brief, unpublished account of VChK operations against Cossack counterrevolutionary activities in southern Russia, in which he portrayed 'semiliterate' VChK officers interested chiefly in boozing, womanising, and executing prisoners. Kiselev was assigned as chief of a VChK unit responsible for fighting 'anti-Soviet parties', in which capacity he received orders to go to a nearby village where counterrevolutionaries had reportedly been active. He was ordered to arrest the village residents and demand that they reveal the locations of the counterrevolutionaries. If they refused, he was to execute some of them and repeat the demand. If they still refused, he was to execute every tenth resident in front of all the others. He evaded the assignment by feigning sickness.[11]

Dissonance was not limited to officers who began their careers with divergent views. Even true believers experienced disenchantment with the tasks they were ordered to fulfil. As military attaché in Vienna, Nesterovich, a decorated civil war leader, was responsible for Razvedupr and Comintern operations in the Balkans, among which was the Soviet-sponsored bombing of the St Nedelya Church in Sofia, Bulgaria, on 16 April 1925. The attack killed 120 and injured nearly 500 people.[12] The operation irreparably shook Nesterovich's faith in his mission, and Grigoriy Zinovyevich Besedovskiy, a Soviet diplomat who defected in Paris in 1929, wrote that the Sofia operation left Nesterovich a sullen, changed man. Besedovskiy, who was a consul at the Soviet Embassy in Vienna when Nesterovich served as military attaché, indicated that Nesterovich had begun to have doubts about his tasks even before Sofia. Speaking of his operations in Ukraine during the civil war, Nesterovich reportedly told Besedovskiy, 'Sometimes it seemed to me that I was in command of Mikhelson's hussars who were pacifying the Pugachev peasant uprising. The only difference was that now the senseless revolt was on both sides.'[13] But the Sofia operation was too much for Nesterovich. A few weeks after the bombing, he wrote a letter to his colleagues explaining that his conscience would not allow him to continue in his career, and he disappeared from the embassy.

Dumbadze draws a detailed picture of VChK 'cellars', where interrogators used a variety of psychological and physical means to elicit information from detainees. The first cracks in Dumbadze's idealistic view of Bolshevism began to form when his job required participating in VChK interrogations and summary executions. He described feelings of guilt and repulsion when he witnessed the interrogation of an old woman who refused to reveal the whereabouts of her own son; she was subsequently executed.[14] Echoing descriptions given by Karpov and Sipelgas, Dumbadze reported that a detainee's exit from a 'cellar' was usually for only one of two reasons: the detainee had either been coerced into becoming a VChK informant or was en route to execution. Dumbadze was assigned as a duty officer to witness execution sessions, where VChK executioners would shoot over a dozen people at a time and let the dead bodies fall into shallow common graves. The extreme behaviour of some OGPU officers and party officials created further doubts in his mind about the justness of the Bolshevik system. One individual, whom he named Shulman, was an executioner who used cocaine to dull his senses while fulfilling his deadly assignments.[15] Dumbadze claims that these scenes of brutality and bloodlust 'had a decisive influence on my decision to break with the Bolsheviks'.[16]

Several other defectors expressed their perceptions of hypocrisy and immorality amongst their Soviet colleagues as the reason for their decision to leave the system that attracted such people. Anti-Bolshevik émigré publications were quick to highlight this theme and may have embellished it to some extent. But the consistent flow of stories about Soviet diplomats and government officials living bacchanalian lives while people in the Soviet Union enjoyed few material benefits gives some credence to the accounts.

Dzevaltovskiy's defection grew out of his disenchantment with communist ideas and his confliction with living in a Soviet regime that he viewed as being ruled by intrigue and envy, and which exploited the Russian people. Dzevaltovskiy began his career as an ardent communist supporter, and he probably replaced Nesterovich in Vienna just after the latter's defection. But Nesterovich's disappearance may have affected Dzevaltovskiy. Articles in émigré newspapers after Dzevaltovskiy's defection indicated that he had become convinced of the venality and self-centredness of Bolshevik officials.[17] He had also sent complaints to Moscow earlier in his career about bickering and inaction while he served in the Far Eastern Republic, likely sowing seeds of doubt that contributed to his eventual decision to defect.[18]

Sipelgas complained of the hypocrisy among Soviet representatives who lived luxuriously while the people in Russia struggled. He disparaged the priceless antiques confiscated from the homes of executed aristocratic families and placed in the extravagantly refurbished Russian embassy in Helsinki. He claimed to have witnessed the Soviet military attaché in Helsinki, Ardalyon Aleksandrovich Bobrishchev, frequenting an expensive nightclub with beautiful women on his arm. Sipelgas speculated, 'What if I sent a photo to the Moscow "*Pravda*" and showed the hoodwinked proletariat how the military representative of the Workers and Peasant Army "lives and works".'[19]

Sobolev was also vocal in his negative descriptions of his Soviet colleagues. He described how party чистки ('*cleansings*') gradually stripped the party of sincere members and replaced them with 'enviers, loafers, and grabbers'. He wrote, 'The party is more and more filled with people very low in moral terms . . . who came to the party just for the "rank"'. He asserts that amoral party members reserved for themselves the right to think for the whole country, and that those who did not join the party – including himself – were prohibited from thinking.[20]

A theme of corruption and immorality ran through Stefens' story as well. He described the abusive language used by OGPU superiors to subordinates. Women were especially vulnerable to supervisors' whims: he related a situation where one of his supervisors, a gloomy, brutal man named Evdokimov, would walk through the office, point to a female clerk, and say, 'You are coming to my place today.' Stefens described typical OGPU employees as losers and dropouts whose behaviour as officers reflected their unrefined nature. Stefens never reached a high rank, and he portrayed a sense of being subjugated to a group of crude, boorish supervisors.[21] Nikitin's description of his supervisors was similar, and he claimed his defection resulted from the fear that they might try to kill him.[22] After defecting, he complained that junior OPGU officers toiled in deplorable conditions, being forced to work twenty-hour days with an unbearable workload. Nikitin chose defection to escape those conditions.[23]

Arutyunov discussed love triangles, embezzlement, and laziness that typified life in a Soviet embassy. He especially highlighted extramarital affairs, describing animosity and intrigue surrounding the few women assigned abroad, which often led to recalls to Moscow for inappropriate behaviour.[24] These unflattering accounts of Soviet personnel and brutality fed into a growing antagonism that defectors felt about the party and system as a whole.

Illegal Activities

Soviet intelligence employment offered numerous opportunities to misuse *rezidentura* funds and exact 'fees' from suspects and local citizens, and defectors were not immune to the temptation. Several defectors in this group may have absorbed some of the OGPU's mentality of impunity. In some cases, defectors' own indiscretions and failings were factors in their decision to renounce the Soviet Union.

Karpov's ideological and personal motivations may have been compounded by financial improprieties involving *rezidentura* funds that threatened to have him recalled to Moscow.[25] Russian historian Aleksandr Zdanovich interpreted Karpov's decision to defect as being based on rumours about his illegal activities circulating within the diplomatic mission, leading to his recall to the Soviet Union for punishment.[26] Soviet-inclined sources assert that Karpov's profligate lifestyle in Germany, made possible by $50,000 in OGPU operational funds he brought with him to Berlin, prompted his defection.[27] On the other hand, Karpov himself indicated that he had become the target of a 'web of intrigue, denunciations, slander, and lies' within the Soviet diplomatic mission.[28] Whether his activities were actually illegal or only reported as such by his embassy colleagues is unclear, but a recall to Moscow prompted his decision to defect.

Kozhevnikov's ultimate motivation for defection in 1927 may have been a thirst for fame and fortune. A former Japanese intelligence officer who worked with Kozhevnikov during World War II characterised him as a volatile individual who desired position and honour.[29] He turned to criminal activities to make a living after his defection, including posing as a Shanghai police official and extorting money from businesses, possibly because his revelations were losing their lustre. In one case, Kozhevnikov, along with an American named Maurice Levitsky, demanded 12,000 dollars from a Chinese businessman for a forged licence to set up a gambling house.[30] His post-defection criminal activities likely had roots in relationships that he developed while still active as an intelligence officer.

The defector known only as 'Vasiliy Petrovich' was among a team of OGPU operatives sent to 'arrest' Yuriy Alekseyevich Prasolov, an OGPU officer who was operating in Paris as an illegal using the name Viktor Kepp. Prasolov had considered defecting after gambling away over 9 million francs that he was supposed to use to set up and operate an OGPU cover company. OGPU officers, including 'Vasiliy Petrovich', forcibly returned him to the Soviet Union before he could consummate his plan. Ironically, 'Vasiliy Petrovich' became the defector instead.[31]

Foreign Intelligence Recruitment

Defectors were often accused of espionage on behalf of a foreign power, and in a few cases these accusations were accurate. During the first decade of Soviet intelligence, the countries most often identified as targeting Soviet intelligence officers for recruitment were Britain, Germany, and Finland, which occasionally enticed intelligence officers to defect and took advantage of their insider information for counterintelligence purposes. However, while almost all of the defectors in this group cooperated with at least one foreign intelligence service after their defection, that cooperation was only occasionally instrumental in the decision to defect itself and pre-defection espionage recruitment was the exception, not the norm.

German police, for example, may have facilitated Karpov's defection, making contact with him through his girlfriend Miss Dümmler, who was believed to be a German intelligence agent.[32] He subsequently revealed intelligence about Soviet intelligence activities in Germany, particularly Soviet financing of intelligence operations. Finnish police similarly summoned Sipelgas in the fall of 1921 for questioning about Bolsheviks in Finland. Based on this and other contacts with the Finnish police, he appears to have become a double agent, cooperating with the Finnish political police against Soviet intelligence. The information he revealed to the Finnish authorities led in 1923 to the expulsions of Bolshevik officials from Finland, including the chief of mission, Aleksey Sergeyevich Chernykh, and Sipelgas' Razvedupr supervisor, Bobrishchev.[33] Sipelgas took credit for prompting the expulsions of almost twenty chekists from Finland over a three-year period.[34] Kozhevnikov also had an espionage relationship with a possible SIS officer in the British-run Shanghai Municipal Police, yielding intelligence that contributed to a police raid on the Soviet consulate in Shanghai in May 1927.[35] Espionage relationships gave a foreign country leverage over an officer, sometimes leading to their defection.

Some defectors attempted to assist foreign intelligence services but were received with suspicion rather than being welcomed. Arutyunov approached the British military attaché in Turkey in February 1930, offering to reveal how the OGPU was intercepting British diplomatic mail in Constantinople.[36] The attaché rebuffed him because of suspicions about his bona fides, and because of the objections of his fiancé, Isabel Streater's, family members, who tried their best to separate Isabel from Arutyunov, whom they saw as repulsive.[37]

Not all defectors voluntarily surrendered themselves. Some were captured in the act of fulfilling their intelligence mission and then broke under interrogation. Such was the case with Eduard Miller, a Soviet military intelligence operative specially trained to penetrate Baltic countries. Miller had spent time in Riga in 1928 organising labour demonstrations;[38] he was arrested in March 1930 as he illegally crossed into Latvia for a similar mission.[39] This type of defection became a common phenomenon a decade later during World War II, when many individuals turned against the Soviet Union after being captured by German forces (see Chapter 3).

Recalls to Moscow

The proximate catalyst for defection was often an unexpected 'recall'. A sudden, unexplained summons to return to Moscow often meant that a Soviet official had fallen into disfavour and could expect punishment upon arrival. Recalls could be in the form of a formal message that offered a new position in Moscow, or an abduction that forcibly returned the officer to Moscow. But based on experience seeing their colleagues summoned, along with their knowledge of how the Soviet system operated, intelligence officers understood and dreaded the recall. For some defectors, a recall cemented in their minds the decision to defect that they had been considering for some time.

Sobolev reportedly received instructions from Razvedupr chief Jan Karlovich Berzin, dated 6 April 1930, upbraiding him for unsuccessful collection operations during his previous assignment in Turkey, and directing him to collect military intelligence and to obtain weapons plans, drawings, and manufacturing secrets in Sweden.[40] Within a week after this message arrived he received another communication recalling him to Moscow, ostensibly to take a new position in the People's Commissariat of Foreign Affairs.[41] Just days later, Sobolev announced that he refused to return to the Soviet Union.[42]

Sometimes a 'recall' involved capturing the offender and forcibly returning him to Moscow. Kozhevnikov's proximate motivation for defection was to save his own skin from such an operation. On 18 May 1927, Kozhevnikov was taken to a hospital in the French Concession of Hankow, China, with a sword wound to his head.[43] Kozhevnikov's OGPU supervisor had invited him to a meeting in a safe house, but Kozhevnikov soon recognised a trap where the OGPU, assisted by Chinese thugs, planned to capture him and return him to the Soviet Union. He escaped by jumping out of a window and climbing over a wall, but not before one of the Chinese thugs sliced him with a sword.[44] He subsequently became known for the Tatar skullcap that he wore to hide the scar on his head.[45]

The defector known as 'Vasiliy Petrovich' was not the target of a kidnapping himself, but participated in the forcible recall of another OGPU officer, Prasolov/Kepp. 'Vasiliy Petrovich' was posted to the Berlin OGPU *rezidentura* at the time of Prasolov's operation in Paris, and he, along with two other Berlin-based OGPU officers, travelled to Paris as a 'flying team' to locate and 'arrest' Prasolov/Kepp.[46]

A recall could precipitate from a variety of suspicions, ranging from a simple lack of enthusiasm to embezzlement or espionage. But whether by force or by administrative notice, recalls put fear into the minds of Soviet officials abroad and continued to be a catalyst for defections throughout the rest of Soviet history.

Receiving Countries

Soviet intelligence officer defectors during this period escaped while they were working in a variety of Soviet legal and illegal positions both inside and outside the Soviet Union. Six defectors worked in Soviet government establishments abroad, often under diplomatic cover (Karpov, Berlin; Kozhevnikov, Shanghai; Nesterovich and Dzevaltovskiy, Vienna; Sobolev, Stockholm; and Dumbadze, Istanbul). Six other officers were under illegal cover when they defected (Arutyunov, Istanbul; 'Vasiliy Petrovich' and Stefens, Paris; Sipelgas, Helsinki; Miller, Latvia; and possibly Hendler).

However, the country where Soviet intelligence officers resided when they defected was not necessarily their final destination, which was a more definitive indicator of Soviet perceptions and relations at the time. Defectors chose ultimately to go where they felt they would be safe from Soviet pursuit and where their information would be used effectively against the Soviet Union. Consequently, France was the primary destination of Soviet intelligence officer defectors during the first decade of the Soviet Union. Seven of the sixteen defectors in this group either defected while already in France (Stefens and 'Vasiliy Petrovich'),[47] travelled to France immediately after defection (Sipelgas, Dumbadze, Drugov, and Arutyunov), or defected into French custody (Nesterovich).[48]

However, it was not always the French government that attracted these defectors, but rather the presence of active, vocal, anti-Bolshevik émigrés, particularly former White Army leaders. In addition to these seven who landed in French-controlled territory, other Soviet intelligence officer defectors also sought out anti-Bolshevik émigrés: Karpov, who defected in Germany, approached a White Army officer to announce his defection. He subsequently cooperated with well-known anti-Bolshevik activist Vladimir Grigoryevich Orlov, contributing his OGPU knowledge to Orlov's anti-Bolshevik operations, which landed him in jail. Orlov's autobiography indicates that anti-Bolshevik émigrés in Germany debriefed Karpov for several months, during which he disclosed 'everything that he knew about Bolshevist activities'.[49] Sobolev, who defected in Sweden, also published extensively in anti-Bolshevik émigré publications after he moved to Belgium.

In reality, these individuals defected not to a foreign power, but to an anti-Bolshevik cause, which loomed large in the early Soviet national security threat calculus. Soviet intelligence collection, influence, and assassination operations were predominantly directed against Russian anti-Bolshevik émigrés and White Army leaders wherever they resided, particularly in Western Europe, even though the White Army leadership was divided and posed little military threat to the Soviet Union after its evacuation from Ukraine in 1923. This fixation on external opposition drove defectors' choices of post-defection destination and was a unique aspect of this early period.

Britain and the United States factored significantly less as destinations for these early defectors than France, contrary to the situation that developed ten years later. In the case of Britain, this was more a result of British policy than a reflection of defectors' intentions. Although Kozhevnikov and Arutyunov approached British representatives to offer information, they were viewed with suspicion and neither was admitted into Britain. Arutyunov would have preferred to land in the UK, both because of his British fiancé Isabel Streater and because Britain was his primary target through most of his career and he possessed information of interest to the British government, but he was blocked. Hendler was alone in ending up in the United States, first offering his services to the US embassy in Havana in May 1926 using the name Miguel (Mikhail) Stein, to little effect, and eventually travelling to New York, albeit not contacting the US government until several years after he arrived.[50]

At least three of these defectors were not posted abroad when they defected, but instead crossed an international border from within the Soviet Union and surrendered themselves to foreign authorities. Nikitin walked into Latvia and surrendered.[51] Drugov[52] and Kiselev[53] crossed into Finland, although Finland was not their final destination; Drugov continued to France and Kiselev travelled to Germany and then Czechoslovakia.[54] Miller also crossed the border into Latvia, but his border crossing was originally intended for operational purposes, not defection. These border-crossers viewed Latvia and Finland as easily accessible safe havens from Soviet revenge, possibly reflecting a common perception among Soviet intelligence officers, corresponding to Nikitin's information, which indicated that the OGPU labelled people across the border as the 'enemy'.[55] Defectors may have viewed surrendering to the 'enemy' as the safest course because they could feel most sure that the receiving power would not turn them back. These threat perceptions derived from OGPU operational priorities at the time, and translated into the materials that these officers revealed after their defection.

Operational Priorities

Over the 1920s, Soviet national security priorities evolved from initial anxiety about internal threats to an ever-widening circle of external threats. Soviet state security was established initially to secure the revolutionary regime at home, but grew to neutralise anti-Soviet forces in the civil war, then to counter foreign sponsorship of those anti-Soviet forces, and finally to penetrate foreign adversaries abroad. Concurrent with these priorities was the mission of exporting the Bolshevik revolution around the world, which often conflicted with the simultaneous objective of securing worldwide recognition of the Soviet regime. Soviet intelligence officer defectors' information illustrated this evolution of priorities.

Internal Security

From its foundation, the VChK focused its attention on solidifying the Bolshevik revolution inside the Soviet Union. The VChK's full name – the All-Union Extraordinary Commission to Combat Counterrevolution, Profiteering, and Corruption – reflected the internal enemies that the newly formed Bolshevik regime faced. As Bolsheviks fought to establish control over the former Russian empire, Soviet state security organisations fanned out across Soviet territory to defeat anti-Bolshevik influences. Arutyunov, Drugov, Dumbadze, Karpov, Kiselev, Kozhevnikov, Sipelgas, and Stefens all joined a Soviet intelligence or security organisation between 1917 and 1921, when the Bolshevik regime faced strong resistance from White forces in Ukraine, Southern Russia, and the Far East, and from Poland, which entered into a war with the Bolshevik regime in 1919. Arutyunov, Dzevaltovskiy,

Nesterovich, and Sobolev, as well as the unnamed officer who defected in August 1926 and probably Nikitin, also served in or led Soviet military units that countered White forces before they joined a Soviet intelligence organisation. They all illustrate the formative period of Soviet state security, including leadership, finances, and operations against deserters, oppositionists, and insurgent groups like Ukrainian and Georgian nationalists and Central Asian Basmachis.

Internal security operations led to the detention of thousands of people in VChK 'cellars' and to executions that the VChK used to control the population and deter opposition. Defectors gave first-hand accounts of 'cellars': Karpov, Sipelgas, and Stefens spent time in VChK detention facilities themselves before being coerced into cooperation; Drugov was in charge of disposing of thousands of detainees in Petrograd; Arutyunov and Dumbadze witnessed detainee interrogations and executions as VChK officers; and Kiselev worked as a prison officer in the Directorate of Northern Special Purpose Camps (*Управление Северных Лагарей Особого Назначения*; USLON) corrective labour complex. All of these defectors painted a grim picture of existence in a Soviet detention facility and the unhappy fate of many detainees.

Drugov claimed the VChK's internal security methods looked uncomfortably similar to those of the dreaded Okhrana, which had pursued, arrested, and exiled Bolsheviks and SRs before the revolution. According to Drugov, the VChK inherited many of the Okhrana's deception and interrogation techniques, but took them to a higher level because of the VChK's larger budget and its greater willingness to use violence. Drugov was well placed to expose the cognitive contradictions that early revolutionaries sensed between the new regime's foundational ideals and the necessity of using violence and deception to secure the revolution's future. He wrote about early VChK officers' soul-searching that the similarity with the Okhrana caused:

> Each of us felt in the depth of our souls that that we were called upon to create something similar to the old Okhrana – and we were ashamed of the thought. It was completely obvious that the very character of the task before us would make it necessary to employ a system

of surveillance and denunciations (of the latter, by the way, we had already accumulated quite a few). Who will fill the role of 'stoolies'? On the one hand, the thought sickened the revolutionaries, but on the other, such a task could only be assigned to people who were devoted to the revolution. How could that be?[56]

While many VChK officers, including several in the *Yezhovshchina*-era group (see Chapter 2), endorsed the brutal 'Red Terror' methods employed by VChK and its successors, the methods were too much for these early defectors and contributed to their decision to break with the Soviet Union.

Foreign Ties to Anti-Bolshevik Resistance

As the Bolshevik regime pushed opposition forces out of Russian territory and the immediate threat of internal collapse subsided, the circle of Soviet state security priorities widened to include Russian émigrés abroad and their external support. Foreign actions that attracted VChK/GPU/OGPU wrath ranged from benign, like a foreign government welcoming anti-Soviet émigrés, to provocative, like harbouring White generals, to belligerent, like providing weapons and material support to insurgent operations.

The VChK's International Section (*Иностранный отдел*; INO) was formed in late 1919, nearly two years after the VChK's foundation. It was initially focused on hunting anti-Soviet émigrés and defectors abroad, luring them back to the Soviet Union if possible, or assassinating them if necessary. Assassinations abroad were reserved for prominent White Army commanders and high-level defectors, such as Nesterovich and Dzevaltovskiy, whom the INO tracked down a few months after their defections in 1925; tsarist General Aleksandr Pavlovich Kutepov in France in 1930; and Razvedupr illegal agent Vitold Shturm de Shtrem, who threatened to defect in 1933. Arutyunov claimed involvement in the 1922 assassination of Enver Pasha, who was leading a Basmachi revolt in Turkestan.[57] Later, Arutyunov himself avoided an assassination plot in 1932, but disappeared and was presumed killed in 1937.

Sipelgas monitored foreigners' connections to White émigrés as an OGPU officer in Finland. His intelligence collection objectives included the following:

- List all Russian émigrés with their addresses.
- Become familiar with and trusted by White Army leaders in Finland.
- Report on the address and activities of Colonel Mitskevich, a close associate of White General Yevgeniy-Ludvig Karlovich Miller. Obtain his photograph.
- Recruit attractive young women among local Russian émigrés.[58]

Foreign intelligence service support to oppositionists was of particular concern, and the INO launched multiple operations to identify, deceive, and neutralise that support. As early as 1923, Arutyunov was tasked to collect evidence to validate a Soviet perception that the British were supplying weapons and money to Basmachis to fight the Bolsheviks in Turkestan.[59] By the late 1920s, OGPU operations targeted British, French, Finnish, Chinese, German, and Baltic republics' intelligence services, viewing them as enemies giving aid to anti-Soviet émigré groups abroad.

Conversely, while the INO tried to interrupt foreign support to anti-Soviet oppositionists, defectors revealed Soviet efforts to foster and assist other countries' oppositionist and revolutionary movements, including Comintern-sponsored covert influence and terrorist operations, particularly in countries with vulnerable anti-Soviet regimes. By 1923, Sipelgas had become the Razvedupr illegal *rezident* in Finland and was involved in planning a Bolshevik uprising that occurred but failed in Reval (Tallinn), Estonia, in December 1924.[60] Nesterovich, Dzevaltovskiy, Hendler, and Kozhevnikov all had connections to Soviet sponsorship of Bulgarian communist revolutionaries, including the bombing of St Nedelya church in Sofia in April 1925. Kozhevnikov was also involved in Soviet support to Chinese revolutionaries from 1925 to 1927, and Kozhevnikov and Arutyunov both participated in Soviet support to Indian revolutionaries in 1927.[61] Miller supported labour demonstrations in Latvia in 1929, and was en route to a similar mission when Latvian border police arrested him crossing the border in 1930.[62] Later defectors cast additional light on these revolutionary activities, as well as others in Germany, Hungary, and Persia (see Chapter 2).

However, assassination and revolutionary support operations came with a cost, and the Soviet Union was forced to balance covert operations against political blowback. Arutyunov recounts that several planned assassinations, like those against Besedovskiy and former Soviet official Boris Georgiyevich Bazhanov, were suspended because of the sensitivity of committing violent acts abroad and the possibility that the diplomatic and public relations consequences could outweigh the benefit of eliminating an irritating individual.[63]

Great Britain, France, and Germany

Of the countries that Soviet intelligence viewed as most threatening, Great Britain stood at the forefront, followed by France and Germany. Soviet intelligence saw a British hand behind anti-Soviet events around the world, and British influence in South Asia, the Middle East, China, and the Balkans weighed heavy in Soviet national security decision-making, and correspondingly in Soviet intelligence operations.

Both Dzevaltovskiy's and Kozhevnikov's missions in China involved counterweighing British, French, and German influence as early as 1921. When Dzevaltovskiy was posted to Beijing representing the nominally independent Far Eastern Republic, he was responsible for persuading China to contradict its powerful allies, notably Great Britain and France, and recognise the new Bolshevik regime. Although he failed to convince China, he did reach a compromise in which China would disestablish diplomatic recognition of the former tsarist government and close the Russian embassy until a stable government took control in Moscow.[64]

The INO sought to discredit Nesterovich after his defection by claiming he was tied to British intelligence. Within a few months of Nesterovich's assassination his name appeared in a group of purported OGPU memos, called the 'Trilisser documents', made public by Karpov. One of the documents, dated 1 October 1925, claimed that Nesterovich had maintained a secret relationship with the famous British adventurist Sidney Reilly for several years.[65] The apparent purpose for the intentionally leaked forgeries was to cast a shadow on Nesterovich's revolutionary record and paint him as a British intelligence collaborator even before his defection.

After the mid-1920s, Britain dominated Arutyunov's activities, as the OGPU assumed British involvement in China, Turkestan, Afghanistan, Iran, Palestine, and Turkey. According to Arutyunov, the OGPU saw nefarious motives in any British move in Asia.[66] Arutyunov's decision to approach the British in Constantinople to request asylum was an indicator of the place that Britain occupied in Soviet national security thinking. According to Arutyunov, when British Secretary of State for Foreign Affairs Austen Chamberlain sent a diplomatic note to the USSR threatening to sever diplomatic relations in retaliation for Soviet interference in UK internal affairs, the Politburo ordered all Soviet covert influence activities in the Far East suspended.[67] Britain followed through on the threat on 12 May 1927, after MI5 raids on the All-Russian Cooperative Society (ARCOS) in London uncovered evidence of Soviet clandestine activities in the UK. The concurrent exposure of Soviet support to Chinese nationalists directly fed this break in Soviet–British relations. The previous month, Chinese troops, supported by European powers, raided the Soviet Embassy in Peking, seizing documents showing Soviet instigation of revolutionary activities in China. Samples from the contents of this raid showing Soviet interference in the Nationalist government were published on 11 May 1927, the day before the ARCOS raid, in the *North China Daily News*, an English-language newspaper in Shanghai affiliated with the British consulate.[68] A short time later, the Shanghai Municipal Police raided the Soviet Consulate in Shanghai, informed by Kozhevnikov's information about espionage operations being run from the consulate and by information seized in the Peking raid.[69] According to a statement by Chamberlain in the British House of Commons, the raid was partially based on the 'intensity of hostile feeling against the Soviet Consulate and its activities in Shanghai'.[70] The raid led to prosecutions of 15 Russians in September 1927, for 'agitating to produce internal disturbances in China'.[71]

British influence in Europe also drew Soviet intelligence interest. Karpov provided a detailed list of Soviet military, diplomatic, and economic intelligence collection priorities showing that, as of 1924, Soviet intelligence focused resources on what he called the 'Big and Little Ententes'.[72] The Big Entente, known in English as the Triple Entente, consisting of Great Britain, France, and pre-revolutionary Russia, was formed before World War I as a counterweight to the triple alliance of Germany, Austria-Hungary, and Italy. The Little Entente, consisting of Czechoslovakia, Yugoslavia, and Romania, was founded through a series of interlocking treaties in 1921 and 1922, designed to counter a resurgence of the Austro-Hungarian Empire. The OGPU *rezidentura* in Berlin was the centre of Soviet operations in Europe directed against these alliances, in which Great Britain played a key role.

Sipelgas's collection priorities from 1921 to 1925 also included Britain in conjunction with other Western powers. He was tasked to recruit agents in the Helsinki-based consulates of Great Britain, along with the USA, France, and Italy; to report any changes in the appearance of those countries' visas, stamps, signatures, and secret marks; and to be alert for British and American agents working in Finland.[73] Soviet intelligence viewed Britain and its allies as the primary foreign threat to the Bolshevik regime.

United States

Although Sipelgas's operational priorities in Finland included collection against the US consulate, the United States held a significantly less prominent place in Soviet intelligence targeting in the 1920s than European powers. OGPU operations in relation to the United States divided into two primary categories: clandestine influence campaigns to persuade the US government to recognise the Soviet regime diplomatically, and operational support activities using US territory and passports. When Karpov defected in 1924, most major Western European countries had established diplomatic relations with the Bolshevik regime. Within the United States, however, the question of diplomatic recognition was a topic of heated debate, and the United States withheld recognition until November 1933. In the absence of US diplomatic recognition, the

Soviet Union maintained the Amtorg Trading Company in New York, which represented Soviet commercial interests and acted as a *de facto* diplomatic representation. Hendler revealed some of the first information exposing Amtorg as a Soviet intelligence operational platform, which, during the 1920s, focused much of its operations on persuading the US government to recognise the Soviet regime.[74]

Karpov's 1929 trial in Germany promoted a Soviet narrative claiming widespread, spontaneous US support for diplomatic recognition. The trial was to determine whether documents that Karpov and his co-defendant Vladimir Grigoryevich Orlov had sold to a journalist were forgeries. The documents in question claimed that two American senators, William Borah and George Norris, both vocal proponents of opening US diplomatic and commercial relations with Moscow, had received bribes from the Soviet Union for their support.[75] The court convicted Karpov and Orlov of fraud, effectively diverting attention from allegations of Soviet collusion in the US diplomatic recognition process and shielding Borah and Norris from criticism for their pro-Soviet positions.[76] Soviet press at the time stated that Karpov's and Orlov's convictions 'deprived non-recognition of all of its props'.[77] Simultaneously, it discredited Karpov, the first intelligence officer defector in Soviet history.

Conclusion

The sixteen men in the Early Group of Soviet intelligence officer defectors represented the diversity of early Soviet officials, ranging from ardent young Bolsheviks who enthusiastically joined a Soviet intelligence service to anti-Bolsheviks whose induction into the service was by coercion. They revealed a gradually broadening ring of threats, initially focused internally in reaction to opposition to the Bolshevik takeover. As the civil war wound down, threats expanded to foreign powers' and émigré groups' support to the anti-Bolshevik opposition, and then to the foreign powers themselves. By 1925, collection requirements included military and political information about the entities that the Soviet Union perceived as posing the greatest threats, particularly the anti-Bolshevik opposition abroad, Great Britain, and France. These defectors also revealed the relationship between the Comintern and Soviet intelligence and state security services, initially the Razvedupr and then the OGPU, and those services' use of the Comintern for intelligence collection and covert revolutionary support. They offered some of the first indicators of direct Soviet participation in attempted revolutions in Germany, Bulgaria, Estonia, Latvia, and China at a time when the Soviet Union claimed the Comintern was a spontaneous gathering of like-minded socialist parties. Even ardent Bolsheviks lost their enthusiasm when they recognised that Soviet state security had inherited many methods from the hated Okhrana and was conducting violent operations around the world.

Interim Period from 1930 to 1937

Before proceeding to the second chapter, some explanation is needed to account for the longest gap in time between Soviet intelligence officer defectors in the entire history of the Soviet Union, which lasted from 1930 to 1937. During that time, no defectors who fit the criteria for this study broke with the Soviet Union. This absence may be explained by recognition within the Soviet leadership that defectors and 'non-returnees' had become a serious problem and needed a solution.

The year 1930 was the peak time for Soviet intelligence officer defectors. Information about and by seven of the sixteen defectors in this group appeared in print in 1930. Miller, Drugov, Kiselev, Sobolev, and Arutyunov all defected in 1930 and prompted press references to their defections. In addition, Sipelgas and Dumbadze, who had defected in previous years, published writings, and Hendler made himself known in 1930. This followed Karpov's highly publicised trial just a few months earlier in late 1929.

The peak in 1930 was the culmination of a disturbing trend in numbers of 'non-returnees' and defectors during the 1920s. Russian historian Vladimir Genis, in his study of Soviet

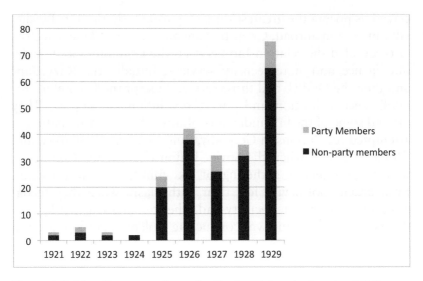

Figure 1.2 Non-Returnees from the Soviet Union during the 1920s

'non-returnees' in the 1920s and 1930s, showed that numbers were small in the first few years after the revolution, but by 1926 the numbers began to grow. By 1929, seventy-five Soviet citizens refused to return to the Soviet Union, of which ten were Communist Party members. Genis states that the problem peaked in the late 1920s, with 190 people refusing to return to the Soviet Union between October 1928 and August 1930.[78] Although intelligence officers were only a small part of this overall number, their defections showed similar trends and were particularly irritating because of the sensitive, and often unflattering, information they revealed.

Defectors publicity embarrassed the Soviet leadership. In typical Stalinist fashion, the response to this trend was to make refusal to return to the Soviet Union a crime against the state. In November 1929, the Presidium of the USSR Central Executive Committee adopted the 'Resolution on Declaring as Outlaws Official Citizens of the USSR Abroad Who Defect to the Camp of the Enemies of the Working Class and Peasants and Refuse to Return to the USSR', which defined any Soviet citizen sent abroad on official business who refused to return to the Soviet Union as a traitor.[79]

Stalin addressed the problem of 'non-returnees' publicly with the party leadership for the first time at the 16th Party Congress in the fall of 1930.[80] The law on non-returnees resulted in a significant drop in the number of non-returnees, with only eleven registered in 1932 and five in 1933.[81]

In March 1934, a Soviet military pilot named Vakhromeyev flew his airplane across the border into Manchuria and defected.[82] This event prompted another angry reaction from Stalin, and only a few weeks later the Politburo adopted a resolution, 'Proposal of Comrade Gamarnik in Connection with the Vakhromeyev Case', which partially restored Party control over military units. In June, the Politburo adopted another resolution, 'Addition to the All-Union Law on State Crimes of Articles on Betrayal to the Homeland', which amended Section 58 of the Soviet penal code and treated flight across the border, either on foot or by air, as a treasonous act that inflicted damage on the state power and independence of the USSR.[83] The penalty for treason for a civilian was ten years' imprisonment and confiscation of all property at the least, and a death sentence at the most severe. For a military or state security member, the option of ten years in prison was omitted, leaving only the death penalty.[84] All travel abroad for personal reasons was forbidden. Any foreign travel required official sanction, which included a check on the traveller's trustworthiness and accompaniment by state security minders.[85]

OGPU/NKVD officers during this time were entrusted with monitoring and ensuring loyalty among the few Soviet citizens authorised to travel abroad. These measures had a chilling effect on defectors, especially those given the special privileges of intelligence officers, until a force even more intense than being labelled a traitor began again to drive Soviet intelligence officers to consider defecting. That force was the Great Purge.

Notes

1. No information is available about the personal backgrounds of Hendler and the defector known as 'Vasiliy Petrovich'.
2. SIS memo dated 11 January 1927, TNA, KV 3/11, serial 50a.

3. Lutz Häfner, 'The Assassination of Count Mirbach and the July Uprising of the Left Socialist Revolutionaries in Moscow, 1918', *Russia Review*, vol. 50, issue 3 (July 1991), 324–44.

4. Sobolev discussed this at length; see 'Их Шансы' ('Their Chances'), *Vozrozhdenie*, 18 May 1930, 4–5.

5. See, for example, 'Дело Советских Шпионов в Латвии' ('The Case of Soviet Spies in Latvia'), *Vozrozhdenie*, 24 July 1928, where Nikitin makes this claim.

6. Partial transcript of the trial of Vladimir Orlov and Peter Pawlonowski, 3 July 1929, sent to Washington as an enclosure to US Embassy Berlin cable number 4736, dated 19 July 1929, which reported the results of the trial; NARA, RG 59, Central Decimal Files, 1910–1949, 811.44, Borah, William E.

7. Feodor Drugoff, 'Моя Биография' ('My Biography'), handwritten statement given to Finnish police, National Archives of Finland, State Police (Valpo I) files, Box 102, folder 11033.

8. 'Беседа с сотрудником газеты «Известия» о разоружении анархистов в Москве' ('Conversation with an *Izvestiya* Colleague about the Destruction of Anarchists in Moscow'), *Izvestiya VTsIK*, 16 April 1918. Aleksandr N. Yakovlev Archive, <http://www.alexanderyakovlev.org/fond/issues-doc/1018183> (last accessed 13 March 2020).

9. L. Benar (pseudonym of Drugov), 'Нации в Плену' ('Nations in Captivity'), 20 March 1930, National Archives of Finland, State Police (Valpo I) files, Box 102, folder 11033; Fedor Pavlovich Drugov, 'С Дзержинским в ВЧК: Исповедь раскаявшегося чекиста' ('With Dzerzhinskiy in the VChK: The Confession of a Repentant Chekist'), *Иллюстрированная Россия* (*Russia Illustrated*), 7 February 1931, 8–9.

10. N. I. Kiselev-Gromov, *Лагери Смерти в СССР: Великая братская могила жертв коммунистического террора* (*Death Camps in the USSR: The Mass Grave of the Victims of Communist Terror*) (Shanghai: N. P. Malinovskiy, 1936), 152.

11. N. Kiselev, *Борьба с Бандидатами на Кубани?* (*Fight against Bandits in Kuban?*), HIA, Boris Nicolaevsky Collection, Box 182, Folder 27 (microfilm reel 155).

12. Richard J. Crampton, *A Short History of Modern Bulgaria* (Cambridge: Cambridge University Press Archive, 1987), 101–2.

13. Gregory Bessedovsky, *Revelations of a Soviet Diplomat* (London: Williams & Norgate, 1931), 54–5. Nesterovch was referring to the 1773–5 peasant uprising lead by Emelyan Ivanovich Pugachev against Catherine the Great. General Ivan Ivanovich Mikhelson, a

Russian imperial cavalry commander, was tasked with leading the campaign to quell the revolt.

14. Yevgeniy Dumbadze, *На службе Чека и Коминтерна. Личные воспоминания* (*In the Service of the Cheka and Komintern: Personal Reminiscences*) (Paris: Mishen, 1930), 50–2.

15. Ibid. 60–4. Igor Simbirtsev described probably the same Shulman, who eventually went insane, see *ВЧК в ленинской России. 1917–1922: В зареве революции* (*VChK in Lenin's Russia, 1917–1922: In the Glow of the Revolution*) (Moscow: Tsentropoligraf, 2008), Chapter 9, '*Кровавые Годы*' ('The Bloody Years').

16. Dumbadze, *In the Service of the Cheka and the Komintern*, 59.

17. 'Развал Изпутри: Большевик Дзевалтовский Бежал из Советской России' ('Crumbling from Within: Bolshevik Dzevaltovskiy Escaped from Soviet Russia'), *Vozrozhdenie*, 14 November 1925, 1; 'Вечерние Известия' ('Evening News'), *Последние Новости* (*Latest News*), 14 November 1925, 1.

18. Telegram from Dzevaltovskiy to the Politburo, 14 March 1920, HIA, Soviet Communist Party and Soviet State Microfilm Collection, 1903–1992: Russian State Archives of Social and Political History (RGASPI), Reel 2.1501, File 86: Far Eastern Republic.

19. Andrey Pavlovich Smirnov (pseudonym of Sipelgas), 'Записки агента Разведупра' ('Notes of a Razvedupr Agent'), *Vozrozhdenie*, 11 March 1930, 4; 26 April 1930, 3. Throughout 'Notes of a Razvedupr Agent' Sipelgas refers to the exorbitant amounts of money the VChK/GPU spent on operations in Finland, as well as on expensive food, clubs, gala balls, and the luxurious refurbishment of the Russian Embassy in Helsinki. See also Ben Hellman, 'Писатель Алекцандр Сипельгас, он же разведчик А. Смирнов. Русско-финско-эстонская загадка' ('Author Alexander Sipelgas, also known as Intelligence Officer A. Smirnov: Russo-Finno-Estonian Riddle'), in *Встречи и столкновения: Статьи по русской литературе* (*Meetings and Clashes: Articles on Russian Literature*), Slavica Helsingiensia 36 (Helsinki: Helsinki University Press, 2008), 216.

20. A. Sobolev, 'Записки Невозвращенца' ('Notes of a Non-Returnee'), *Vozrozhdenie*, 17 May 1930, 2.

21. 'Нравы и Работа ГПУ' ('The Mores and Work of the GPU'), *Vozrozhdenie*, 11 September 1926, 2.

22. US Embassy, Riga, Latvia, dispatch, 10 September 1928; NARA, RG 59, M-316, 861.20260 P/5 (microfilm reel 89).

23. 'The Case of Soviet Spies in Latvia', *Vozrozhdenie*, 24 July 1928.

24. See, for example, Agabekov, *The ChK at Work*, 72–3.

25. Interregional Public Assistance Foundation of Strategic Security (IPAFSS), 'Сумароков Михаил Георгиевич' ('Sumarokov, Mikhail Georgiyevich'), in the series Turncoats and Traitors, 5 January 2013, <http://www.fssb.su/history-state-security/history-state-secu rity-traitors/41-1924-sumarokov-mihail-georgievich.html> (last accessed 13 March 2020).

26. Aleksandr Aleksandrovich Zdanovich, *Свои и чужие: интриги разведки* (*Ours and Theirs: Intrigues of Intelligence*) (Moscow: OLMA Media Group, 2002), 195–202.

27. IPAFSS, 'Sumarokov, Mikhail Georgiyevich'.

28. Biography of Peter Pavlonovsky (Sumarokov), submitted as a statement in his trial in July 1929, HIA, Boris Nicolaevsky Collection, Box 217, Folder 6 (Microfilm 187).

29. US Strategic Services Unit (SSU), *Japanese Intelligence Organizations in China*, 4 June 1946, 87, NARA, RG 263, Entry ZZ-19, box 40 (CIA FOIA site).

30. 'Mysterious Capt. Pick: Strange Story of a Man of Many Names', *The Daily Herald* (Shanghai), 10 July 1929; clipping in TNA KV 2/1895, serial 9a.

31. 'Les Conjurés du Destin' ('The Conspirators of Destiny'), *Détective*, 14 February 1930, 4–5; Grigoriy Z. Besedovskiy, 'Гепеу за Границей' ('GPU Abroad'), *Russia Illustrated*, 15 February 1930, 1–2. Prasolov/Kepp's kidnapping was also briefly mentioned in N. Alekseyev, 'Темные Дельцы на Службе СССР' ('Dark Dealers in the Service of the USSR'), *Vozrozhdenie*, 14 May 1931, 2.

32. Igor Anatolyevich Damaskin, *100 великих разведчиков* (*100 Great Intelligence Officers*) (Moscow: Veche, 2001), published online at <http://fisechko.ru/100vel/razved/60.htm> (last accessed 13 March 2020); Tsarev and Costello, *Deadly Illusions: The KGB's Orlov Dossier Reveals Stalin's Master Spy* (New York: Crown, 1993), 52–3.

33. Hellman, 'Author Alexander Sipelgas', 215. Bobrishchev was expelled from a subsequent assignment in Iran four years later, as discussed by Arutyunov, see Georges Agabekov, *OGPU: The Russian Secret Terror* (New York: Brentanos, 1931), 105.

34. A. I. Sipelgas-Olshanskiy, 'Г.П.У. в Париже: Записки бывшего "секретного сотрудника"' ('The GPU in Paris: Notes of a Former "Secret Collaborator"'), *Russia Illustrated*, 6 August 1932, 2.

35. Frederic Wakeman, Jr., *Policing Shanghai, 1927–1937* (Berkeley: University of California Press, 1995), 160.

36. Agabekov, *OGPU: The Russian Secret Terror*, 247.

37. British Consulate General, Paris, 'Memorandum on the Case of Isabel Streater and Guicha Serguevitch Agabekof', 3 July 1930, TNA, KV 2/2398.
38. Matthew Worley, *In Search of Revolution: International Communist Parties in the 'Third Period'* (London: I. B. Tauris, 2004), 137–8.
39. 'Verhaftung eines Spions' ('Arrest of a Spy'), *Rigasche Rindschau*, 22 March 1930, 14.
40. 'Письмо заведущего шпионажем' ('Letter from the Spy Chief'), *Vozrozhdenie*, 30 November 1930, 1
41. Nikita Anatolyevich Kuznetsov, 'Старший Лейтенант Флота А. А. Соболев – не легкий путь в эмиграцию' ('Senior Navy Lieutenant A. A. Sobolev – Hard Path to Emigration'), in *Труды II Международных Исторических Чтений Посвященных памяти профессора, Генерального Штаба Генерал–Лейтенанта Николая Николаевича Головин (1875–1944)* (*Proceedings of the Second International Historical Readings Dedicated to the Memory of Professor, General Staff General Lieutenant Nikolay Nikolayevich Golovin (1875–1944)*) (St Petersburg: Scriptorium, 2012), 282.
42. 'Alexander Sobolev plötsligt återkallad. Fruktar nu för livet' ('Alexander Sobolev Suddenly Withdrawn. Now Fears for His Life'), *Svenska Dagbladet*, 16 April 1930.
43. Wakeman, *Policing Shanghai, 1927–1937*, 160.
44. Report on Kozhevnikov (Pick), written by Andrey Terentyevich Belchenko to the French Consul General in Hankow on 31 May 1927, HIA, Andrei Terent'evich Bel'chenko Papers, 1898–1962, Box 24, Folder 8. In October 1927, the French Foreign Ministry provided a copy to the UK Foreign Office, which sent it to the British Military Attache in Shanghai, 4 October 1927, TNA KV 3/146, serial 52a. An English translation is contained in TNA KV 2/1895, serial 5a. A variation on this story appeared in a US SSU assessment that claimed that Kozhevnikov's injury came when Soviet officers tortured him by pouring boiling oil on his head: see SSU, *Japanese Intelligence Organizations in China*, 82, 91. The Belchenko report, made immediately after Kozhevnikov's visit to a French hospital, is more reliable.
45. Viktor Nikolaevich Usov, *Советская разведка в Китае. 20-е годы XX века* (*Soviet Intelligence in China: The 20s of the 20th Century*) (Moscow: OLMA Media Group, 2002), 187–91.
46. 'Les Conjurés du Destin' ('The Conspirators of Destiny'), *Détective*, 14 February 1930, 4–5. The same story was published under the name 'P.R.' (full name not provided), 'По Следам Похитителей ген.

А. Р. Кутепова' ('On the Trail of Gen. A. P. Kutepov's Kidnappers'), *Russia Illustrated*, 22 February 1930, 11–13.

47. 'The Mores and Work of the GPU', *Vozrozhdenie*, 11 September 1926, 2.

48. Dmitriy Prokhorov, *Сколько Стоит Продать Родину* (*What Is the Cost of Betraying One's Homeland?*) (St Petersburg: Neva Publishing, 2005), 20.

49. Vladimir Orloff, *Underworld and Soviet* (New York: Dial Press, 1931), 266. This is an English translation of Orlov's autobiography, *Im Kampf Mit Mördern und Betrügern* (*In the Fight with Murders and Swindlers*) (Berlin: Brücken-Verlag, 1929). The German version was also serialised in *Beiblatt des 8 Uhr-Abendblatt der National-Zeitung* (*Supplement to the 8 o'clock edition, National Newspaper*) (Berlin), 7–30 November 1929.

50. Letter from Mikhail Hendler to Chairman Hamilton Fish, 23 November 1930, in University of Notre Dame, Hesburgh Libraries, the Richard J. O'Melia Collection, Correspondence Box XVI, item 55.

51. 'Разоблачения Чекиста Никитина' ('Disclosures of the Chekist Nikitin'), *Vozrozhdenie*, 29 October 1927.

52. V. K. Vinogradov, Aleksey L. Litvin, Vasiliy S. Khristoforov (managing eds), *Архив ВЧК: Сборник документов* (*The VChK Archive: A Collection of Documents*) (Moscow: Kuchkovo Pole, 2007), 673. See also Feodor Drugoff file, National Archives of Finland, State Police (Valpo I) files, Box 102, folder 11033.

53. Kiselev-Gromov, *Death Camps in the USSR*, 187–8. See also Nikolai Kiseleff file, National Archives of Finland, State Police (Valpo I) files, Box 105, folder 11055.

54. Sergey Maslov, foreword to Kiselev-Gromov, *Death Camps in the USSR*.

55. 'Creation of a Minor Trans-Frontier System of Agents', Circular from the Pskov Provincial Branch, OGPU, 22 August 1927; enclosure to US Embassy, Riga, Latvia, dispatch, 18 May 1929; NARA, RG 59, M-316, 861.20260 P/73 (microfilm reel 89).

56. Drugov, 'Confession', 31 January 1931, 1.

57. Agabekov, *The ChK at Work*, 33–40.

58. Smirnov, 'Notes of a Razvedupr Agent', *Vozrozhdenie*, serialised from 4 March to 3 May 1930.

59. Agabekov, *The ChK at Work*, 62–3.

60. Smirnov, 'Notes of a Razvedupr Agent', 15 March 1930, 3; 29 April 1930, 2.

61. Belchenko, Report to French Consul General; Agabekov, *The ChK at Work*, 81–5; Agabekov, *OGPU: The Russian Secret Terror*, 77–9, 92–3.

62. 'ГПУ в Прибалтике» ('GPU in the Baltics'), *Vozrozhdenie*, 26 March 1930, 2.

63. Agabekov, *The ChK at Work*, 95–101.

64. Robert Carver North, *Moscow and Chinese Communists* (Palo Alto: Stanford University Press, 1963), 47. See also Allen S. Whiting, *Soviet Policies in China, 1917–1924* (Palo Alto: Stanford University Press, 1954), 155–67, which describes Dzevaltovsky's (Yurin's) mission to China.

65. HIA, Boris Nicolaevsky Collection, Box 217, Folder 6 (Microfilm 187).

66. Agabekov, *The ChK at Work*, 50–4; Agabekov, *OGPU: The Russian Secret Terror*, 35–6, 44.

67. Agabekov, *The ChK at Work*, 81–5; Agabekov, *OGPU: The Russian Secret Terror*, 77–9, 92–3. Chamberlain's note was dated 23 February 1927; see Xenia Joukoff Eudin and Harold Henry Fisher, *Soviet Russia and the West, 1920–1927: A Documentary Survey* (Palo Alto: Stanford University Press, 1957), 370–1, for discussion of the Soviet reaction to Chamberlain's diplomatic note.

68. *The Soviet in China Unmasked: Documents Revealing Bolshevistic Plans and Methods, Seized in the USSR Embassy, Peking, April 6, 1927* (Shanghai: North China Daily News and Herald Ltd, 1927). A copy of this document is contained in TNA, KV 3/145.

69. John Powell, 'Consuls Meet to Protest Picketing Soviet Office', *Buffalo Courier Express*, 10 April 1927, 1.

70. House of Commons Debate, 11 April 1927, vol. 205, cc10-2, <http://hansard.millbanksystems.com/commons/1927/apr/11/russian-consulate-shanghai> (last accessed 13 March 2020).

71. 'The Soviet Embassy Raid', *North China Daily News*, 17 September 1927; forwarded by UK military attaché to the War Office on 27 September 1927, TNA, KV 3/145, serial 50a.

72. *Организация ГПУ (The Organisation of the GPU)*, undated typescript, 16–18, HIA, Boris Nicolaevsky Collection, Box 217, Folder 6 (microfilm reel 187).

73. Smirnov, 'Notes of a Razvedupr Agent'.

74. Hendler letter to Chairman Hamilton Fish, 23 November 1930; US Embassy Havana to Department of State, Despatch 1437, 25 May 1926, NARA, RG 59, Central Decimal File 1910–1929, Box 7330, 811.00B/585; Department of State to Ambassador Enoch

H. Crowder, Despatch 741, 14 July 1926, NARA, RG 59, Central Decimal File 1910–1929, Box 7330, 811.00B/585.

75. Richard B. Spence, 'Senator William E. Borah: Target of Soviet and Anti-Soviet Intrigue, 1922–1929', *International Journal of Intelligence and CounterIntelligence*, vol. 19 (2006), no. 1, 134–55.

76. Prokhorov, *What is the Cost of Betraying One's Homeland?*, 28.

77. US Embassy Riga dispatch number 6380, 3 September 1929; NARA, RG 59, Central Decimal Files, 1910–1949, 811.44, Borah, William E.

78. Vladimir Leonidovich Genis, 'Невозвращенцы 1920-х- начала 1930-х годов' ('Non-returnees in the 1920s and Early 1930s'), *Вопросы Истории (Questions of History)*, 2000, no. 1, 46–63.

79. 'Материалы по Разработке Инструкции "О Порядке Применения Постановления Президиума ЦИК СССР о Перебежках за Границу"' ('Materials on the Drafting of an Instruction "On the Order of Implementing the Resolution of the Presidium of the USSR Central Executive Committee on Defectors Abroad"'), HIA, RGASPI, Reel 3.7401, Delo 11.

80. Ivan Tolstoy, 'Кому нужен берег турецкий: первые советские невозвращенцы' ('Who Needs the Turkish Coast: The First Soviet Non-Returnees'), interview with Vladimir Genis, aired on *Radio Liberty*, 11 January 2010, <http://www.svoboda.org/articleprint view/1929236.html> (last accessed 13 March 2020).

81. Genis, 'Невозвращенцы 1920-х- начала 1930-х годов'.

82. 'Освобождение бежавшихъ из СССР летчиков' ('Freeing of the Airmen who Escaped from the USSR'), *Vozrozhdenie*, 6 April 1934, 1; 'Бежавшие летчики' ('Escaped Airmen'), *Vozrozhdenie*, 14 April 1934, 1; 'Бегство Советских летчиков' ('The Flight of the Soviet Airmen'), *Vozrozhdenie*, 21 April 1934, 5.

83. Prokhorov, *What is the Cost of Betraying One's Homeland?*, 75–6.

84. Government of the Russian Soviet Federated Socialist Republic, *Уголовный кодекс РСФСР. Официальный текст с изменениями на 1 июля 1950 г. и с приложением постатейно систематизированных материалов (Penal Code of the RSFSR. Official Edition with Changes up to 1 July 1950 and with Additional Materials, Systematised According to Paragraphs)* (Moscow: RSFSR Government, 1950), 35–43.

85. Gery Kern, *The Kravchenko Case: One Man's War on Stalin* (New York: Enigma Books, 2007), 11.

2 *Yezhovshchina*-Era Defectors, 1937–1940

The second group of Soviet intelligence officer defectors includes eight individuals who escaped the deadliest purge in Soviet history, known as the Great Purge and labelled colloquially in the Soviet Union as the *Yezhovshchina* after Nikolay Ivanovich Yezhov, the People's Commissar of State Security from 1936 to 1938. Six of the eight defectors in this group broke with the Soviet Union within a twelve-month period in 1937 and 1938. The remaining two defected in 1940, after the purge had subsided, but were directly influenced by their colleagues' executions and continuing fear for their own lives. All of these defectors began as loyal Bolshevik revolutionaries; they proved themselves in the civil war, and their careers flourished into the 1930s. Unlike the defectors in the previous chapter, they remained loyal while Stalin took control of the Soviet government. But their perseverance was finally tested when the Great Purge took the lives of many of their colleagues and threatened to liquidate them and their families.

Personal Backgrounds

These eight individuals shared many experiences that ultimately led to their decisions to break with the Soviet regime despite the dangers inherent in such a decision. *Yezhovshchina*-era defectors' age and rank distinguished them from other chronological groups. They represented the old guard of the VChK/GPU/OGPU/NKVD and Razvedupr. All but one were born in the decade between 1895 and 1904. Most had served in the civil war and became intelligence officers during Lenin's lifetime, and

Table 2.1 *Yezhovshchina*-Era Defectors, 1937–1940

Name	Best-Known Alias	Service	Became Intel Officer	Date of Defection	Location of Defection	Receiving Country
Natan Markovich Poretskiy	Ignatiy (Ignace) Stanislavovich Reiss	Razvedupr/ OGPU	1921	17 July 1937	France	France
Aleksandr Grigoryevich Graff	Alexander Grigoryevich Barmin	Razvedupr	1923	18 July 1937	Greece	France/ United States
Samuel Gershovich Ginzberg	Walter Germanovich Krivitsky	Razvedupr/ OGPU	1921	October 1937	France	United States
Iosif Volfovich Volodarskiy	Armand Labis Feldman	OGPU/NKVD	1933	April 1938	United States	Canada
Genrikh Samoilovich Lyushkov		OGPU/NKVD	1920	13 June 1938	Japan	Japan
Leyba Lazarevich Feldbin	Alexander Mikhailovich Orlov	OGPU/NKVD	1918	12 July 1938	France	United States
Lev Borisovich Helfand		OGPU/NKVD	~1920	15 July 1940	Italy	United States
(??) Chivin	Smith	OGPU/NKVD	??	15 August 1940	United States	??

had served for fifteen or more years when they defected. They averaged over thirty-seven years old at the time of their defection, and six were senior officers.[1] Most were contemporaries of Genrikh Grigoryevich Yagoda and Yezhov, successive OGPU and NKVD chiefs, and several worked directly with INO chief Abram Aronovich Slutskiy. Lyushkov, for example, was the most senior intelligence officer to defect in Soviet history, having commanded NKVD operations in two different regions. While this rank brought privileges, it also brought risks; as the Great Purge eliminated many senior NKVD officers, their associates, including these defectors, were immediately brought under suspicion.

Yezhovshchina-era defectors also shared similar origins; most were born on the western edge of the Russian empire in what is now Ukraine and Belarus. Their defection was in part a reaction to an increasing trend towards Russian nationalism under Stalin in the 1930s. Ginzberg and Graff noted how Stalin was positively impressed by Hitler's decisive, ruthless action against opponents in the Nazi Party in June 1934, which became known as the 'Night of the Long Knives', and that this inspired him to root out unreliable elements from the Bolshevik Party.[2] This growing respect for Hitler and consequent Russian nationalism also highlighted another commonality among *Yezhovshchina*-era defectors – seven of the eight were Jewish. Although Stalin's purges were not overtly anti-Semitic, many of the victims of the purges were Jews. For example, ten of the sixteen defendants in the first major purge show trial in August 1936 were Jews. Feldbin noted ironically that all eight of the defendants in the 1937 show trial of Soviet military leaders were convicted of cooperating with Hitler, yet three were Jews.[3]

Ginzberg interpreted Stalin's purge of senior Soviet military leaders in 1937 as being based on Stalin's view that they would never agree with his plan for a pact with Hitler.[4] Several defectors related personally with those senior military leaders and were deeply shaken by their executions.[5] Helfand had gained an anti-German reputation when he was working as chargé d'affaires at the Soviet embassy in Rome in 1939, and he was a Jew, both of which drew unfavourable attention and gave the German government reason to lobby Moscow for his removal.[6] That lobbying

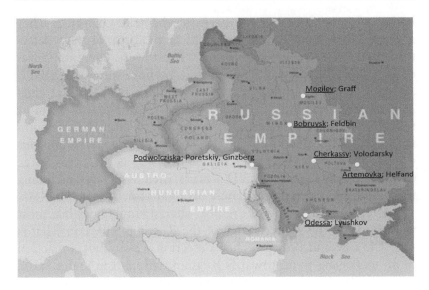

Figure 2.1   Origins of *Yezhovshchina*-Era Defectors, 1937–1940

resulted in Helfand's recall to Moscow, which prompted him to defect in July 1940.

Another commonality among *Yezhovshchina*-era defectors was the decisive role that their families played in their defections. Because of Soviet laws holding family members liable for a defector's actions, threats to defectors' family members weighed heavily on their minds and influenced their decisions about whether and when to defect. Each defector in this group made some plans for family members before defecting. This family consciousness may reflect the older, more mature men who made up the *Yezhovshchina*-era Soviet intelligence officer defectors. However, these same men were also active at the foundations of the Bolshevik revolution nearly twenty years earlier, fought in the civil war, and were reportedly involved in the brutal violence in the 1920s and early 1930s, including arrests, assassinations, and kidnappings. Despite being family men, they viewed their service to a Soviet intelligence organisation as honourable and necessary in the pursuit of a socialist future, and they accepted, and in some cases participated in, the excesses that characterised Soviet state security in the 1920s and early 1930s.

Lyushkov and Feldbin were OGPU counterintelligence officers in the early 1920s, enforcing revolutionary order and pursuing spies for liquidation.[7] Helfand was also rumoured to have been involved in repressive actions in the 1920s and to have played a role in the disappearance and death of tsarist General Kutepov in France in 1930.[8] Prokhorov asserts that Poretskiy was involved in the assassination of defector Vladimir Nesterovich in 1925 (see Chapter 1), and that both Ginzberg and Poretskiy were involved in the disappearance of Razvedupr illegal agent Vitold Shturm de Shtrem, who was suspected of planning to defect in December 1933.[9]

These men, however, drew a distinguishing line between the violence they viewed as an integral part of the revolution, which they considered honourable, and the terror sponsored by Stalin's regime, in which they were involved but later condemned. They regarded their role in the revolution with pride, but expressed shame at having played a role in Stalin's purges. Feldbin, for example, participated in investigations that led to the first purge show trial in 1936 and was reported to have been engaged in eliminating 'Trotskyist' elements among foreign fighters in Spain.[10] However, he denied having taken part in purges and strongly condemned Stalin's tactics in his book *The Secret History of Stalin's Crimes*. Lyushkov took part in those same investigations and led purges in Ukraine, the North Caucasus, southern Russia, and the Soviet Far East. He oversaw the forced migration of ethnic Chinese and Koreans from the Far East to Central Asia.[11] Unlike Feldbin, however, Lyushkov admitted his involvement, leading some to question why the 'repentant purger' carried out Stalin's orders for so long before defecting.[12] He recognised this inconsistency, explaining: 'Guilty as I am of collaborating in Stalin's foul terror, I shall risk everything, flee to the nearest country, seek asylum as others had done, and carry on the good fight against Stalin from the outside. The dictator's toadies will libel me and say I sold my soul but, one day, when the despot has been overthrown, I shall go home to a bright new Russia.'[13] He never fulfilled this prediction.

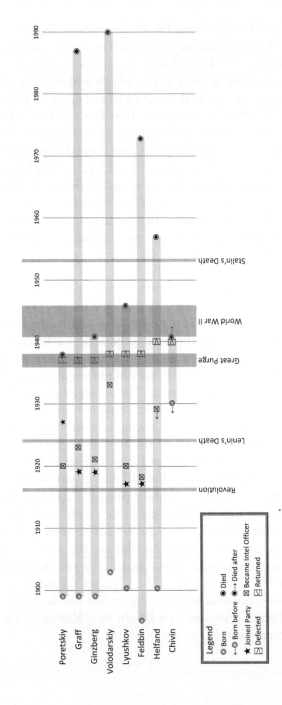

Figure 2.2 Lives of *Yezhovshchina*-Era Defectors, 1937–1940

Motivations

Yezhovshchina-era defectors showed almost universally a single motivation for defection – fear of execution, combined with philosophical disagreement with the course on which Stalin was steering the country. The fear was founded on their identities as early revolutionaries who entered Soviet state security during Lenin's lifetime, and who had personal relationships with old Bolsheviks purged in the three public trials in 1936 and 1937. They often counted themselves among the old Bolsheviks: Feldbin's biographer Edward Gazur characterised this view:

> Orlov always considered himself to be a loyal member of the Communist Party and had no reservations whatsoever that the ideals promulgated by Lenin and his followers were the appropriate and fairest course for the Russian people. He also had no reservations about his work for the KGB [sic] as he saw this as one of the means to secure the end. However, as the trial [of the Sixteen in July 1936] progressed, seeds of doubt came into his mind, and for the first time he sensed that he was not completely in accord with the hidden objectives of the trial.[14]

No firm data are available about the number of intelligence and state security officers who fell victim to the purges, but the results were catastrophic. Prokhorov quotes Yezhov as saying at a closed session of the USSR Supreme Court, 'I count 14,000 chekists.' Prokhorov claims that 275 out of 450 officers in the INO disappeared, paralysing Soviet foreign intelligence collection.[15] A 2005 history of Soviet foreign intelligence assessed that the 'INO collapsed into such confusion during 1938 that for 127 consecutive days not a single foreign intelligence report was forwarded to Stalin'.[16]

The fear that these actions created compounded defectors' increasing dissonance with Stalin's policies, which they saw as betraying the revolutionary ideal they had fought for in the early Soviet years. These defectors perceived that Stalin was charting a major redirection in Soviet policies, minimising and often contradicting the Bolshevik revolution and even seeking to join forces with Nazism, despite public propaganda to the contrary. They viewed themselves as defenders of Leninist principles who were obliged to illuminate and counter Stalin's policies.

Poretskiy was first to issue an anti-Stalinist manifesto with his letter to the Central Committee of the Communist Party, dated 17 July 1937: 'The working class must defeat Stalin and Stalinism so that the USSR and the international workers' movement do not succumb to fascism and counter-revolution. This mixture of the worst opportunism, devoid of principles, and of lies and blood threatens to poison the world and the last forces of the working class.' He further demanded a 'return to Lenin's international!'[17] Ginzberg recommended during debriefings in 1940 that the British government prepare anti-Soviet propaganda to counter Comintern messaging, trumpeting that 'Bolshevism, Leninism, and socialism are dead in the Soviet Union, [and] no genuine attempt is now being made to carry out the teachings of Karl Marx. The Soviet Union has become a rigid dictatorship maintained by a system of wholesale purges, and Stalin is attempting to maintain his unstable position by a policy of military aggression.'[18] Graff wrote in an open letter in December 1937: 'Had I consented to remain in the service of Stalin I should have felt myself morally defiled, and should have had to take a share in the responsibility for crimes committed daily against the people of my country. It would have meant betraying the cause of Socialism to which I have dedicated my life.'[19] For Helfand, the betrayal was manifest in the Molotov–Ribbentrop Pact. Soon after defecting, Helfand sent Molotov a letter explaining his actions and predicting that an alliance with Germany would lead to the downfall of the Soviet Union and the destruction of the revolutionary movement for which Helfand and other old Bolsheviks, who had nearly all been liquidated, had fought so hard.[20]

These defectors' socialist idealism also aroused a mistrust of the West and its capitalist ways, which impeded some from making full revelations. Poretskiy and Ginzberg discussed their reluctance to surrender themselves into the hands of capitalist secret services in 1936, although Ginzberg did later allow himself to be debriefed by French, British, and American intelligence services.[21] Volodarskiy initially hid from US authorities before making his way to Canada, where he opened up only when the Canadian government interned him as an undocumented foreigner. Feldbin waited fifteen years, and then only partially opened up to US authorities, withholding the most important information he possessed and remaining faithful to the promise he had made to Yezhov in 1938. Although Chivin reportedly refused to return to the Soviet Union, there is no indication that he surrendered himself to the West. However, defectors' conflict with Stalinism outweighed their philosophical dissonance with capitalism, and fear for their lives pushed them to their final decision to break with the Soviet Union.

Receiving Countries

Yezhovshchina-era Soviet intelligence officer defectors' destination after their break with the Soviet Union was initially the same as the majority of defectors before 1931: they made for Paris. Accordingly, Poretskiy, Graff, and Ginzberg all initially planned to settle in France after their defections. However, by late 1937, it was clear that France was no longer a safe haven, as demonstrated by the ease with which the NKVD tracked down and assassinated Poretskiy in September. Brook-Shepherd noted: 'Hitherto, the runaways had nearly all made for Paris, centre of the largest and most variegated Russian community in exile. From 1937 on, defectors began to head across the Atlantic, using the French capital only as a transit stage in their journey.'[22] Correspondingly, Feldbin passed through Paris on his way to Canada and then the United States in July 1938.

Whereas only one defector prior to 1931 settled in the United States (Hendler), all of the *Yezhovshchina*-era defectors had some connection to the United States in the late 1930s, most viewing it as the new safe haven. Graff, Ginzberg, Feldbin and Helfand all immigrated to the United States, and Lyushkov expressed interest in doing so, although he died before he realised that aspiration. Volodarskiy and Chivin were already in the United States when they defected. Volodarskiy hid in the United States from 1938 to 1940 before he left for Canada out of fear that US authorities would arrest him for his past anti-US operations. Chivin was also operating in the United States when he refused to return to the Soviet Union, but his further whereabouts are unknown.

However, the sense of the United States as a refuge was short-lived. Ginzberg's death under suspicious circumstances in February 1941 shattered defectors' illusions of safety in the United States. Although the Soviet hand in Ginzberg's death remains a mystery, the incident frightened others, driving them either underground or into the arms of the US government. At the time of Ginzberg's death, three other Soviet intelligence officer defectors were already living in the United States. Feldbin was hiding under a special immigration status, obtained with the personal intervention of Attorney General Francis Biddle, allowing him to register for the Alien Registration Act of 1940 without identifying his whereabouts.[23] Graff published a book before leaving France, and made himself known to US authorities when he arrived. By late 1942 he was working for the US Army translating a Soviet guerrilla manual and monitoring Soviet radio transmissions,[24] and he began working for the US Office of Strategic Services (OSS) in 1942. Helfand melted into the business world in the United States and assumed the name Leon Moore. Both US and British officials debriefed him, and the US government probably helped him resettle.[25]

By the late 1940s, the shock of Ginzberg's death had subsided somewhat and most of these defectors again felt more secure in the United States. Graff began working openly as the chief of the Russia Section at Voice of America in 1948. Helfand later developed a personal relationship with CIA Director Allen Dulles, which gave him some level of protection. From 1951 to 1956, he and his wife made at least seven trips to France and Italy, indicating that he felt sufficiently secure to travel to Europe.[26] Volodarskiy lived the rest of his life in Canada and reverted to using his real name. Only Feldbin continued to claim to be under threat; although he made his presence known publicly after Stalin's death in 1953, he still wrote, 'The death of Stalin has not diminished the threat to my life.'[27]

Operational Priorities

In 1963, Feldbin published a short book titled *Handbook of Intelligence and Guerrilla Warfare*.[28] Not long before the book was released, CIA's *Studies in Intelligence* published an excerpt accompanied by the endorsement: 'a thoughtful former insider examines in depth Soviet (and Western) intelligence services'. It was commended as warranting special presentation to the Intelligence Community.[29]

Feldbin described eight Soviet intelligence emphases during his career that showed the Soviet mindset of merging intelligence and covert action into a unified state security enterprise. While Feldbin's information was over twenty-five years old when his writings appeared, they nevertheless gave insights into the Soviet intelligence activities that had not changed significantly in the intervening years. His eight Soviet intelligence missions were:

1. Diplomatic intelligence
2. Military intelligence
3. Economic warfare
4. Misinformation
5. Infiltrating foreign intelligence and security services
6. Political action
7. Industrial intelligence
8. Guerrilla Warfare[30]

These missions reflected an ever-present assumption that Western countries were dangerous enemies bent on destroying the Soviet Union. These included primarily Great Britain and Germany, and secondarily the United States, Japan, Italy, and France. Although in the 1963 context this was not a startling revelation, Feldbin's information, combined with reporting from other defectors like Ginzberg, Graff, and Volodarskiy, showed a Soviet adversarial approach to the West as early as the 1930s, long preceding the Cold War.

United Kingdom

Based on the operations that *Yezhovshchina*-era intelligence officer defectors revealed, the Soviet Union viewed Great Britain in the 1930s in terms that would approach the Cold War-era phrase, the 'main enemy'. According to Ginzberg, from 1935, Stalin considered the Soviet Union to be at war with Great Britain, and Stalin directed both the OGPU and Razvedupr to prepare for war: 'The aim of Stalin's war is the destruction of the British Empire.'[31] Six of the eight *Yezhovshchina*-era defectors ran a wide variety of operations targeting the British government. The exceptions are Lyushkov, who spent most of his career in internal security, and Chivin, whose mission was mainly operational support.

Diplomatic Intelligence
Soviet intelligence sought sources with access to protected information to inform the Soviet leadership about capitalist countries' intentions towards the Soviet Union and their contemplated political moves. Prominent among these sources were diplomats; foreign ministry staff, including code clerks, secretaries, etc.; private secretaries to cabinet members; members of parliament; and ambitious politicians seeking financial aid and left-wing support.[32] *Yezhovshchina*-era defectors cited some notable successes of these operations directed against British political activities in particular.

When Graff served in Resht, Persia, in 1923 and 1924, he echoed Arutyunov's assessment from the same period that Great Britain was the primary adversary of Soviet interests in Persia. Further corroborating Arutyunov, Graff reported that the OGPU greatly valued sources with direct access to British diplomatic correspondence, both for what they revealed about British policy and because British diplomats were well-informed observers of the politics within whatever country they served, especially about Germany. *Yezhovshchina*-era defectors had ties to several sources of British diplomatic correspondence and cipher materials. Helfand referred to a source with access to British diplomatic communications in Italy that had access to all British diplomatic telegrams from Rome, as well as internal communications and minutes of meetings between the ambassador and the commercial counsellor. Helfand stated that the operation had run for over seven years, and that the Soviets had similarly penetrated other missions in Rome, notably the Japanese and Romanian.[33] Helfand related a similar account to the FBI, stating that from conversations he had with Italian officials it appeared that the Italians likely also had access to the same information.[34] MI5 took issue with Helfand's allegations, casting doubt on their credibility and asking that an MI5 Soviet specialist be allowed to 'properly interrogate' him.[35] There is no record of a further debriefing.

Operations inside the UK were also a priority. Before Great Britain extended diplomatic recognition to the Soviet Union in 1924, ARCOS informally represented Soviet interests in London. ARCOS was ostensibly an international trade brokerage, but also served as a platform for intelligence and Comintern operations, which led to the British raid on the London ARCOS office in May 1927. Feldbin arrived in France in mid-1926 and, although resident in Paris, he ran operations at least partially focused towards Britain. A letter intercepted by Scotland Yard in 1928 stated that Feldbin was involved in discussions about ARCOS staffing prior to its closure, and that he was similarly in a position to approve the transfer of a Soviet agent to Amtorg in New York.[36] The ARCOS raid forced the OGPU to transfer what remained of the London *rezidentura* to Paris, when Feldbin became even more involved in British operations.[37] Despite Feldbin's denials of ever having visited or operated against the UK,[38] he hinted about involvement in British operations when he told US authorities that he recognised a photograph of Soviet illegal William August Fisher/ Rudolf Abel during Fisher/Abel's well-publicised 1957 espionage trial, and that Feldbin had met him briefly at OGPU headquarters.[39] An August 1958 *Studies in Intelligence* article noted further details of Feldbin's relationship with Fisher/Abel, indicating that Feldbin was involved in handling Fisher/Abel when the latter was first assigned to London in 1927 for training as a future illegal.[40]

Ginzberg offered MI5 valuable intelligence about Soviet operations against British diplomatic information. He described a British Foreign Office cipher clerk who passed confidential documents to the OGPU until he committed suicide in the early

1930s.[41] Helfand reportedly met and interviewed a British man who fit the same description, who walked into the Soviet embassy in Paris in 1929 offering to sell Foreign Office cipher materials.[42] Both Ginzberg and Helfand were referring to Ernest Holloway Oldham, about whom MI5 had some suspicion, but whose trail went cold when Oldham committed suicide in 1933. Defectors' information corroborated MI5's suspicions.

Ginzberg also identified another Foreign Office cipher clerk, whom he named 'King', who was 'selling everything to Moscow'.[43] Ginzberg's revelations pointed unmistakably to John Herbert King. Ginzberg partially identified a Soviet intelligence agent named Henri Christiaan Pieck who was involved in handling King under Poretskiy's direction. Pieck initially met King in early 1934 when King was working at the British delegation to the League of Nations in Geneva, Switzerland. King returned to London in 1935, but Pieck's cover as an artist allowed him to travel frequently to the UK and maintain contact. Pieck offered an ostensible business deal, in which King would supply copies of British diplomatic communications and Pieck would use the information for insider trading on stock markets and currency exchange markets. Poretskiy and Pieck had chosen a willing target; King saw bleak career prospects for himself as a non-permanent Foreign Office employee with no pension and he was eager to build a better financial future. He agreed to the business deal and began to pass sensitive Foreign Office documents to Pieck, for which he received £50–£200, a significant sum for a low-level employee.[44] Some of King's material was sent directly to Stalin because of its high value, especially information about British diplomatic interaction with Nazi Germany.[45]

In 1936, Pieck transferred the handling of King to an illegal officer he knew as Mr Peterson, with whom King continued to do business until mid-1937. Peterson took control of the operation and began requesting that King pass ciphers and cipher tables in addition to diplomatic cables, but King claimed to have refused.[46] Peterson was the cover name for Theodore Stephanovich Maly, an NKVD officer who arrived in London in March 1936 to replace Feldbin as OGPU illegal *rezident*.[47] Maly received King's information and passed it to Poretskiy, sometimes using Pieck as a courier, and Poretskiy forwarded it to Moscow. MI5 used Ginzberg's information to launch a whirlwind investigation that led to King's arrest and prosecution in October 1939.[48]

Maly inherited from Feldbin responsibility for two other valued British sources: another Foreign Office employee, later identified as Donald Maclean; and a journalist, later identified as Harold A. R. 'Kim' Philby.[49] Ginzberg reported having seen a compartmented report from one of these sources in Moscow in spring 1937 that discussed British defence measures and memos on the situation in Germany from the British ambassador in Berlin. The report also identified five Soviet Foreign Ministry officials supposedly working for British intelligence, supplying information of such a secret character that it convinced the NKVD that British intelligence had penetrated the upper levels of the ministry. The report was printed and bound in five copies – for Stalin, Yezhov, INO Chief Slutskiy, People's Commissar for Defence Kliment Yefremovich Voroshilov, and Commander-in-Chief of Naval Forces Vladimir Mitrofanovich Orlov.[50] The fact that reports from this agent were delivered directly to the most senior Soviet military and security leaders shows that the information was highly valued and, like the information from King, is an indicator that high-level British national security information was of the utmost Soviet interest at the time.

Because Ginzberg did not handle the source himself he could give only the barest description, tentatively identifying him as working in the 'Political Committee Cabinet Office' or 'Council of State'.[51] After further debriefing, MI5 interpreted this as being the Committee of Imperial Defence (CID). MI5 showed Ginzberg the cover of a CID report, and Ginzberg recognised it as being like the one he saw in Moscow.[52] Feldbin similarly recounted seeing a document in Moscow in fall 1935 that contained minutes of a CID meeting regarding British perceptions about German rearmament, stating that Winston Churchill possessed information showing that Germany's rearmament had progressed further than other sources had indicated. Feldbin remembered seeing other reports from the same source compiled into a loose-leaf binder,[53] resembling what Ginzberg described.

This information likely originated from Donald Maclean,

whose reporting Feldbin read in his headquarters position after his return to Moscow. Maclean's reporting also included minutes of British–German diplomatic exchanges and information about British decryption capabilities. At the same time that Maclean was providing photos of plain text Foreign Office cables, King compromised Cipher Office copies, which when put together would have enabled Soviet decryption operations targeting British communications. Costello and Tsarev corroborate the assertion that Maclean was the source of these reports and claim that the information was voluminous and highly valued, providing Soviet leadership with insights into British and German military planning.[54]

Feldbin was directly involved in Donald Maclean's early espionage career and took over his handling in February 1935, according to information made available to Tsarev.[55] The NKVD cultivated Maclean hoping that he would receive a posting in the Foreign Office, and Feldbin learned that Maclean achieved that goal just before Feldbin left Britain.[56] However, Ginzberg's ambiguous information and Feldbin's incomplete revelations were too little, too late. By the time Feldbin talked, MI5 had already concluded that Maclean was the source of these reports, but he was safely in the Soviet Union.[57]

Military Intelligence

Soviet intelligence also provided insights into British military plans, intentions, and vulnerabilities, which were of the utmost priority for the Soviet Union. The Soviet Union anxiously followed British colonial affairs, and the Razvedupr had a specific section dedicated to studying British colonial influence, especially in the Near and Far East, focusing on military vulnerabilities that the Soviet Union could exploit in case of war. According to Ginzberg, Razvedupr analysts compiled reports for the Soviet General Staff about movements of troops, conditions of native populations, and religious and economic issues. Ginzberg remembered seeing a report on 1929 Arab uprisings, presumably referring to the 'Western Wall' riots in August 1929.[58]

Ginzberg claimed that the Razvedupr had no illegal *rezident* in Great Britain in 1935 for two reasons: the Razvedupr could not find anyone with proficient enough English language skills who could be 'legitimised' as an illegal, and the OGPU was gaining primacy over the Razvedupr. Ginzberg stated that in 1935, Stalin directed the OGPU to begin collecting military intelligence in parallel with the Razvedupr.[59] Nevertheless, the Razvedupr continued its British collection, and from 1935 it interviewed British Communist Party leaders Harry Pollitt and William Gallacher whenever they visited Moscow, questioning them about the political situation in Great Britain, the British General Staff, conditions in the British Army, and other military-related topics.[60]

Infiltrating Foreign Intelligence and Security Services
Soviet intelligence organisations sought sources inside foreign intelligence services for several reasons: foreign intelligence officers could identify spies inside the Soviet Union; they could inform Soviet decisions about how much the foreign government knew about Soviet plans; and they had broad access to classified information not only from their own organisation but also from other government departments, such as the military and diplomatic services.[61] The SIS was of particular Soviet intelligence interest because of its global reach and professional reputation. The NKVD's aspiration for Philby was to steer him into a career in the SIS. The NKVD files on which Oleg Tsarev based his research reportedly indicate that Feldbin proposed avenues for Philby to gain SIS employment as early as 1935.[62] He did join SIS a few years later, and the SIS material he provided the NKVD resulted in the interruption of at least two would-be Soviet intelligence officer defectors – Konstantin Dmitriyevich Volkov in 1945 and Vladimir Aleksandrovich Skripkin in 1946 – and suppression of reporting from a third, Izmail Guseynovich Akhmedov (see Chapter 3). Philby also had access to documents containing Foreign Office information about British policy towards Germany.[63]

Feldbin also directed Soviet illegal Arnold Deutsch to recruit Guy Burgess, first proposing him as a potential recruit as early as August 1934.[64] Like Philby, Burgess's primary target during Feldbin's time was the SIS, which he joined in 1938. Feldbin viewed Burgess's flamboyant homosexuality as a hook that Soviet intelligence could use to entrap others into working as sources. Feldbin later wrote, '[Homosexuals] who agreed to work for the Russian network were instructed to approach other homosexual members of the diplomatic corps, a strategy which was remarkably successful.'[65] Correspondingly, Feldbin used Burgess initially to identify other potential recruits who shared both Burgess's left-wing political views and blatant homosexuality, and who had access to the diplomatic and SIS information that Soviet intelligence highly valued.[66]

Guerrilla Warfare

Ginzberg also discussed at length the concept of 'decomposition work', which entailed infiltrating communist and Soviet sympathisers into military and critical infrastructure facilities to conduct anti-military agitation during peacetime and sabotage during war. Ginzberg noted that in the 1920s the Razvedupr was responsible for instigating 'decomposition' activities, which it viewed as an element of world revolution. Anti-military propaganda work had traditionally been more successful in France than it was in Britain, because it initially used unsophisticated methods. But when Stalin discarded the concept of world revolution, the purpose for agitation transitioned into preparing for war with Great Britain and it became more effective. Ginzberg surmised that there were military officers in the British Forces at the time of his defection who were prepared to work for the Soviet Union to the detriment of British interests.[67]

Ginzberg claimed that Soviet intelligence fully exploited the Communist Party of Great Britain, facilitated by Soviet propaganda portraying the Soviet Union as the world anti-fascist leader. Although communist agents in Great Britain were not as numerous as Moscow would have liked, those who were there would act as sabotage agents upon orders from Moscow; he predicted that as many as 500 British workers would sabotage factories and key infrastructures if war broke out between the Soviet Union and Britain.[68] Ginzberg warned that, while the British Government might be right to think that during peacetime the Communist Party of Great Britain appeared weak, the Soviet Union would use it as a tool against Great Britain during wartime.[69]

Industrial Intelligence/Economic Warfare

Volodarskiy's first overseas assignment began when he and his young family arrived in the UK in September 1930 working for Russian Oil Products, a Soyuzneft subsidiary.[70] He was probably not an OGPU agent at the time,[71] but he returned to the Soviet Union from late November 1931 until March 1932[72] and was likely co-opted as a secret collaborator (*секретный сотрудник*; *seksot*) then. With his expertise in oil engineering and his position as a Soviet oil company employee, he had good access to information about the British oil industry, which fit into two of the OGPU's intelligence priorities: industrial intelligence, which the OGPU collected to strengthen Soviet industrial enterprises, and economic warfare, through which the OGPU sought to uncover foreign collusion against Russian companies.

Volodarskiy first came to the attention of MI5 in September 1932 when, posing as 'Olsen', a Romanian journalist, he introduced himself to Marcus Weinstein, an employee of the Shell-Mex oil company in London, and offered £20 per month for detailed sales figures for all grades of petroleum products from each of the company's branches.[73] Volodarskiy levied specific information requirements about Shell-Mex's production and sales, and Weinstein's first impression was that he was well informed about the British oil industry.[74] Weinstein was suspicious of the contact and informed his superior, who engaged MI5. MI5 began to monitor Volodarskiy's meetings with Weinstein, and the company created falsified sales data for Weinstein to pass to Volodarskiy. On 10 November, Volodarskiy left a meeting with Weinstein with a package of Shell-Mex financial documents and went to the ARCOS office, from which he re-emerged after a few hours with the package;[75] he presumably used ARCOS photographic and communications equipment to copy the documents and transmit them to Moscow. Scotland Yard arrested Volodarskiy at the next meeting with Weinstein. MI5 suspected industrial espionage, but a court ruled Volodarskiy acted alone, prosecuted him for bribery under the Prevention of Corruption Act of 1906, and fined him £50.[76] The British government did not further pursue the case, despite Volodarskiy's evident relationship with the

Soviet government and even though it occurred only five years after MI5 had raided the ARCOS office.

Germany

Yezhovshchina-era defectors revealed that the Soviet Union, under Stalin's orders, conducted a two-pronged policy towards Germany both as a hostile operating environment and a hopeful ally. Throughout most of the 1930s, Soviet intelligence operated against Germany along several lines of operation, while simultaneously cooperating with German intelligence. But in 1937, Soviet intelligence organisations temporarily disengaged from offensive operations against Germany based on Stalin's hope of turning Germany into an ally.

Industrial Intelligence

German technology was a valuable commodity for the Soviet Union. However, advanced technology was expensive and sometimes dissemination was restricted, so Soviet intelligence organisations were dispatched to obtain needed technology in a less costly manner, particularly in the 1920s and early 1930s. The Soviet Union routinely expected capitalist powers to overcharge and cheat Soviet purchasers, so it employed intelligence operations to circumvent disadvantageous deals. Feldbin wrote of an incident when the Soviet Union was negotiating with the German company Krupp to buy artificial diamonds. According to Feldbin's account, the company knew how desperate the Soviet Union was for industrial diamonds and charged a staggering price for them. During Politburo discussions, Stalin reportedly turned to Yezhov and said, 'The bastards want too much money. Try to steal it from them. Show what the NKVD can do.'[77]

Whether this anecdote is real or apocryphal is unknown, but it is clear that the Soviet government eagerly sought German technology. Feldbin served in the Soviet Trade Delegation in Berlin from early 1928 until April 1931, where his operations particularly focused on collecting science and technology (S&T) information, including manufacturing processes to advance the Soviet Union's armaments industry and to bolster the industrial base. At times, the Trade Delegation acquired not only technology but also recruited the associated German experts to travel to the Soviet Union because of a lack of expertise in the Soviet Union to apply the technology. Feldbin accompanied his anecdote about artificial diamonds with another story about enticing a German scientist to the Soviet Union. The scientist had been fired from Krupp, and Soviet intelligence played on his disgruntlement to convince him to travel to the Soviet Union. Feldbin later wrote, 'The fees paid by the Russians for such trips ran sometimes as high as $10,000,' but 'the savings amounted to millions.'[78] Lyushkov claimed to have served in a foreign assignment in Germany in 1930. He boasted about drawing praise from Stalin himself for analysing Junkers aircraft factories in Germany, using his proficiency in the German language.[79]

Ginzberg worked as a Razvedupr illegal in Germany in 1926–7, running operations against Germany and German allies, particularly collecting military and technological intelligence. He subsequently operated in France (1927–8), Italy (1928–30), and Austria (1931), primarily targeting Germany and technology, and he received recognition for his outstanding achievements: in 1928 he was awarded an honorary military weapon for successful operations, which was inscribed 'to a steadfast defender of the proletarian revolution, from the Revolutionary Military Committee of the Soviet Union'.[80]

Such operations could be risky. Ginzberg reported running two agents in Germany who disclosed the plans for a new aircraft engine. The Razvedupr passed the plans to a Soviet aircraft factory, which implemented them directly without any alteration or obscuring of the source. Unfortunately for Ginzberg's agents, Germany had recruited an agent inside that same Soviet factory who reported their existence to German intelligence, leading German counterintelligence to arrest and execute the Soviet agents in Germany. The Soviet officers who were responsible for providing the unaltered plans to the aircraft factory, and thereby compromising the agents, were also shot.[81]

Poretskiy reported as an illegal officer in Berlin in 1931. Due to the rise of nationalism and militarism in Germany, German strategic information, especially economic and industrial information, became high on Poretskiy's priority targeting list, placing him at risk of German counterintelligence scrutiny. An SIS source reported that Poretskiy began in 1931 to discuss economic subjects and that he was formulating a variety of economic projects, including targeting the German chemical company IG Farbenindustrie. Poretskiy left Berlin in 1933 when Hitler took control of the German government, but he continued running operations into Germany from his new base in Paris, where he operated under cover of a Soviet Planning Committee (GOSPLAN) specialist and journalist. His cover gave him access to German economic information and was sufficiently convincing to fool an SIS source who encountered Poretskiy in 1933 and assumed that he had left intelligence work altogether and joined the GOSPLAN full time.[82]

Although the Soviet Union was always suspicious of German corporate collusion against the Soviet Union, by 1937 Stalin was increasingly cautious about antagonising Germany. Graff reported that he presented a plan to Moscow in January 1937 to counterweigh German influence by using the force of the Soviet market, which the government controlled completely, to dominate Greek exports in exchange for cash or wheat. The plan would increase Soviet economic power in Greece at Germany's expense. The People's Commissariat of Foreign Trade welcomed Graff's plan, but he later learned that it had been buried, for what he believed was Stalin's preference to reach a trade agreement that would make Germany an ally instead of a competitor.[83]

Diplomatic Intelligence

Nevertheless, German politics and relations with both its allies and its potential adversaries were of paramount importance to Soviet decision-makers to navigate the changing European political environment. As noted above, highly valued Soviet intelligence sources reported on German–British relations and negotiations, providing forewarning of possible connivance between the two world powers that the Soviet Union feared the most. German relations with Japan and Italy were of similar importance to understand the developing axis alliance and its implications for the Soviet Union. Defector information cast light on these efforts from a variety of perspectives.

In addition to Great Britain, Germany was also a target for Feldbin when he returned to Moscow in 1932 to take the position of section chief in the OGPU Economic Department. He would have been aware of a German delegation that travelled to the Soviet Union in August 1932 ostensibly for trade negotiations under an organisation called the Society for a Planned Economy, led by the leftist German political activist Arvid Harnack. Harnack was recruited as a Soviet source and later formed the nucleus of the *Rote Kapella* ('Red Orchestra') Soviet intelligence network that became famous for operating inside Nazi Germany early in World War II.[84] Feldbin may have played a role in cultivating Harnack during his trip to Moscow, and Feldbin's later assistant in Spain, Naum Markovich Belkin, was Harnack's initial handler.[85] Unfortunately, Feldbin obscured this period in his revelations with the fictitious title of an employee in the Soviet export flax trust and never discussed it directly.

When Ginzberg was assigned to his final Soviet intelligence post as the illegal *rezident* in the Netherlands from October 1935 until his defection in September 1937, he focused most of his effort on collecting intelligence about Germany, along with running sources into Spain during the Spanish Civil War. Obtaining German ciphers and intercepting German diplomatic communications were high on the list of Soviet intelligence priorities, similar to Great Britain. This had also been the case during Ginzberg's previous assignment to Germany in the early 1930s, and he reportedly acquired the decryption key for German diplomatic communications, giving Moscow the ability to intercept German secret negotiations with other countries.[86] Then, in 1936, Razvedupr received reports about German–Japanese talks to create an anti-Comintern agreement. Information about the agreement was a high-priority intelligence requirement and Moscow pressed for documentary proof throughout 1936. In August 1936, Ginzberg's agent network obtained a file from Berlin containing German intercepts of Japanese communications with Tokyo during the anti-Comintern pact negotiations. The Razvedupr in Holland already possessed a Japanese codebook to decode the messages. And thus, Stalin received direct information about German–Japanese collaboration before the pact was signed on 25 November 1936.[87]

As Nazi Germany's aggressiveness intensified in the late 1930s, Helfand was in a position to view and report to Moscow Germany's plans and Italy's reactions. Helfand wrote a dispatch to Moscow dated 14 September 1938 summarising the Italian views of the Nazi *Anschluss* with Austria, claiming that Italy was torn between its political obligations to Germany and its desire to avoid entering into a war in Germany's favour. Helfand expressed confidence that Britain and France would not go to war over Czechoslovakia, but that Italy would use the Sudetenland crisis as a public propaganda opportunity, declaring for the benefit of foreign journalists that French military interference in Czechoslovakia would attach ideological significance to the crisis and force Italy to join on Germany's side.[88] Helfand's placement in Italy offered highly valuable access, but as Graff and Ginzberg noted, Moscow might have had other priorities by 1938 that obscured Helfand's reporting.

Guerrilla Warfare

Covert activities to counter Germany were integrated into the Soviet intelligence operations soon after the Bolshevik revolution. Ginzberg confirmed Lenin's belief that successful revolutions would install Bolshevik regimes across Europe within a year of the Russian revolution. Several *Yezhovshchina*-era Soviet intelligence officer defectors were direct participants in the early Bolshevik revolutionary activities in Germany in particular. Short-lived Soviet republics were even established in Bavaria and Hungary as early as 1919, and in Persia in 1920. But the Bolshevik regime in Russia was heavily burdened with a civil war and was unable to support these fledgling republics, which soon collapsed.

Poretskiy took a Comintern assignment in the Ruhr region of Germany in 1921, where he posed as a journalist and gained a reputation for opposing nationalism.[89] His tasks included supporting the German Communist Party in planning an armed uprising to protest the Weimar Republic's failed economic policies and the increasing power of German nationalists. Ginzberg and a group of Razvedupr officers joined Poretskiy in Germany to reignite Comintern operations that had been pushed underground after a Bolshevik Republic in Bavaria failed in 1919. They were there when French and Belgian forces occupied the Ruhr region of Germany in January 1923, and the Soviet Union hoped to capitalise on German anger over the move, which compounded humiliation induced by the Treaty of Versailles. The Comintern, operating through the Razvedupr, worked throughout 1923 to organise a Soviet-style revolution in Germany. Ginzberg and Poretskiy established clandestine cells among German communists and organised militant units that the Soviets planned to form the foundation of a future German Red Army.[90] Graff remembered hearing Soviet propaganda in Moscow during the summer of 1923 in which Soviet propagandist Karl Berngardovich Radek lectured on the imminent workers' revolution that would overturn German nationalist ideology, and Grigoriy Yevseyevich Zinovyev, the leader of the Comintern, predicted the establishment of a German Soviet republic.[91] Comintern representatives in Germany received launch dates from Moscow several times in September and October 1923, only to receive cancellation orders soon thereafter. Finally, a date was set and cells were ready to act. But, according to Ginzberg, the uprising was called off yet again at the last moment due to power struggles within German leftist parties and indecision in Moscow. However, this time, the cancellation reached the Hamburg cell too late and it unilaterally launched a labour insurrection, which was quickly quashed. Workers did not join in a general uprising against the government as the Comintern planned.[92] The faltered insurrection left the communists discredited: Communist-Left Socialist politicians were expelled from parliament and Comintern representatives, including Poretskiy, were forced to flee Germany.[93]

The failed German revolution was on a par with other attempts to produce Bolshevik uprisings in Europe, and abortive communist revolutions in Estonia (1924) and Bulgaria (1925) had similar results. Ginzberg adds that failures in Hungary, Poland, Germany, Estonia, and Bulgaria were analysed in depth in Moscow; however, in no case did Soviet leaders view their own policies as the reason for the failures. They blamed local leaders instead, always upholding a myth of Soviet leaders' infallibility.[94]

Poretskiy soon departed Germany, but Ginzberg stayed after the failed insurrection as a member of a Razvedupr cell that retained the best remaining German agents for clandestine operations. Ginzberg believed that if the Soviet Union and Germany were to go to war, a sabotage capability would be more valuable than an espionage network. Correspondingly, he organised his agents so that some who were assigned to espionage missions during peacetime could transition to sabotage operations during war.[95] Ginzberg noted that the Comintern's Lenin School, established in 1926, trained specially selected foreigners in espionage and sabotage methods, initially focusing mainly on students from Germany and Central Europe.[96] As Stalin retreated from Leninist policies in the 1930s, operations to export revolution to Germany and Central Europe faded, replaced by influence operations against other capitalist countries like Britain, France, and the United States.[97]

Misinformation

Covert revolutionary activities were replaced with misinformation and propaganda operations against Germany designed for two contradictory but related purposes: to persuade Germany that the Soviet Union was a power to be reckoned with and thus a worthy ally, and to persuade Western powers and foreign leftists that the Soviet Union was a bastion of anti-Nazism. Defectors asserted that anti-Nazism was for public consumption, while wooing Germany was the real goal.

Outside the Soviet Union, anti-Nazism was a useful hook for recruiting intelligence sources who would not naturally have cooperated with the Soviet regime. It broadened the pool of potential intelligence recruits to more than just overt adherents to communism. According to Ginzberg, up to the early 1930s, 80 per cent of OGPU agents were recruited from among communist circles. However, as the Nazi Party began to take hold in Germany, OGPU used public fear of Nazism to draw recruits, and by the time Ginzberg defected in 1937, he estimated that only 50 per cent of OGPU recruits were active communists, the rest coming from other anti-fascist circles.[98] Feldbin similarly asserted that OGPU *rezidenturas* in the 1930s focused their recruitment attention on young people from influential families who were receptive to anti-fascism.[99] Ginzberg and Feldbin both described

Philby as an example of an anti-Nazi who was susceptible to offers of opportunities to secretly work against Germany.[100]

Soviet propaganda portrayed Germany as a threat to the Soviet Union throughout the 1930s. This was manifest in the June 1937 trials of Chief of the General Staff Mikhail Nikolayevich Tukhachevskiy and seven other senior Red Army officers, who were charged with espionage on behalf of Germany and quickly executed.[101] Although Germany unquestionably did direct its intelligence resources against the Soviet Union, it would have been unrealistic for Germany to penetrate the People's Commissariat of Defence to the extent that purge trials alleged. Nevertheless, these charges allowed the Soviet Union to portray itself as the victim of an aggressive Germany, affording Soviet intelligence numerous opportunities to recruit anti-Nazi sources.

Lyushkov added that anti-German propaganda also had an internal audience. As Soviet military leaders disappeared in the purge, Stalin replaced them with younger officers, attracting them with 'the possibility of a rapid career and dazzling promotions'. Soviet propaganda rallied these young people by demonising Germany and Japan as enemies intent on infiltrating Soviet forces with spies, whipping up nationalistic fervour among the soldiers and young military commanders.[102]

However, according to Ginzberg, anti-fascist propaganda was only one half of the two-sided Soviet foreign policy that approached Germany simultaneously as a public enemy and a private ally. In 1934, Stalin enlisted Radek to articulate the public line of this policy. He wrote articles excoriating Nazi Germany and Imperial Japan, linking them to a Soviet-concocted British scheme to oppose the Soviet Union. However, even as Radek was articulating the public line, he was fully aware of negotiations underway with Berlin towards a pact of alliance. Ginzberg recalls Radek talking about the secret side of the Soviet relationship with Germany: 'Only fools can imagine we could ever break with Germany. What I am writing here is one thing – the realities are something else. No one can give us what Germany has given us. For us to break with Germany is simply impossible.'[103]

During this period, the Soviet Union advocated the policy of collective security, which encouraged Western countries, especially

Britain and France, to join forces against an aggressive Nazi Germany. Yet, in December 1936, just a month before Graff's economic plan for Greece was buried in Moscow, INO Chief Slutskiy instructed Ginzberg to reduce operations against Germany. Stalin expected good news regarding behind-the-scenes negotiations for a Soviet–German trade pact, and he did not want clandestine operations to spoil his chances. Ginzberg quoted OGPU chief Yezhov, echoing Stalin, as saying, 'We must come to terms with a superior power like Nazi Germany.'[104] The agreement finally came in August 1939, when the Soviet Union and Germany suddenly announced the Molotov–Ribbentrop Pact.

Cooperation with Germany

Ginzberg claims that Stalin was impressed by Hitler's decisiveness in eliminating internal opposition in 1934 and he studied Hitler's tactics closely, laying the foundation for Stalin's purges over the following four years.[105] Stalin considered that Hitler's purge was the sign of a strong leader, the type of leader Stalin wanted to be.[106] Ginzberg wrote, '[Stalin] had a profound contempt for the "weakling" democratic nations and an equally profound respect for the "mighty" totalitarian states. And he was guided throughout by the rule that one must come to terms with a superior power.'[107] Graff added that the lack of international reaction to Hitler's 1934 'Night of the Long Knives' encouraged Stalin to apply the same methods in the Soviet Union.[108]

Even before the Nazi purge, Soviet intelligence organisations were both working against and cooperating with German intelligence. Ginzberg described a relationship between the two countries' intelligence services that had existed since the Treaty of Versailles, and he reported that Berlin was a clearinghouse for intelligence of common interest to both the Soviets and Germans. Until the Nazi Party took control in Germany, Soviet intelligence ran operations against Poland and Great Britain from Berlin with the full awareness of, and in some cases support from, the German government.[109] However, while Soviet and German services shared some information at the government level, their cooperation did not extend to the field level and they did not typically share agents, although they did inadvertently recruit the same agents at times. Ginzberg recounted an instance when Austrian counterintelligence identified a Soviet intelligence network in December 1931. It turned out that German intelligence was also running one of the agents in that network. Razvedupr chief Berzin dispatched Ginzberg to Vienna to sort out the ensuing flap and to prevent the existence of German–Soviet intelligence cooperation from becoming public knowledge.[110] Ginzberg told MI5 that, in the wake of the Molotov–Ribbentrop Pact, he was convinced that Soviet and German intelligence were still cooperating, although he was speaking in 1940, over a year after his defection, and thus was providing his opinion rather than inside knowledge.[111]

Spanish Civil War

The Spanish Civil War was a peculiar manifestation of Soviet policy towards Germany. Soviet intervention in the war aligned with Soviet propaganda that portrayed the Soviet Union as the world's protector against fascism. While Adolf Hitler and Benito Mussolini were making agreements with Nationalist forces, Stalin ordered clandestine Soviet support to the Republican faction, both in the form of military supplies and through the Comintern-sponsored International Brigade that attracted anti-Nazi fighters from across Europe and North America. Anti-Nazism became the rallying cry for International Brigade volunteers.

Ginzberg was initially hopeful that the Soviet intervention in Spain would bring a return of Leninist world revolution. In July 1936, after the trial of the Sixteen in Moscow, Ginzberg met in Paris with a shaken Poretskiy, who proposed that the two old friends make a break with Stalin together to protest the executions. Ginzberg, however, persuaded Poretskiy to remain loyal to the Soviet Union. He argued that Soviet participation in the Spanish Civil War was a positive sign that Stalin's philosophy of 'socialism in one country' was being rejected; he encouraged Poretskiy to await results in Spain to see whether the proponents of international revolution would defeat Stalin.[112]

The NKVD operated aggressively against Francoist forces, giving reason to believe the Soviet policy was genuine. While in Spain, Feldbin handled Philby when the NKVD sent him as a freelance journalist to report on the civil war in February 1937.

Philby's NKVD assignment was to gather information about the Francoist military and about German and Italian troops supporting Spanish General Francisco Franco. Additionally, Maly instructed Philby to 'discover the system of guards, primarily of Franco and then of other leaders' to identify vulnerabilities in Franco's security measures, Franco's routines, and places where he stayed, and in general to get close enough to Franco to develop information that could be used in an eventual assassination plot.[113] Ginzberg gave a similar account in his 1940 MI5 debriefing, stating that Yezhov instructed Maly to recruit an English source to arrange for Franco's assassination. Although Ginzberg did not know the name of the individual Maly chose, he described him as 'a young Englishman, a journalist of a good family, an idealist and fanatical anti-Nazi', which MI5 over twenty years later realised was Philby.[114] Feldbin never mentioned Philby and denied knowledge of any Englishman being sent to Spain to assassinate Franco, although he did admit that the Soviets had a source with almost daily access to Franco.[115] Maly and Deutsch questioned whether Philby possessed the internal fortitude to perform such a risky mission,[116] and their concerns proved justified; the NKVD never attempted an assassination operation. Nevertheless, Philby's intelligence from inside Franco's headquarters was valuable in informing the Soviet leadership about the plans and strategies of Nationalist troops.

The Razvedupr also received orders to arrange clandestine arms shipments to Spain from every source possible.[117] The need for aircraft was particularly urgent to counter imported Italian and German planes flown by Franco's forces. Ginzberg's agents unsuccessfully approached the French Foreign Ministry to obtain transit clearance for weapons en route to Spain, but later found Latin American governments to be more amenable, and they succeeded in securing import certificates to cover the weapons' ultimate destination in Spain. In July 1936, Poretskiy sent Henri Christiaan Pieck to Athens to persuade the Greek government to participate in a weapons trade deal in support of Spanish Republicans in the civil war.[118] Graff was serving as a Razvedupr officer under the cover of chargé d'affaires in Athens at the time of Pieck's visit, and Poretskiy possibly chose Athens as the venue for such a deal specifically because a senior Razvedupr officer experienced in weapons sales was there to oversee it. Although Graff never mentioned the deal in his writings, he was likely to have at least been aware of it and possibly supervised it.

Ginzberg's initial hope that Soviet intervention in Spain signalled a return to Leninist internationalism was eventually replaced with a realisation that it was actually only a foreign policy manoeuvre to strengthen Stalin's bargaining position in Europe. He wrote that the problem of world revolution – the dream of the old Bolsheviks – had long since ceased to be a priority for Stalin, as evidenced by purges of Lenin's associates. Stalin continued to cover his intervention with Comintern rhetoric, claiming, 'The Spanish struggle is not a private affair of Spaniards. It is the common cause of all advanced and progressive mankind.' But Ginzberg connected, somewhat circuitously, Soviet intervention in Spain with Stalin's efforts to woo Germany. He claimed that Stalin intended the intervention to bring Spain into Moscow's political sphere of influence, which would persuade Paris and London to accept stronger ties with Moscow, ultimately to become bargaining chips with Hitler.[119] Feldbin similarly wrote of an operation during the Spanish Civil War when what he called the NKVD 'Misinformation desk' was ordered to insert information into German military intelligence channels claiming that the Soviet aircraft flying against Franco's forces in Spain were not the latest or most capable in the Soviet inventory. The operation was intended to persuade Hitler that the Soviet Union was powerful, with thousands of second- and third-generation aircraft that could fly faster and higher than anything the Germans saw in Spain, and thus was worthy of becoming a German ally.[120] Both defectors perceived the real reason for the intervention as being the opposite of how Soviet propaganda portrayed it.

Public Comintern rhetoric attracted thousands of foreigners to Spain to fight in the International Brigade. Ginzberg wrote, however, that the Comintern soon faded into the background and the NKVD took charge of the volunteers and conducted a purge in Spain similar to what was happening in the Soviet Union. Stalin used the NKVD in Spain to filter the volunteers and identify which ones supported him personally and which did not. Ginzberg described Feldbin's job in Spain as identifying and eliminating dissidents, independents, and anti-Stalinists, which Moscow collectively labelled 'Trotskyists'.[121] Feldbin denied having anything to do with purges in Spain,[122] but Ginzberg illustrated the 'countless disappearances' of International Brigade volunteers by noting one particular example of a communist volunteer whom he described using the code name FRIEND. FRIEND was Brian Goold-Verschoyle, a young British communist who was eager to support Moscow in any way he could. He was trained as a radio technician, and on Ginzberg's recommendation, enrolled in an NKVD radio-operator course and travelled to Spain to support NKVD operations. After a short time in Spain, the NKVD accused Goold-Verschoyle of having Trotskyist sympathies, arrested him, and sent him to prison in Russia.[123] Many other similar stories emerged from the Soviet presence in Spain, belying Feldbin's denials.

Support Operations

Germany was a crossroads for Soviet intelligence operations during the early 1930s, and Soviet intelligence organisations used Germany's central location for operational travel and communication until Nazi control made operating there too risky. Poretskiy, for example, assigned one of his agents, Hede Massing, logistical support tasks, including locating safe houses and mail drops. Massing returned to Germany from Moscow in early 1930, and Poretskiy tasked her with meeting Russian officers who were travelling through Germany en route to foreign assignments and 'attempt[ing] to rub off some of the obviously Russian characteristics' so they could more successfully fit into Western society. Poretskiy also tasked her with contacting several targeted people and setting up meetings for them for developmental purposes.[124]

Ginzberg and Feldbin both discussed a Soviet operation in the late 1920s and early 1930s to counterfeit US currency, which they described as an attempt by Stalin to increase the Soviet Union's hard currency reserves, in which Germany played a role.[125] The operation resulted in arrests of OGPU agents in Germany in 1929. On 11 February 1941, the day after Ginzberg was found dead, the FBI interviewed Joseph Dorn, a businessman who had worked at the Bank Sass and Martini in Berlin, which Ginzberg mentioned in his writings as an institution through which the Soviet Union laundered counterfeit US currency in Germany.[126] Many data points and names in Dorn's story align with Ginzberg's account, although there were some differences in recollection.[127] Dorn told the FBI his first encounter with Ginzberg was in 1929, when Ginzberg came to the recently chartered bank and wanted to deposit money. Dorn stated that he was apprehensive about the deposit, because Ginzberg had brought newly printed, small-size US $100 bills, which Dorn had never seen before; the new bills entered circulation in the fall of 1929. Feldbin was in Germany when the plot became public, prompting an increasingly hostile counterintelligence environment in Germany. German counterintelligence began to more energetically pursue industrial espionage, forcing Feldbin to withdraw from Berlin and return to OGPU headquarters in April 1931.[128]

Japan and Italy

Intelligence operations against Germany were closely related to operations against Germany's allies, Japan and Italy. Several defectors noted Soviet intelligence activities directed against those countries, often in connection with Germany.

Soviet intelligence ran a variety of operations against Japan, heavily emphasising diplomatic/political intelligence and later counterintelligence. As noted above, Ginzberg reported that the Razvedupr in Holland obtained a Japanese codebook, which it used to intercept Japanese diplomatic communications in the mid-1930s.[129] Feldbin may have also used his position in Germany to target Japan in the early 1930s. Possibly referring to his own operation, Feldbin wrote about a Russian-born German manufacturing expert who had fallen on hard times, whom Soviet intelligence approached to woo him to the Soviet Union to supervise the construction of a pencil-making plant. Pencils were not the ultimate objective, however, as the man's daughter worked in the Japanese embassy in Berlin and had access to the chargé d'affaires and the ambassador. The OGPU informed the man that his employment was contingent on his ability to convince his daughter to supply information from inside the Japanese embassy. The operation fell apart when the man's wife halted the deal, reportedly saying that the daughter 'would never be a spy'.[130]

In the years preceding World War II, the Soviet Union often included Japan alongside anti-Nazi Soviet propaganda narratives. When Stalin interviewed Lyushkov and gave him orders for his final assignment in the Far East in 1937, his instructions included the task of rooting out Japanese spies and saboteurs, along with remnants of Tukhachevskiy's supporters and Trotskyites. Stalin also told Lyushkov that Japan maintained an espionage and sabotage network in the Soviet Far East using Korean and Chinese agents.[131] This suspicion precipitated the forced resettlement of over 135,000 Korean residents from the Soviet Far East to Kazakhstan and Uzbekistan and 25,000 Chinese residents to Xinjiang beginning in December 1937, overseen by Lyushkov.[132] Lyushkov chose Japan as a destination for defection because of proximity, but once there he exploited Japan's anti-Soviet stance as a willing platform from which to launch two unsuccessful assassination attempts on Stalin's life.[133]

Several of the *Yezhovshchina*-era defectors also discussed operations in or against Italy during the 1930s, directed at military, industrial, and diplomatic/political intelligence. Ginzberg served as an illegal officer in Italy in 1928–30, under cover as a scholar doing research in the Vatican library on the history of slavery. His intelligence mission included obtaining the plans for an Italian submarine.[134] Mussolini had agreed to sell the Soviet Union the plans for an outmoded model, but Stalin wanted the most recent. In 1928, Ginzberg used a communist sympathiser to establish contact with an Italian engineer who was willing to sell the plans.[135] For the effort, Ginzberg received the Order of the Red Banner in 1931. While awaiting a visa to enter Belgium in 1931, Graff also temporarily worked in Milan as director general of imports, where he negotiated purchases of Fiat cars, airplane engines, dockyard equipment, and ships. He also observed air force manoeuvres in Italy and reported to Moscow the tactical advantages of night-time air attacks.[136]

Feldbin briefly discussed an operation in the 1930s to recruit a key member of Mussolini's cabinet, not mentioning his own involvement.[137] Costello and Tsarev indicate that Feldbin himself ran the operation in December 1933 when he was sent to Rome to cultivate the Italian Minister of Corporations, Giuseppe Bottai. Stalin had personally issued instructions to recruit Bottai; however, the operation failed, reportedly because the OGPU offered insufficient inducement money.[138]

Helfand arrived at the Soviet embassy in Rome during the same month that Feldbin made his attempt on Bottai,[139] and Helfand remained in Italy for the next seven years until his defection. In his cover position as a diplomat in Rome, Helfand was involved in a series of events leading up to the initiation of World War II, including explaining Soviet support to Spanish Republicans, reporting on negotiations related to the Munich Accords in September 1938 and fallout from Nazi Germany's annexation of the Sudetenland from Czechoslovakia, and reporting Italy's reaction to the Soviet invasion of Finland in December 1939. Italian security officials suspected Helfand of being involved in more than purely diplomatic functions.[140] Helfand cultivated Italian Foreign Minister Galeazzo Ciano, Mussolini's son-in-law, becoming a close friend and meeting him informally for social activities. This relationship placed Helfand in a position to learn much about internal Italian political thinking and to influence Ciano in a Soviet direction. Helfand was a direct witness to the Italian government's fear of the Soviet Union as a communist threat, especially after its involvement in Spain directly opposite German and Italian troops. When the Soviet Union invaded Finland on 30 November 1939 with Germany's tacit acceptance, Helfand could report that Italy was inclined to view Germany in the same negative light as it did the Soviet Union, and that pro-Finnish demonstrations broke out in Italy and the Italian press was critical of both the Soviet Union and Germany.[141] Although Soviet intelligence operations treated Fascist Italy as an extension of Nazi Germany, Helfand was in a position to report the seams that Soviet activities created between the two Axis powers.

United States and Canada

Yezhovshchina-era defectors' choice of the United States over France as a post-defection residence revealed a shift in Soviet thinking in the 1930s. This shift was manifested in an evolution in the categories of operations that Soviet intelligence organisations conducted in and against the United States, from an initial emphasis on support operations, to industrial collection, and later anti-defector operations and political/diplomatic intelligence.

Support Operations

Soviet intelligence operations in the United States before diplomatic recognition in 1933 were mostly directed at obtaining US and Canadian passports for clandestine travel in support of other operations around the world. Ginzberg reported that, although the Razvedupr used German or British passports for operational travel throughout much of the 1920s, it came to realise in 1928–9 how easy it was to counterfeit US and Canadian passports and began using them extensively after that.[142] Feldbin wrote that US passports were the most popular among Soviet intelligence travellers because Americans could travel around the world without suspicion and could enter many countries without a visa.[143] They were also popular for couriers, as Americans were viewed as world travellers and would not draw suspicion: 'immigration officers of European and Asiatic countries are not surprised at all if an American lady pops up again and again with her little pet dog on their borders'.[144] From the late 1920s, the Razvedupr and OGPU looked to the Communist Party of the USA (CPUSA) as a supplier of US passports and travel documents in exchange for the operating funds that the party received from the Comintern.[145]

In the early 1930s, the OGPU recruited a Russian émigré named Jacob Golos who became a major supplier of false US passports. Golos ran a travel agency called World Tourists in New York that specialised in facilitating international travel to and from the United States by Soviet agents and CPUSA members. World Tourists was also deeply involved in passport fraud.[146] Chivin reportedly played a role in Golos's recruitment. From what few details are available about Chivin, it appears that his primary mission in New York was to recruit operational support agents, including document forgers and couriers, among whom was Golos. Chivin met Golos in 1930,[147] and although another OGPU illegal, Abram Osipovich Eingorn (variant Einhorn), formally recruited Golos, Chivin and Eingorn likely worked together as they were both in New York at the same time.[148]

Feldbin personally benefited from Golos's services when he travelled to the United States from September to November 1932 under the cover of a Soviet trade specialist. Obtaining a false US passport for future operational use was Feldbin's main reason for travelling to the United States, along with improving his English language proficiency.[149] Golos supplied him with a US passport in the name William Goldin, under which name Feldbin later worked as the illegal *rezident* in London.[150]

US State Department officials debriefed Ginzberg on 28 June 1939 and asked questions primarily about the Soviet use of fraudulent US passports. He described the activities of another OGPU contact named Adolph Arnold Rubens, whom he knew as Ewald, the leader of a network of about twenty agents that obtained approximately 100 to 150 US passports for Soviet operational use. The network also acquired birth certificates and naturalisation certificates to support Soviet intelligence cover operations.[151]

During this time, Soviet intelligence organisations viewed Canada practically as an appendage to the United States, and Canada played a similar role as a source of passports in the 1930s. Ginzberg reported that the Razvedupr placed one officer in Canada who was there expressly to run passport operations.[152] Volodarskiy later had first-hand experience facilitating cover documentation for OGPU illegals in Canada. He worked with two lawyers in Montreal, Aaron Marcovitch and Adolph Stark, who were specialists in obtaining false naturalisation certificates, and thence false passports.[153] He also had contact with Fred Rose, a leading Canadian communist and member of the Canadian Parliament, whom defector Igor Gouzenko identified as a GRU contact in 1945 (see Chapter 3).[154] His most prominent document operation came in September 1936, when he accompanied OGPU illegal Mikhail Borovoy from New York to Montreal to facilitate Borovoy's false Canadian passport. The passport was issued in October 1936 under the name of Willy Brandes, a naturalised Romanian with his wife, Mary.[155] Borovoy used this passport to cover his illegal identity when he and his wife arrived in the UK in November 1936 to replace Theodore Maly as illegal OGPU *rezident*.[156] Volodarskiy revealed his involvement in facilitating Borovoy's cover documents during his RCMP/FBI interrogations in 1940, although the Canadians were aware of Borovoy as early as 1938.[157] While escorting Borovoy to Canada, Volodarskiy also received new Canadian naturalisation certificates for himself and his own family members. Using the identity Armand Labis Feldman, Volodarskiy returned to the United States on 5 January 1937 with a passport that he later used to re-enter Canada in 1940.[158]

Ginzberg further wrote that one of the valuable aspects of American and Canadian foreign fighters volunteering in the International Brigade during the Spanish Civil War was their passports. He wrote that when an International Brigade volunteer arrived in Spain, the NKVD confiscated his passport and told the volunteer it had been 'lost'. The NKVD sent the 'lost' passports to Moscow and used them for operational purposes.[159] Feldbin characteristically denied any NKVD involvement in mishandling passports in Spain.[160] However, many International Brigade volunteers complained that their passports were confiscated and never returned, and several NKVD and GRU operatives assumed the names of those volunteers and travelled on their passports. For example, Ramón Mercader, the NKVD-hired assassin who killed Lev Trotsky in Mexico in 1940, used a passport that had originally belonged to Canadian International Brigade volunteer Tony Babich.[161] Soviet Razvedupr illegal Zalman Volfovich Litvin also travelled to the United States in 1938 using the passport taken from a Canadian International Brigade volunteer, Ignacy Samuel Witczak. Litvin's status as an illegal in the United States was cut short when Gouzenko defected in 1945 and provided a lead about his use of a false passport (see Chapter 3).[162]

The United States was also a venue for funds transfers and economic counterintelligence. In February 1936, Volodarskiy, on instructions from Gaik Badalovich Ovakimyan, his OGPU supervisor operating under Amtorg cover, purchased shares in a company in New York City called Round the World Trading Company, which Volodarskiy subsequently used to hide Soviet money transactions. Ovakimyan gave Volodarskiy money to deposit in the company's accounts and then Volodarskiy wrote checks from the company to recipients all over the world.[163] Additionally, as noted with Germany and Great Britain, Soviet leaders assumed that Western trade partners colluded to over-charge and bilk the Soviet Union.[164] Correspondingly, Volodarskiy stated that NKVD also used Round the World Trading Company for economic counterintelligence inquiries. When Amtorg received an offer from an American company to purchased machinery, Volodarskiy, using Round the World Trading as cover, contacted the same American suppliers and asked for price quotations for the same products. Amtorg could then compare prices and determine whether Amtorg was being overcharged as a Soviet entity.[165]

Industrial Intelligence
As the 1930s progressed, Soviet intelligence operations in the United States increasingly turned from operational support to industrial collection, targeting industrial production processes, new inventions, and secret technological breakthroughs in the United States.[166] In the 1920s and early 1930s, the OGPU focused much of its industrial collection in Europe. But in subsequent years, the United States grew as a source of technological intelligence, and eventually overtook Europe. The OGPU began to view the United States as a 'storehouse of industrial know-how', according to Ginzberg.[167] He quoted a Razvedupr official in the United States as saying, in response to the question of why he used CPUSA functionaries so much for industrial espionage, 'Why not. They receive good Soviet money. They'll never make a revolution, so they might as well earn their pay.'[168] Graff wrote that the Soviet Union was feverishly purchasing industrial machinery to fuel Stalin's industrialisation programme, hoping to 'catch up to and surpass America'.[169]

Volodarskiy's engineering background corresponded closely with the Soviet priority on collecting industrial and technological information. Volodarskiy's supervisor Ovakimyan, also a trained engineer, openly stated that he was in the United States to 'investigate American methods of producing chemicals. If I believe such methods would prove beneficial to my country and satisfactory arrangements can be made, I recommend license be obtained so we may produce under patent rights. In some cases, we ask

83

your manufacturers to design and sell to us chemical produc-ing machinery.'[170] Ovakimyan's transactions were not always as above board as he made them sound.

When Ovakimyan could not obtain technology openly, he passed collection tasks and operating funds to Volodarskiy. Volodarskiy then dispatched agents to factories and engineering facilities around the United States to acquire sketches or drawings, sometimes trav-elling with them.[171] Volodarskiy downplayed the significance of the industrial information he received. But Simon A. Rosenberg, Volodarskiy's assistant, informed the FBI that Volodarskiy col-lected sensitive information from sources in strategic industries, including steel foundries, precision machine manufacturers, and explosives and chemical companies, fulfilling high-priority Soviet requirements when Stalin's second five-year plan was stressing the need to grow Soviet military-related industries.[172]

Operations in Pursuit of Defectors

Soviet intelligence officer defectors chose to immigrate to the United States because of a sense that they would be safer there than in France. However, as the NKVD extended its reach into the United States for technology collection, it also expanded its base of agents who could track down and monitor wanted indi-viduals, like defectors, in the United States.

On 7 March 1939, Sergey Basov, known in the United States as 'Serge Basoff', approached Ginzberg in New York City 'to have a friendly chat'.[173] Ginzberg interpreted the encounter as an ominous signal that the NKVD was following him. Basov appeared only a few months after Ginzberg had arrived in in the United States, and a month before his first public revelations in the *Saturday Evening Post*. Basov was a former Soviet sailor who had joined Soviet state security in 1920. He immigrated to the United States as an illegal Razvedupr officer and gained US citi-zenship, through which he obtained a US passport that gave him freedom to travel internationally. He worked as an NKVD courier between the United States and Europe,[174] and Ginzberg had previ-ously worked him in the Netherlands.[175] His appearance in New York frightened Ginzberg, who never again felt safe and predicted his own assassination on multiple occasions.

The NKVD also pursued Helfand when he first arrived in the United States. Elizabeth Bentley reported that Jacob Golos and another NKVD agent, Joseph Katz, met Helfand's boat and tried to follow him after he disembarked, but they confused the licence number of the vehicle in which he was riding and lost him. They identified the apartment in Manhattan where Helfand was staying, but they lost him again.[176]

Both Volodarskiy and Feldbin believed that the NKVD was capable of following them in the United States. Volodarskiy told RCMP debriefers that the NKVD 'would not hesitate to get rid of a person if they had any reason for doing so and knew where he was ... It is well known that they got rid of many persons.' He was afraid of being ordered back to the Soviet Union and suspected that Soviet agents were searching for him. The FBI commented that it appeared Volodarskiy was more afraid that the NKVD would find him and 'take him to account' than that US authorities would find him and arrest him.[177] He decided in August 1940 to move to Canada.

Feldbin went to great lengths to hide from Soviet pursuit. Soon after defecting he sent a letter to Yezhov promising to maintain secrecy, while appealing to him for his own and his mother's safety: 'If you leave me alone, I will never embark on anything harmful to the Party or the Soviet Union. I have not committed, nor will I commit, anything damaging to the Party and our country. I solemnly swear to the end of my days not to utter a word that may harm the Party that brought me up or the country in which I grew up.' His letter went on to enumerate sensitive operational details covering operations in France, Britain, and Spain, including information about Maclean and Philby, demonstrating the harm he could inflict if the NKVD failed to honour the agreement.[178] He stayed true to his side of the bargain and took many of those Soviet operational details to his grave.

Political Intelligence

Yezhovshchina-era defectors possessed some information about Soviet intelligence operations directed at collecting US political intelligence in the 1930s, although their revelations were sparse. This was partially a factor of defectors' accesses, but also an indicator of the lower position that the United States held in Soviet priorities.

In addition to handling sources of technological intelligence, Volodarskiy was also involved with an agent named Abraham Glasser, who provided inside information about FBI investigations into Soviet activities in the United States. Glasser worked as a research attorney in the Department of Justice, and in 1938 he authored a report titled 'The Use of Military Force by the Federal Government in Internal Disturbances', which examined the federal government's use of force in race riots, strikes, and other domestic security events.[179] Glasser's research duties gave him access to US intelligence about Russian émigré activities and communist recruitment for the Spanish Civil War. Volodarskiy told the FBI about Glasser's status as an NKVD agent and Glasser was fired from his position at the Department of Justice in June 1941, although he was never prosecuted.[180]

Graff claimed peripheral knowledge of operations to collect US-related political intelligence. Graff told the FBI about a conversation he had with Razvedupr chief Berzin about Razvedupr interest in recruiting American, British, and French citizens who resided in China, like those who were connected with a chamber of commerce, research commission, or trade commission. The Razvedupr initially approached potential agents and gave them an overt task to write a report on economic conditions in China, and subsequently offered an all-expenses-paid research trip to Soviet-aligned Mongolia. Berzin told Graff the Razvedupr already had a network of agents in an organisation called the Institute of Pacific Relations in China. After defecting, Graff met fellow intelligence officer defector Ginzberg in Paris who, in the course of conversation about Soviet intelligence operations directed at the United States, indicated that the Razvedupr was successfully using the Institute of Pacific Relations as cover for intelligence operations.[181]

Feldbin's role in setting up intelligence and sabotage schools for International Brigade volunteers who displayed exceptional loyalty to the Soviet Union and aptitude for clandestine operations had long-ranging implications in the United States.[182] A number of American intelligence agents began their careers in the Abraham Lincoln Battalion and were likely graduates from an NKVD espionage school in Spain. These included Morris Cohen, William Weisband, Amadeo Sabatini, Zalmond David Franklin, and Michael Sidorovich. Additionally, several US Army officers who ran OSS anti-fascist operations during World War II were International Brigade volunteers in the late 1930s.[183] After World War II, the FBI began to recognise the connections between Americans who had served in the Abraham Lincoln Brigade in Spain and communist activities in the United States, and Feldbin supplied some background information for the resulting investigations.

France

France continued to be both a venue for and target of Soviet intelligence operations in the 1930s, although its priority had receded somewhat from the 1920s. As noted earlier, one of the reasons defectors chose to immigrate to the United States rather than stay in France was that the Soviet intelligence presence was too intense to allow them to live in France safely. Poretskiy's assassination in September 1937 underlined the Soviet threat, and Arutyunov's disappearance just a short time later added to defectors' fears. Graff's and Ginzberg's experiences of being under Soviet surveillance gave further evidence of the intensity of Soviet counter-defector operations in France.[184]

Those operations were the outgrowth of operations to pursue anti-Soviet émigrés, which was one of the enduring Soviet missions in France from the 1920s. Paris continued to be the hub of the White and anti-Soviet emigration, which attracted a significant amount of Soviet intelligence attention into the late 1930s. The prominent Russian émigré journalist Vladimir Lvovich Burtsev identified L. L. Nikolayev (a pseudonym for Feldbin) as the OGPU chief in France from August 1926 to February 1928 who handled several valuable sources in Paris.[185] One of these was a Russian émigré businessman who targeted the monarchist military organisation Russian All-Military Union (*Русский Обще-Воинский Союз*, ROVS), dealing a devastating blow to the organisation's finances.[186] Feldbin also discussed the NKVD role in the September 1937 kidnapping of tsarist General Yevgeniy-Ludvig Karlovich Miller, who had taken over leadership of the ROVS after Kutepov's disappearance. Miller was later taken to Moscow and executed, effectively ending the monarchist threat to the Soviet Union.[187]

France was also a source of military and industrial intelligence. According to Feldbin, the NKVD had long sought to obtain information from the Second Bureau (military intelligence) of the French General Staff, and the Paris *rezidentura* jumped at opportunities to recruit sources with access.[188] Ginzberg similarly claimed to have participated in collecting the plans for a French submarine.[189] France was also a cover venue for Stalin's interaction with Germany and a recipient of misinformation related to Soviet policy towards Germany. Feldbin described an operation in which OGPU inserted fabricated information into the French General Staff alleging that Germany planned to invade the Rhineland in 1936 and occupy it.[190]

Conclusion

Although the smallest group in this study, *Yezhovshchina*-era defectors furnished glimpses into the reality of the Great Purge, in several cases speaking from their first-hand experience as senior officers in charge of purge operations. These defectors described the impact of the *Yezhovshchina* on Soviet intelligence and security services themselves, leaving large gaps in personnel that were filled with officers who were either blindly loyal to Stalin or less well vetted and more inclined to defect later. But in addition to the emphasis on internal security, these defectors revealed that by the late 1930s, Soviet intelligence operations had expanded into many parts of the world, shifting from prompting Bolshevik-type revolutions to collecting intelligence and conducting 'decomposition work'. Over 400 INO officers and a similar number of Razvedupr officers ran thousands of recruited agents and numerous technical collection operations focused on political, military, scientific, and economic intelligence. Britain and Germany dominated Soviet intelligence attention, with other countries, like the United States, Japan, France, and Italy, all taking secondary but still prominent places in Soviet priorities. Despite initial distrust from receiving countries, several *Yezhovshchina*-era defectors became valuable sources for foreign counterintelligence services, leading to intensified counterespionage actions and arrests in Europe, Japan, and the United States. While their motivations for defecting were similar to many of the officers in the next group – those who defected during World War II – *Yezhovshchina*-era defectors differed from World War II-era defectors mostly because the latter group persevered just long enough to fight in the war.

Notes

1. The only defector in this group that was clearly not a senior officer was Volodarskiy. Chivin, aka Smith, may have been a senior officer, but his rank is unknown.
2. Krivitsky, *I Was Stalin's Agent*; 204–5; MI5 compilation of Ginzberg's debriefings, 'Information Obtained from General Krivitsky During His Visit to This Country, January–February 1940', TNA, KV 2/805, serial 55x, 72 (hereafter 'Compilation of Ginzberg's MI5 Debriefings'); Barmine, *One Who Survived: The Life Story of a Russian under the Soviets* (New York: G. P. Putnam's Sons, 1945), 251.
3. Orlov, *The Secret History of Stalin's Crimes*, 234.
4. Krivitsky, *I Was Stalin's Agent*, 245–7, 254–7.
5. Barmine, *One Who Survived*, 7.
6. Gerhard L.Weinberg, *Germany and the Soviet Union* (Leiden: E. J. Brill, 1954), 92–6.
7. For Lyushkov: Nikita Vasilyevich Petrov and Konstantin Vladislavovich Skorkin, *Кто руководил НКВД 1934–1941* (*Who Led the NKVD 1934–1941*) (Moscow: Zvenya, 1999), published online at <http://www.memo.ru/history/nkvd/kto/index.htm> (last accessed 13 March 2020); for Orlov: Alexander Orlov, *The March of Time: Reminiscences* (London: St Ermin's, 2004), 34.
8. Foreign Office minute, 2 June 1937, TNA, KV 2/2681, serial 10a.
9. Prokhorov, *What is the Cost of Betraying One's Homeland?*, 74–5, 78.
10. Krivitsky, *I Was Stalin's Agent*, 105, 110–11.

11. Alvin D. Coox, 'An Intelligence Case Study: The Lesser of Two Hells: NKVD G. S. Lyushkov's Defection to Japan, 1938–1945', Part I, *The Journal of Slavic Military Studies*, vol. 11 (1998), no. 3, 155–6; 'Постановление политбюро ЦК ВКП(б) "о корейцах"' ('Resolution of the Politburo of the CC VCP (b) "On the Koreans"'), 21 August 1937, Aleksandr N. Yakovlev Archive, <http://www.alexanderyakovlev.org/db-docs> (last accessed 13 March 2020).
12. Coox, 'The Lesser of Two Hells', Part I, 172.
13. Ibid. 159–60.
14. Edward Gazur, *Alexander Orlov: The FBI's KGB General* (New York: Carroll & Graf, 2002), 43.
15. Prokhorov, *What is the Cost of Betraying One's Homeland?*, 76–7.
16. Yevgeniy Primakov (managing ed.), *Очерки Истории Российской Внешней Разведки* (*Essays on the History of Russian Foreign Intelligence*), vol. 3 (Moscow: Mezdunarodnye Otnosheniya, 2007), 17.
17. Elizabeth Poretsky, *Our Own People* (Ann Arbor: University of Michigan Press, 1969), 2.
18. Compilation of Ginzberg's MI5 debriefings.
19. Barmine, *Memoirs of a Soviet Diplomat*, ix–x.
20. MI5 Report sent to the British Consulate General in New York, 12 August 1940, TNA, KV 2/2681, serial 22a.
21. Poretsky, *Our Own People*, 150.
22. Brook-Shepherd, *The Storm Petrels*, 164.
23. Costello and Tsarev, *Deadly Illusions*, 324–5.
24. Memo from Donald C. Downes to Major David Bruce, 3 November 1942 (CIA FOIA site).
25. See Helfand debriefing, TNA, FO 371/24845; and FBI memo, 'Soviet War Plans', 9 August 1946, FBI file 100-343044, serial 109.
26. Helfand and his wife are listed in ships' manifests as Leon and Sophie Moore; see New York, New York Passenger and Crew Lists, 1909, 1925–1957, contained on FamilySearch.org.
27. Orlov, *The Secret History of Stalin's Crimes*, xvi.
28. Alexander Orlov, *Handbook of Intelligence and Guerrilla Warfare* (Ann Arbor: University of Michigan Press, 1963).
29. Alexander Orlov, 'The Theory and Practice of Soviet Intelligence', *Studies in Intelligence*, vol. 7, no. 1 (Spring 1963), 45–65.
30. Orlov, *Handbook*, 164–83.

31. MI5 Krivitsky Debriefing Notes, 3 and 10 February 1940, TNA, KV 2/804, serials 28a and 42a; MI5 Krivitsky Debriefing Notes, 2 February 1940, TNA, KV 2/804, serial 25a.
32. Orlov, 'The Theory and Practice of Soviet Intelligence', 50.
33. 'Record of a Conversation with Mr. H.', 14 April 1941, TNA, KV 2/2681, serial 17a.
34. Ricardo Maffei, 'Il "Caso Helfand"': La Defezione nel 1940 del Diplomatico Sovietico a Roma nei Documenti Americani' ('The "Helfand Case": The Defection in 1940 of a Soviet Diplomat to Rome from American Documents'), *Nuova Storia Contemporanea*, vol. 18, no. 5 (September–October 2014), 54.
35. MI5 memo, 23 June 1941, TNA, KV 2/2681, serial 22a.
36. SIS information quoted in New Scotland Yard memo, 12 December 1928, TNA, KV 2/2878, serial number unclear.
37. Costello and Tsarev, *Deadly Illusions*, 54.
38. Feldbin maintained throughout his debriefings that he had never been to Britain; see, for example, FBI memo 17 December 1953, TNA, KV 2/2878, serial 28a.
39. Gazur, *Alexander Orlov: The FBI's KGB General*, 435.
40. [Author's name redacted], 'A Stone for Willy Fisher', *Studies in Intelligence*, vol. 30, Winter 1986, 21; see also Costello and Tsarev, *Deadly Illusions*, 482, n13.
41. SIS telegram, 4 September 1939, TNA KV 2/1585, serial 22a.
42. JIC, 'Study of Defectors from the USSR', 11–12.
43. SIS telegram, 4 September 1939, TNA, KV 2/1585, serial 22a.
44. Sworn statement of John Herbert King, 28 September 1939, TNA, KV 2/809, serials 133b and 133c.
45. William E. Duff, *A Time for Spies: Theodore Stephanovich Mally and the Era of the Great Illegals* (Nashville; London: Vanderbilt University Press, 1999), 81.
46. Sworn statement of John Herbert King, 28 September 1939, TNA, KV 2/809, serials 133b and 133c.
47. Duff, *A Time for Spies*, 190.
48. SIS telegram, 4 October 1939, TNA, KV 2/1585, serial 25a.
49. Duff, *A Time for Spies*, 100–1.
50. Preliminary MI5 summary of Krivitsky's information, 26 January 1940, TNA, KV 2/804, serial 9a; MI5 Krivitsky Debriefing Notes, 5 February 1940, TNA, KV 2/804, serial 33a.
51. SIS telegram, 4 September 1939, TNA, KV 2/1585, serial 22a.
52. MI5 Krivitsky Debriefing Notes, 3 February 1940, TNA, KV 2/804, serial 29a.

53. FBI memo, 'Intelligence Activities in England', 1 October 1953, TNA, KV 2/2878, serial 7a.
54. Costello and Tsarev, *Deadly Illusions*, 201–2.
55. Ibid. 187–9.
56. Ibid. 192.
57. Memo from MI5 to the FBI, 18 November 1953, TNA, KV 2/2878, serial 15a.
58. MI5 Krivitsky Debriefing Notes, 3 February 1940, TNA, KV 2/804, serial 29b.
59. MI5 Krivitsky Debriefing Notes, 2 February 1940, TNA, KV 2/804, serial 25a.
60. Compilation of Ginzberg's MI5 debriefings, 64.
61. Orlov, *Handbook*, 23–5.
62. Costello and Tsarev, *Deadly Illusions*, 151.
63. Ibid. 160–1.
64. Ibid. 223.
65. Orlov, *Handbook*, 16.
66. Costello and Tsarev, *Deadly Illusions*, 227–32.
67. MI5 Krivitsky Debriefing Notes, 3 February 1940, TNA, KV 2/804, serials 28a, 29b.
68. MI5 Krivitsky Debriefing Notes, 3 February 1940, TNA, KV 2/804, serial 28a.
69. Compilation of Ginzberg's MI5 debriefings, 64.
70. Intercepted letter from Russian Oil Products headquarters, 21 September 1930, TNA, KV 2/2880, serial 3x.
71. Telegram from British Consulate General Moscow to MI5, 30 August 1930; response telegram dated the same day; TNA, KV 2/2880, serial 5b.
72. Immigration notices for Joseph Volkovich Volodarksy, TNA, KV 2/2880, serials 12a and 13a.
73. Marcus Weinstein contact report, 4 October 1932, TNA, KV 2/2880, serial 19a.
74. Marcus Weinstein contact reports, 4 and 12 October 1932, TNA, KV 2/2880, serials 19a and 21a.
75. 'Corrupt Gift Allegation', *Daily Telegraph*, 24 November 1932.
76. 'Russian Fined £50 for Bribery', *Daily Express*, 25 November 1932.
77. Orlov, *Handbook*, 32.
78. Ibid. 31–8.
79. Coox, 'The Lesser of Two Hells', Part I, 148. Coox draws from

interviews with former Japanese intelligence officers and from Lyushkov's post-defection notes.

80. Prokhorov, *What is the Cost of Betraying One's Homeland?*, 89.
81. MI5 Krivitsky debriefing report, TNA, KV 2/804, serial 29b, 56; Compilation of Ginzberg's MI5 debriefings, 5.
82. Cross-reference from MI6 intelligence reports, 23 and 24 May 1933, TNA, KV 2/1898, serial 2a; 'Ignace Reiss Personal History', 17 October 1949, TNA, KV 2/1898, serial 15a.
83. Barmine, *One Who Survived*, 308–9.
84. Costello and Tsarev, *Deadly Illusions*, 72–3.
85. Ibid. 75.
86. Mariya Aleksandrovna Pankova, Inga Yuryevna Romanenko, Ilya Yakovlevich Bagman, and Olga Aleksandrovna Kuzmenko, *100 знаменитых загадок истории* (*100 Famous Mysteries of History*) (Moscow: Directmedia, 2014), 363–4.
87. Krivitsky, *I Was Stalin's Agent*, 20, 32–3.
88. USSR Ministry of Foreign Affairs, Документы и Материалы Кануна Второй Мировой Войны *1937–1938* (*Documents and Material on the Eve of the Second World War*), vol. 1 (Moscow: Politizdat, 1981), 153–4.
89. Statement by Moritz Bardach to French police, in Hede Massing's compilation of the French and Swiss investigations of Poretskiy's murder, HIA, Hede Massing Papers, Box 1, Folder 7.
90. Krivitsky, *I Was Stalin's Agent*, 62–3.
91. Barmine, *Memoirs of a Soviet Diplomat*, 185–6.
92. Krivitsky, *I Was Stalin's Agent*, 62–3.
93. Peter Schwarz, 'The German October: The Missed Revolution of 1923', *World Socialist Web Site*, three-part series, 30–1 October, and 1 November 2008, published online at <https://www.wsws.org/en/articles/2008/10/1923-o30.html> (last accessed 13 March 2020).
94. Krivitsky, *I Was Stalin's Agent,* 67.
95. Compilation of Ginzberg's MI5 debriefings, 29.
96. MI5 Debriefing Notes, TNA KV 2/804, serials 10a and 52a; Compilation of Ginzberg's MI5 debriefings, 58–60. See also Krivitsky, *I Was Stalin's Agent*, 75–6.
97. Compilation of Ginzberg's MI5 debriefings, 59.
98. MI5 Krivitsky debriefing report, TNA, KV 2/804, serial 25a.
99. Orlov, *Handbook*, 108–9.
100. MI5 Krivitsky Debriefing Notes, 10 February 1940, TNA, KV 2/804, serial 41a. Also extracted from Krivitsky debriefing and

cross-referenced to MI5 file on Yezhov, TNA, KV 2/583, serial 21a. Costello and Tsarev, *Deadly Illusions*, 146–7.

101. Krivitsky, *I Was Stalin's Agent*, 254–7.
102. Enclosure to US military attaché Moscow dispatch, 'Interrogation of Liushkov G. S. November 1938', 12 May 1939, 6, NARA, RG 165, Correspondence of the Military Intelligence Division Relating to General, Political, Economic, and Military Conditions in Russia and Soviet Union 1918–1941, MID number 2037-1997/11, microform series M-1443, roll 17.
103. Krivitsky, *I Was Stalin's Agent*, 26.
104. Ibid. 38–9, 236.
105. Ibid. 204–5.
106. Ibid. 249.
107. Ibid. 19.
108. Barmine, *One Who Survived*, 251.
109. Compilation of Ginzberg's MI5 debriefings, 72.
110. Ibid. 73. See also Boris Volodarsky, *Stalin's Agent: The Life and Death of Alexander Orlov* (Oxford: Oxford University Press, 2014), 47.
111. Compilation of Ginzberg's MI5 debriefings, 71.
112. Poretsky, *Our Own People*, 150; see also Duff, *A Time for Spies*, 148.
113. Costello and Tsarev, *Deadly Illusions*, 165.
114. MI5 Krivitsky Debriefing Notes, 10 February 1940, TNA, KV 2/804, serial 41a.
115. Letter from the US Embassy in London to MI5, 24 July 1953, TNA, KV 2/2878, serial 1a; letter from US Embassy, 30 September 1953, TNA, KV 2/2878, serial 5z.
116. Costello and Tsarev, *Deadly Illusions*, 169.
117. MI5 Krivitsky debriefing report, TNA, KV 2/804, serial 39a.
118. SIS memo to MI5 summarising data about Henri Christian Pieck, 25 March 1938, TNA, KV 2/908, serial 107a. See also Krivitsky, *I Was Stalin's Agent*, 105, 110–11.
119. Krivitsky, *I Was Stalin's Agent*, 94.
120. Orlov, *Handbook*, 22–3.
121. Ibid. 119.
122. 'Comments of Alexander Orlov about Walter Krivitsky's Book "In Stalin's Secret Service"', 13 October 1954, 6, TNA, KV 2/2879, serial 45b.
123. Sylvia M. Goold-Verschoyle's letters to Krivitsky, TNA, KV 2/804, serial 7a. See also Brian Goold-Vershoyle's MI5 file, TNA,

2/817, and the MI5 file of Goold-Vershoyle's girlfriend, Margarete Charlotte Moos, TNA, 2/1248.

124. *Personal History of Hede Massing*, 15–17, HIA, Hede Massing Papers, Box 1, Folder 1.

125. Krivitsky, *I Was Stalin's Agent*, 135–58; Feldbin: US Congress. Senate. Committee on the Judiciary. *Scope of Soviet Activity in the United States*, 85th Congress, First Session, Part 50 (Washington, DC: Government Printing Office, 1957), 3441–2.

126. Krivitsky, *I Was Stalin's Agent*, 138–41.

127. FBI New York report of interview, 12 February 1941, file number 100-11146, serial 1.

128. Feldbin discusses the counterfeit operation in US Congress. Senate. Committee on the Judiciary. *Scope of Soviet Activity in the United States*, 85th Congress, First Session, Part 50 (Washington, DC: Government Printing Office, 1957), 3441–2. See also Arnold Krammer, 'Russian Counterfeit Dollars: A Case of Early Soviet Espionage', *Slavic Review*, vol. 30, no. 4 (December 1971), 763–73. Krammer relies partially on Ginzberg's writings for his account.

129. Krivitsky, *I Was Stalin's Agent*, 20, 32–3.

130. Orlov, *Handbook*, 99–102. Costello and Tsarev assert that Feldbin was the case officer in this operation, but did not find specific evidence in his file to prove their assertion; Costello and Tsarev, *Deadly Illusions*, 62, 438 n18–19.

131. 'Interrogation of Liushkov G. S. November 1938', 1.

132. Coox, 'The Lesser of Two Hells', Part I, 155–6.

133. Yoshiaki Hiyama, 'Японские планы покушения на Сталина' ('Japanese Plans to Assassinate Stalin') *Проблемы Дальнего Востока (Problems of the Far East)*, no. 5 (1990), 109–11. See also Iosif Telman, 'Бегство чекиста' ('Flight of the Chekist'), *Русский Базар (Russian Bazaar)*, 2012, no. 34 (853), 23 August 2012, published online at <http://russian-bazaar.com/ru/content/98483. htm> (last accessed 13 March 2020).

134. Gary Kern, *A Death in Washington: Walter G. Krivitsky and the Stalin Terror* (New York: Enigma Books, 2003), 34.

135. Brian R. Sullivan, 'Soviet Penetration of the Italian Intelligence Services in the 1930s', in Tomaso Vialardi di Sandigliano and Virgilio Ilari (eds), *The History of Espionage: Italian Military Intelligence, Electronic Intelligence, Chinese Intelligence* (Biella: Associazione Europea degli Amici degli Archivi Storici, 2005), 87.

136. Barmine, *One Who Survived*, 189.

137. Orlov, *Handbook*, 81.

138. US Congress. Senate. Judiciary Committee, *The Legacy of Alexander Orlov*, 93rd Congress, First Session (Washington, DC: Government Printing Office, 1973), 68–9. See also Costello and Tsarev, *Deadly Illusions*, 109–10.

139. Maffei, 'Il "Caso Helfand"', 49–74.

140. Ibid. 52–3.

141. Weinberg, *Germany and the Soviet Union*, 91.

142. MI5 Krivitsky Debriefing Notes, 31 January 1940, TNA, KV 2/804, serial 20a.

143. Orlov, *Handbook*, 58–9.

144. Ibid. 150.

145. US Congress. House. Special Committee on Un-American Activities. *Investigation of Un-American Propaganda Activities in the United States*, vol. 9 (hereafter Krivitsky Congressional Testimony) (Washington, DC: Government Printing Office, 1939), 5740.

146. Frank J. Rafalko (ed.), *CI Reader: American Revolution into the New Millennium* (Washington, DC: Office of the National Counterintelligence Executive, 2004), 23. See also Costello and Tsarev, *Deadly Illusions*, 93.

147. Alexander Vassiliev, 'Vassiliev White Notebook #1 Translated', 140, 2009, History and Public Policy Program Digital Archive, Alexander Vassiliev Papers, Manuscript Division, Library of Congress <http://digitalarchive.wilsoncenter.org/document/112564> (last accessed 13 March 2020).

148. Teodor Kirillovich Gladkov, *Наш человек в Нью-Йорке. Судьба резидента* (*Our Man in New York: The Fate of a* Rezident) (Moscow: Yauza EKSMO, 2007).

149. Gazur, *Alexander Orlov: The FBI's KGB General*, 22. FBI Summary of Orlov's information provided to MI5 in Washington, 26 October 1953, 8, TNA, KV 2/2878, serial 9a.

150. Volodarsky, *Stalin's Agent*, 37; see also Duff, *A Time for Spies*, 77.

151. FBI memo, 5 June 1948, transmitting transcripts of Ginzberg's State Department debriefings, file number 100-11146, serial 84.

152. MI5 Krivitsky Debriefing Notes, 31 January 1940, TNA, KV 2/804, serial 20a, 12. This changed only a few years later when Canada became involved in atomic research (see Chapter 3).

153. FBI investigative summary, multiple pages, TNA, KV 2/2881, serial 115a.

154. 'The Corby Case', 14, MI5 summary of Gouzenko interrogations, TNA, KV 2/1420.

155. RCMP response to MI5 enquiry about Willy Brandes, 24 January 1938, TNA, KV 2/1004, serial 6a.

156. Investigative summary of Mr and Mrs Willy Brandes @ Mr and Mrs Stevens, TNA, KV 2/1004, serial 7a; Newspaper clipping from the *Daily Telegraph*, 5 January 1937, TNA, KV 2/1004, serial 1a.

157. In February 1938, the Canadian Secretary of State for External Affairs sent dispatches to Canadian legations in Paris, Tokyo, and Washington informing them to impound Borovoy's passport if it came into their possession; see Library and Archives of Canada, RG 25, File number 1938-194, Control Number, FIND025/40494.

158. Immigration record, Vermont, St Albans Canadian Border Crossings, contained on FamilySearch.org.

159. Krivitsky, *I Was Stalin's Agent*, 113. See also Krivitsky Congressional Testimony, 5736.

160. FBI memo titled 'Comments of Alexander Orlov about Walter Krivitsky's Book "In Stalin's Secret Service"', 13 October 1954, 9, TNA, 2/2879, serial 45b.

161. Peter Worthington, 'Canadian Passport: No Spy Lacks One', *Sunday Star* [Washington, DC], 13 October 1968; quoted in US Congress. Senate. Judiciary Committee, Subcommittee to Investigate the Administration of the Internal Security Act and Other Internal Security Laws, *Testimony of Frances G. Knight*, 92nd Congress, Second Session (Washington, DC: Government Printing Office, 1972), 28–9.

162. US Congress. House. Committee on Un-American Activities, *The Shameful Years: Thirty Years of Soviet Espionage in the United States*, 82nd Congress, 2nd Session (Washington, DC: Government Printing Office, 1952), 25–6.

163. FBI investigative summary, 16, 35, 36, TNA, KV 2/2881, serial 115a

164. FBI memo, 'Comments by Alexander Orlov Regarding Information Furnished by Walter Krivistky', TNA, KV 2/2879, serial 64b, 13.

165. FBI investigative summary, 19, TNA, KV 2/2881, serial 115a.

166. Orlov, 'The Theory and Practice of Soviet Intelligence', 50–60.

167. FBI memo, 'Comments by Alexander Orlov Regarding Information Furnished by Walter Krivistky', 13.

168. Krivitsky, *I Was Stalin's Agent*, 90. See also Krivitsky Congressional Testimony, 5740.

169. Barmine, *One Who Survived*, 173.

170. FBI investigative summary, 53, TNA, KV 2/2881, serial 115a.

171. US Congress, *The Shameful Years*, 16; FBI investigative summary, 23, TNA, KV 2/2881, serial 115a.

172. John Earl Haynes, Harvey Klehr, and Alexander Vassiliev, *Spies: The Rise and Fall of the KGB in America* (New Haven; London: Yale University Press, 2010), 382–4, citing Volodarsky's FBI interrogation. See also FBI interview of Thomas L. Black, 7 July 1950, FBI Headquarters file, 'Thomas L. Black, Espionage – R', 65-59191, serial 77; and 24 July 1950, serial 87.

173. Krivitsky, *I Was Stalin's Agent*, 296–7.

174. Kern, *A Death in Washington*, 183. Information about Basov's earlier operations as an illegal in the Netherlands is noted in Christopher Andrew and Oleg Gordievsky, *KGB: The Inside Story* (New York: HarperCollins, 1990), 183.

175. FBI memo, 22 April 1944, FBI file number 100-11146, serial 46.

176. Signed statement by Elizabeth Bentley to the FBI, 30 November 1945, FBI file number 65-56402, serial 220, 9–10.

177. FBI investigative summary, 17, 65, TNA, KV 2/2881, serial 115a.

178. Operational Record File no. 76659, vol. 1, 245–58, Archives of the Foreign Intelligence Service of Russia, quoted in Costello and Tsarev, *Deadly Illusions*, 308–12.

179. NARA, RG 60, Entry A1 126.

180. Haynes, Klehr, and Vassiliev, *Spies: The Rise and Fall of the KGB in America*, 203–4.

181. FBI Case Summary, Owen Lattimore, file number 100-24628, serial 1447, 4 April 1950, 11.

182. Costello and Tsarev, *Deadly Illusions*, 276–7; FBI Summary of Orlov's information provided to MI5 in Washington, 26 October 1953, 4, TNA, KV 2/2878, serial 9a.

183. FBI, Summary of Special Investigation of William J. Donovan, 15 July 1953, 16, file number 77-58706, serial 47.

184. Barmine, *One Who Survived*, 25–6; Krivitsky, *I Was Stalin's Agent*, 294.

185. Vladimir Burtsev, 'Парижская сеть ГПУ с 1925 г. с сетками коминтерна' ('The Paris GPU Network from 1925 with the Comintern Nets'), HIA, Boris Nicolaevsky collection, Box 800, Folder 16 (microfilm reel 744).

186. Vladislav Ivanovich Goldin, *Солдаты На Чужбине: Русский Обще-Воинский Союз, Россия и Русское Зарубежье в XX-XXI Веках* (*Soldiers in a Foreign Land: The Russian All-Military Union,*

Russia, and the Russian Abroad in the 20th and 21st Centuries) (Electronic Publication: Russian All-Military Union, 2011), 136, 401.

187. US Congress, *The Legacy of Alexander Orlov*, 8.
188. Orlov, *Handbook*, 142.
189. Compilation of Ginzberg's MI5 debriefings, 16.
190. Orlov, *Handbook*, 21.

3 World War II-Era Defectors, 1941–1946

Soviet intelligence and state security officers in the third group of defectors fled Soviet control or were captured between 22 June 1941, when German forces invaded the Soviet Union, and the end of 1946. This group includes forty-one officers who either defected while on assignments outside the Soviet Union or decided to collaborate with Germany after they were captured on the battlefield, effectively becoming defectors to the German government. Prisoner-of-war (POW) defectors were forced to navigate the choice of remaining loyal to the Soviet Union and Stalin, whose Great Purge was fresh in their minds, or collaborating with Hitler, who stabbed the Soviet Union in the back with Operation Barbarossa. Many struggled with this choice, and a few decided to throw in their lot with Germany, hoping that someday they would see a new Russia free from both Stalin's and Hitler's rule.

The timeframe for this group extends beyond the formal end of World War II to the end of 1946 for several reasons. First, a wartime atmosphere endured in Europe past the end of hostilities, especially in Germany, due to the level of destruction, lack of infrastructure, and continued presence of millions of troops and refugees. Second, the repatriation clause in the February 1945 Yalta Agreements, by which the Allies committed to hand all Soviet citizens liberated by US or British forces over to Soviet authorities,[1] put wartime Soviet defectors at risk of being sent back to the Soviet Union. For any Soviet citizen who had cooperated with Germany, this was a frightening prospect. The post-war environment for Soviet defectors did not begin to change significantly until Allied forces recognised the ramifications of the Yalta

Table 3.1 World War II-Era Defectors, 1941–1946

Name	Best Known Alias	Service	Became Intel Officer	Date of Defection	Location of defection	Receiving Country
Ivan Georgiyevich Bessonov		NKVD	1926	August 1941	Germany	Germany
Alexander Yakovlevich Zhigunov		NKVD	1938	August 1941	Germany	Germany
Rafail Illych Bekker	Khrenov	NKVD	1920	September 1941	Germany	Germany
Aleksandr Vladimirovich Anokhin	Aleksandr Glebovich Brazhnev; Nikolay Potapov	NKVD	1937	September 1941	Germany	Germany
Georgiy Petrovich Ryabtsev	Aleksandrov	OGPU/ GRU	1920	September 1941	Germany	Germany
Ivan Matveyevich Grachev	Vladimir Alekseyevich Kopylov	GRU?	1941	September 1941	Germany	Germany/ United States
Mikhail Alekseyevich Kalugin		NKVD	1922	fall 1941	Germany	Germany/ United States
Aleksandr Petrovich Kurayev				1941	Germany	??
Nikolay Fedorovich Lapin		NKVD	1936	October 1941	Germany	Germany
Vasiliy Grigoryevich Kiselev		NKVD	1941	December 1941	Germany	Germany/ United States
Kirill Vasilyevich Dovydenko		NKVD		December 1941	Germany	Germany
Petr Vasilyevich Kashtanov	Mikhail Vasilyevich Shatov	NKVD	1942	February 1942	Germany	Germany/ United States
Konstantin Fedorovich Povarov		NKVD		March 1942	Germany	Germany/ United States
Vadim Andreyevich Denisov		GRU?	1936	March 1942	Finland	Germany/ United States
Izmail Guseynovich Akhmedov	Izmail Ege	GRU	1930	May 1942	Turkey	Turkey/ United Kingdom/ United States
Nina Ilinichna Chaplygina		GRU	1941	June 1942	Germany	

Table 3.1 *continued*

Name	Best Known Alias	Service	Became Intel Officer	Date of Defection	Location of defection	Receiving Country
Khelge Eynarovich Vainio		GRU	1942	August 1942	Finland	Finland
Lidiya Pavlovna Yesenina	Maria Arsenyeva	NKVD	1936	October 1942	Germany	Germany
Vladimir Dmtriyevich Fomenko		GRU		October 1942	Germany	??
Yuriy Ivanovich Sedashov		GRU?		1942	Germany	??
Nikolay Vasilyevich Sivtsov		GRU		1942	Germany	??
Viktor Aleksandrovich Dubkov	Victor Nottbusch	NKVD	1942	April 1943/ November 1952	Germany	United States
Vyacheslav Pavlovich Artemyev		NKVD	~1934	September 1943	Germany	Germany/ United States
Boris Alekseyevich Morozov	Boris Aleksandrovich Gai		1934	September 1943	Germany	Germany/ United States
Aleksandr Grigoryevich Kopatskiy	Igor Grigoryevich Orlov	NKVD	1941	October 1943	Germany	Germany/ United States
Aleksandr Fedorovich Chikalov	Igor Almazov	NKVD/ GRU	1924	November 1943	Germany	Germany/ United States
Gasan Artemovich Arabadzhev		NKVD	1936	During WWII	??	??
Aleksandr Yakovlevich Trikoz		NKVD		July 1945	Germany	??
Unknown	Konstantin Dmitriyevich Volkov	NKVD		August 1945	Turkey	United Kingdom
Mikhail Dmitriyevich Mondich	Nicola Sinevirsky	NKVD	1944	August 1945	Germany	United States
Igor Sergeyevich Gouzenko		GRU	1942	September 1945	Canada	Canada
Michael Pines	Stefan Janeczek	NKVD	1945	September 1945	Austria	United States
Unknown	"Vladimir"	NKVD		November 1945	Germany	United States

102

Name	KGB Wanted List	Agency	Year	Date		
Unknown	KGB Wanted List 75	NKVD	1945	December 1945	Germany/Canada	Canada
Aleksandr Stepanovich Kirsanov	KGB Wanted List 338	GRU	1942	1946	Hungary/Canada	Canada
Vladimir Vasilyevich Kulagin		MVD		March 1946	Germany	Germany
Sergey Naumovich Perlin	KGB Wanted List 81	NKVD	1941	March 1946	Germany/Israel	??
Petr Berngardovich Roze	KGB Wanted List 304	NKVD	1945	May 1946	Germany/Venezuela	United States/Venezuela
Vladimir Aleksandrovich Skripkin		GRU		May 1946	Japan	United States
Anatoliy Mikhailovich Granovskiy		MGB	1939	September 1946	Sweden	United States
Yevgeniy Viktorovich Abryutin	KGB Wanted List 107	MGB	1945	November 1946	Germany/United States	United States
Mikhail Vasilyevich Gorshkov		MGB		late 1946	??	United Kingdom

policy and ended the forced repatriation of Soviet citizens in 1947 (see Chapter 4).

Personal Backgrounds

World War II-era Soviet intelligence officer defectors fall into two subcategories: those who defected, or attempted to defect, directly to an Allied or neutral power; and those who were captured while engaging in military operations against Germany and collaborated with German forces after their capture.

The first subcategory consisted of thirteen Soviet intelligence officers whose defection was similar to those in other groups. Gouzenko, Volkov, and Skripkin were serving in Soviet diplomatic establishments; Akhmedov was under cover as a Soviet press attaché; Granovskiy was on the crew of a Soviet merchant ship; and eight others were serving in Soviet occupation forces in Germany and Eastern Europe after the war. They turned to Allied governments that were hesitant to accept them out of fear of irritating the Soviet Union, which was an ally in the fight against Hitler. They faced the dual risk of being involuntarily repatriated or falling victim to Soviet penetrations of the Western intelligence services to which they turned, which in two cases – Volkov and Skripkin – allowed the Soviets to intercept them before they fully consummated their defections.

The second subcategory came from among an estimated 5.7 million Soviet POWs captured during the war. During the first year of the war, German forces penetrated deep into Soviet territory, and it is likely that thousands of Soviet intelligence and state security personnel fell into German captivity during this time. But only a small number of them are known to have collaborated with the Nazis once they were in German custody. Twenty-six are identified in this group, of which fifteen defected during the first year of the war. Two others – Povarov and Morozov – voluntarily crossed the line to surrender to German forces, and one – Anokhin – escaped when German bombing damaged the Soviet prison camp where he was detained, and he subsequently turned himself over to the Germans. These also include twelve officers who were left as stay behind agents or dispatched on covert missions behind German lines and who subsequently were arrested or surrendered themselves to the Germans, or in the case of Vainio, to the Finns. One of those, Dubkov, was captured on the battlefield but never collaborated with Germany; his affiliation with a Soviet intelligence service became known only in 1952.

Little is known of the last two defectors in this group, Gorshkov and Arabadzhev. Gorshkov was an MGB lieutenant who defected probably in late 1946 and wrote an essay for SIS about the MGB. Kim Philby, who was in charge of the SIS's Russia section, signed a transmittal memo forwarding the essay to MI5, although the essay itself is not available. Unfortunately for Gorshkov, the British handed him back to the Soviets as a deserter and nothing further is known of him.[2] Arabadzhev was an NKVD officer in Ajaria before World War II, and his name appears in Krasnov's alphabetic list, but is absent from Krasnov's research papers. Consequently, he probably defected at some time during World War II, although nothing further is known of his defection.[3]

Captured Soviet intelligence and state security personnel were operating in four general missions:

- NKVD border guard and internal security/counterintelligence units
- Tactical military intelligence officers in troop units
- SMERSH counterintelligence officers and interpreters embedded in troop units
- NKVD covert action and penetration forces working behind German lines for intelligence collection and sabotage purposes

The first Soviet personnel exposed to the German onslaught were NKVD border guards and internal security troops. While border guards had regular exposure to foreigners, and some had defected in the past (Nikitin, for example; see Chapter 1), NKVD military forces officers were a category of defectors unique to the wartime period. Four of the defectors early in the war – Bessonov, Ryabtsev, Kiselev, Kashtanov – had commanded NKVD internal security and border guard troops and were captured in the first eight months of the war. Two additional troop commanders – Artemyev and Chikalov – defected in 1943.

Defection requires access to a foreign power to which an aspiring defector can offer him- or herself. Tight control over the Soviet population and severe limitations on interaction with foreigners before the war meant that a defector had to make a conscious decision to approach a foreign power, either while posted outside the Soviet Union or by walking across an international border into a neighbouring country. That changed when German forces invaded the Soviet Union, and millions of Soviet personnel were suddenly exposed to foreigners not by their own choice, but by a foreign power coming to them.

This dynamic forced Soviet POWs into a wrenching choice: return to an unwelcoming Soviet Union, suffer in a Nazi POW camp, or collaborate with the enemy. To the Soviet government, Soviet POWs were traitors. When asked about providing Red Cross postal services for Soviet POWs, Stalin is reported to have responded, 'There are no Russian prisoners of war. The Russian soldier fights on till death. If he chooses to become a prisoner, he is automatically excluded from the Russian community. We are not interested in a postal service only for Germans.'[4] On the other hand, many Soviet POWs existed in horrendous conditions of starvation and exposure, and they faced brutality and open contempt as *Untermenschen*, or subhumans. Approximately 3.3 million died in German captivity.[5]

A small number of POWs collaborated after they received better treatment under German control than that to which they were accustomed in the Soviet Union. Soviet intelligence officer POWs found that the Germans, despite viewing Slavs contemptuously, could tolerate those who cooperated and revealed details of Soviet security and counterintelligence procedures and information about Soviet tactics to infiltrate German-held territory, conduct sabotage operations, and direct partisan bands operating against German forces. Bessonov, for example, was singled out for positive treatment and offered a degree of freedom in exchange for planning anti-Soviet operations.[6] Artemyev looked back at his time in a German POW camp with relief, both because of the respectful treatment offered by the Germans, and because detention as a POW gave him the luxury of time to think.[7] Anokhin claims that the Germans treated him well, although they watched him closely and never fully trusted him; he referred to the Germans as 'pig-headed'.[8] Yesenina initially lied to German interrogators, but changed her mind about cooperating after several months of being treated well in German captivity.[9] In each of these cases, Soviet officers contrasted life in the Soviet Union to the treatment they received under German control and found the latter to be preferable.

The better treatment shown to certain Soviet POWs was an element of the German Operation ZEPPELIN, through which the Reich Main Security Office (*Reichssicherheitshauptamt*; RSHA) selected Soviet soldiers in German POW camps, trained them for covert operations behind enemy lines, and sent them into the Soviet Union. ZEPPELIN began early in the war and extended almost until the German capitulation, and identified hundreds of Soviet soldiers who were willing to support German missions. According to Walter Schellenberg, Chief of the RSHA,

> The purpose of this organization [ZEPPELIN] was to choose from a selection of Russian prisoners intelligent and suitable men to be deployed on the eastern front behind the Russian lines. This work was done by our own Commandos of the Operation ZEPPELIN. The PW's thus selected were turned over to Commandos in the rear, who trained the prisoners. They were trained in assignments of the secret messenger service and in wireless communications. In order to furnish these prisoners with a motive for work, they were treated extremely well. They were shown the best possible kind of Germany. This was accomplished by trips around Germany where they were shown industry and farms and super-highways.[10]

Under this construct, the Germans allowed Soviet POWs to establish anti-Stalin military formations, under close German supervision. Bessonov viewed himself as a future leader in a new Russia freed from Bolshevik rule and he founded, with German consent, the Political Centre for the Struggle with Bolshevism (*Политический центр борьбы с большевизмом*; PTsB), to unite anti-Stalinist formations and organisations and prepare for the overthrow of the Bolshevik regime. Others, like Grachev and Kashtanov, joined the German-sponsored Russian National People's Army (*Русская Национальная Народная Армия*; RNNA), also known as the Osintorf Brigade. Senior Russian émigrés had created the RNNA in March/April 1942, and by fall 1942 the unit had reached 3,300 members. Like Bessonov's PTsB, the Soviet POWs that participated in the RNNA envisioned it as becoming the core of a future anti-Stalinist Russian army, but the Germans viewed it as a pool from which to select soldiers to infiltrate behind the Soviet lines.[11] Fifteen of the officers in this group gravitated towards the most prominent German-sponsored Russian unit, the Armed Forces of the Committee for the Liberation of the Peoples of Russia (*Вооруженные Силы Комитета Освобождения Народов России*; VS KONR), led by Soviet dissident General Andrey Andreyevich Vlasov. The KONR's Prague Manifesto in November 1944 espoused the principles of removing Stalin and the Bolsheviks from power in Russia, returning to the precepts of the February (as opposed to October) revolution, and reaching an honourable peace with Germany.[12] Several officers in this group served in senior KONR command and staff positions.

Generational Shift

This group represents two different generations of Soviet officials: older officers born between 1894 and 1904 and younger officers born between 1912 and 1923. The older officers closely resemble the defectors in the first two chronological groups: they were old enough to have active memories of the Bolshevik revolution, fought in the civil war, and began their Soviet careers during Lenin's lifetime. They had achieved senior ranks in the Red Army or NKVD, and although some were demoted during the *Yezhovshchina*, they persevered long enough to be captured by German forces. They also tended to defect early in the war, most in the first year. Only two of the older generation – Artemyev and Chikalov – defected after mid-1942.

Whereas the older defectors averaged over forty-one years old at the time of their defection, the younger officers' average age was twenty-five. They were often in their teens or early twenties

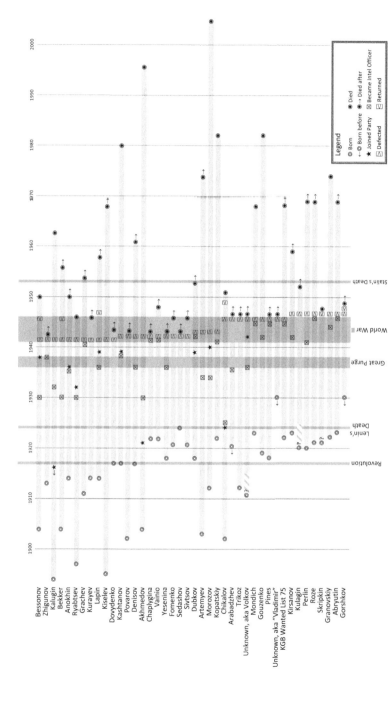

Figure 3.1 Lives of World War II Defectors, 1941–1945

at the beginning of World War II, and many were born after the revolution. They began their military or intelligence careers during the *Yezhovshchina* years or early in the war, and they were junior officers when they defected. Nevertheless, they revealed the priorities of Soviet intelligence in the wartime setting.

Motivations

A variety of factors drove World War II-era defectors' decisions to break with the Soviet Union, most important of which were experiences in their past that led to disenchantment with Soviet power. Some, like Skripkin, were simply disgruntled. Skripkin admitted to a US contact that he had become 'sick and tired' of the Stalinist regime and was waiting for his wife to arrive in Japan so he could defect.[13] Others had deeper dissensions with the Soviet government born from the effects of collectivisation and the *Yezhovshchina* on them or their families. At least eight of the defectors in this group had direct experience with collectivisation and the purges, either as participants or victims. World War II-era defectors experienced family and personal cataclysms during the 1930s similar to much of the rest of the Soviet population, and their losses left a lasting mark on them that contributed to ideological dissonance and their eventual decision to escape Soviet control. Anokhin, Zhigunov, Denisov, and Granovskiy wrote about their parents' arrests and doubts that developed from those experiences. Artemyev, Chikalov, Anokhin, Granovskiy, and probably Morozov were arrested themselves. This is a significant distinguishing characteristic that separates World War II-era from *Yezhovshchina*-era defectors: members of the earlier group were personally involved in violent state security operations, but never experienced the effects on their own families. World War II-era defectors persevered through the purges rather than escaping them, although not always unscathed.

Akhmedov was largely spared the purge himself, and upon graduation from the Higher Military Electro-Technical School of the Red Army Command Staff in Leningrad in 1936 he was accepted for postgraduate work in the electro-technical and radio control research division of the Signal Corps Central Scientific Research Institute in Moscow. However, the *Yezhovshchina* still affected him. He arrived at the time of the first purge trial in Moscow, and he rose quickly in position at the institute chiefly because those above him were arrested.[14] As a Red Army officer, the 1937 trial of Tukhachevskiy and other senior military leaders had a profound impact on Akhmedov, although he claims to have immersed himself in his work to avoid politics as much as the Soviet system would allow.

Russo-Finnish War Experiences

The defectors in this group also saw the *Yezhovshchina*'s effects on Soviet military capabilities, and several witnessed first-hand Soviet deficiencies in Finland during the period 1939–40. Five World War II-era defectors had combat experience in the Russo-Finnish War, which left a strong impression of the purge's negative impact on Soviet military power. For some officers, the Soviet invasion also damaged their careers as the Soviet Union sought culprits for its military failure.

In November 1939, Akhmedov was among students at the Soviet General Staff Academy who deployed to Leningrad for duty on the Finnish Front. He mobilised with an Army headquarters staff, and he complained to his commander about the flaws that led to the defeat of Soviet troops on the Finnish frontier. His comments led to his assignment to an inspection team to look into the shortcomings. The team compiled its report in concert with the NKVD, which participated to determine whether any criminal wrongdoing or treason had led to the defeat.[15]

Bessonov may have been a victim of such an investigation. His career flourished leading up to the Russo-Finnish War because of his association with Mikhail Petrovich Frinovskiy, who served as Yezhov's deputy from 1936 to 1938. After conducting a purge of the Soviet Navy Fleet in 1938, Frinovskiy himself was arrested in April 1939, placing Bessonov in jeopardy by association.[16] Bessonov initially avoided Frinovskiy's fate by denouncing his associates and members of his family.[17] He was returned to the NKVD, promoted to *kombrig*, and assigned as Chief of Training for the NKVD Border and Internal Troops. But his career took a sudden turn for the worse in early 1940 when he deployed to the Finnish front.[18] That, combined with Frinovskiy's execution in February 1940, may have been enough for Bessonov to spend a short period in the Ukhto-Pechorsk prison camps in northern Russia.[19] When he was released, Bessonov was demoted to colonel and assigned not to NKVD troops, but as chief of staff of the 102nd Rifle Division of the 21st Army, which was hastily formed immediately after the Nazi German attack in June 1941. He was captured in action with that unit near Gomel in August 1941.

Denisov deployed to Murmansk during the Russo-Finnish War to prepare covert action groups to infiltrate into the Finnish rear area. He trained a group of thirty Finns for infiltration work, but the war ended before the NKVD launched his mission. During that time, Soviet intelligence reported that the Soviet Union could not count on Finnish communists to incite internal resistance activities against the Finnish government. However, Soviet leaders, refusing to accept unpleasant news, ignored the reports and proceeded to form a communist-based Finnish National Army, which Denisov states 'didn't do a single bit of good'.[20]

Kalugin participated in the Soviet–Finnish war in 1939–40, probably with NKVD troops on the Northwest Front. This service apparently temporarily damaged his career, because during the summer of 1940 he was transferred to the regular Red Army and assigned as a company commander in the Second Slutsk Infantry Regiment. In 1941, he was promoted to major, this time probably as a regular army officer, not a state security officer.[21]

Chikalov never deployed to the Finnish front, but he did consider volunteering. He was released from prison in March 1938 and assigned to Vladikavkaz in the Caucasus to teach at the NKVD military school. But he wrote that 1939 and 1940 were hardest years of his life. He felt that he was living under a constant cloud of suspicion, leading him to consider suicide and to volunteer for service on the front line of the Russo-Finnish war, deliberately looking for a dangerous assignment.[22] Chikalov, like other officers, saw the Finnish Front as a career-ending assignment.

Soviet Propaganda vs Reality

Several World War II-era defectors' motivation was based on the contrast they witnessed between what they heard in the Soviet Union about the ills of the West, and what they saw with their own eyes. Three defectors in this group, Denisov, Gouzenko, and Yesenina, remarked about the divergence they perceived between their personal experiences and the Soviet propaganda that demonised capitalist countries. The Soviet government had enacted strict laws and applied ever-present state security measures to prevent Soviet people from seeing and recognising that contrast. As noted in the next chapter, many who were repatriated to the Soviet Union after the war were sent to forced labour camps to prevent them from infecting Soviet society with pro-Western attitudes after their return.

Denisov travelled several times outside the Soviet Union as a merchant marine cadet, including port calls in the Netherlands in 1932 and England in 1935, and he was struck by the more prosperous living conditions in the West compared to the Soviet Union. He compared the poverty in the Soviet Union with Soviet propaganda claiming that Western societies were threatening and exploitative. The contrast weighed heavily on his mind.[23] Gouzenko's first impressions of Canada highlighted the contrast between life in Canada and the environment in which he grew up; 'I wonder where the workers live?' he recalled his colleague asking as they saw the cleanliness and orderliness of Edmonton, Alberta.[24] During the first year of Gouzenko's stay in Canada he got used to living in a culture where the people 'all seem so pro-Soviet' and 'don't seem to be the least bit scared of secret agents'.[25] Yesenina appears to have been a sincere Soviet believer based on the course of her career and her clandestine assignments. When she was captured in German-occupied Poland in October 1942, she initially resisted interrogation and gave two false names before giving what was likely her real name. But she eventually relented and cooperated, claiming to have realised that Soviet propaganda about Germans did not correspond with reality and that the German system was not as bad as she had always heard.[26] This contrast affected many other Soviet individuals who were exposed to the reality of life outside the Soviet Union, even those who served on the Finnish Front in 1939–40 and with Soviet forces in a devastated Germany after the war.

Personal Differences and Recalls to Moscow

Although disillusionment with the Soviet system was at the foundation of many of these defectors' motivations, it was often compounded by more superficial experiences that prompted their final decision to defect. These catalysing events included a variety of personal disagreements with supervisors or peers or misdeeds that placed defectors in danger of being disciplined or recalled to the Soviet Union in disgrace. In some cases, such as Akhmedov, Chikalov, Volkov, and Gouzenko, defectors had privately harboured the idea of escape for some time, but a disagreement or abrupt recall prompted their final decision to put thoughts to action. For Pines, Granovskiy, and Mondich, NKVD operational experiences soured them to the Soviet cause, although Mondich had entered his NKVD experience with anti-Soviet motivations from the outset. Although each of these defectors came to their decision to defect from different circumstances, dissatisfaction with their Soviet mission and fear of supervisors was a common motivation. In some cases, this pushed them into the arms of the Germans, who used their anti-Soviet attitudes to German advantage.

Receiving Countries

The World War II period was unique in its collection of receiving countries and was divided into two phases: during the war and after the war. The temporary alliance between the Soviet Union and the Western Allies dissuaded defectors from choosing the typical pre-war countries. Many during the war instead chose the destination that was most likely to use their information to do the maximum harm to the Soviet Union: Germany.

Twenty-three of the officers in this group offered their services to Germany. However, thirteen of these did not deliberately choose Germany; Germany chose them when they were captured on the battlefield as POWs. Their choice was not which country to approach, but whether to defect at all. Only Povarov, Morozov, Zhigunov, and Anokhin actively chose to cross the line and surrender themselves to German forces. Others had crossed the line on covert operational missions, but were arrested once they were there.

In all of these cases, defectors' decisions to collaborate with Germany were based on a mixture of self-preservation and a belief that Germany was the only country that could defeat Stalin. They contributed to the German cause by providing intelligence, planning anti-Soviet operations, and developing propaganda messages that would resonate with a Soviet audience. Many threw their support behind the German-sponsored KONR. When Germany capitulated and allied forces occupied German territory in 1945, their belief in Germany as a last resort against Stalin evaporated, and Germany quickly lost its allure as a recipient of defectors.

Chuev describes four reasons why Soviet citizens were drawn into collaboration with the Nazi government. Soviet intelligence officer defectors demonstrated all four of these traits in varying degrees: (1) the growth of pro-Soviet partisan and covert action in the German rear area prompted Germany to recruit cooperative Soviet citizens into counter-partisan military formations; (2) the horrendous conditions of Soviet POWs in German camps convinced many to accept the German offer of fighting against the Soviet Union to escape the suffering; (3) Nazi Germany used anti-Soviet Russian émigrés to persuade POWs to fight against the Soviet Union; and (4) internal social upheaval caused by Soviet leaders' errors and miscalculations turned some Soviet citizens against their government.[27] Most defectors attributed their actions to reason 4 – they believed their collaboration with Nazi Germany represented the only chance to remove Stalin, whom they had grown to hate. The Germans employed pre-war Russian émigrés to solidify defectors' anti-Stalin mindset and to persuade them to cooperate, as articulated by reason 3. This was related to reason 1, as shown by pro-German formations of Russian POWs, like the RNNA, which Germany employed in countering Soviet partisan operations, with pre-war Russian émigrés often in command positions. However, despite these ideological and propaganda drivers, reason 2 may have been the primary motivator for defectors' collaboration – they found that they could receive tolerable and even respectable treatment if they cooperated with their German captors, while being uncooperative could lead to starvation.

None of these reasons implies a pre-existing ideological inclination towards Nazism, which was seldom a motivation for collaboration. Nevertheless, some Soviet and neo-Soviet writers label all defectors to Germany during World War II as Nazis, assuming that anyone who collaborated was automatically pro-Hitler. Sidorov, for example, calls Bessonov a 'Hitlerite chekist'.[28] Prokhorov proclaims that defectors betrayed the great heroism and selflessness that the Soviet people showed in the face of German invasion, and he states, 'With that in the background, instances of betrayal and treason appear even more criminal.'[29] That assumption, however, dismisses the possibility that a Soviet officer might have entered into a temporary alliance with Germany expressly to sweep Stalin from power. These writers ignore Stalin's temporary alliance with Hitler in 1939, which he replaced with another temporary alliance with the United States and Great Britain during the war. If Stalin was willing to enter into temporary alliances with various foreign powers to achieve his objectives, it should come as no surprise that defectors, who grew up in Stalin's regime and had a similar mindset vis-à-vis alliances, considered a temporary relationship with Nazi Germany to achieve their aim of removing Stalin from power.

Some World War II-era defectors expressed views towards Nazi Germany that were far from sympathetic, and they deliberately distinguished their anti-Stalin sentiments from pro-Nazism, although their avowals came after the war and they may have intended them to distance themselves from Nazi crimes. Grachev, for example, claimed members of the RNNA often resisted German supervision because most of the Russian soldiers were motivated by Russian nationalism, not affinity to Germany. He claimed to have served as the chief of police in Mogilev, Belarus, in 1943 under German control, but used his position to help residents avoid the worst of the German occupation. He later said: 'I pride myself on having helped a great many people in Mogilev.' Grachev noted that one of the Russian RNNA commanders, former Soviet Army colonel Vladimir Gelyarovich Bayerskiy (pseudonym Boyarskiy), was openly anti-German, and other Russian officers tried to persuade him to be more discreet.[30] Growing anti-German feelings resulted in some RNNA units re-defecting en masse back to the Soviet Union, leading to the disestablishment of the RNNA altogether in spring 1943.[31]

Artemyev wrote that, although he was treated well in German custody, he had no sympathy for Nazi ideology and was not swayed by German propaganda, which he called 'so stupid, so idiotic, so base that it could not have influenced anyone'.[32] He eventually became a unit commander in the KONR, and he indicated that Vlasov often disagreed with the Germans about plans for using the KONR. Vlasov even instituted a signal to his commanders about whether to obey or sabotage a German order; if Vlasov disagreed with the order, he would sign his name with the last line curving down; if he agreed with it, the last line of the signature would curve up.[33]

Bessonov became one of the leading anti-Stalinist voices in German POW camps, vying with Vlasov for pre-eminence, but his intentions were towards a new Russia, not a stronger Germany. He refused to cooperate with Vlasov, viewing himself as senior militarily and politically. His stated goal was to use Germany to defeat Stalin and then make an agreement by which Germany would recognise Russia's borders as they existed on 1 September 1939, with Bessonov in a leadership role in post-Bolshevik Russia.[34] He wrote about his view of a future Russia:

> Heavy industry, transport, post, and telegraph will be run by the government. Kolkhozes will be dissolved, personal ownership of land will be introduced and personal initiative permitted: in those circumstances, foreign trade will also be under government control. Russia should retain its full territorial, economic and political independence. After the overthrow of Soviet power, military dictatorship will be introduced until the end of the war, established by leaders of the Liberation forces, and then general elections.[35]

Bessonov gathered around himself likeminded officers such as Colonel Viktor Viktorovich Brodnikov, the former chief of staff of the 18th Cavalry Division, who reportedly 'dreamed of the throne of the Chief of Staff of "New Russia"'.[36]

Others did not initially intend to defect but were persuaded after their capture to join German-sponsored anti-Stalinist groups. Kashtanov, for example, hid in the forest for two weeks with freezing hands and feet after his unit was defeated in battle in February 1942. He later told a colleague that he joined the RNNA only to get food and a warm place to stay, planning to escape back into the forest to join the partisans. He stayed instead, saw action in RNNA anti-partisan operations, and later joined the KONR military forces, even leading Vlasov's personal security detail.[37]

Of the defectors in this group, only Zhigunov displayed pro-Nazi sympathies during his interrogation. He blamed the *Yezhovshchina* on a cabal of Jews at the head of Soviet state security, and he told his interrogators, 'The whole period, i.e., the period of VChK-OGPU-NKVD, can be regarded as one of Jewish predominance . . . The period of Yagoda was one of Jewish predominance in the NKVD.' During this period in which he claimed that Jews were in charge, the NKVD used 'perverted methods' and arrested innocent people and forced them to testify against their friends and family.[38] Zhigunov stated that when Beriya became chief of the NKVD, Armenians and Georgians, whom he also called 'Semites', replaced Jews in senior positions, while Jews remained as deputy section chiefs and subsection chiefs. Nevertheless, Zhigunov accredited Beriya with establishing order in the NKVD and stopping the practice of beating prisoners except under direct authorisation.[39]

Still others were driven as much by opposition to Hitler as they were by opposition to Stalin, and for those whose defection occurred outside the battlefield, the preferred destination was either Great Britain or the United States, as it had been before the war. Defectors' choices, however, forced British and US wartime representatives into the awkward position of engaging with 'renegade' officers from an allied power. The British and US governments were loath to anger their Soviet ally and responded by turning away Soviet intelligence officers requesting asylum or hesitating to the point of disaster for the defector. Only after 1946 did they begin to accept Soviet defectors, and even then, with suspicion (see Chapter 4).

Akhmedov's case is particularly remarkable because of its timing – he defected within the first year of the Soviet Union's participation in the war. But Akhmedov did not consider Germany as a recipient country because of the treatment he had received at Nazi hands. Akhmedov was assigned to the Soviet embassy in Germany in May 1941 and was interned along with other Soviet diplomatic personnel when Germany declared war on the Soviet Union the following month. Having been raised as a Muslim, Akhmedov was circumcised, and thus treated as a Jew in German custody and assigned duties to clean latrines and sweep sidewalks.[40] The Soviet Union and Germany exchanged interned diplomats in neutral Turkey in July 1941, and Akhmedov remained there to run clandestine operations. Akhmedov made his first attempt at defection in Istanbul in December 1941, just after the United States declared war on Japan. He walked into the US consulate in Istanbul, introduced himself with his real name, identified himself as a Soviet military intelligence officer, and offered his services to the US government. He met a small, frail, elderly gentleman who listened politely but responded that he could do nothing for him.[41] When Akhmedov received a recall notification in May 1942, he made contact with a British official in Istanbul, but received only a well-wishing gesture.[42] When neither the Americans nor the British accepted his approach, he contacted the Turkish government, which readily granted him asylum. Five years later, when a British intelligence official (Philby) finally debriefed him, Akhmedov thought, 'where have you been since 1942?'[43]

Dubkov was captured in June 1943, 'while fulfilling a combat intelligence mission' behind German lines. He was held in a German POW camp until the end of the war, working as a common labourer in a brush factory. He insisted that he never collaborated with the Germans and especially denied having served in the KONR under Vlasov, considering the KONR 'just as he viewed Hitler's Army, not as a liberator of Russia from Bolshevism, but even more of an oppressor and enslaver of the Russian people'.[44] He joined the US Army Air Corps in March 1945 and served as an aircraft mechanic until July 1946. He was discharged when the US government reversed a decision that had allowed foreign nationals to enlist in the US Army. He did not reveal his intelligence affiliation until 1952, when German police arrested him for a petty crime. He described his background and offered to serve as a US counterintelligence agent during debriefings, but US interrogators never recognised his value.[45]

After the war, the United States and Great Britain again took the primary place as defector recipient countries. Volkov and Skripkin both initially approached British representatives. Volkov contacted the British consulate in Istanbul in August 1945, but Philby intercepted his asylum request at SIS headquarters and reported it to his Soviet handlers, and Volkov returned to Moscow strapped to a stretcher.[46] Skripkin initially approached a British representative in Tokyo in May 1946 and later talked to Americans, but he too was betrayed, probably through a Soviet penetration of British intelligence, and sent back to Moscow before he could defect.[47]

KGB Wanted List number 75 and Abryutin escaped to the American zone of Germany after the war, in December 1945 and November 1946 respectively. They had both taken jobs with the MVD in spring 1945 as interpreters. Abryutin later immigrated to the United States, and number 75 immigrated to Canada.[48]

Gouzenko and Granovskiy chose different defection routes due to their circumstances. Gouzenko was already in Canada, and his first choice was to approach the press, not the government, thinking he could publicise his disagreements with the Soviet system. He was influenced by the defection in the United States in April 1944 of Viktor Andreyevich Kravchenko, who published an anti-Soviet manifesto in the *New York Times* soon after his defection.[49] Gouzenko turned to the Canadian government for asylum only after a newspaper rejected his story.[50] Granovskiy's first defection attempt was to French representatives in Prague in May 1946; however, he did not ultimately defect to the French.[51] A few months later he joined the crew of a Soviet merchant vessel, planning to sail with the ship until it made a scheduled port call in Spain, thinking the Spanish were sufficiently anti-Soviet to accept him.[52] However, the ship's schedule changed suddenly while it was in refit in Stockholm, and he made a hasty decision to approach the US military attaché in September 1946 instead. The US attaché turned him over to the Swedish government to allow the Swedes to vet him and determine whether he was a bona fide defector. The Swedish government permitted him to leave Sweden in November 1946 and he was smuggled to a US interrogation facility in Germany and later resettled in Brazil.[53]

Post-War Careers

Most of those who had collaborated with Germany during the war landed in US or British POW camps after the war, placing them at risk of repatriation. US forces repatriated three World War II-era Soviet intelligence officer defectors: Bessonov, Bekker, and Lapin. British forces repatriated Gorshkov. Ryabtsev committed suicide to avoid repatriation. Chikalov avoided repatriation by accepting US intelligence recruitment in 1946 and initially settled in Germany. But he was kidnapped, probably by MGB personnel, and forcibly returned to the Soviet Union in September 1949. Nothing is known of the post-war whereabouts of Zhigunov or Yesenina.

Others were more fortunate, partially benefiting from drawn-out bureaucratic processes surrounding the repatriation of a huge volume of Soviet POWs. Delays allowed some POWs to remain in US or British camps until after the Allies reconsidered their repatriation policy in 1947. Still others benefited from wilful disobedience by US servicemen, who either intentionally obstructed the fulfilment of the order or facilitated Soviet POWs' escape and disappearance into German society.[54]

Every individual in the World War II-era defector group who was not repatriated had some post-war connection to the United States, Great Britain, or both, either through cooperation with a US or British intelligence organisation, emigration to the United States, participation in a US-sponsored Soviet research programme, or a combination of the three. Five individuals in this group – Anokhin, Artemyev, Denisov, Grachev, and Kashtanov – were interviewed in 1950 or 1951 for the Harvard Project on the Soviet Social System (HPSSS), a project that consisted of social scientists from Harvard University travelling to West Germany to debrief Soviet DPs.[55] David Dallin, who managed the HPSSS, also interviewed Artemyev and Anokhin separately in Germany in

1951 for his research into Soviet state security.[56] After their participation in the HPSSS, Artemyev, Grachev, and Denisov settled in Germany; Kashtanov immigrated to the United States in 1952 and worked at Columbia University. Nothing further is known of Anokhin's whereabouts after his interviews.

Columbia University sponsored another programme – known as the Research Program on the USSR, and run by David Dallin's son Alexander – which attracted Soviet refugee scholars who wrote on a wide variety of political, arts, and economics topics. Artemyev and Kashtanov wrote articles and monographs on Soviet intelligence and state security topics for the Research Program. Additionally, Boris Nikolayevskiy, who supported the Columbia programme through his association with David Dallin, conducted years-long correspondences with Chikalov, Artemyev, Kashtanov, and Denisov, soliciting specific information about Soviet intelligence and state security operations and organisations.

Several defectors in this group obtained full-time employment with a US intelligence or counterintelligence organisation as experts and contributed their Soviet intelligence expertise as instructors. Artemyev, Denisov, and Anokhin taught at the US Army intelligence school at Regensburg, Germany. Mondich immigrated to the United States and married émigré actress Viktoriya Grigoryevna Semenova, and both moved back to Germany to work at the US-sponsored Radio Liberty.[57] Morozov immigrated to the United States and worked for the CIA recruiting assets to infiltrate the Soviet Union.[58] Pines, Abryutin, and the unknown defector named 'Vladimir' approached either American or British intelligence representatives between December 1945 and November 1946, agreeing to cooperate. Akhmedov had a long career in the CIA. He moved to Germany in 1951 and worked in the Defector Reception Center near Frankfurt, participating in interrogations of Soviet defectors and Iranian refugees. He also wrote anti-Soviet propaganda materials targeted at Muslims in the Soviet Union, and the CIA valued his knowledge of Islam in preparing anti-Soviet operations.[59]

Kopatskiy was also hired as a CIA contractor, first in Germany and then in the United States. But he was later suspected of being re-recruited by the KGB to infiltrate the CIA. Mitrokhin's notes indicate that Kopatskiy walked into the Soviet Military Mission in Baden-Baden, Germany, in 1949 and offered his services.[60] No suspicion fell on Kopatskiy at the time, and he and his wife were transferred to the United States in 1957 to continue working for the CIA until 1960, when he was released and took a job driving a newspaper delivery truck.[61] He fell under suspicion in 1962 when defector Anatoliy Mikhailovich Golitsyn provided partially identifying information about a mole inside the CIA that seemed to point to Kopatskiy. He remained under suspicion for the rest of his life, although no conclusive evidence against him surfaced until Mitrokhin's notes came to light in the 1990s, eight years after his death.

Beginning as early as April 1946, Chikalov worked for a US intelligence operation called Operation RUSTY, run by the G-2 US Forces European Theater in Frankfurt, Germany, to collect intelligence about Soviet occupation forces in Germany.[62] However, he fell victim to a lack of coordination between US intelligence and counterintelligence organisations, and the US Army Counterintelligence Corps (CIC) launched an investigation into Chikalov, suspecting that his intelligence activities were in support of the Soviet Union, not the United States. He was held in a CIC detention facility for ten months in 1947–8, and then released with no evidence of Soviet espionage. He was kidnapped and forcibly returned to the Soviet Union about a year later.[63]

Operational Priorities

World War II-era defectors picked up where *Yezhovshchina*-era defectors left off in discussing the targets against which Soviet intelligence and security services directed their efforts. According to defectors' revelations, major targets remained Germany, Japan, and Great Britain, with the United States, Canada, and Turkey emerging as priority targets. Not surprisingly, Germany was the primary target early in the war. But by 1942, near the time that the Soviet Union began to advance westward against a retreating German army, Soviet intelligence priorities began to shift back to Great Britain, combined with the United States as Britain's ally.

Intelligence activities against Germany were directed at winning the current war and were thus largely tactical, combining intelligence collection with sabotage operations in support of military missions. Intelligence activities against Great Britain and the United States were strategic, directed at political and technological targets that would help to win what the Soviets predicted would be the next war.

Germany

World War II-era defectors' revelations depicted three distinct time phases of Soviet operations against Germany: before, during, and after the war. Operations during these periods showed some similarities with each other but noteworthy differences that indicate an evolving role that Germany played in Soviet thinking. Germany understandably drew the lion's share of Soviet intelligence and counterintelligence attention during the war. But Germany was a priority target even before the war, despite the formal friendship denoted by the Molotov–Ribbentrop Pact.

Pre-War Collection

Based upon World War II-era defectors' revelations, the cautious approach to Germany indicated by an NKVD order in late 1936 to reduce intelligence targeting against Germany (see Chapter 2) was short-lived.[64] Denisov, for example, wrote that in the time between Yezhov's ouster from the NKVD and the Soviet Union's entry into World War II (1938–41), Soviet intelligence concentrated its efforts on Axis countries.[65] Akhmedov also indicated that Germany was the Razvedupr's prime target while Akhmedov was at headquarters from mid-1940 to mid-1941.[66] The pre-war NKVD training curriculum included skills specifically needed to operate against Germany: Zhigunov and Yesenina reported that German was one of the primary languages taught to new officers during NKVD training in the late 1930s, and NKVD trainees were taught to view Germany as an enemy bent on destroying the Soviet Union.[67] Lectures during Anokhin's NKVD training from September 1937 to November 1939 contained frequent references to 'capitalist encirclement' and depicted the Nazi system as the epitome of injustice, exploitation of workers, and persecution of communists, with Gestapo spies as the villains.[68]

According to Akhmedov and Zhigunov, in the late 1930s, Soviet intelligence expected war to break out between Germany and other capitalist powers, through which they would weaken each other and leave the world ripe for Soviet dominance. Zhigunov told his German interrogators that Soviet policy was directed against Germany even after Molotov–Ribbentrop, and that Soviet leaders viewed the pact as a marriage of convenience, not of love. He asserted that the Soviet Union concluded the agreement to drive Germany into war with the UK and to profit from the consequent weakening of Germany.[69] Zhigunov claimed that if Germany had not attacked the Soviet Union, the Soviet Union would eventually have attacked Germany, although it was not ready in 1941.[70]

Zhigunov's assessments contained an element of obsequiousness to the Germans. But Akhmedov, who had no affinity for Germans, gave a similar appraisal of Soviet intentions. He wrote that in mid-December 1940 Razvedupr predicted Hitler would quickly bring Great Britain to its knees and British colonial possessions would be divided between Germany and Japan. The Razvedupr assessed that Germany would not attack the USSR: Hitler and his marshals, the Razvedupr believed, were not 'maniacs or lunatics' and 'were not going to attempt suicide'.[71]

The Razvedupr, according to Akhmedov, predicted that the United States would come to Great Britain's aid and attack Germany, and that capitalist states would fight among themselves until the USSR would come and liberate the rest of the world in their wake. In line with these assessments, the USSR developed two alternative plans concerning which capitalist side the Soviet Union would temporarily join to defeat the other: Plan A – the USSR would enter the fight on the side of Germany and Japan against the United States; and Plan B – the USSR would enter into a 'temporary' alliance with the United States to fight Germany. Akhmedov's and Zhigunov's views corresponded with Ginzberg's interpretation of Soviet intentions towards Germany, which saw Soviet intervention in Spain in 1936 as an effort to play Germany off of Britain and France, with the ultimate goal of attracting Germany as a strong partner – in line with the Plan A that Akhmedov described. But even before Operation Barbarossa, the USSR settled on Plan B, initiating a series of efforts to increase intelligence networks against Germany and identify intelligence cooperation opportunities with the United States.[72] Anokhin's NKVD training elaborated on a similar theme, claiming that it would be easy to deal with America later because the 15 million unemployed there already supported the Soviet Union. Similarly, the Soviet Union would easily bring British colonies into the Soviet fold because 'the enslaved peoples practically pray to Lenin and Stalin'.[73]

The Balkans region was also a major element of the Soviet plan. Akhmedov claimed that the USSR planned to 'liberate' the Balkans, 'our brothers in blood', and thereby open a way to the Middle East and its oil resources and strategic routes.[74] As part of the 'liberation' policy, Akhmedov was sent on a mission to the western Ukrainian city of Kamenets-Podolskiy in June 1940 to courier a classified order for the Soviet military commander there to attack Romanian forces if Romania refused to cede northern Bukovina and Bessarabia to the Soviet Union. The plane in which Akhmedov was riding got caught in fog and could not proceed to the meeting point, and when he landed and tried to reach the commander by car, he received a radio message that the order was rescinded because Romania had assented to the demand.[75]

Zhigunov claimed that the Soviet Union was attempting to instigate a war between Hungary and Romania so that Soviet troops would have a pretext to enter the conflict and occupy the oil fields at Ploieşti, Romania, to keep them out of German hands. The Hungarian ambassador to Moscow, Jozsef Kristoffy, wrote a report about this scenario and naively threw a draft of it in the rubbish. The NKVD recovered the draft.[76] The plan ultimately failed, because the German Army took control of the Ploieşti oil fields in November 1940 and they became a source of oil for Germany during the war. Soviet forces did not capture the region until August 1944.

Both Akhmedov and Zhigunov also discussed the Soviet use of Latvia as a recruiting ground for anti-German intelligence operations. Zhigunov worked in Riga from December 1940 to July

1941,[77] and Akhmedov deployed there from January to April 1941.[78] Their assignments were a direct result of the Soviet Union's annexation of the Baltic republics in June 1940 and the subsequent agreement to forcibly resettle Germans living in the occupied territory. This resettlement, known as the *Nachumsiedlung* ('after resettlement'), became an intelligence windfall for the Razvedupr and NKVD, which competed with each other to find recruits among Baltic Germans before they departed. Zhigunov claimed success during his time in Latvia: he reported recruiting an agent in the German embassy in Riga.[79] Agents recruited among resettlees later turned up in various places around Europe and the Middle East. Akhmedov mentioned that when he was posted in Turkey he encountered a young Russian girl travelling on a Polish passport. She was the daughter of a wealthy Russian family who had escaped to Latvia during the Bolshevik revolution, and the Razvedupr recruited her during the resettlement period in 1940–1. The Razvedupr later used her to spot and assess potential targets in bars and clubs in Istanbul.[80]

Wartime Intelligence

When Akhmedov returned to Razvedupr headquarters after his deployment to Latvia, he received a report dated 17 April 1941 from a Czech agent indicating that Germany was making plans to attack the Soviet Union, possibly in June. Stalin interpreted the report as a British provocation and ordered the Razvedupr to investigate its source.[81] Akhmedov was dispatched to Berlin in May under *Tass* cover using the alias Georgiy Petrovich Nikolayev to fulfil Stalin's order.[82] When he arrived in Germany, he learned that the Berlin GRU *rezidentura* had received another agent report in April claiming that about 180 German divisions were grouping on the Soviet border. The ambassador, Vladimir Georgiyevich Dekanozov, dismissed it as a figment of someone's imagination.[83] Akhmedov later wrote, 'We were praised for our second-rate information, but when we got something really important, nobody was even allowed to prepare for invasion.'[84] Denisov stated similarly that Soviet intelligence mistrusted a 'beautiful piece' of intelligence, meaning a single agent report that reveals an adversary's plan in its entirety.[85]

Immediately after Germany's attack on the Soviet Union, Germany transitioned overnight from an important target to the 'main enemy'. In July 1941, just a few weeks after Operation Barbarossa, Akhmedov began working in Turkey under cover as a press attaché, leading a *rezidentura* with four case officers working against Germany.[86] The *rezidentura*'s mission was to recruit sources among European expatriates, especially from countries under Axis control (Poles, Czechoslovaks, Yugoslavs, French, Italians), and instruct them to return home and operate against Germany. He was also to obtain German identity cards, birth certificates, and ration cards to support future illegal operations in Germany. Akhmedov identified a number of Soviet agents in Istanbul who were primarily targeting Germany.[87]

Wartime Soviet intelligence activities concentrated more heavily on tactical targets than before the war. Interrogations of German and other Axis POWs were a valuable source of battlefield intelligence, and POWs became a pool from which to spot penetration opportunities. Soon after Germany attacked the Soviet Union, Yesenina was assigned to Odessa under cover as a nurse but with the mission to conduct POW interrogations. Her questioning of POWs yielded information about unit strengths, morale, armaments, and political orientations of soldiers. Yesenina identified former German communists and socialists among the POWs who had hidden their political views after the Nazi takeover of the German government in 1933.[88] She reported about operations to recruit these left-wing German POWs, train them as propaganda agents, and send them back to their units to foment communism among the German soldiers, subsequently to return to the Soviet side bearing intelligence.[89] Gouzenko similarly indicated that Soviet interrogators recruited German and Italian POWs and either put them to work in Razvedupr headquarters or used them to infiltrate German-held territory.[90] Yesenina further reported that Soviet propaganda encouraging desertions bore fruit among German and Axis soldiers, particularly among non-German units that sometimes defected en masse. She found that Italian, Romanian, and Slovak POWs were less resistant during interrogation.[91]

Yesenina was later airdropped behind German lines near Rovno, Ukraine,[92] to monitor German troop movements and replenishment activities and the sentiment of the local population in the area around Lvov, Rovno, and Lutsk. She relied on over a dozen NKVD agents, mostly Ukrainians and Jews, whom she identified to German interrogators.[93] As the only woman among the World War II-era defectors, Yesenina also appears to have operated as a honey trap, using her language ability and her femininity to elicit information from German, Italian, and Slovak troops fighting along the Eastern Front. Yesenina recounted an instance when she met a German lieutenant with whom she struck up a conversation and who was impressed by her mastery of German. He invited her to his quarters for drinks. He drank a lot, and when he fell asleep, Yesenina stole military orders, notes, a photo ID, and a train ticket from his briefcase and left him sleeping.[94] In August 1942, Yesenina travelled to German-occupied Poland, first spending a week in Warsaw, where she observed and reported military equipment and movements, particularly anti-aircraft batteries, and then moving to Kraków, where she was soon captured.[95]

German scientific intelligence continued to be a priority during the war, as it had been before the war. Gouzenko claimed that atomic energy had been high on the Soviets' priorities for several years before his defection. He wrote that 'the word "uranium" was listed among the more frequently used phrases in the secret cipher codebook of the Director of Military Intelligence in Moscow when I began to work in the communications section there in 1942'.[96] Alan Nunn May, whom Gouzenko identified as a GRU source in Canada late in the war, claimed to have first come into contact with Soviet intelligence through communist circles in 1942 after being asked to analyse a US report (later proven false) that the Nazis were planning to create radioactive 'dirty bombs'.[97]

After the war, the Soviet Union saw Germany as a repository of industrial and consumer goods to turn to Soviet use, and Soviet intelligence officers were employed in seizing German technology and transporting it to the Soviet Union. Soviet troops were astounded by the prosperity they found compared with the Soviet Union, even in a Germany devastated by war. In late April 1945, Granovskiy was sent to Berlin to confiscate vehicles and bring them back to Kiev for the NKGB's use. He also witnessed the

Soviet Union's efforts to dismantle German factories and round up German scientists and send them to the Soviet Union,[98] which, along with the United States and Great Britain, made extensive use of German scientists in developing military-related technologies after the war.

Guerrilla and Partisan Warfare

In addition to collection operations, Soviet intelligence services activated a network of covert sabotage operatives and partisans behind German lines soon after the war began, as *Yezhovshchina*-era defectors had predicted.[99] Six of the defectors in the World War II-era group – Akhmedov, Chikalov, Denisov, Granovskiy, Kopatskiy, and Pines (as well as several in the Early Cold War group, see Chapter 4) – conducted or were involved with sabotage operations targeting German military objectives, such as ammunition and supply depots, roads and bridges, and military leaders.

Akhmedov's tasking included identifying cache sites in Ankara, Istanbul, Izmir and other Turkish cities, as well as in the open country near the Soviet border, in which to store weapons, communications equipment, and money for future use by guerrillas. He was also to identify officers of the defeated Yugoslav royalist army and induce them to go to Moscow for guerrilla training, later to be airdropped into Yugoslavia to lead partisan units.[100] Denisov was assigned in late 1941 to select and train sabotage teams to infiltrate German-allied Finland. His mission was to lead a group to Petsamo (now called Pechenga) north of Murmansk to disrupt communications lines and destroy warehouses, especially those used to store aircraft spare parts and fuel. Petsamo was a staging point for Finnish and German attacks on Murmansk, making it an important point for Soviet military action.[101] Chikalov was ordered to stay behind and establish intelligence, partisan, and sabotage operations when German troops surrounded Kharkov, Ukraine, in July 1942, which he did until his capture in November 1943. He claimed that his unit inflicted considerable losses on the Germans, for which he was decorated multiple times.[102]

A seventh World War II-era defector may have been a partisan leader, but the identifying data is inconclusive. A 2010 study of the Bryansk region during World War II identified a K. Povarov as a leader of the anti-German underground in the town of Seshcha, north-west of Bryansk, soon after the German invasion in 1941. This could be a reference to Konstantin Fedorovich Povarov in this group. The study does not give enough identifying information to determine conclusively that the two are identical, although the coincidence of names and Povarov's status as an NKVD officer make it possible.[103]

Gouzenko never conducted sabotage missions himself, but because he had some acquaintance with the German language, his cipher work at GRU headquarters involved processing messages from partisans operating inside German-held territory. He noted in particular anti-German sabotage operations directed at disrupting railways, demolishing bridges, cutting telegraph and telephone communications, and collecting intelligence on German strengths and weaknesses. Gouzenko also recalled having processed a series of telegrams detailing an operation in which a Soviet agent who was working as a medical inspector in German barracks in Belarus reportedly used his position to introduce poison into the German soldiers' food. The operation was apparently a success, and the agent was subsequently safely exfiltrated.[104]

Granovskiy conducted several short-duration sabotage missions, including a mission to destroy a Gestapo headquarters in western Ukraine. But he also indicated that the NKGB considered exploiting a sabotage mission as cover to dispatch a false defector and establish a long-term infiltration of Germany. Granovskiy described a proposed plan by which he would parachute behind German lines with a team of four other men. Each team member would drop separately and make his way to a designated rendezvous point. But instead of going straight to the rendezvous, Granovskiy would locate and kill three of the others and seriously wound the fourth. He would then surrender to the Germans, claiming to have deserted and abandoned his sabotage mission. The fourth man would be left alive to be captured by Germans and corroborate Granovskiy's story.[105]

Granovskiy's plan was never carried out, but two World War II-era defectors – Kopatskiy and Chikalov – were suspected of being false defectors posing as captured sabotage agents. Kopatskiy was trained to conduct partisan operations behind German lines and he was parachuted into German-held territory in October or December 1943 to lead partisans.[106] The operation did not last long, because he was wounded almost immediately and sent to a German hospital, where he recuperated for several months. Some have surmised that Kopatskiy was dropped into German territory intentionally as a false defector with a mission to penetrate German intelligence.[107] However, Kopatskiy was more likely a legitimate but reluctant defector. Aleksandrov notes that he was among a few officers within the KONR military forces known for openly declaring their Soviet patriotism even after joining the KONR. These officers' attitudes were motivated less by anti-Stalinism than by anti-Nazism, and they hoped to return someday to the Soviet Union to 'atone for their sins to the Motherland'.[108] Expressing pro-Soviet views and aspirations would be incompatible with the objectives of a dispatched false defector, who would rather have avoided drawing attention to himself to reduce the risk of German counterintelligence scrutiny.

Chikalov was also widely suspected of being a Soviet agent posing as a defector, but none of the suspicions was ever substantiated. The US CIC opened a major investigation named Operation HAGBERRY in 1947 based on allegations that Chikalov was involved in Soviet espionage activities.[109] The CIC arrested him and extensively interrogated him from December 1947 to October 1948, but then released him without charge. Aleksandrov cites a separate incident that he claims as evidence that Chikalov was a Soviet agent dispatched as a defector. According to Aleksandrov, the CIA obtained intelligence that Chikalov travelled to Athens, Greece, at some unspecified time in 1948 or 1949, and the CIA sent Grachev, with whom Chikalov had worked in the KONR, to Athens to identify him. Grachev supposedly spotted him, but Chikalov sensed the surveillance and disappeared.[110] Aleksandrov uses this reported incident to show that Chikalov was operating clandestinely on Soviet orders. However, inasmuch as Chikalov was regularly writing letters to Boris Nikolayevskiy from Germany until late August 1949 and he was kidnapped and forcibly returned to the Soviet Union in September 1949, there is no support for the CIA's suspicion that Chikalov travelled to

Greece.[111] Although the Soviet Union may have sparingly used covert operators as false defectors, it more often used them for real missions to destroy German military objectives and create havoc in the German rear.

Counterintelligence

Six officers in this group were involved in counterintelligence missions during the war, including military counterintelligence in Special Sections (*особый отдел*; OO) that preceded the creation of SMERSH – Bekker, Denisov, Granovskiy, Kalugin, Povarov, and Zhigunov. Soviet propaganda built up the threat of German espionage as an element of a concerted effort by capitalist countries to penetrate and destroy the Soviet Union, and several defectors described the concept of 'capitalist encirclement' as a driver behind Soviet counterintelligence activities.[112] Propaganda about 'capitalist encirclement' was reinforced by public proclamations of German espionage, which were used to justify vigilant and omnipresent counterintelligence. As noted in Chapter 2, purge arrests in the late 1930s were often rationalised with claims of espionage on behalf of Germany as well as other capitalist countries like Poland, Japan, and Great Britain. Denisov explained that the Soviet regime based the need for an economic counterintelligence capability on several perceived threats: capitalist encirclement; counterrevolutionaries and oppositionists who hated the USSR; and a continued reliance on specialists from the pre-revolutionary regime due to the lack of communist specialists.[113]

Some defectors seem to have honestly believed the proclamations of German espionage even after they arrived in the West. Chikalov, for example, wrote that the case against Tukhachevskiy was based on bona fide information about a coup plot that Tukhachevskiy was planning with military officers who were disgruntled by the Soviet system and angered by collectivisation. The plot was supposedly widespread and involved a plan to assassinate Stalin and surround Moscow with military forces.[114] Chikalov wrote that Tukhachevskiy had been under the influence of the German General Staff since 1924, and that it was rumoured Tukhachevskiy lived in luxury and kept what amounted to a harem of women, among whom were reportedly German, Polish, and Japanese spies.[115] While there is no credible evidence of Tukhachevskiy's association with foreign intelligence services, many in the Soviet Union, including Chikalov, accepted the espionage allegations presented at the purge trials as legitimate.

Similarly, Zhigunov expressed a firm belief that the purge allegations against Nikolay Nikolayevich Krestinskiy, a prominent old Bolshevik who had served as the Soviet ambassador in Berlin during the 1920s and who was executed as a German spy, were legitimate.[116] Even when his German interrogators confronted him with definitive knowledge that Krestinskiy was not a German spy, Zhigunov stuck to the Soviet party line.[117]

SMERSH ran counterintelligence operations against Soviet troops who fell into German captivity, including several of the defectors in this group, especially those who cooperated with Vlasov. Among these was Bekker, who was probably among those who yielded to SMERSH re-recruitment offers while he worked as an instructor at a German-sponsored intelligence school. He reportedly passed information about Soviet POW students at the school, which led to the neutralisation of KONR intelligence activities behind Soviet lines.[118] Operations like these increased in priority as Soviet forces advanced westward and the Soviet Army replaced Germany as the occupying power in Eastern European countries. Soviet counterintelligence viewed captured Soviet troops as a serious threat, affecting defectors in this group and those in the Early Cold War group (see Chapter 4).

The Soviet Union eventually shifted its focus from Germany as the 'main enemy' towards Germany as a defeated power. Soviet counterintelligence conducted extensive operations to punish Germany for its role in the war and to pursue Nazi officers and collaborators. Near the end of the war, the NKVD began intensifying interrogations of German POWs to locate and arrest SS and SD officers, German saboteurs, and Nazi Party members. Granovskiy reported how SMERSH used captured German files to recruit agents in what would become the Western zones of Berlin with the intention of pre-positioning collection networks before the establishment of occupation zones.[119] Mondich was assigned as an interpreter in a POW screening centre recruiting sources among German POWs to penetrate back into Germany.[120] In May 1945, Mondich was among a SMERSH detachment dispatched to Prague, and his unit arrived just after the KONR had freed Prague from Nazi troops. The unit's primary mission was to identify potential spies and to initiate arrest operations to clear former Nazis and collaborators out of the city. The unit descended on a building that had previously housed a Gestapo headquarters, hoping to find documents that would identify the subjects of Gestapo investigations. But the documents had been removed before they arrived. These networks were later to become the platform for targeting Western occupation forces. The unit also sought refugees who specialised in the field of nuclear fission and collected economic intelligence about German industry and agriculture.[121]

As the Soviet army was poised to enter Vienna in March 1945, Pines offered information to SMERSH about German forces remaining in the city. Pines approached Aleksey Vasilyevich Blagodatov, the Soviet commandant in Vienna, along with his NKVD and NKGB staff, proposing to identify clandestine SS networks and conduct a large-scale eradication of Nazis from Vienna. Pines claimed that Blagodatov initially offered Pines the position of police chief of Vienna to carry out his plan, but later withdrew the offer because Pines was not an Austrian citizen. He did, however, extend a personal invitation for Pines to join the NKVD as a captain in May 1945. Pines agreed, on the condition that his mission would be to kill Nazis.[122] He had personal experience with Nazi brutality; his parents were deported from a Jewish ghetto in 1942, and he joined anti-Nazi partisans organised by the Polish Workers' Party, which cooperated with Soviet forces in Poland. However, he was soon disappointed with the dedication of other NKVD officers who did not share his anti-Nazi fanaticism, but rather cared more about looting. He decided to end his NKVD career after only two months and return to Poland in mid-July.[123]

Nazi hunting increased in importance over the following several years, but counterintelligence among Soviet occupation troops in Germany became a dominant theme after the war (see Chapter 4).

Great Britain, the United States, and Canada

Although Soviet intelligence turned its full attention to Germany after Operation Barbarossa, Stalin redirected part of his intelligence apparatus back towards the Western allies as early as 1942, primarily targeting Great Britain and the United States, and secondarily, Canada and Australia. Stalin continued to see the Allies as capitalist enemies with which the Soviet system could never fully reconcile. He was suspicious of the West from the outset of the war, and his alliance with the Allies was never much deeper than his nonaggression pact with Germany. Stalin's continued mistrust of Western allies was fuelled by questions; for instance, why did the Allies delay launching a second front in the West, and what was Rudolf Hess really doing in Great Britain? Before Germany surrendered, Soviet intelligence leaders reminded their troops that the Soviet Union's alliance with the Western Allies was temporary.

Defectors' revelations about Soviet intelligence targeting before World War II indicate that Soviet intelligence viewed Great Britain and the United States as sources of different broad types of information: collection in Britain leaned towards political and counterintelligence information, while collection in the United States emphasised S&T information.[124] But despite this divergence, Soviet intelligence often viewed Great Britain and the United States as a combined entity, even before the war. Akhmedov wrote that recruitment operations involving German resettlers in Latvia in early 1941 targeted more than just Germany. A few of the recruited agents, particularly Jews, were forced to emigrate to other Western powers, and Akhmedov reported receiving praise for his efforts to recruit agents bound for Great Britain and the United States.[125] As the war progressed, Soviet priorities in the two countries gradually converged – collection targeting Britain increasingly focused on S&T, and penetrations of US political institutions grew in priority, with Canada and Australia being venues for both. Soviet intelligence perceptions of the two countries as a single capitalist entity became even more apparent after the war (see Chapter 4).

Political Collection Directed at Great Britain

Adding to reporting from *Yezhovshchina*-era defectors, World War II-era defectors revealed a number of Soviet intelligence agents before the war with access to British political information. Artemyev identified a Soviet intelligence agent in Iran nicknamed 'Arvad' who worked as a courier for the British consulate in Mashhad and disclosed information from British diplomatic correspondence.[126] More significantly, Gouzenko identified Kathleen Willsher, who worked in the British High Commission in Ottawa and similarly provided access to British diplomatic correspondence. She initially met Canadian Communist Party leader Fred Rose in the mid-1930s, at which time Rose asked her to supply her views about British policy on world events, including the Spanish Civil War and British attitudes towards Germany and Italy. Her interaction with Rose ended in 1939 when the war began in Europe.[127] But GRU agent handler Eric Adams re-established contact in 1942 and again began asking for general information about British policy, which she derived from the diplomatic cables she read at the High Commission. Willsher stated that Adams asked about US–UK relations and for information that might help the Soviet Union convince the Allies to open a second front in Europe.[128] Gouzenko handed Canadian authorities a telegram, supplied by Willsher, dated 3 November 1944 from Dana Wilgress, the Canadian Ambassador to Moscow, describing financial credits for trade assurances between the USSR and Great Britain after the war.[129]

Soviet intelligence taskings also extended to collecting information about and countering British intelligence operations. Zhigunov wrote that his counterintelligence training included Great Britain among the primary threats the NKVD faced, and that he was aware of Soviet counterintelligence operations targeting the British embassy in Moscow.[130] Anokhin's counterintelligence training described Great Britain as a threat on par with Germany.[131] In a similar vein, as Pines was offering his services to the NKVD to hunt Nazis in Vienna in May 1945, Blagodatov, the Soviet commandant in Vienna, asked him whether he knew of any British agents in Vienna and whether he could locate them.[132]

The Canadian government investigation of Gouzenko's allegations uncovered further Soviet attempts to collect on British intelligence. Eric Adams tasked Willsher in November 1944 to report any information she could about SIS activity at the High Commission; however, she declined because her access did not include SIS information.[133] Gouzenko later revealed a vague description of a Soviet source inside British intelligence codenamed 'Elli', whose existence he learned about at GRU headquarters before leaving for Canada in 1943. Gouzenko had little identifying information about 'Elli' except that he worked in 'five of MI', which could have either been MI5 or Section Five of SIS. The vagueness of the information led to various hypotheses about the identity of 'Elli', including Roger Hollis, who worked in MI5, and Philby, who worked in Section Five of SIS. But despite years of searching, including passionate arguments by British counterintelligence investigator Peter Wright, the culprit was never identified.[134]

Akhmedov also provided peripheral information about 'Elli'. As of September 1940, Akhmedov was Acting Chief of the Razvedupr Fourth Section, which was responsible for technical intelligence operations in the West. His deputy was Mariya Iosifovna Polyakova, a GRU officer who managed Razvedupr illegals in the West, and who later became known for handling the *Rote Drei* espionage ring in Switzerland during World War II.[135] Akhmedov's acquaintance with Polyakova became an item of counterespionage interest years later when, in the mid-1960s, MI5 invited Akhmedov to London to question him about Polyakova.[136] In her position, she had reviewed communications from the London-based 'Elli', who Akhmedov claimed worked in British counterintelligence. The communications were of such importance that Polyakova would show some of them directly to Stalin.[137] Akhmedov's information, however, added little to what Gouzenko had revealed and did nothing to resolve the identity of 'Elli'.

Volkov also hinted about Soviet assets within British intelligence, although his defection was thwarted and he never passed the details. Volkov offered the identities of 314 Soviet agents, including two in the British Foreign Office, seven 'inside the

British intelligence system', and another one of which was 'fulfilling the function' of head of a section of counterespionage in London, likely a reference to Philby. He also claimed, as had Arutyunov and Helfand before him, that the Soviet Union had broken British diplomatic ciphers and had been listening to correspondence with London since approximately 1943.[138]

Gouzenko's defection revealed voluminous details about Soviet political collection and influence operations in Canada, which was an indicator of Soviet intelligence priorities in other Western countries. When an assignments officer briefed Gouzenko about his future mission in Canada, he informed Gouzenko that the Soviet Union's goal was to infiltrate communist workers loyal to the Soviet Union into labour unions, who would agitate from within and take leading labour positions, providing a platform for Soviet manipulation.[139] The GRU's most valuable political and influence source in Canada was Fred Rose, who had been arrested for communist labour agitation in 1929 and again in September 1942, after which he was released on the condition that he would not participate in any Communist Party activities. However, he contacted the GRU *rezidentura* just weeks after his release to offer his assistance, and on instructions from New York-based Pavel Petrovich Melkishev (aka Pavel Petrovich Mikhailov), he became a hub of a GRU source network in Canada. Melkishev, otherwise known by his cover name Moliere, managed GRU operations in Canada until an independent Ottawa *rezidentura* opened in June 1943. Rose was thus already serving as a GRU agent when he was elected to the Canadian Parliament in August 1943 and re-elected in June 1945.[140] In addition to source handling work, Rose disclosed information about parliamentary and political matters, including the details of a secret session of Parliament that occurred near the end of 1944.[141]

S&T Collection

As noted in Chapter 2, collection in the United States emphasised S&T information before the war. Akhmedov's revelations about pre-war Soviet intelligence collection focused primarily on military-related technology. Akhmedov's responsibilities at Razvedupr headquarters in 1940 involved managing S&T

collection operations in the United States, based at Amtorg in New York City.[142] When Akhmedov appeared at a US Senate hearing in 1953, he testified that he had received reports and pictures of American tanks from Aberdeen Proving Grounds in Maryland, collected by Amtorg-based Razvedupr officers.[143] Akhmedov also provided a biography of Artak Armenakovich Vartanyan, a Razvedupr officer experienced both in intelligence work and electronics, who had been posted to Amtorg from 1934 to 1939 to collect S&T intelligence. Akhmedov knew Vartanyan well, because after Vartanyan left the United States he served for a time as Akhmedov's assistant at Razvedupr headquarters.[144] Denisov similarly claimed that just before the outbreak of World War II, Stalin ordered an urgent increase in political and military intelligence collection against the United States and Europe, particularly focusing on military-related technology, with aviation technology as the highest priority and shipbuilding a close second.[145]

As the war progressed, Canada began to rise as a prominent operational venue for S&T collection, partially serving as a venue for collecting US and increasingly British research. Gouzenko's extensive revelations showed Soviet intelligence collection in three broad military-related S&T fields: electronics and radar, explosives, and, most prominently, atomic R&D. Gouzenko identified multiple sources working in Canadian military research and development institutions, particularly the National Research Council (NRC), with access to classified information about electronics research, including radar and microwave, submarine detection, and aerial photography. One of those sources, Durnford Smith, had access to the NRC library and passed about 700 pages, including secret and top secret material, about magnetic and radio locators for field artillery on 25 August 1945.[146] Multiple Razvedupr sources also focused on the development of the explosive RDX, for which a new method of production was formulated in Canada during World War II. Raymond Boyer, a professor at McGill University, gave a classified report on the new process, described as 'a process different from that previously employed anywhere else'.[147] In 1943 and 1944, he provided information about ingredients, proportions for preparing, and uses for new

Canadian RDX. He also gave general information about an RDX pilot-plant near Grand-Mère, Quebec.[148]

The technology that brought Great Britain more into the Soviet S&T collection spotlight than any other was atomic R&D, which became the most prominent item in the public's perception of Gouzenko's revelations. Gouzenko claimed that atomic energy had been high on the Soviets' priorities for several years before his defection. The Ottawa *rezidentura*'s largest step towards fulfilling atomic collection requirements was its recontact with British atomic scientist Alan Nunn May in the spring of 1945 to renew a clandestine relationship that the Soviets had initiated with him as early as 1942. Soon after the Ottawa *rezidentura* contacted Nunn May, he provided a survey of atomic energy and the uranium research structure in Canada and the United States. Gouzenko later described Nunn May's information: 'The message described the whole set-up of the American atomic bomb project, naming Major General Leslie R. Groves as its director and Robert Oppenheimer as "the brains", listing the other scientists engaged in the work and locating the plants and experimental stations at Oak Ridge, Tennessee; Los Alamos, New Mexico; Chicago University, Chicago, Illinois; and Hanford, Washington.'[149]

Moscow again ordered Ottawa on 22 August 1945 – just two weeks before Gouzenko's defection – to collect all possible atomic information by the end of 1945, including technological processes, drawings, and calculations related to the atomic bomb. The message designated information on the atomic bomb as 'Task Number 1'.[150] The previous week it had ordered Ottawa to send a more detailed description of the exterior of a plant, possibly referring to a facility associated with the atomic programme.[151] The GRU recognised Nunn May's enduring value after he returned to Great Britain, and Moscow ordered Ottawa to develop a contact plan for him in London.[152]

Collection of US Political Information

Just as S&T collection grew in Canada and Great Britain, defectors reported that political information increasingly arose in their training and taskings related to the United States. Granovskiy's 1943 training as an illegal prepared him for his ultimate target:

Western European countries or the United States. The curriculum included reading foreign books about espionage, such *The Dark Invader: War-Time Reminiscences of a German Naval Intelligence Officer*, written by Franz von Rintelen, a German intelligence officer who operated clandestinely in the United States during World War I.[153] He also indicated that he was trained to seduce women, especially women in the West, who could be valuable as agents by influencing their husbands and through powerful women's organisations.[154] Near the end of the war, Granovskiy was instructed to prepare for a mission to penetrate Czechoslovakian society, and from there to become a 'refugee' and immigrate to the United States. He was tasked to use his training in satisfying women to gain control over a Czech woman named Margarita Rachkova,[155] who owned a restaurant in Uzhgorod in Carpathian Ruthenia. He was to court and marry her, and then suggest that they 'escape' to the West together. His NKGB supervisor reportedly told him, 'Your real work, and the object of all this will be in the United States of America, where such a wife will be very useful to you.' Once he got to America, the NKGB would invest funds to establish a restaurant, which would provide cover for intelligence activities in the United States.[156] At the same time as he was developing a relationship with Rachkova, Granovskiy met an American soldier named Bill who was staying in Uzhgorod. The NKGB viewed this encounter as fortuitous, because Granovskiy could contact Bill once he arrived in America and Bill could vouch for his identity as a Czech émigré. The operation failed because Rachkova had other suitors who became jealous and obstructed Granovskiy's attentions.[157]

Gouzenko also described political collection in the United States, including alleged penetrations at high levels of the US government. He learned from the officer sent to replace him in June 1945 that an assistant to Edward Stettinius, the US Secretary of State, was a Soviet intelligence agent; however, Gouzenko never learned the individual's name.[158] The FBI suspected Alger Hiss, who had participated in the US delegation headed by US delegation headed by Stettinius at the February 1945 Yalta Conference, and chaired the US delegation to the San Francisco United Nations Conference in April to June 1945. The FBI never proved Hiss to be the agent that Gouzenko mentioned and no other candidate was ever conclusively implicated. Nevertheless, whoever it was, the GRU reportedly had a Soviet agent close to the US Secretary of State, and thus knowledgeable of US negotiating strategies for post-war diplomacy. Soviet intelligence interest in the San Francisco Conference was also manifested by the travel of Nikolay Zhiveinov code name MARTIN, a GRU officer operating in Ottawa under Tass cover, to San Francisco to cover the conference.[159] Gouzenko reported that the Soviet embassy viewed the San Francisco Conference as being of little significance except as a platform for Soviet propaganda to lull Western powers into a false view of Soviet intentions.[160]

Preparation for Future War

Soviet collection near the end of World War II showed a Soviet urgency to prepare for the next war. S&T collection had direct relevance to Soviet weapons development, much of it applicable to weapons destined not for use against Germany, but in a war that Soviet leaders foresaw against Great Britain and the United States. Soviet intelligence instructed its personnel to view Great Britain and the United States as potential enemies even while they were allied in fighting Germany, and to prepare for war that would follow soon after Germany's defeat. The Soviet view of Great Britain was encapsulated in instructions Akhmedov received from Moscow: 'never trust the British'.[161] Similarly, Akhmedov wrote that in January 1942 the NKVD *rezident* in Turkey briefed the Istanbul consulate-based intelligence staff that the United States, as the wealthiest of the imperialist countries, was thus the enemy number one. The *rezident* instructed Akhmedov that, although he could be friends with British and Americans in 1942, the World War II alliance was a temporary phenomenon until the defeat of Germany and he should always remember that the Soviet Union would fight them later.[162]

On the day Mondich's unit learned that the war in Europe had ended, a colonel called the unit together to congratulate them on the successful defeat of the Nazis. He then warned them that for Soviet counterintelligence, the war was not over. The Soviet Union was still surrounded by the capitalist world and 'the

143

enemy is not sleeping'.[163] Gouzenko similarly recounted a belief among the Ottawa Embassy staff that the Soviet Union was preparing for World War III even before World War II was over.[164] Gouzenko quoted the NKVD *rezident* in Ottawa as telling the embassy staff, 'Remember that here in Canada you are surrounded by enemies.'[165] He quoted the GRU *rezident* as saying, 'They [the Canadians] don't seem to get it into their heads that today we are friends, but tomorrow we might be enemies.'[166] Gouzenko stressed that collection requirements for information about the atomic bomb, troop movements, coastal maps, tank production, etc., were related to preparation for a future war. He also claimed that post-war Soviet industrial capacity was not being converted to peacetime requirements but continued in full war production.[167]

As the war drew to a close, British- and US-related collection topics transitioned from strategic information to tactical information that could be used in a direct military conflict. On 11 August 1945, two days after Soviet troops rolled into Manchuria and one day after the Japanese government informed the Allies that it would accept the surrender terms articulated in the Potsdam Declaration, the GRU sent a telegram instructing the Ottawa *rezidentura* to collect information about US troop units in Europe and transfers of units to the Pacific Theatre. The requirement tasked the collection of the locations, strengths, and future plans of specific US divisions and corps. It also requested information about the establishment of a US Army headquarters in Germany, its location, and the identity of its new commanding officer. The GRU headquarters telegram began with the caveat, 'It is very important that we receive this information.'[168]

Although this collection ballooned as the war closed, the GRU had begun military intelligence collection against Great Britain and the United States several years earlier. As noted above, the GRU *rezidentura* in Ottawa was activated in 1942 and became fully manned in 1943. During the same year, a GRU illegal Witczak, who was originally sent to the United States in 1938 to recruit sources with access to Japan, asked an American source, Dr Arnold Krieger, to supply information about his military training in the Army Air Corps during World War II.[169] In August

1945, the Ottawa *rezidentura* received instructions from Moscow to expedite a passport for Witczak through GRU agent Sam Carr, and Gouzenko handed this telegram to Canadian authorities when he defected.[170] Gouzenko's lead was sufficient for the FBI to launch an investigation and locate Witczak, although delays in the decision to pursue arrests gave Witczak time to flee the United States. Witczak's real identity was unknown publicly until 1990, when former GRU general Petr Ivanovich Ivashutin published an article in which he identified Witczak as GRU officer Zalman Volfovich Litvin.[171]

Sovietising Newly Occupied Territory

Another principal Soviet objective during the late 1930s and 1940s was to Sovietise newly occupied Eastern European and Baltic territories and root out anti-Soviet elements and Nazi sympathisers. The Soviet Union had long suspected Poland of anti-Soviet agitation in western regions, and the 1939 partition of Poland and the Soviet occupation of the Baltic republics that resulted from the Molotov–Ribbentrop Pact extended the Soviet internal security apparatus into territory from which the Soviet Union suspected Poland of staging espionage operations. As the war progressed and Soviet troops moved westward, Soviet security forces took control of governing functions in newly occupied countries to ensure no anti-Soviet agitation could survive.

Soviet intelligence operations on the territory of Eastern Europe dated from long before World War II. From 1924 to 1933, Chikalov served in various assignments of increasing rank and authority in the OGPU border guards along the Soviet–Polish border. In May 1929, he was promoted to captain, and he led a detachment whose mission included guarding against British, French, German, and Polish spies crossing the western Soviet border. From April 1936 to September 1937, he was assigned to Timkovichi, Belarus, to command a border guard sector, and he wrote a description of the interrogation of Vladislav Iosifovich Golubok, a Belarusian actor and stage director who was arrested for alleged association with Polish intelligence. Chikalov witnessed Golubok's interrogation during the spring of 1937, and while Golubok disclaimed espionage on behalf of Poland, an NKVD interrogator administered an injection that induced Golubok to talk openly about his Belarusian nationalist sentiments and to admit contacts with Belarusian nationalists in Poland. His openness led to a sentence in a prison camp, where he eventually died.[172]

Yesenina's NKVD training included an emphasis on Poland. She took an NKVD-sponsored month-long training tour through Europe during the summer of 1938 to become familiar with European culture in preparation for future operations. At the end of the trip, Yesenina passed through the province of Volhynia, in modern-day north-western Ukraine and south-eastern Poland, where she was informed that her future operating area would be in case of war. While in Volhynia, she collected information about military facilities, transportation infrastructure, and the attitudes of the local residents. She also disseminated Soviet propaganda, which she claimed was easy because most of the population were Ukrainians and Jews, many of whom were inclined towards the Soviet Union anyway.[173]

Yesenina graduated from the NKVD school in May 1939 and reported to her first assignment as a counterintelligence officer in an office in Kiev that oversaw the management and construction of military facilities in Ukraine. Her cover position was as a secretary for the office chief, but her NKVD mission was to familiarise herself with the military facilities in the region in preparation for future conflict. In September 1939, when Soviet forces entered Lvov, Yesenina moved her operation to an office there that performed the same function. In Lvov, she had the added task of monitoring the office staff to identify those who had become too fond of capitalist pre-Soviet conditions.[174]

Anokhin reported that the Soviet Union began priming the intelligence and security staff for an invasion of Poland while negotiations for the Molotov–Ribbentropp Pact were still in progress. In July 1939, lectures at Anokhin's NKVD school began to vilify Polish spies and intensify the urgency of counterintelligence vigilance. He writes that it was clear that the instruction was preparing the ground for some action against Poland. The Soviet population watched as Germany crossed the Polish border in

September 1939. The Soviet government did not oppose the move and even increased rhetoric about mutual support between Nazi Germany and the Soviet Union. Anokhin writes that Soviet people were unsure how to accept the Soviet Army's invasion of Poland later the same month, which he labelled a 'monstrous act'.[175]

In February 1940, Anokhin was selected from his NKVD unit to participate in a mass operation to arrest anti-Soviet agitators in areas of western Ukraine and Belarus that had, until September 1939, been part of Poland. Based on an order from Beriya, on Stalin's prompting, the NKVD mobilised a force of thousands of officers to subdue those regions to 'endear them to us and our laws' and to look after our 'brothers and sisters who have been liberated from the Polish yoke'.[176] Anokhin led a team of thirty-six NKVD and militia soldiers assigned to 'cleanse' a portion the town of Rava-Russkaya, north-west of Lvov.

After he returned from this assignment, Anokhin's job for the remainder of his time in the NKVD was to issue internal passports to Soviet citizens. He initially worked in Kharkov as an NKVD liaison to a militia office, where people requesting internal passports were mostly former military personnel who had been arrested during the *Yezhovshchina* and released from prison under Beriya. He later worked in Latvia in the autumn of 1940, issuing Soviet documents to Latvians who came under Soviet rule when the Soviet Union annexed Latvia.[177]

Mondich and Granovskiy provided corroborative information about Soviet operations to occupy Carpathian Ruthenia and Czechoslovakia. According to Mondich, who was a native of Carpathian Ruthenia, many Ruthenians looked forward to Soviet occupation in 1944, hoping that the Soviet Union would develop and modernise their small, backward province, and pro-Soviet voices predicted great achievements under communist rule.[178] On 23 October 1944, Soviet troops entered Carpathian Ruthenia and anti-Hungarian partisans initially welcomed them. The Soviet Union soon placed NKGB and NKVD personnel in key positions throughout the nominally independent provincial government to pave the way for eventual annexation. Granovskiy was among them, and he served as an advisor to the local city government in the provincial capital Uzhgorod, where he described himself as 'practically speaking, the governor of Uzhgorod'. His job entailed convincing the local population that the Soviet government was a better option than what they had experienced previously.[179]

However, soon after Soviet troops arrived, SMERSH counterintelligence personnel began arresting potentially anti-Soviet elements, including people of Hungarian and German origin, Ruthenian non-communist intellectuals, and Ukrainian nationalists. Many were interrogated and shipped to forced labour camps in Russia or eastern Ukraine. SMERSH recruited Mondich as a Czech and Hungarian translator and interpreter for interrogations with the rank of junior lieutenant.[180] His position in SMERSH gave him insights into how the NKVD inserted sources into Eastern European countries as Soviet troops occupied them and how the NKVD monitored and vetted Russian refugee populations.[181] Mondich was attached to a SMERSH unit under the Fourth Ukrainian Front as it advanced westward from Carpathian Ruthenia through Czechoslovakia and southern Poland. His first assignment was to translate captured documents about nationalist and anti-Soviet organisations, which gave him a glimpse of how much SMERSH knew about nationalist groups that opposed Soviet occupation, like the People's Labour Union of Russian Solidarists (*Народно-Трудовой Союз Русских Солидаристов*; NTS), to which Mondich himself belonged. A fellow NKVD officer discussed with him the threat that the Soviets perceived from NTS, and the officer claimed: 'we know what they're up to'.[182]

Granovskiy similarly wrote that Soviet intelligence operations late in the war took advantage of the population of Eastern Europe as it had done among German returnees from Latvia in 1940. He described Soviet efforts to recruit agents among Eastern Europeans fleeing the advancing Soviet army. He wrote, 'Our agents had to "flee" and "escape" while the world thought that confusion reigned and before the iron curtain could clamp down along the eastern perimeter of Western Europe.'[183]

In July 1945, Granovskiy travelled with an NKGB team to Czechoslovakia, where he operated under a Czech identity and received papers identifying him as a Czech citizen originally from Carpathian Ruthenia. The team set up operations in Dobříš Castle, owned by the Czech nobleman Count Colloredo-Mansfeld, whom the NKGB had recruited as an agent. The Communist Party of Czechoslovakia had taken over the castle and offered it as a Soviet intelligence cover location.[184] Granovskiy's mission at this time was to prepare Czechoslovakia for communist rule, which he did by running agents with access to the Czech government. Among these was reportedly Klement Gottwald, the long-time Czech Communist Party leader who led the Czech underground during the period of German occupation. Granovskiy stated that his mission included spreading rumours about Czech officers in military units trained by the British and the Americans to discredit the officers and sow discord among the troops.[185]

Pines reported that NKVD missions in Vienna included operating against émigré Hungarians and Serbian Chetniks. In June 1945, Pines also came into contact with a special NKGB unit that arrived from Moscow to 'loot' a topographic and cartographic institute, which possessed dies used to print currency for the national banks of Balkan countries. The unit packed up every map, coin, die, and specimen of money from the institute, catalogued them, and sent them to Moscow.[186] This activity gave the Soviet Union control over local currency that would assist in subsuming local economies under the Soviet Union.

After he returned to Poland, Pines commanded security troops in the Danzig district, including those involved in investigations, intelligence collection, and clandestine operations. While he nominally led the department, an NKGB officer, Colonel Kulikov, was assigned as a liaison. The Russian officer did not directly interfere in Polish operations, but Pines felt it was wise to inform him of all significant developments. Any crimes committed by occupying Soviet troops or reports of Russian, White Russian, or Ukrainian nationalists were immediately handed to Soviet officers.[187] In November 1944, Perlin was assigned as one of those Soviet liaison officers in the Main Information Department of the Polish Army (*Główny Zarząd Informacji Wojska Polskiego*), which was the foundation of the Soviet-sponsored communist Polish military intelligence service and was initially manned heavily by Soviet intelligence officers.[188] Coincidentally, the early Polish leaders of the Main Information Department, such as Michał Rola-Żymierski and Marian Spychalski, were the same people that Pines had worked with when he ran Soviet-sponsored anti-German partisan operations during the war.[189]

The Soviet Union also tasked collection platforms in other parts of the world to report on Eastern European plans and strategies. Beginning about October 1944, Emma Woikin, a GRU source uncovered by Gouzenko, passed unencrypted versions of diplomatic cables that had originated in the Dominion Office in London. She earmarked cables that she thought might be of interest to the Soviets, including on Spain, Yugoslavia, Hungary, and Central European states. According to Amy Knight, she gave general information dealing with political conditions in Austria and Eastern Europe.[190] Gouzenko also reported that GRU *rezident* Colonel Nikolay Zabotin ran an agent named Zasansky in the Czechoslovakian Mission in Ottawa in 1945.[191] These sources detailed Soviet foundational preparations for the occupation of Eastern European countries after the war.

Japan/China

The Far East experienced some of the same Soviet operations as Eastern Europe. Several World War II-era Soviet intelligence officer defectors had experience in the Soviet Far East during the 1930s. World War II-era defectors provided little information about Soviet intelligence in the Far East during the war, but they revealed two thrusts of Soviet intelligence activity before the war: counterintelligence against perceived Japanese espionage and Soviet influence operations in China and Mongolia. Their assignments in the Far East were short, so the information they revealed was not as detailed, or in some cases as reliable, as information about European operations. But it shed some light on Soviet priorities in the Far East.

Bessonov and Chikalov both served in positions in Xinjiang and neighbouring Mongolia during the early to mid-1930s, suppressing anti-Soviet resistance and establishing Soviet control in the region. Bessonov participated in action against the Chinese Muslim warlord Ma Zhongying in 1936, for which he was awarded an honorary weapon.[192] Chikalov served a two-month assignment in Xinjiang in 1932 as part of an operation to Sovietise the region, and then on a temporary duty assignment to Mongolia for three months in 1936 to teach border guard troops about Japanese espionage.[193] Rastvorov was involved in operations in China during the war to solidify Soviet influence further (see Chapter 4).

Before his assignment to Canada, Gouzenko worked at GRU headquarters in Moscow processing reports from officers at the Russian mission in China. He saw messages that indicated unfriendly relations between the official Soviet representatives and the local Chinese government, discord and competition amongst the Soviet staff at the embassy, and overall unpleasant living conditions.[194] Gouzenko was initially informed that his first foreign assignment would be China and he began studying about China, but he soon learned that his assignment would be Canada instead.[195]

Japan was viewed less as a zone of influence than as a looming threat. Artemyev wrote about an experience he had with a Japanese cavalry officer named Major Doi who visited his regiment for several months during the summer of 1933 as an exchange officer while Artemyev was serving as a squadron commander. Even though Doi was part of a formal military-to-military exchange programme, Artemyev's regiment prepared for his visit by warning the officer staff to avoid Doi as much as possible, to evade conversations, to walk the other direction when they saw him coming, and to report any interchanges to the Party leadership. The *politruk* and NKVD OO chief described Doi as a representative of a capitalist military who only wanted to conduct espionage. The regiment prepared for all foreseeable contingencies to avoid contaminating the Soviet officers. Doi had come to observe military training; however, rather than showing him real Soviet military tactics, the regiment staged military manoeuvres to impress Doi, while hiding genuine, substantive exercises. This led to some uncomfortable situations, like when the unit was scheduled to be part of a combined arms exercise, which was considered a military secret, and was forced to revise the training plan to prevent Doi from seeing anything real.[196] Artemyev was likely referring to Doi Akio, who served as the Japanese military attaché in Moscow in 1939 and eventually rose to the rank of lieutenant general in the Japanese army. Doi became known as an expert on

Soviet affairs and served as the head of a Japanese think tank, the Continental Affairs Research Institute, which was responsible for Soviet issues. Artemyev gives what is likely an account of the beginning of Doi's career as a Soviet specialist.

Denisov graduated from the Institute of Water Transport in 1938, and his first assignment was as an NKVD OO officer in the Pacific Fleet investigating Japanese espionage in the Soviet Pacific ports. He arrived in Vladivostok in January 1938 while Lyushkov, who defected to Japan later that year, led the Far Eastern NKVD district (see Chapter 2), although Denisov never mentions Lyushkov. Denisov participated in what he called the Far Eastern Operation, one of four major NKVD purge operations that led to mass arrests and executions.[197] He also wrote about a border post north of Vladivostok that handled hundreds of low-level informants and agents inside Korean and Chinese territory who cooperated in exchange for packets of opium and through which the NKVD monitored Korean border guard patrols.[198] Later, when Denisov was in Germany supporting US intelligence, he wrote a detailed description of the Pacific Fleet, including an annotated map of ports and details of the types of naval ships positioned there.[199]

The GRU also dispatched illegals to target Japanese information and to facilitate communications with Japanese agents. As noted above, Witczak/Litvin, a Razvedupr illegal whose existence Gouzenko revealed, was sent to the United States in 1938 to recruit sources in southern California among people who had family or business ties to Japan. Initially, the United States was only a venue for his operations, and it became the target only during the war. Witczak/Litvin discussed his selection as an illegal to travel to the United States during a recorded interview in the early 1990s. He stated that he was selected because of his experience in Far Eastern affairs – he had graduated from the Far Eastern Institute in Vladivostok.[200] Witczak/Litvin's potential agent, Dr Arnold Krieger, testified before the US House of Representatives that Witczak/Litvin had initially attempted to recruit him to be a letter drop in China, Japan, or Latin America.[201]

Soviet intelligence during the war emphasised Europe over China and Japan. But operations in the Far East grew in importance again after the war, when the Soviet Union supported communists in China and Korea and monitored the US occupation of Japan (see Chapter 4).

Turkey/Iran

Although Soviet intelligence used Turkey and Iran to a great extent as venues to collect against other priority targets, like Germany and Great Britain, several World War II-era defectors discussed Soviet intelligence activities against Turkey and Iran themselves. Akhmedov in particular wrote about Soviet operations in Turkey, since he directly targeted Turkey in the 1930s and served there personally during the war. Volkov could have been a similarly valuable source, and he offered a list of Soviet agents in Turkey and information about Soviet intelligence operations in the Near East and Iran, but his defection was cut short and he never revealed the information.

Akhmedov operated against Turkey early in his Razvedupr career, and his first task as a new intelligence officer in 1930 was to become familiar with Razvedupr operations in Turkey. He worked as a ham radio operator, making contact with other ham operators in Turkey and Iran and recruiting them to assist with clandestine communications. One of these agreed to travel to Tabriz under Soviet diplomatic cover to work as a Razvedupr radio operator. In 1931, Akhmedov began studying Kurdistan, including details of Kurdish tribal chieftains, travel routes and paths, sources of water, local history and folklore, the origins of conflicts among the tribes and generally among the people of the Middle East, and the struggles between the various political parties. He planned operations for infiltrating insurgents and identified ways for Soviet advisors to appeal to the national and religious feelings and customs of local populations. He also learned of Razvedupr radio communications equipment buried in remote locations outside the Soviet Union for use in future Soviet-sponsored insurgent activities.[202]

Early in the war, the Soviet Union viewed Turkey as a potential ally of either Great Britain or Germany, and the NKVD mobilised to counter the Turkish threat on its southern border. Soon after the war began, Chikalov was assigned to Batumi, Georgia, to participate in forming a special NKVD division to prepare for an invasion of Turkey in case Turkey joined the war on the German side. However, after only two weeks of this assignment, the Soviet Union became convinced that Turkey intended to remain neutral, and the formation of the division was postponed. He was then sent briefly to Iran, but was subsequently sent to Moscow to assist in forming a different special unit to defend Moscow, which was mobilised in October 1941.[203]

When Akhmedov was posted to Turkey in July 1941 after his expulsion from Germany, the Soviet ambassador in Turkey, Sergey Aleksandrovich Vinogradov, ordered him to recruit a prominent Turkish journalist to write pro-Soviet press stories and mobilise Turkish public opinion in favour of the Soviet Union. This order revealed a divergence between NKVD and Razvedupr missions in Turkey; Akhmedov's Razvedupr instructions did not include operating against Turkey itself during the war, but rather using Turkey as a venue from which to launch operations against Germany. Akhmedov refused Vinogradov's order on the grounds that he was a Razvedupr officer and was not obliged to take orders from the NKVD.[204]

On 24 February 1942, while Akhmedov was in Turkey, a Yugoslav refugee attempted to assassinate the German ambassador to Turkey, Franz von Papen, revealing another NKVD mission in Turkey. The would-be assassin detonated a bomb prematurely, killing himself but not seriously injuring the ambassador. Nevertheless, the event caused commotion in Turkey: the British and Soviets accused the Gestapo; the Germans pointed at the British.[205] However, the Turkish police quickly identified the assassin and arrested his accomplices, including an NKVD officer under diplomatic cover at the Soviet trade delegation. The trial of the suspects commenced in April 1942, to great Soviet embarrassment.

Soviet counterintelligence in Moscow also targeted Turkish officials. Zhigunov discussed the September 1939 visit by Turkish Foreign Minister Sukru Saracoğlu to Moscow to negotiate a mutual assistance treaty with the Soviet Union. Zhigunov indicated that Saracoğlu was under NKVD observation during his entire visit and noted a long car ride he took with a British embassy official through the streets of Moscow, during which he claimed the British persuaded Saracoğlu to refuse Soviet overtures. Saracoğlu did, in fact, reject the treaty, including a demand to allow the Soviet Union to station troops in the Dardanelles, which Turkey was unwilling to accept regardless of British or French influence. Saracoğlu left Moscow after a few days with no agreement.[206]

Artemyev never directly served in Turkey or Iran during his career, but he wrote an essay for the Research Program on the USSR based on second-hand information that touched on overseas trade and intelligence activities, with a particular emphasis on the Soviet trade representation in Iran. He wrote that the Soviet Union used whatever Soviet personnel had access to Iran, like fur traders or businessmen, to collect intelligence about market conditions and prices for commodities that the Soviet Union wanted to buy or sell. Soviet trade officials took advantage of Iranians who were willing to take bribes to falsify trade arrangements or reveal inside information. Iran's road and rail infrastructure was a particularly prominent collection target for Soviet intelligence. An intelligence officer named Bazikov, who was covered as an economist at the Soviet Trade Mission in Tehran, ran sources in Iranian government institutions, including a senior official in the Ministry of Railroads, who reported information about the construction of the Trans-Iranian Railway. Chauffeurs passed information about bridge-building and the status of rivers and reservoirs. The Soviet trade mission staff sponsored excursions into the countryside for picnics and hunting, during which topography specialists collected cartographic information. Artemyev claims that this collection greatly assisted the Soviet army when it entered Iran in 1941, because Soviet maps were more accurate than the Iranians' own.[207]

Operational Support

World War II-era Soviet intelligence officer defectors also revealed some insights into operational support networks through which Soviet intelligence services communicated information, passed funds, and moved people. Denisov wrote that Soviet intelligence used the Soviet merchant fleet to courier instructions to and from agents, and for sending valuables to agents abroad for operational financing. He claimed that the Soviet Union had used the long-distance merchant marine fleet for intelligence purposes since its earliest founding. The detail with which he described this intelligence activity indicates that Denisov himself may have been one of the sailors chosen for this special duty.[208] Denisov gave as examples a 2–3 kg package of gold jewellery with precious stones that a merchant ship carried to London in 1935 and passed to an agent to support striking workers, and propaganda literature carried to Asian countries in 1935–6. He also noted an instance when a merchant ship delivered a Swedish passport to an agent in Antwerp, Belgium, for operational use. Among Denisov's papers is a chart that lays out the Soviet intelligence organisation in Antwerp, suggesting that Denisov himself was familiar with this operation.[209] He also gave an example of a merchant ship that pulled into Singapore in 1938 and transported agent reports about British military forces and civilian establishments in Singapore and India. The Soviet source in Singapore was a port husbandry agent, providing plausible cover for transferring goods onto the ship; Denisov claims to have seen the documents when the merchant ship delivered them to Vladivostok.

In addition to being a communications method, merchant ships were also assigned to observe and collect intelligence about military ships anchored in port and, where possible, to ascertain their previous and future destinations. In lesser-visited ports, sailors were instructed to observe defensive measures, port infrastructure, and channel lengths and depths. Denisov gives a specific example of a navigator and an institute student on board a ship that pulled into the Irish port of Limerick in 1936, tasked with making observations about the port. Although he does not identify the Soviet sailors involved, Denisov himself may have been the student.[210]

Along with being an emerging intelligence target, Canada continued as an operational support hub, serving as a source of false documents for clandestine travellers. In May/June 1944, GRU Colonel Mikhail Abramovich Milshteyn travelled to the Soviet embassy in Ottawa to conduct an inspection. Milshteyn encouraged the *rezidentura* to revive networks of specialists who had assisted the GRU to obtain false travel documents and passports in the past, but who had drifted out of use.[211] A note in Sam Carr's GRU file indicates that Carr met Milshteyn in June and Milshteyn asked about the availability of people to assist with producing passports for GRU use.[212] Witczak/Litvin was a beneficiary of the Ottawa *rezidentura*'s document services. The *rezidentura* also explored the possibility in April 1944 of using relatives of GRU agent Harold Gerson's wife, some of whom were doctors and other professionals living in Romania and Bukovina, for operational purposes. The idea originated with Gerson's request to send money to the relatives through Red Cross channels. The *rezidentura* recommended to Moscow to take advantage of the relatives' presence and use them as mail drops for passing operational mail along with the Red Cross packages.[213] No further information is available about the GRU's reaction to the proposal, but Gouzenko's compromise of Gerson likely prevented any follow-up.

In 1946, Kirsanov, a Navy lieutenant stationed in Budapest, Hungary, made contact with US representatives through his girlfriend, a local Hungarian, with the goal of immigrating to the United States. He was working as a radioman in a special purpose radio detachment of the Red Banner Danube Fleet Headquarters in Budapest. Such units supplied radio communications for GRU operations, so he could probably reveal information about GRU operations and communications procedures in Europe.[214]

Conclusion

Most World War II-era defectors took advantage of the proximity to a foreign power on the battlefield to escape their intelligence and state security positions rather than continue to support Stalin. Several of the defectors early in the war had long careers and served in senior NKVD positions, but their experiences in the *Yezhovshchina* left them disenchanted with Stalin. When they were captured in battle, their *Yezhovshchina* experiences, calculated against the prospect of dying in a Nazi

POW camp, persuaded them to collaborate with Nazi Germany in defeating the Soviet regime. They portrayed Soviet planning for relations with Germany and the next war against Great Britain and the United States even before World War II ended, foreshadowing the Cold War and continuing Soviet antipathy for capitalist powers, even those with which the Soviet Union had entered into a 'temporary alliance'. As the war ended, members of this group fell into US and British custody, only to find themselves at risk of being repatriated to the Soviet Union. For four members of this group, repatriation led to death sentences. Those who avoided that fate made new lives for themselves in Germany or immigrated to the United States, similar to the members of the next, Early Cold War group, all of whom defected after the United States and Great Britain stopped forced repatriations.

Notes

1. Charles I. Bevans (ed.), 'Care and Repatriation of Liberated Prisoners of War and Civilians', in *Treaties and Other International Agreements of the United States of America, 1776–1949*, vol. 11 (Washington, DC: US Department of State, 1978), 1286–9.
2. SIS memo, 16 January 1947, TNA, KV 5/105, serial 3a.
3. Krasnov, *Soviet Defectors*, p. 171.
4. Nikolai Tolstoy, *The Secret Betrayal* (New York: Charles Scribner's Sons, 1977), 34.
5. Thomas Earl Porter, 'Hitler's Forgotten Genocides: The Fate of Soviet POWs', *Elon Law Review*, vol 5, no. 2 (2013), 359–87.
6. Sergey Gennadiyevich Chuev, Проклятые Солдаты. Предатели на Стороне III Рейха (*Cursed Soldiers: Traitors on the Side of the Third Reich*) (Moscow: EKSMO, 2004).
7. Harvard Project on the Soviet Social System (HPSSS). Schedule A, vol. 11, Case 136, 15–16.
8. HPSSS, Schedule B, vol. 10, Case 147, 1–3.
9. Yesenina interrogation report, 11 March 1943, Gestapo/RSHA file number 173-b-16-12/126, 6a; located in Gestapo records that fell into US custody after World War II, now stored in NARA, RG 242, Entry UD 23B, Box 13.

10. Lt Col Smith W. Brookhart, Jr., 'Excerpts from Testimony of Walter Schellenberg, taken at Nurnberg, Germany, 13 November 1945', 1623, <https://www.historiography-project.com/nca/nca0B/Supplement-B.php> (last accessed 2 April 2020).

11. Kirill Mikhailovich Aleksandrov, *Генералитет и Офицерские Кадры Вооруженных Формирований Комитета Освобождения Народов России 1943–1946 гг.* (*General and Officer Corps of the Armed Formations of the Committee for the Liberation of the Peoples of Russia 1943–1946*), dissertation for the Russian Academy of Sciences, St Petersburg History Institute, 2015, 249–51. Grachev recounted the same sequence of events in his Harvard interview; see HPSSS, Schedule B, vol. 10, Case 219, 2–3 Grachev referred to the RNNA as the *Русская Освободительная Народная Армия* (Russian Liberation People's Army; RONA).

12. Kirill Mikhailovich Aleksandrov, *Армия Генерала Власова 1944–1945* (*General Vlasov's Army 1944–1945*) (Moscow: Yauza EKSMO, 2006), 38–9.

13. Brook-Shepherd, *The Storm Birds*, 61.

14. Ismail Akhmedov, *In and Out of Stalin's GRU: A Tatar's Escape from Red Army Intelligence* (Frederick, MD: University Publications of America, 1984), 101–2.

15. Akhmedov, *In and Out of Stalin's GRU*, 119–21.

16. Aleksandr Antonovich Petrushin, 'Призраки Приполярного Урала' ('Ghosts of the Polar Urals'), *Тюменский курьер* (*Tyumen Courier*), nos 104–7 (16–21 June 2011), published online at <http://a-pesni.org/grvojna/kr/a-prizraki.php> (last accessed 17 Janaury 2019).

17. Dmitriy Aleksandorvich Zhukov and Ivan Ivanovich Kovtun, *1-я Русская Бригада СС 'Дружина'* (*First Russian SS 'Druzhina' Brigade*) (Moscow: Veche, 2010), 47.

18. Aleksandr Anatolyevich Sidorov, *Великие битвы уголовного мира. История профессиональной преступности Советской России. Книга вторая (1941–1991 г.г.)* (*Great Battles of the Criminal World: The History of the Professional Crimes of Soviet Russia, Book 2 (1941–1991)*) (Moscow: EKSMO, 1999).

19. Petrushin, 'Ghosts of the Polar Urals'.

20. HPSSS, Schedule B, vol. 1, Case 105, 17.

21. Information about Kalugin's career is derived from Kirill Mikhailovich Aleksandrov, *Офицерский Корпус Армии Генерал-Лейтенанта Ал. Власова, 1944–1945* (*Officer Corps of the Army of General Lieutenant Vlasov, 1944–1945*) (St Petersburg: Russo-Baltic Information Center 'BLITs', 2001), 166–7.

22. Manuscript biography of Almazov/Repin (pseudonym of Chikalov), 7, HIA, Boris Nicolaevsky Collection, Box 497, Folder 35 (microfilm reel 386).

23. HPSSS, Schedule A, vol. 8, Case 105, 28, 53–4.

24. Gouzenko, *The Iron Curtain*, 184.

25. Ibid. 187.

26. Yesenina interrogation report, 11 March 1943, 6a.

27. Chuev, *Cursed Soldiers*.

28. Aleksandr Sidorov, 'Мюнхгаузен "в законе": история одного предательства' ('Munchausen "in law": The Story of One Betrayal', *Index*, no. 27 (2007), published online at <http://index.org.ru/journal/27/sid27.html> (last accessed 13 March 2020).

29. Prokhorov, *What is the Cost of Betraying One's Homeland?*, 151.

30. HPSSS, Schedule B, vol. 10, Case 219, 3–4.

31. Aleksandrov, *General and Officer Corps of the Armed Formations of the Committee for the Liberation of the Peoples of Russia 1943–1946*, 249–51.

32. HPSSS, Schedule A, vol. 11, Case 136, 15–16.

33. HPSSS, Schedule B, vol. 15, Case 136, 12.

34. Aleksandrov, *General Vlasov's Army 1944–1945*, 38–9.

35. 'Десант на ГУЛАГ' ('Airborne Assault on the GULAG'), *Новая Газета* (*New Journal*), 1 March 2004.

36. Yakov Abramovich Chugunov, 'Объяснительная Записка о Пребывании в Плену Немецко-Фашистской Армии Батальонного Комиссара Чугунова Якова Абрамовича' ('Explanatory Note about Battalion Commissar Yakov Abramovich Chugunov's Time in German-Fascist Captivity'), 29 July 1943, Yaroslavl Historical and Genealogical Society, published online at <http://forum.yar-genealogy.ru/index.php?showtopic=9248> (last accessed 13 March 2020).

37. Konstantin Grigoryevich Kromiadi, *За Землю, За Волю: Воспоминания соратника генерала Власова* (*For Land, For Freedom: Reminiscences of General Vlasov's Comrade in Arms*) (Moscow: Veche, 2011). See also Aleksandrov, *Officer Corps of the Army of General Lieutenant Vlasov, 1944–1945*, 324.

38. Zhigunov, 'NKVD-VChK-OGPU-NKVD-NKGB-NKVD', in *Testimony of the NKVD Official Zhigunov*, German file number EAP 3-a-11/2, 57, 59, 64; NARA, RG 242, Entry UD 282AV, Box 18.

39. Ibid. 61–2, 68–9.

40. Akhmedov, *In and Out of Stalin's GRU*, 149.
41. Ibid. 159.
42. Ibid. 169.
43. Ibid. 189.
44. Dubkov written statement, Headquarters Region VI, 66th Counterintelligence Corps Group, 22 December 1952, NARA RG 319, Entry 134A, Box 173, Dubkov file.
45. Dubkov statement, 10 January 1953; and Case Summary, Headquarters Region VI, 66th Counterintelligence Corps Group, 24 March 1953, NARA RG 319, Entry 134A, Box 173, Dubkov file.
46. JIC, 'Study of Defectors from the USSR', 22–3; Andrew and Mitrokhin, *The Sword and the Shield*, 138–40; Kim Philby, *My Secret War* (New York: Grove Press, 1968), 147–60; Brook-Shepherd, *The Storm Birds*, 48–56.
47. Brook-Shepherd, *The Storm Birds*, 61.
48. 'KGB Wanted List', Entry numbers 75 and 107.
49. 'Soviet Official Here Resigns: Assails "Double-Faced" Policies', *New York Times*, 4 April 1944. Kravchenko was not an intelligence officer.
50. Igor Gouzenko, *The Iron Curtain*, 262–77.
51. Granovskiy gave two different accounts of his approach to the French in Prague: one in Stockholm Police debriefing report, dated 11 October 1946, 79, National Archives of Sweden, Statens Utlänningskommission (State Immigration Commission), Hemliga Arkivet (Classified Archive), F4, Volume 7, Granovski, Anatoli Michailovitj; and the other in Anatoliy Mikhailovich Granovskiy, *I Was an NKVD Agent: A Top Soviet Spy Tells His Story* (New York: Devin-Adair, 1962), 262.
52. Granovskiy, *I Was an NKVD Agent*, 269.
53. Kevin C. Ruffner, 'On the Trail of Nazi Counterfeiters', *Studies in Intelligence* (2002), 51, n46. Ruffner cites Granovskiy's book, *I Was an NKVD Agent*, in several CIA internal publications.
54. Donna E. Dismukes, *The Forced Repatriation of Soviet Citizens: A Study in Military Disobedience*, thesis for the US Naval Postgraduate School, December 1996.
55. Denisov was respondent #105; Artemyev, #136; Anokhin, #147; Grachev, #219; and Kashtanov, #220.
56. Interview with Vladislav Artemyev, in David J. Dallin Papers 1948–1959, New York Public Library Archives and Manuscripts, Box 1, Folder 1950–1951; Interview with Aleksandr Vladimirovich Anokhin (Brazhnev), David Dallin Notes on the NKVD, David

Dallin Manuscripts 1947–1951, Columbia University Rare Book and Manuscript Library.

57. Pyotr Vail, 'Лицом к событию. Золотой юбилей русской службы Радио Свобода' ('Facing the Events: The Golden Jubilee of the Russian Service of Radio Liberty'), *Radio Liberty*, 1 March 2003, <http://www.svoboda.org/content/transcript/24197826.html> (last accessed 13 March 2020).

58. Vadim Andryukhin, 'Судьба резидента' ('The Fate of the *Rezident*'), *Zemlya Nizhegorodskaya*, 14 May 2012, published online at <https://zem-nn.ru/?p=3556> (last accessed 5 February 2019).

59. CIA Memo, 'Request for Amendment "1 to Project AEACRE for the Fiscal Year 1957', 30 January 1957 (CIA FOIA site).

60. Andrew and Mitrokhin, *The Sword and the Shield*, 149.

61. David E. Murphy, Sergei A. Kondrashev, and George Bailey, *Battleground Berlin: CIA vs. KGB in the Cold War* (New Haven: Yale University Press, 1999), 241.

62. Geoffrey E. Duin, 'Operation Rusty: The Gehlen–US Army Connection', *MilitaryHistoryOnline.com*, 15 July 2007, <http://www.militaryhistoryonline.com/wwii/articles/operationrusty.aspx#> (last accessed 13 March 2020).

63. HQ Region IV Case Summary, 'Operation Hagberry', 24 December 1947, NARA, RG 319, Entry A1 314B, Box 810; also CIC Case summary, 'TUKHOLNIKOV, Wjatcsheslav, aka TUKHLNIKOV, Byatscheslaw (Slavko), SOKOLOW, Walentin and other Variations', undated, but written between mid-1953 and mid-1954, 1, NARA, RG 319, Entry A1 314B, Box 810–11.

64. Krivitsky, *I Was Stalin's Agent*, 38, 236.

65. Vadim Denisov, *Советская Тайная Работа Вне СССР* (*Soviet Secret Work Outside the USSR*), HIA, Alexander Dallin Papers, Box 71, Folder K, Aparat II. Another version of the same paper is also contained in HIA, Boris Nicolaevsky Collection, Box 293, Folder 10 (microfilm reel 253).

66. FBI Washington Field Office memo, 'Ismail Akhmedov, aka Ismail Ege, Internal Security – R', 27 October 1953, file number 100-351199 (FBI FOIA site).

67. Zhigunov, 'My Studies in the Central School of the NKVD', in *Testimony of the NKVD Official Zhigunov*, 28–44; Yesenina interrogation report, 7 December 1942, 5.

68. Aleksandr Brazhnev, *Школа Опричников* (*Oprichniki School*) (Kiev: Diokor, 2004), 15, 40, 72 (originally published in 1951); HPSSS, Schedule B, vol. 1, Case 147, 6.

69. *Testimony of the NKVD Official Zhigunov*, 15.
70. Ibid. 17.
71. Akhmedov, *In and Out of Stalin's GRU*, 134.
72. Ibid. 133–5.
73. Brazhnev, *Oprichniki School* (2004), 15.
74. Akhmedov, *In and Out of Stalin's GRU*, 134.
75. Ibid. 123–4.
76. *Testimony of the NKVD Official Zhigunov*, 16.
77. 'Sketch of the Interrogation of the GPU Official Zhigunov on 18 September 1941', in *Testimony of the NKVD Official Zhigunov*, 6.
78. Akhmedov, *In and Out of Stalin's GRU*, 135.
79. 'Intelligence Report on Zhigunov', 18 August 1941, in *Testimony of the NKVD Official Zhigunov*, 6.
80. Akhmedov, *In and Out of Stalin's GRU*, 153–4.
81. Ibid. 137.
82. US Congress. Senate. Judiciary Committee. *Scope of Soviet Activity in the United States*, 84th Congress, Second Session, part 3 (Washington, DC: Government Printing Office, 1956), 60–72.
83. Akhmedov, *In and Out of Stalin's GRU*, 145.
84. Ibid. 148.
85. HPSSS, Schedule B, vol. 1, Case 105, 17–18.
86. CIA, *GRU Legal Residencies*, August 1960, 1 (CIA FOIA site).
87. Akhmedov, *In and Out of Stalin's GRU*, 155–7.
88. Yesenina interrogation report, 11 December 1942, 20.
89. Ibid. 22.
90. Gouzenko, *The Iron Curtain*, 132–3.
91. Yesenina interrogation report, 11 December 1942, 26.
92. In her December 1942 interrogation, Yesenina claimed to have been airdropped near Zhitomir and travelled by land to Rovno. She stated in her March 1943 interrogation that her initial story was false.
93. Yesenina interrogation report, 10 March 1943, 1–3.
94. Yesenina interrogation report, 7 December 1942, 29.
95. Yesenina interrogation report, 11 December 1942, 31.
96. Igor Gouzenko, 'I Was Inside Stalin's Spy Ring', *Cosmopolitan*, March 1947.
97. Jeevan Vasagar, 'Spy's deathbed confession: Atom physicist tells how secrets given to Soviet Union', *The Guardian*, 27 January 2003. See also Amy Knight, *How the Cold War Began: The Igor Gouzenko Affair and the Hunt for Soviet Spies* (New York: Carroll & Graf, 2005), 149.

98. Granovskiy, 'Eu Fui Espião de Stalin' ('I Was Stalin's Spy'), *A Noite*, 5 April 1949.

99. Ginzberg, see Compilation of Ginzberg's MI5 debriefings, 29; Feldbin, see Orlov, *Handbook*, 164–83. Feldbin himself established counterintelligence and sabotage schools in Spain to organise attacks on Franco's forces, see FBI Summary of Orlov's information provided to MI5 in Washington, 26 October 1953, 3, TNA, KV 2/2878, serial 9a. The NKVD also ran a training course for radio operators and saboteurs in the Far East directed against Japan, according to Lyushkov ('Interrogation of Liushkov G. S. November 1938', 24–5).

100. Akhmedov, *In and Out of Stalin's GRU*, 156–7.

101. HPSSS, Schedule B, vol. 1, Case 105, 8; HPSSS, Schedule B, vol. 10, Case 105, 2.

102. Boris Nikolayevskiy's notes from his first encounter with Chikalov, 'Из Записной Книжки' ('From a Notebook'), 17 August 1947, 8–9; HIA, Boris Nicolaevsky Collection, Box 233, Folder 9 (microfilm reel 199).

103. E. N. Shantseva, V. V. Dzyuban, and Yu. T. Trifankov, *Брянщина в Период Оккупации 1941–1943 гг.: Генезис Партизанского Движения и Коллаборационизма* (*The Bryansk Region in the Occupation Period, 1941–1943: Genesis of Partisan Movements and Collaborationism*) (Bryansk: BGTU Publishing, 2010).

104. Gouzenko, *The Iron Curtain*, 102–3.

105. Ibid. 148–54.

106. Murphy, Kondrashev, and Bailey say October, *Battleground Berlin*, 111. It is December in Andrew and Mitrokhin, *The Sword and the Shield*, 149; and David Wise, *Molehunt: The Secret Search for Traitors That Shattered the CIA* (New York: Random House, 1992), 184.

107. James Angleton, CIA Chief of Counterintelligence from 1954 to 1975, was among these; see Wise, *Molehunt*, 273.

108. Aleksandrov, *General and Officer Corps of the Armed Formations of the Committee for the Liberation of the Peoples of Russia 1943–1946*, 628–9.

109. Telegram from HQ EUCOM Frankfurt, Germany to HQ US Army, 29 November 1947, establishing the codename Operation HAGBERRY (available on BrillOnline Primary Sources).

110. Aleksandrov, *General Vlasov's Army 1944–1945*, 47, 48.

111. Chikalov's correspondence with Nikolayevskiy is in HIA, Boris Nicolaevsky Collection, Box 497, Folder 35 (microfilm reel 386).

112. Brazhnev, *Oprichniki School* (2004), 15, 40, 65–6, 72; HPSSS, Schedule B, vol. 1, Case 147, 6.

113. Vadim Denisov, Экономическое Управление ГУГБ НКВД СССР, Сокращение ЭКУ НКВД (*The Economic Directorate of the GUGB NKVD USSR, abbreviation EKU NKVD*), HIA, Boris Nicolaevsky Collection, Box 293, Folder 5 (microfilm reel 252).

114. Almazov, 'По Делу Тухачевского' ('On the Tukhachevsky Case'), essay number III in an undated collection of essays contained in HIA, Boris Nicolaevsky Collection, Box 233, Folder 8 (microfilm reel 199).

115. Letter from Chikalov to Nikolayevskiy, 30 March 1949, HIA, Boris Nicolaevsky Collection, Box 497, Folder 35 (microfilm reel 386).

116. Zhigunov, 'English Intelligence in the USSR and the Activity of the English Embassy in Moscow', in *Testimony of the NKVD Official Zhigunov*, 124, 127.

117. *Testimony of the NKVD Official Zhigunov*, 16; Zhigunov, 'NKVD-VChK-OGPU-NKVD-NKGB-NKVD', 59. See also Orlov, *The Secret History of Stalin's Crimes*, 286–92.

118. Aleksandrov, *General Vlasov's Army 1944–1945*, 53–5.

119. Granovskiy, *I Was an NKVD Agent*, 226.

120. Nicola Sinevirsky (pseudonym of Mondich), *SMERSH* (New York: Henry Holt and Co., 1950), 108–10.

121. Sinevirsky, *SMERSH*, 105–6.

122. US Forces Austria, Project SYMPHONY, file number LVX 231, 9 May 1946, 8–9 (CIA FOIA site).

123. Ibid. 14.

124. There were exceptions to this, such as the Woolwich Arsenal case, which involved Soviet collection of military technology in Great Britain, and Elizabeth Bentley's and Whittaker Chambers' revelations, which detailed political collection in the United States. But defector information provided a general trend and emphasis.

125. Akhmedov, *In and Out of Stalin's GRU*, 135.

126. Viacheslav P. Artemiev, *Selection and Training of Personnel for Trade Missions Abroad and the Soviet Trade Mission in Iran: Two Brief Essays*, Mimeographed Series no. 68 (New York: Research Program on the USSR, 1954), 17–18.

127. Kellock-Taschereau Commission, *Report of the Royal Commission Appointed under Order in Council P.C. 411 of February 5, 1946 to Investigate the Facts Relating to and the Circumstances Surrounding the Communication by Public Officials and*

Other Persons in Positions of Trust of Secret and Confidential Information to Agents of a Foreign Power (Ottawa: Privy Council, 1946), 232–3.

128. Ibid. 236, 240.
129. GRU telegram, Moscow to Ottawa, number 12200, 24 August 1945; TNA, 2/1427, item 107; SIS telegram, Ottawa to London, number 179, 20 February 1946; TNA, KV 2/1421, serial 67a.
130. Aleksandr Zhigunov, 'My Studies in the Central School of the NKVD', in *Testimony of the NKVD Official Zhigunov*, 28–44.
131. Brazhnev, *Oprichniki School* (2004), 15.
132. US Forces Austria, Project SYMPHONY, file number LVX 231, 9 May 1946 (CIA FOIA site).
133. SIS telegram, Ottawa to London, number 186, 21 February 1946; TNA, KV 2/1421, serial 70a.
134. Peter Wright, *Spycatcher: The Candid Autobiography of a Senior Intelligence Officer* (New York: Viking, 1987), 290.
135. 'The Rote Drei: Getting Behind the "Lucy" Myth', *Studies in Intelligence*, vol. 13 (1969), no. 3.
136. Akhmedov, *In and Out of Stalin's GRU*, 130.
137. Wright, *Spycatcher*, 281–2.
138. Brook-Shepherd, *The Storm Birds*, 50.
139. Gouzenko, *The Iron Curtain*, 172.
140. GRU telegram, Ottawa to Moscow, number 209, 12 July 1945; TNA KV 2/1247, item 73.
141. 'Register of Materials Sent to the Director', January 1945, TNA, KV 2/1427, serial 8a, item 108.
142. Akhmedov, *In and Out of Stalin's GRU*, 132–3.
143. US Congress. Senate. Judiciary Committee. *Interlocking Subversion in Government Departments* (Washington, DC: Government Printing Office, 1953), 1014.
144. Undated memo, 'Arshak Armenakovich Vartanian, with aliases Artak A. Vartanian, A. A. Vartagnian', forwarded to the 7970th CIC Group, 4 October 1949, NARA, RG 319, Entry 134A, Box 822.
145. Denisov, *Soviet Secret Work Outside the USSR*, 3.
146. GRU telegram, Ottawa to Moscow, number 266, 27 August 1945, TNA, KV 2/1427, item 89.
147. 'Second Interim Report of the Royal Commission to the Governor General in Council, March 14, 1946', in *Documents Relating to the Proceedings of the Royal Commission* (Ottawa: Edmond Cloutier, 1946), 15.

148. SIS telegram, Ottawa to London, number 196, 22 February 1946; TNA, KV 2/1422, serial 71a; SIS telegram, Ottawa to London, number 323, 8 March 1946; TNA, KV 2/1422, serial 120a; 'Second Interim Report of the Royal Commission to the Governor General in Council, March 14, 1946', 15.
149. Gouzenko, 'I Was Inside Stalin's Spy Ring', 25.
150. GRU telegram, Moscow to Ottawa, number 11931, 22 August 1945; TNA, KV 2/1427, item 105; 'The Corby Case', 3–4, SIS summary of Gouzenko interrogations, TNA, KV 2/1420.
151. GRU telegram, Moscow to Ottawa, number 11438, 14 August 1945; TNA, KV 2/1427, item 102.
152. GRU telegram, Moscow to Ottawa, number 10458, dated 30 July 1945; GRU telegram, Ottawa to Moscow, number 244, undated (probably 9 or 10 August 1945; GRU telegram, Moscow to Ottawa, number 11955, dated 22 August 1945; TNA, KV 2/1427, items 77, 97, 106.
153. Stockholm Police debriefing of Granovskiy, 48–9; see Captain Franz von Rintelen, *The Dark Invader: War-Time Reminiscences of a German Naval Intelligence Officer* (London: Taylor & Francis, 1933).
154. Granovskiy, *I Was an NKVD Agent*, 138–42. Granovskiy did not mention this training during his Swedish debriefings.
155. She is referred to by the name Patjkova in Stockholm Police debriefing of Granovskiy, 69–70.
156. Granovskiy, *I Was an NKVD Agent*, 200.
157. Granovskiy, *I Was an NKVD Agent*, 216–17; Stockholm Police debriefing of Granovskiy, 70.
158. Bruce Craig, 'A Matter of Espionage: Alger Hiss, Harry Dexter White, and Igor Gouzenko. The Canadian Connection Reassessed', *Intelligence and National Security*, vol. 15 (2000), no. 2, 215.
159. GRU telegram, Moscow to Ottawa, number 11295, 14 August 1945; TNA KV 2/1427, item 99.
160. SIS telegram, New York to London, 24 September 1945, TNA, KV 2/1421, serial 28a.
161. Akhmedov, *In and Out of Stalin's GRU*, 156–7.
162. Ibid. 160.
163. Sinevirsky, *SMERSH*, 144.
164. SIS telegram, Ottawa to London, number 419, 22 March 1946; TNA, KV 2/1421, serial 157a.
165. Gouzenko, 'I Was Inside Stalin's Spy Ring', 25.
166. Gouzenko, *The Iron Curtain*, 220.

167. SIS telegram, New York to London, 24 September 1945, TNA, KV 2/1421, serial 28a.
168. GRU telegram, Moscow to Ottawa, number 11273, 11 August 1945, TNA, KV 2/1427, item 98; Telegram from British Embassy in New York to Foreign Office, 10 September 1945, TNA, KV 2/1419, serial 3a.
169. US Congress. House. Committee on Un-American Activities, *Communist Infiltration of the Hollywood Motion-Picture Industry*, Part 5 (Washington, DC: Government Printing Office, 1951), 2104–10.
170. GRU telegram, Moscow to Ottawa, number 11436, 14 August 1945; TNA, KV 2/1427, item 100.
171. Petr Ivanovich Ivashutin 'Докладывала точно' ('Reported Precisely'), *Военно–Исторической Журнал* (*Journal of Military History*), 1990, no. 5. Anatoliy Georgiyevich Pavlov also mentioned him in 'Советская военная разведка накануне Великой Отечественной Войны' ('Soviet Military Intelligence on the Eve of the Great Patriotic War'), *Новая и Новейшая История* (*Modern and Contemporary History*), 1995, no. 1. USC professor Mike Gruntman published a biography of Litvin in *Enemy Amongst Trojans: A Soviet Spy at USC* (Los Angeles: Figueroa Press, 2010).
172. Almazov, *Голубок* (*Golubok*), undated manuscript and typescript, HIA, Boris Nicolaevsky Collection, Box 497, Folder 35 (microfilm reel 386); see also Almazov, 'На Службе в Советской Разведке' ('In the Service of Soviet Intelligence'), undated typescrypt, HIA, Boris Nicolaevsky Collection, Box 233, Folder 7 (microfilm reel 199), 8–12.
173. Yesenina interrogation report, 7 December 1942, 12–13.
174. Ibid. 13–14.
175. Brazhnev, *Oprichniki School* (2004), 57.
176. Ibid. 77–8.
177. HPSSS, Schedule A, vol. 12, Case 147, 7.
178. Sinevirsky, *SMERSH*, 13.
179. Granovskiy, *I Was an NKVD Agent*, 204.
180. Mondich notes his rank in Sinevirsky, *SMERSH*, 167 and 176–7. See also 'KGB Wanted List', Entry number 439.
181. Sinevirsky, *SMERSH*, 78–82, 95.
182. Ibid. 131–3.
183. Ibid. 194–8.
184. Stockholm Police debriefing of Granovskiy, 75.

185. Granovskiy, *I Was an NKVD Agent*, 256; see also Statement attributed to Granovskiy in July 1961 in a compilation of statements about the John Birch Society, 'Conservative Critics of Robert Welch and the Birch Society', 17 August 2017, 116, <https://archive.org/details/JohnBirchSocietyReportAugust2017?q=%22 Conservative+Critics+of+Robert+Welch+and+the+Birch+Society %22> (last accessed 13 March 2020).

186. US Forces Austria, Project SYMPHONY, file number LVX 231, 9 May 1946, 13 (CIA FOIA site).

187. Ibid. 18.

188. 'KGB Wanted List', Entry number 81.

189. US Forces Austria, Project SYMPHONY, file number LVX 231, 9 May 1946, 3 (CIA FOIA site).

190. Knight, *How the Cold War Began*, 121.

191. SIS letter to British Embassy in Washington for passage to FBI, 5 December 1949, TNA, KV 2/1424, serial 268a.

192. Chuev, *Cursed Soldiers*.

193. Letter from Chikalov to Nikolayevskiy, 26 April 1949, HIA, Boris Nicolaevsky Collection, Box 497, Folder 35 (microfilm reel 386).

194. Gouzenko, *The Iron Curtain*, 110–15. Shorokhov provided further information about Soviet activities in China; see Petrov and Petrov, *Empire of Fear*, 59–66.

195. Gouzenko, *The Iron Curtain*, 168–72.

196. Vyacheslav Pavlovich Artemyev, *Майор Дои Сан* (*Major Doi San*), undated typescript, HIA, Boris Nicolaevsky Collection, Box 233, Folder 15 (microfilm reel 199). Artemyev sent the story to Boris Nicolaevsky in September 1950, hoping it would be publishable. However, there is no indication that it was ever published; letter from Artemyev to Nikolayevskiy, 25 September 1950, HIA, Boris Nicolaevsky Collection, Box 233, Folder 17 (microfilm reel 199).

197. Vadim Denisov, *Mass Persecutions by the NKVD in 1932–1938*, HIA, Alexander Dallin Papers, Box 71, Folder K, Aparat II. The four operations were the Kuban Operation (1932–1933), Tambov-Voronezh Operation (1933–1934), Six Cities Operation (Moscow, Leningrad, Kiev, Kharkov, Rostov, and Odessa) (1935–1936), and Far Eastern (Vladivostok) Operation (1938). Denisov also described these operations in 'Массовые акции КРУ и СПУ НКВД' ('Mass Operations of the NKVD KRU and SPU'), *Народная правда* (*Narodnaya Pravda*), September 1950, nos 9–10, 29–30.

198. Denisov, *Soviet Secret Work Outside the USSR*, 5.

199. Vadim Denisov, *Тихоокеанский Военно-морской Флот Советского Союза* (*The Pacific Fleet of the Soviet Union*), HIA, Boris Nicolaevsky Collection, Box 293, Folder 8 (microfilm reel 252).

200. A video of the interview is available at <http://www.net-film.ru/film-25738/> and <https://www.net-film.ru/film-25737/> (last accessed 13 March 2020).

201. US Congress, *Communist Infiltration of the Hollywood Motion-Picture Industry*, 2104–10.

202. Ibid. 84.

203. Letter from Chikalov to Nikolayevskiy, 16 June 1949, HIA, Boris Nicolaevsky Collection, Box 497, Folder 35 (microfilm reel 386).

204. Akhmedov, *In and Out of Stalin's GRU*, 161–2.

205. Agostino von Hassell, Sigrid MacRae, *Alliance of Enemies: The Untold Story of the Secret American and German Collaboration to End World War II* (New York: Macmillan, 2013), 130.

206. *Testimony of the NKVD Official Zhigunov*, 15–16; see also Zhigunov, 'English Intelligence in the USSR and the Activity of the English Embassy in Moscow', in *Testimony of the NKVD Official Zhigunov*, 129–30.

207. Artemiev, *Selection and Training of Personnel for Trade Missions Abroad and the Soviet Trade Mission in Iran*, 18–19.

208. Vadim Denisov, *Использование Моряков Советского Торгового Флота в Целях Разведки* (*The Use of Soviet Merchant Fleet Sailors for Intelligence Purposes*), HIA, Boris Nicolaevsky Collection, Box 293, Folder 6 (microfilm reel 252).

209. Vadim Denisov, *Внешний Оперативный Центр ИНУ НКВД Западноевропейского Отдела в Антверпене, Белгия* (*INU NKVD Foreign Operational Center of the Western Department in Antwerp, Belgium*), handwritten chart, HIA, Alexander Dallin Papers, Box 71, Folder K, Aparat II.

210. Denisov, *The Use of Soviet Merchant Fleet Sailors for Intelligence Purposes*, 8.

211. *Report of the Royal Commission*, 40–1.

212. *Report of the Royal Commission*, 41. See also 'Gouzenko Takes Stand in Trial of Sam Carr', *Ottawa Citizen*, 6 April 1949, 28; 'The Corby Case', 39, SIS summary of Gouzenko interrogations, TNA, KV 2/1420, redacted; SIS telegram, New York to London, 22 September 1945, TNA, KV 2/1421, serial 24a.

213. 'Second Interim Report of the Royal Commission to the Governor General in Council, March 14, 1946', 17.

214. 'KGB Wanted List', Entry number 338.

4 Early Cold War Defectors, 1947–1951

The Early Cold War group of Soviet intelligence officer defectors consists of twenty-three individuals who defected from the beginning of 1947 to 1951. These defectors had many similarities with defectors in the World War II-era group and provided some of the same information. But the Early Cold War group benefited from a gradual shift in Allied policy away from repatriation and towards exploitation of defectors for intelligence purposes.[1] The information they revealed shed light on the Soviet Union's transition from wartime to peacetime intelligence and counterintelligence, targeted predominantly at the 'Anglo-American bloc' and the Sovietisation of Eastern Europe.

Less is known about most of the individuals in this group than about defectors in other groups due to several factors. Fifteen of the defectors in this group have never appeared in any published literature, the names of four of them are still not publicly available, and the existence of five of them is known only from the KGB Wanted List.[2] Only three officers in this group published their stories, and all three used pseudonyms. One of them (Baklanov) waited twenty-five years to publish his book, and another (A. A. Petrov) published under a pseudonym and only in French.[3] Only two were interviewed for the Harvard Program on the Soviet Social System, primarily because the HPSSS focused on wartime refugees.[4] Instead, British and American intelligence services debriefed them, and their information went into intelligence and counterintelligence files that remained classified for over forty years.

This lack of publicly available information has led some writers to draw incorrect conclusions about intelligence officer defectors

Table 4.1 Early Cold War Defectors, 1947–1951

Name	Best-Known Alias	Service	Became Intel Officer	Date of Defection	Location of Defection	Receiving Country
Unknown	A. A. Petrov	NKVD/MGB	1936	Early 1947	Germany	United States
[Aleksandr Nikolayevich?] Rebrov		NKVD		1947	Germany	United States
Isaak Moiseyevich Genrikh	KGB Wanted list 153	MVD		March 1947	Romania	United States
Aleksandr Stepanovich Kravchenko		MGB	1945	June 1947	Germany	United States
Boris Ivanovich Baklanov	A. I. Romanov	MGB	1942	July 1947	Austria	United Kingdom
Mikhail Filipovich Denisov		GRU	1944	August 1947	Hungary	United States
Veronika Feodorovna Takacs		NKVD	1945	August 1947	Hungary	United States
Vasiliy Mikhailovich Sharandak	Laszlo Baksa	??	1945	August 1947	Austria	United Kingdom
Simas Pečiulionis	Algimantas Mažeika	NKVD	1946	April 1948	Germany	United States
Aleksandr Ivanovich Ryabenko	KGB Wanted list 307	MGB	1945	April 1948	Germany	United States
Vasiliy Pavlovich Korniyevskiy		MGB		April 1948	Austria	United States
Aleksandr Nikolayevich Mikheyev	Aleksandr Nikolayevich Vorontsov	MGB	1945	August 1948	Germany	United States, France, Australia
Unknown	KGB Wanted list 21	MGB	1944	August 1948	Germany	United Kingdom?
Boris Kupriyanovich Gurzhiev		MGB	1938	November 1948	Germany	United States?
Georgiy Ivanovich Samusev	Franz Ulrich	MGB	1942	December 1948	Germany	United States
Unknown	Harvard Case 525	MGB	1948	February 1949	Germany	United States
Vadim Ivanovich Shelaputin	Viktor Gregory	GRU	1942	March 1949	Austria	United Kingdom
Rafail Illych Goldfarb		MGB	1948	June 1949	Germany	United States
Nikolay Ivanovich Bondarev	KGB Wanted list 278	MGB		July 1949	Germany	United States
Ivan Matveyevich Grigoryev	KGB Wanted list 55	MVD		October 1949	Germany	United Kingdom
Nikolay Ivanovich Marchenkov	KGB Wanted list 367	GRU	1941	March 1950	Germany	United States
Georgiy Vasilyevich Salimanov	Icarus	MVD		May 1950	Germany	United States
Unknown	Nikolay Grishin	MVD?		late 1951	Germany	United States

172

in the late 1940s. Brook-Shepherd, for example, wrote, 'For nine years after these cases [Gouzenko, Volkov, and Skripkin] had occurred almost simultaneously, the roll call of defectors remains nearly blank. Only two Soviet intelligence officers are recorded as having reached the West from any jumping-off point during this period, and neither was of great significance.'[5] The two to which Brook-Shepherd referred were Granovskiy (see Chapter 3) and Baklanov. Prokhorov lists only Vadim Ivanovich Shelaputin during this period.[6] Nigel West erroneously claimed, 'Between the receipt of Grigori Tokaev in 1946 and Oleg Lyalin in August 1971, not a single Soviet intelligence defector chose to come to Great Britain.'[7] In reality, Gorshkov, Baklanov, Shelaputin, Roze, Korniyevskiy, Mikheyev and Harvard Case 525 surrendered to British authorities in the late 1940s, and Yuriy Aleksandrovich Rastvorov planned to defect to the British in Japan in 1954, but a heavy snowstorm delayed his departure and he approached the Americans instead (see Chapter 5).[8] Mikhail Grigoryev (see Chapter 5) also defected to the British in Germany in 1954. This study does not claim to present an exhaustive list of defectors, to avoid drawing similarly inaccurate conclusions. But it presents a more complete list than has previously been available.

Personal Backgrounds

Defectors in the Early Cold War group continued the trend of young, junior officers that began at the end of the World War II-era group. Over half of the twenty-three defectors in the Early Cold War group were born after the Bolshevik revolution and were in their twenties when they defected; eleven defectors were twenty-five years old or younger. Their experience in Soviet intelligence and state security organisations was correspondingly short: sixteen became Soviet intelligence officers or interpreters during or after the war. Because of their low average rank and age, their professional experience was often limited to only one or two assignments.

Only two defectors in this group are known to have held a rank higher than captain – Petrov was a major when he defected and Salimanov was a colonel. Others may have held more senior ranks, but little information is available about their careers. Grigoryev graduated from an artillery officers' academy in 1931 and was old enough to be a major or higher, but the KGB Wanted List does not give his rank or when he became an NKVD officer. Information about the careers of Gurzhiev, Grishin, and Genrikh is sparse, but they may have held higher ranks as well.[9]

Even with the low average experience level of most of the Early Cold War Era defectors, Dana Durand, Chief of CIA's Berlin Operations Base (BOB), assessed in April 1948 that 'through a series of carefully encouraged low-level defections (of interpreters and secretaries) [a British intelligence officer] paved the way for interrogations covering in great detail all the principle RIS [Russian intelligence service] headquarters in Berlin and the Soviet Sector, with names and descriptions of hundreds of staff and agent personnel.' Durand's report listed Granovskiy (defected in September 1946 and arrived in Germany in November 1946) and Kravchenko (defected in June 1947) as the two principal counterespionage defections of 1947. Granovskiy was BOB's first Soviet intelligence officer defector, and BOB and CIC jointly debriefed Kravchenko.[10] Kravchenko's information was valued to the point that a report of his debriefing indicated: 'A lucid and consecutive compilation . . . was not possible without the additional and strategic information of this source.'[11]

Eight of the defectors in this group were involved in Soviet counterintelligence operations, working in SMERSH until it was renamed the Counterintelligence Directorate (*Управление Контрразведки*; UKR) in 1946. These defectors provided significantly corroborative stories about their experiences investigating espionage and screening Soviet citizens for repatriation. Their revelations made it clear that the Soviet Union viewed the Western Allies as intelligence adversaries even before the end of the war.

Foreign Language Interpreters

Thirteen of the Early Cold War era defectors were interpreters/translators, either hired because of previously obtained language capabilities or trained in a military language institute.

Nine were German linguists, three Hungarian, one Czech, and one Lithuanian.[12] The trend of interpreters defecting began just after the war, with six World War II-era defectors also working as linguists: Mondich (Czech, Ukrainian, and Ruthenian); and Gouzenko, Dubkov, Roze, Abryutin, and KGB Wanted List number 75 (all German) (see Chapter 3).

As Soviet forces moved westward beginning in 1943, they occupied Eastern and Central European countries, creating an urgent need for expertise in corresponding foreign languages. According to Petrov, who studied German and French before being drafted into the NKVD, Soviet troops were handicapped after the war because they were operating in foreign environments where few Soviet troops could communicate with locals or with Allied occupying forces.[13] Mikheyev, a SMERSH interpreter hired in Germany in 1945, similarly reported that the Soviet Union was in dire need of German speakers at the end of the war. The NKVD was often forced to rely either on locally recruited agents or on Soviet citizens proficient in a foreign language, even some who were 'contaminated with the Western way of life'.[14] The need for linguists sometimes compelled the NKVD and GRU to hire young Soviets who had not undergone thorough vetting for loyalty and security. Simultaneously, the NKVD allowed interpreters more freedom of movement than other intelligence personnel, according to Goldfarb.[15] These two factors compounded to create an environment ripe for defections.

Several defectors took advantage of that greater freedom to sidestep situations in which other Soviet citizens would typically have suffered punishment. Kravchenko, for example, was labelled pro-Western after unwisely showing overt interest in learning English and making careless comments sympathetic to the West. However, he claimed his usefulness as a German linguist saved him from prison.[16] When Harvard 525 took home leave in 1946, she violated regulations by telling a friend about life in Germany, and a militiaman came to her house and arrested her. She was released and allowed to return to Germany; she vaguely states 'somehow I got out of this', but others were not allowed to return to Germany after such incidents. Her tour of duty in Germany was scheduled to end in 1946 and she would have preferred to go home, but even after her run-in with the MVD, she was retained in Germany because of the lack of German linguists.[17] The priority need for linguists took precedence over normal security rules.

Soviet troops advancing into Hungary initially arrested Takacs because she had been born in Russia but had moved to Hungary with her mother as a child. However, an NKVD officer hired her as his interpreter, and she travelled with him to Czechoslovakia and Austria. She complained to the officer's superiors about his uncontrolled and licentious behaviour, and in the summer of 1945, she returned to Budapest as an interpreter for the Allied Control Commission Inspectorate, a Soviet intelligence cover organisation. She was working there when she met Denisov, also a Hungarian linguist. Takacs and Denisov decided to get married in late 1946, but Denisov's superiors forbade them from marrying or even seeing each other, and the GRU transferred Denisov back to Moscow in January 1947 to break off the engagement. But Soviet intelligence urgently needed Hungarian linguists, and in April, only three months later, the GRU assigned him back to Hungary as an interpreter in the GRU section of the Red Banner Danube Fleet. Takacs and Denisov defected together in August.[18]

Experience in Germany during the War

Eight of the defectors in this group spent time in Germany or German custody during the war. But unlike World War II-Era defectors, only one of the Early Cold War Era defectors, Mikheyev, willingly supported German forces, and one other, Pečiulionis, served in an anti-Soviet military group that was briefly allied with Germany. Others were either residents in German-occupied territory, POWs who never collaborated, or foreign labourers who were forced to work in Germany.

Several of these defectors were among the over two million Soviet citizens transported to Germany as forced labourers during the war. The region where Sharandak lived fell under German control in spring 1942, and he volunteered to work in Germany. But rather than being treated as a volunteer, he was sent to Germany as a forced labourer. He attempted to escape several times until 1943 when he was finally arrested under the false name Laszlo Baksa and thrown in prison in Sopron, Hungary, near the border with Austria; here he remained until Soviet troops arrived in March 1945. Kravchenko worked on his father's farm until June 1942, when he was transported as a forced labourer to Germany. He worked in a German factory in Ludwigshafen until US forces liberated him in March 1945.[19] Ryabenko was also taken to Germany as a forced labourer in 1942, and US forces liberated him in July 1945.[20] US forces repatriated Kravchenko and Ryabenko to Soviet control after the war, and the MGB hired them as interpreters.

Petrov spent time as a German POW after being captured with a team of NKVD personnel in June 1941.[21] Unlike World War II-era defectors, Petrov did not collaborate with German forces, but instead hid his NKVD insignia and burned his identity documents and Germans never realised who he was. He escaped during a prisoner movement and made his way back to Soviet-held territory, only to be received with suspicion and arrested. He was held among many other POW returnees suspected of disloyalty and assigned to a penal battalion, in which he fought for the rest of the war.[22]

Takacs lived in German-occupied Budapest during the war, working as a secretary for a construction engineer. When Soviet forces arrived in Hungary in January 1945, NKVD arrested Takacs because she had been born in Russia and spoke Russian, but her proficiency in Hungarian made her an attractive candidate as an interpreter.[23]

Each of these passed the screening process for employment or re-employment with a state security organisation but lasted only a few years after the war (see Chapter 6 for discussion of relaxed vetting standards during times of crisis).

Motivations

Lingering memories and familial connections to Soviet purges of the 1920s and 1930s created doubts about the Soviet system in the minds of Early Cold War defectors just as it had in earlier groups, forming the ideological motivation for at least six defectors in

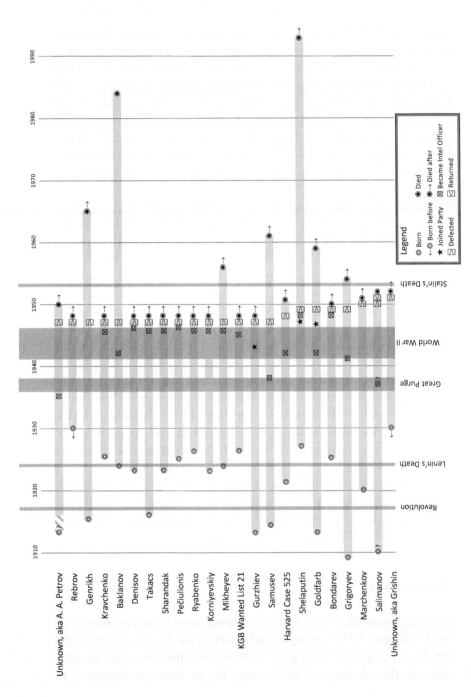

Figure 4.1 Lives of Early Cold War Defectors, 1947–1951

this group. An analysis of Soviet defectors in Germany under-taken by the US European Command in October 1948 identified three additional proximate motivations for defection that often accompanied ideology: imminence of return to the Soviet Union, usually tied to a relationship with a local woman; imminence of a court-martial; and previous collaboration with the enemy or a criminal record just discovered by the Soviet authorities.[24] These motivations were borne out in the Early Cold War Era group of Soviet intelligence officer defectors.

Purge Remnants

While purge connections usually disqualified a Soviet citizen for trusted employment in a Soviet intelligence or security service, the chaos of war often prevented Soviet state security organisations from performing thorough background investigations until the late 1940s, and some politically unreliable individuals made it through the process, later to escape when the opportunity arose.

Several defectors in this group were children or adolescents during the *Yezhovshchina* years and saw their parents and family members arrested. When Sharandak approached British forces in Austria in August 1947, he had in his possession photo-graphs showing his family's poverty, and their hardship played a significant role in his decision to escape Soviet control.[25] Both Mikheyev's and Goldfarb's fathers had been wealthy in the early Soviet years and were arrested as kulaks in the late 1920s or 1930s. Mikheyev said that he gained a dislike for the Soviet gov-ernment from a young age, partially through witnessing the con-trast between the living conditions of normal Soviet citizens and the Communist Party elite, and partially because of his father's embittered political views. Mikheyev volunteered for a German police unit and served in Germany for much of the war, but suc-cessfully hid his background until mid-1948, after over two years working as an MGB interpreter.[26] Goldfarb similarly described his father as an outspoken opponent of the Soviet system, which led to several arrests until he finally died in prison in 1938.[27] When Goldfarb joined the NKVD in 1942, he omitted refer-ences to his father's arrest, and historical NKVD records for the

Leningrad region were not accessible to check his background: NKVD files had been transported from Moscow and Leningrad to Sverdlovsk during the war.[26] Goldfarb told his American interrogators that his defection was the culmination of a long-held repugnance for the Soviet dictatorship: 'It could not be said that I suddenly became disenchanted with the Soviet system.'[29]

Shelaputin described himself as anti-Soviet already when he started working for the GRU.[30] His father was an actor, and Shelaputin described him as 'a little bohemian', forced to perform propaganda roles just to earn a living.[31] Shelaputin's time in the Military Language Institute was a moment of political awakening when he discussed anti-Soviet views with his close friends. By the time he left the institute, he had been accepted as a full party member, but claimed it was only to show superficial obedience and that he had become an 'accomplished double thinker' and careerist.[32] When Shelaputin arrived in Vienna, he and other GRU officers were encouraged to read foreign newspapers to practice their language skills, giving them access to news that most Soviet citizens never saw.[33] This reinforced Shelaputin's existing views about the Soviet Union. His GRU translation work was intended to train him for clandestine agent handling work, and he received orders to go to Czechoslovakia in a cover assignment for that purpose; however, he decided to defect instead.[34]

Petrov's experience with the *Yezhovshchina* was not as a victim but rather as an NKVD officer. Petrov's first NKVD job was in the Secret Political Directorate in 1936, where he witnessed interrogations of political suspects as the Great Purge was just getting started. Petrov's supervisor explained that he had a quota of bringing forty 'enemies of the people' before a tribunal each month.[35] Petrov was later summoned to give a deposition against the same former supervisor, who himself had been declared an 'enemy of the people'.[36] During a month's leave at an NKVD resort on Crimea, Petrov noted, as previous defectors like Ginzberg had, the contrast between the luxuries afforded him as an NKVD officer and the poverty in which the ordinary Soviet citizen struggled to exist. He likened the barbed wire that separated the NKVD resort from the local population to an 'iron curtain' to keep the peasants from intruding on the relaxation of the upper class of Soviet society. Later, after his defection, Petrov asked himself, 'Is this what we fought for?'[37]

Turning Against the Soviet People

The motivations of Early Cold War Era defectors revealed that, despite victory parades and exultation about crushing the fascist foe, the Soviet Union felt a sense of inferiority vis-à-vis the West. Defectors noted that Soviet leadership was concerned about shielding the Soviet population, especially state security officers, from the West's relative economic prosperity and political influences. Even defeated Germany compared positively with the Soviet Union economically, and Soviet leaders were afraid that a Western mindset would infect the Soviet Union.

The Soviet government reacted by applying state security measures to prevent the Soviet people from highlighting the contrast between life in the West and life in the Soviet Union. This included censorship of correspondence passing between the West and the Soviet Union; increased counterintelligence scrutiny on Soviet citizens, especially those who had spent time in Germany during the war, either voluntarily or by coercion; and forced repatriation of Soviet citizens and isolating them from the rest of the Soviet population by banishing them to forced labour camps. Soviet counterintelligence officers from SMERSH and then UKR manned repatriation offices under the philosophy that any Soviet citizen in Europe could have been infected by life in the West and could carry that infection back to the Soviet Union.

This underlying suspicion of Soviet citizens led several defectors to question the direction Soviet state security took after Germany's defeat and to complain that the Soviet government viewed its own people as the enemy, despite the sacrifices they had made during the war. In 1953, US Department of State officials interviewed Bondarev among other border crossers and Eastern European refugees to identify their motivations for breaking with the Soviet Union. Bondarev gave his principal reason for defecting as a realisation that the MGB was not concerned with combatting espionage, but instead with 'persecuting the people who spoke the truth'.[38] Baklanov also became disenchanted with his MGB job and with the Soviet Union in general because of the difference he saw between the mission of a wartime chekist and a peace-time chekist. He felt that fighting a foreign enemy was justified, but fighting one's own people was not. Forcing Soviet citizens to repatriate and dooming them to Soviet prison camps was more than he could stand.[39]

Petrov's SMERSH assignment as a Soviet repatriation officer in Germany was to enforce the Yalta Agreement by locating and identifying Soviet refugees and persuading them to return to the Soviet Union. He wrote that the Soviet Union viewed POWs and refugees as traitors, subject to the 1934 law that prohibited leaving the Soviet Union without authorisation. As a SMERSH officer under Soviet repatriation officer cover, Petrov's mission was to identify all Soviet citizens – including those from the Baltic republics, which the West refused to recognise as Soviet territory – collect them into assembly points, and transport them to the Soviet Union, using force if necessary.[40] Petrov specifically targeted members of the former KONR military forces, enticing them into Soviet control by promising that the Soviet government would forgive them for collaborating with the Germans. Although Soviet urgings and pamphlets showing the Soviet Union flowing with milk and honey had early success among some Soviet citizens who longed to return to their families, DPs soon began to hear about the fate of fellow refugees who accepted the Soviet offer. Others were never convinced. When American forces arrived to repatri-ate a camp filled with former KONR personnel in 1946, they met soldiers who preferred suicide to returning to the USSR. Petrov cited a US *Stars and Stripes* newspaper article from 23 January 1946, which reported that when US troops entered a POW camp, they found Soviet soldiers slicing themselves with broken glass and pleading with American soldiers to shoot them.[41]

Baklanov was in the Soviet occupation zone of Austria on the receiving end of repatriation operations in 1948. His job was to screen repatriated Soviets into three categories: enemies of the people, who were sent directly to prison camps or political prisons; relatively clean people in a political sense, who were either sent home and monitored or sentenced to 2–3 years in a forced labour project; and more or less reliable ones, who were hired as civilians to support Soviet occupation forces.[42] The repatriation mission was so big that extra officers were brought in from Soviet Union-based MGB and MVD units to accomplish the screenings.

Genrikh was involved with the last leg of the repatriation process: the transport of condemned Soviet citizens to labour camps. He slipped away at a railway station in Ploieşti, Romania, while accompanying a POW transport train in March 1947.[43] His debriefing is not publicly available, so his motivation is unclear, although he immigrated to the United States and likely provided insights into operations to dispatch repatriated Soviets to camps inside the Soviet Union.

Several defectors noted restrictions that forbade Europe-based Soviet personnel from telling associates in the Soviet Union about living conditions in Germany or Austria. Goldfarb mentioned that controls were put in place on MGB officers to 'shield Soviet citizens from subversive influences'. Soviet officers' wives were forbidden to travel home without their husbands, and letters to the Soviet Union were censored to avoid giving the impression that Soviet personnel lived in luxury in Germany.[44] As noted previously, Harvard 525 was forbidden to talk to her friends and relatives in the Soviet Union about how people lived in Germany. She knew that she was under surveillance while she was in the Soviet Union, because 'we did not trust each other'. When she returned to duty in Germany, Soviet state security officials questioned her friends about what she had told them.[45]

Baklanov similarly complained that he could not write letters about his life in Austria even to his father, a high-level Party official. But censorship also operated in the opposite direction. Baklanov wrote about Army officers returning to Austria after home leave being arrested for talking openly about dreadful living conditions inside the Soviet Union. Rumours circulated in spite of censorship: Baklanov related an anecdote that passed around among Soviet forces in Austria about a Soviet soldier who returned to his hometown after completing his tour of duty in Europe. The soldier found both his mother and father still alive, and rather than rejoicing, his first thought was 'how am I going to feed you both'.[46]

Because of MGB officers' greater exposure to Western institutions and people, they were closely monitored and isolated from the rest of the Soviet forces in Germany. Harvard 525 noted that she was not allowed to talk to regular army officers, and that most of them did not know what the MGB did, although they were still afraid of it.[47] Shelaputin related that the MGB embedded an informant in his unit to monitor GRU officers' loyalty. Although the informant's identity was not publicly known, Shelaputin and his close confidants suspected one individual who tried to draw out subversive sentiments by telling anti-Soviet jokes and then asking others if they knew any, or dropping by another officer's home and asking what he was reading. The GRU officers avoided him.[48]

The MGB was particularly concerned that repatriation officers, like Petrov, would become 'bourgeoisified'[49] by life in the West and try to defect because of their close contact with Allied personnel. An anonymous author who signed his work only as A.B.V., writing about Soviet intelligence activities in France in the first few years after the war, indicated that MGB officers under repatriation officer cover in Germany were rotated into France for only one-month temporary duties, to prevent them from becoming too comfortable in capitalist France. However, desertions still occurred despite precautions. A.B.V. recalls one high-ranking officer who 'fled' and whom A.B.V. assumed fell victim to a hunt organised by the MGB.[50] It is unknown whether this fleeing officer was Petrov, although he fits the general description.

Fraternisation

As part of the effort to shield MGB personnel from Western influences, they were officially prohibited from fraternising with the local population in an attempt to prevent them from becoming attached to the West. Many Soviet troops regularly ignored the prohibition; Baklanov boasted of his relationships with girls in Vienna and Budapest.[51] Nevertheless, the rule was enforced in some instances, leading to defections. British journalist Steven Dorril asserts that the majority of defectors to British forces up to 1951 were low-level Soviet Army soldiers who fled to the

West because of their associations with local women.[52] A few of these were affiliated with the MGB, like Takacs and Denisov, who defected so they could marry each other.[53] Sharandak also worked as a Hungarian interpreter in security units of the Soviet occupation forces in Hungary from about April 1945 until July 1947. He met a Hungarian girl, and he planned to marry her and settle in Hungary for the rest of his life. They escaped together.[54]

Fraternisation drew Soviet counterintelligence interest because of the risk that a local girlfriend would entice a Soviet officer to defect. Goldfarb related an investigation that his unit conducted involving a Colonel Yarkho, a Soviet engineer who became involved in a convoluted case with his mistress. Yarkho fell in love with a German woman, Lieselotte Wieck, whose husband was a former Nazi bürgermeister. To free themselves of the husband, Yarkho and Wieck planted a pistol on him and had him arrested. Wieck's maid found out about the scheme and blackmailed Wieck. Wieck responded by murdering the maid, and Yarkho and Wieck fled to the West. However, a German who facilitated their escape was an MGB agent, and the UKR used him to lure them back into the Soviet zone and arrest them. Wieck was sentenced to ten years' forced labour and Yarkho was sentenced to execution, although Yarkho's sentence was later commuted to twenty-five years' forced labour.[55]

Recalls to the Soviet Union

As with previous groups, some officers in this group defected to British or US forces in direct response to a recall to the Soviet Union, often prompted by illegal activities such as abetting an investigative suspect, committing espionage, or assault. By the late 1940s, the reassembly of NKVD records prompted reinvestigations of Soviet personnel in Germany, often leading to recalls for hidden past transgressions.

In August 1948, Mikheyev's supervisor summoned him to his office and informed him that he was being transferred back to the Soviet Union in two hours – the MGB had learned of his false identity and anti-Soviet background. An escort accompanied him everywhere he went in those two hours to prevent him from escaping. But Mikheyev slipped a pistol into his pocket, and when he and his minder were away from the office, he shot him and ran.[56] Similarly, Goldfarb received an order to return to the Soviet Union in June 1949. He suspected that his father's arrest as an 'enemy of the people' had finally caught up with him, and he immediately made plans to defect.[57] Goldfarb did not resort to such extreme measures as Mikheyev did, however, and he escaped undetected.

Salimanov learned in May 1950 that he was to be removed from his position and ordered back to the Soviet Union. Nothing is publicly available about the reasons for this sudden reversal, but womanising might have been a factor. Dr Arnold Kramish, an official with the US Atomic Energy Commission who supported CIA intelligence operations, characterised Salimanov as a 'very distasteful character'. Eric Welsh, an SIS officer who specialised in atomic intelligence, regarded him as 'very dangerous'.[58] Rather than return to the Soviet Union, Salimanov slipped away from his MGB minder and fled to West Germany.[59]

Grigoryev received orders to return to the Soviet Union in October 1949, coinciding with a reorganisation of Soviet military units. He had arrived in 1945 at the Soviet Military Administration (SMA) in Germany to work in the Directorate of Internal Affairs, an NKVD cover organisation.[60] The SMA existed until the Soviet government began to transfer some governing functions to the newly established East German government in 1949. Based on the timing, Grigoryev's defection may have been to avoid returning to the Soviet Union when his unit was disestablished,[61] probably having become 'infected' by life in the West.

Other defectors escaped to pre-empt a recall. The US Strategic Services Unit (SSU) recruited Rebrov as an espionage agent in 1947. He was serving as the head of the Soviet intelligence registry in Berlin and passed original copies of messages between Berlin and NKVD Headquarters in Moscow that passed through his office. He took advantage of the inefficient filing system at NKVD headquarters in which communications were frequently lost, and thus a message never showing up at its destination did not raise any particular suspicion. Eventually, Rebrov lost his nerve, and the SSU extracted him from Berlin.[62] Harvard 525 fled her position because she tipped off the subject of an investigation about the suspicions against him, allowing the suspect to escape. Fearing a recall, she ran to Berlin in February 1949 with six MGB personnel suspected of aiding the suspect, and she initially turned herself over to British forces.[63] Nothing further is known of the other six. Rebrov and Harvard 525 recognised the danger of their situations.

Overall, a shift in Soviet state security priority from fighting a wartime enemy to fighting the Soviet people heavily influenced defectors in the Early Cold War Group. The oppressive emphasis on rooting out Western influences, both among POWs and among Soviet intelligence officers, created an intolerable environment. Those who could not endure the new scrutiny escaped and took advantage of the welcome that Western governments had begun to offer.

Receiving Countries

All twenty-three individuals in the Early Cold War Group defected either to the US or British government. They were among a flood of Soviet personnel – mostly low-level soldiers – who crossed an occupation zone boundary, most often in Germany or Austria, in the early years after the war. Defectors chose the US and Great Britain for both practical and political reasons. On the practical side, the British and US occupation zones in Germany and Austria shared a border with Soviet occupation zones, which, along with the four-power division of Berlin and Vienna, gave would-be defectors access to a foreign power. Sixteen Soviet intelligence personnel defected in Germany and four in Austria during this period. Berlin and Vienna were especially conducive locations for defection: six Soviet intelligence personnel are known to have defected to the US zone of Berlin during between 1947 and 1950 – Petrov, Rebrov, Kravchenko, Goldfarb, Ryabenko and Marchenkov. Two others likely defected in Berlin, but available information is less definitive – Gurzhiev was last seen in Berlin before his disappearance,[64] and Salimanov frequently travelled to Berlin and would have had access to the US zone there.[65] Two defectors, Shelaputin and Baklanov, defected to the US CIC in Vienna, and Korniyevskiy defected to the British Occupation Zone in Austria.

Four other defectors – Samusev,[66] Bondarev, Grigoryev,[67] and Harvard 525 – fled to the US occupation zone of Germany in late 1948 or 1949, although the specific location of their defection is not available. Grishin probably defected to US forces in Germany because he wrote a monograph for Columbia University's Research Program on the USSR, but little information is available about the circumstances of his defection.[68] Pečiulionis was also in Germany, but his position was quite different from others. The MGB dispatched Pečiulionis to a US-sponsored DP camp in December 1947 on an operational assignment to penetrate anti-Soviet elements. Rather than complete his mission, he revealed his MGB affiliation to Lithuanian camp leaders, who turned him over to US authorities. There is no indication that US forces tried to delve deeper into his Soviet intelligence mission, and German police arrested him for petty theft in June 1948.[69]

Politically, defectors' choice of the United States and Britain was an indication of the Soviet Union's perception of the world: with the defeat of Germany, the Soviet Union faced what it perceived as an 'Anglo-American' capitalist alliance, with other countries being secondary players.[70] The focus on Great Britain as an adversary was a resumption of Britain's pre-war position in the Soviet threat calculation. The United States was added as an emerging threat during World War II and grew to equal status with Great Britain as the war closed. Soviet personnel, especially intelligence and state security officers, were indoctrinated from the moment Germany surrendered that the next war would be against Great Britain and the United States, and defectors viewed those two countries as the most likely to accept them and use their information.

Further, the United States and Britain attracted defectors because they instituted programmes to target Soviet and other Eastern Bloc individuals and induce them to defect. The JIC began discussing the desirability of inducing defection in mid-1948.[71] By 1949, the SIS's Technical Co-ordinating Section, which ran scientific collection operations, targeted Soviet scientists for their intelligence value.[72] The United States established policy for inducing defectors in 1950 with NSCID 13, which defined induce-ment as 'the commission of an act by, or manifestly at the instiga-tion of, an American official which is demonstrably intended to bring about a defection and for which the US Government might, if the act were discovered, be called upon to account'. It assigned the CIA the responsibility for inducing defections unless another agency was more appropriate. By 1951, the CIA instituted the REDCAP programme, 'a systematic and concentrated program of penetration and defection inducement operations directed at Soviet official installations outside the USSR'.[73]

British and Americans worked together in some cases to safely extract defectors and interrogate them. Mikheyev initially slipped into the British occupation zone of Germany and was held in British custody for several days, but asked to go to the Americans so he could reveal everything he knew.[74] KGB Wanted List number 21 defected to British forces in Germany, although the British allowed the US CIC to interrogate him.[75] Conversely, Baklanov debated in his head whether to defect to the Americans or the British, and decided to initially defect to the Americans because they had a better operational infrastructure in Austria, but to later move to Great Britain.[76]

Denisov and Takacs escaped together and walked across the border from Hungary to Czechoslovakia in mid-August 1947. They approached the British Embassy in Prague and spoke to a military attaché, who told them to come back the next day. While they were walking away, two men met them and told them to be on a certain bridge in Prague later that evening. They followed the instructions and were picked up by a car and taken to a safe house, where they were told that because no British occupation zone shared a border with Czechoslovakia, they would be handed to the Americans.[77]

Although the Allies began to soften their compliance with the Yalta Agreement policy regarding repatriation in 1947, would-be defectors were not fully aware of the shift. Kravchenko first considered defection and eventual emigration to the United States in December 1946 when he realised that he no longer shared the ideals of the Soviet government and could not reconcile his conscience with Soviet counterintelligence methods. However, he was concerned that if he approached the Americans without valuable information to give them, they would doubt his story and turn him away. From the beginning of 1947, he gleaned every piece of information he could about Soviet methods and he gathered names and photographs of Soviet intelligence personnel and licence numbers of Soviet vehicles. He waited until June 1947 to defect.[78]

Petrov recalled that another Soviet repatriation officer had offered to defect to the Americans in 1946, only to be returned to the Soviet government as a deserter. Petrov was more aware than most MGB personnel about the Allies' shift away from forced repatriation. But he was still nervous when he turned himself over to the Americans in early 1947, and he was initially held in a US military prison, but was released to find employment and to try to survive in Germany.[79] Sharandak was unsure about approaching the British because of rumours that the British handed deserters back to the Soviet Union, but he was located near the Hungarian border with the British occupation zone of Austria, so he took the chance and walked to a British military unit in Hartberg, Austria.[80] Goldfarb had also heard that as late as 1946, American forces turned back Soviet defectors; he did not defect until 1949.[81]

Although France also occupied portions of Germany, it had neither the practical nor political draw of Great Britain or the United States. The French zones were not contiguous with the Soviet zone, and thus no Soviet defectors could directly cross into the French occupation zone except in Berlin, and there are few examples of defectors doing that. Kulagin (see Chapter 3) was one who did; he defected to the French zone of Berlin in 1946 and was transferred to the French zone of Germany for debriefing. Additionally, while some defectors numbered France among the Soviet Union's imperialist adversaries, Soviet state security did not view it as presenting the same level of threat as the other allies. Baklanov received briefings claiming that many officers in the French security forces were pro-communist, and thus were often sympathetic to the Soviet Union.[82] US forces handed Mikheyev over to French custody in March 1949, but that was probably due to the intensity of the Soviet pursuit to recapture him, not because of his desire to go to France. He wrote a letter from a

French DP camp in Rastatt, Germany, to the CIC Headquarters in Frankfurt in May 1951 asking the CIC to vouch for him so that he could immigrate to the United States; he eventually emigrated to Australia instead.[83]

Defectors' Perceptions of Western Political Naiveté

Although Early Cold War era defectors exclusively chose the United States and Britain, several expressed negative views of their receiving countries. The Allies' repatriation policies were a topic of particular disdain for defectors. For example, although Petrov surrendered himself to US forces in Germany, he was not entirely pro-American and his writing criticised the United States and Britain for their political naiveté and for being easily manipulated by the Soviets. He claimed Beriya himself had drafted the Yalta Agreement, and that by acceding to it, US President Roosevelt and UK Prime Minister Churchill became unwitting collaborators with SMERSH.[84] Baklanov recalled that during his SMERSH training, his instructor assessed that the Americans had not yet 'managed to set up a respectable intelligence service', but the potential was there, despite Americans' political immaturity.[85] He similarly criticised the US and British governments for naively accepting the Soviet insistence of repatriation. He wrote, 'Our allies were apparently unaware that the members of the missions were regular chekist officers from SMERSH.'[86]

Petrov further criticised Westerners for their willingness to accept the Soviet political line and become intelligence agents. During a tour of duty in Switzerland before the war, Petrov remarked that, although Soviet citizens often had no choice but to cooperate with Soviet state security for fear of losing their jobs or their lives, Western officials had no such threat against them. He attributed their willingness either to political naiveté or greed. He asked himself, do these Westerners actually believe that the Soviet Union is the 'most democratic country in the world', or was Marx correct when he asserted that the capitalist world was motivated only by money?[87] His experience recruiting agents from Western countries convinced him that 'capitalism had reached a stage of complete moral decomposition'.[88]

Shelaputin was disappointed by what he perceived as the West's initial timidity about using him as a propaganda weapon against the Soviet Union. During his interview for the HPSSS in November 1950, he remarked that he was hoping to employ what he considered his journalistic talents in America's fight against Bolshevism. But during his first two years in the West, he felt he was not used effectively, and he considered taking an offer to be resettled in Brazil and start a new life. But he sensed a shift in US policy and did not lose hope.[89] He did get his wish: he worked for the SIS in the early 1950s, and US intelligence used him in an unsuccessful operation to recruit one of his former military language institute classmates who was working at the Soviet embassy in the Netherlands.[90] He later worked for the BBC Russian Service until 1972, using the name Victor Gregory. He then moved back to Germany to work for Radio Liberty, and retired in 1990.

Operational Priorities

Similar to World War II-era defectors, Early Cold War defectors' revelations show a transition from Germany as the wartime adversary to the United States and Great Britain as anticipated post-war adversaries even before the war ended. The division of Germany into occupation zones juxtaposed Soviet and Western military forces, providing an unprecedented venue for intelligence activities directed at the Allies. The Soviet leadership recognised the opportunities that this proximity presented for Soviet intelligence collection, as well as the risks it posed to Soviet forces from foreign intelligence and cultural infiltration. They responded by ordering both aggressive intelligence operations and a tightened counterintelligence environment in Soviet occupation zones of Eastern and Central Europe.

Germany and German Sympathisers

Early Cold War defectors revealed the same three phases of Soviet intelligence targeting of Germany as did World War II-era defectors: pre-war, wartime, and post-war. Of the defectors in this group, only Petrov wrote about pre-war intelligence activities against Germany, including aggressive counterintelligence operations targeting Germans visiting the Soviet Union. Salimanov undoubtedly could have revealed similar information, but his debriefings are not publicly available. Baklanov and Goldfarb discussed Soviet wartime operations against Germany and Soviet support for anti-German partisan activities. As most of the Early Cold War defectors became affiliated with the NKVD or GRU during or after the war, most of their information centred around the post-war treatment of Germany as a defeated adversary, particularly denazification operations and Sovietisation of the newly occupied territories.

Petrov's first case as a new NKVD officer in 1936 in the Secret Political Directorate was an individual whom a previous interrogator had already coerced into confessing to being a Trotskyist associated with the German embassy in Moscow. Petrov just needed to document his story. But when Petrov questioned him, it was clear that he had no knowledge of Trotsky and did not even know where the German embassy was.[91] Petrov cited the case as being typical of NKVD tactics during the *Yezhovshchina*. Several years later, just before the outbreak of war in the Soviet Union, Petrov was ordered to travel to Baku, Azerbaijan, to monitor a German delegation that had come to negotiate a deal for Soviet oil. Petrov indicated that by 1940 the 'honeymoon' between the Soviet Union and Germany that began with the Molotov–Ribbentrop Pact had faded and the Soviet government was growing weary of German demands for raw materials. But the Soviet Union feared Hitler, and made a show of abiding by the pact while underhandedly sabotaging it. The NKVD closely shadowed the visiting German delegation and investigated any Soviet citizen that came into contact with it. Reminiscent of Akhmedov and Zhigunov, Petrov cited a declaration by Stalin that war would break out soon, but that the Soviet Union should welcome it because it would result in the weakening of Germany and the United States to the benefit of the Soviet Union.[92]

Baklanov joined the NKVD soon after the war began and indicated that Germany dominated the curriculum during his first year in the NKVD school in 1942. His instructor presented examples of Soviet operations directed at Germany, including stay-behind agents and false volunteers who were dispatched to penetrate all aspects of the German military and police and to sabotage and paralyse German activities on the front and in the rear. The teacher evaluated the German intelligence system, numbering the total absence of liberal-democratic ethics among its strengths, and the Germans' ethnic arrogance and inability to improvise among its weaknesses.[93] The NKVD training also included material on Hungarian and Romanian secret services as allies of Germany.

Baklanov was transferred to Lvov, Ukraine, in mid-1944, and assigned to support covert operations against German forces. His SMERSH unit dispatched partisans behind German lines and debriefed them when they returned. Baklanov described two types of partisan cells: intelligence-sabotage groups, which conducted observation and reporting operations predominantly, with sabotage being secondary; and operational-sabotage groups, which were directed to destroy military facilities such as bridges, airfields, and buildings, and to target specific German or German-allied individuals for assassination. The NKVD agents also supplied underground communist cells in German-occupied territory with arms, ammunition, medical supplies, and personnel so they could conduct sabotage and assassination operations against the Germans.[94] Baklanov personally participated in a mission behind German lines in Poland while posted to the SMERSH unit in Lvov. He airdropped with a team of SMERSH officers into a remote location in a Polish forest to deliver orders to a covert action detachment. The detachment handled Polish agents who observed German troop movements and concentrations and identified roads suitable for future Soviet tank travel.[95]

Goldfarb reported to the SMERSH office of the Leningrad Front in June 1943 as an interpreter for interrogations and recruitment operations among German POWs. As Soviet forces began to push the Germans out of Soviet territory, Goldfarb's unit moved from the Leningrad Front to Estonia, and then to Poland. His unit supported Polish anti-Nazi partisans, like the Armija Krajowa, and participated in the arrests of thousands of Poles who collaborated with Germany. Goldfarb's job during this time included translating a haul of documents captured from Gestapo offices in territory occupied by Soviet forces.[96]

After the war, defectors revealed that Soviet priorities related to Germany shifted from covert activities to overtly pursuing and arresting Nazis and collaborators. SMERSH personnel were quick to label Germans as Nazis and were inclined to believe any denunciation of a German. Mikheyev's unit was primarily focused on denazification initially, and he claimed the MGB had little problem identifying former Nazis since everyone knew who they were. Mikheyev gave detailed information about MGB investigations, including the identities of Germans coerced into cooperation using MGB threats to reveal their Nazi past.[97] Goldfarb described several investigations of former and alleged Nazis, including one former Nazi officer whom the MGB arrested and executed after he admitted to a friend that he had killed Jews during the war.[98] Goldfarb also described an investigation into unsubstantiated rumours that floated around Germany after the war alleging that Heinrich Himmler had issued an order just before the fall of the Nazi government that Nazi organisations should form into underground sabotage groups called Werewolves. The MGB was quick to believe reports about Werewolf cells and ordered that sixteen people be arrested and interrogated for allegedly creating a cell in the town of Fürstenwalde, east of Berlin. However, the arrestees gave contradictory stories, and the investigation uncovered no conclusive evidence of guilt. When the MGB dug deeper into the original report, it turned out that the individual who initiated it was a fabricator and no such cell existed. To the MGB's embarrassment, all sixteen suspects were released and exonerated, and the MGB never discovered a genuine Werewolf cell.[99]

In addition to pursuing former Nazis, Soviet state security officers were on alert for any anti-Soviet activities among the German and Soviet population. Samusev's operational group investigated people who allegedly opposed the Sovietisation of eastern Germany, including a section that monitored Soviet officials in Germany. His unit recruited sources among German government officials to report on the Soviet officers with whom they had contact.[100] Peciulionis was sent into a DP camp in the US zone of Germany to collect information about organisations and their leaders that agitated against repatriation and any information about German anti-Bolsheviks. He was instructed to make contact with the German Communist Party near Kassel, Germany, which the MGB was using as an operations support hub and where he would receive further instructions.[101]

Great Britain and the United States

Building on the information revealed by World War II-era defectors, defectors in the Early Cold War Era group revealed a deep-seated Soviet mistrust for Great Britain and the United States, which prompted numerous strategic intelligence and counterintelligence operations even as Soviet troops were still fighting Germans on the battlefield. As noted in the previous chapter, Soviet intelligence increasingly viewed Great Britain and the United States as a combined target, partially because of their shared language but also because of what the Soviets suspected to be a unified capitalist front against the Soviet Union. This target unity continued after the war, when the Soviet Union perceived that an 'Anglo-American' alliance opposed the Soviet Union in diplomacy, intelligence operations, and militarily.

According to Petrov, Stalin was concerned in 1938 and 1939 about what he viewed as a capitalist conspiracy against the Soviet Union, and he instructed his intelligence services to watch for the possibility that Roosevelt and UK Prime Minister Neville Chamberlain would reach a separate agreement with Hitler.[102] The NKVD was simultaneously interested in collecting information about British and French negotiating positions towards an alliance with the Soviet Union. At this time, Petrov was involved in Soviet intelligence recruitment in and around the League of Nations in Geneva among foreign delegations, Swiss left-wing intellectuals, and Communist Party members in Switzerland. These sources provided copies of confidential League of Nations correspondences and information from local political parties. The internal messages revealed both strategic intelligence about international negotiations and operational targeting information about the authors, which could be pursued even after the League of Nations dissolved. One of the NKVD's sources was the secretary of a British newspaper correspondent in Geneva. The secretary picked up a particularly valuable piece of intelligence when his boss held a conversation with Seán Lester, an Irish diplomat then serving as Deputy Secretary-General of the League of Nations. The correspondent dictated the contents of the conversation to his secretary, who reported it to his NKVD handler. The NKVD handler received another corroborating confidential report from a different source on the same day giving details of British intentions for future negotiations.[103]

Petrov also described a pre-war operation against the United States involving American visitors to the Soviet Union. When Petrov worked in the NKVD Counterintelligence Directorate in Moscow, he arranged for a professor from Columbia University to visit Moscow so that the professor could acquire first-hand experience in the Soviet Union and build more credibility as a Soviet specialist. The NKVD expected him to use his increased stature as a platform for Soviet propaganda when he returned to the United States, and the professor later wrote a flattering book about the Soviet Union.[104]

Soviet intelligence training during and soon after the war indicated a Soviet transition of priorities from Germany to Great Britain and the United States. For example, Baklanov's training began to include lessons on British and American intelligence services during his second year in the NKVD school in 1943. He never heard NKVD instructors refer to Great Britain or the United States as allies. Instead, they taught that the British intelligence service was the best in the capitalist world and that its strengths included worldwide experience, sound financial backing, and a high level of education among intelligence officers. Among the British weaknesses were dilettantism and a British sense of superiority, although the British were not as ethnically chauvinistic as the Germans. In addition to Britain, Baklanov reported that the NKGB foreign intelligence directorate had 'discovered' America on a large scale for the first time in about 1943 and had dispatched numerous agents to collect intelligence about the United States.[105] Samusev's training showed a similar trend. He also attended NKVD counterintelligence training in 1943, where the curriculum included material on a variety of foreign intelligence services, particularly German, Japanese, American, British, and French. He noted during debriefings, however, that the curriculum had changed since he was in training and that English had replaced German as the primary foreign language for new trainees.[106]

After the war, the transition from Germany to the 'Anglo-American' alliance accelerated. Pečiulionis attended an MVD officer's course in Vilnius, Lithuania, from May to November 1946 and his training in espionage, sabotage, surveillance, interrogations, and fieldwork in political investigations and arrests was primarily focused on Great Britain and the United States. He was assigned to collect information about US occupation forces, including numbers of troops and aircraft; the types and condition of weapons; and what the German population thought about the US occupation. His training included predictions that the Soviet Union would soon be at war with Great Britain and the United States, and that Pečiulionis should be ready to organise and conduct stay-behind sabotage actions in case of war. He was told that when he got settled, the MGB would issue him a firearm with which he was to cause disturbances and fire at passing American trains.[107]

Baklanov also recalled the mood in the MGB at the end of the war. Similar to Mondich, Baklanov's unit commander told SMERSH troops that, while for some the war was over, for chekists it was not. 'The real war, to bring about the final destruction of the capitalist world, was only just beginning. We had annihilated just its ugliest manifestation – Hitler and his empire. The fight to annihilate the rest lay ahead.'[108] SMERSH in Vienna recruited cleaners, translators, secretaries, typists, and other locally hired employees as sources inside Allied institutions to keep Allied units, officials of the Allied Control Commission, military police, and the occupation government headquarters under constant surveillance.[109] America's possession of an atomic weapon caused particular consternation and was the topic of Soviet propaganda spread among Soviet forces. The propaganda declared that the Soviet Union must counter American militarism and prepare to occupy all of Western Europe and the British Isles, assuming that the Americans would not drop their atomic bomb on British or French territory.[110]

Despite this close monitoring, Soviet counterintelligence had only a superficial understanding of American and British intelligence capabilities. Mikheyev reported that most low-level MGB personnel knew little about Western intelligence services, other than that they sent a large number of agents into the eastern zone.[111] The MGB suspected many individuals of being foreign agents, often knowing only that a suspect was 'Anglo-American' without specifying which. Mikheyev noted an investigation of an individual named Grimpe who claimed to have fled to a western zone of Germany to avoid forced labour in the mines at Aue. He was reportedly received by British or American intelligence (Mikheyev did not know which) and dispatched back into the Soviet zone. In other cases, suspects were tied to British intelligence specifically, mostly because Mikheyev's operational group's area of responsibility bordered the British occupation zone.[112]

Samusev stated that the chief of the MGB in Germany, General Lieutenant Nikolay Kuzmich Kovalchuk, who arrived in Germany in September 1946, ordered that the primary task for MGB elements in Germany was to uncover and neutralise foreign intelligence agent networks in the Soviet zone. He strengthened MGB second departments, which were responsible for dispatching agents into the western zones for intelligence operations. The MGB used several categories of agents to support these operations: German POWs repatriated to the Soviet zone; Germans with personal or business connections in the western zones; owners of hotels and restaurants frequented by foreigners; black marketers; prostitutes; and priests, doctors, and teachers who might be able to work or be accepted in the western zones.[113] Mikheyev noted a case of two sisters who worked as typists and interpreters for the British Military Government in Germany, whose father was an MGB agent in the Soviet zone. The girls travelled illegally into the Soviet zone to visit their father, and the MGB planned to approach them for recruitment.[114]

Goldfarb provided summaries of MGB counterintelligence cases that illustrated the MGB's emphasis on investigating American and British espionage, as well as the methods that the MGB used to neutralise foreign threats. Cases involved Germans suspected of passing Soviet information to American intelligence, people who expressed interest in escaping to the American zone of Germany, or even people who were acquainted with escapees.[115] Translators noted that their work often involved intelligence and counterintelligence operations targeting Americans or British. In June 1947, Sharandak was translating a denunciation of a Hungarian named Professor Voland who was working as an interpreter for the British mission in Hungary, and he attempted to approach Voland to ask for assistance in escaping.[116] The GRU seconded Shelaputin as a translator to the MGB, where his work included translating documents about the British SIS and US CIC.[117]

Goldfarb reported that during the summer of 1948, MGB headquarters disseminated a message signed by Minister of State Security Viktor Semyonovich Abakumov to all Soviet state security offices in the Soviet Union and in military units, including in Soviet occupation forces in Germany. Goldfarb assumed that message had actually come from the Politburo itself.[118] The message was highly critical of Soviet counterintelligence officers for their lack of vigilance in pursuing and neutralising foreign threats. Foreign intelligence services of the 'imperialist' powers, it said, particularly American and British, actively used embassy officials and journalists for intelligence purposes. The message censured Soviet counterintelligence officers for their laxity in handling intelligence agents, noting one example of an officer who accepted 'gifts' from his agent, who had gotten the gifts from the foreign counterintelligence target himself. It contended that the majority of Soviet counterintelligence operations were either useless or had been doubled. Soviet counterintelligence officers were ordered to relook all of their agent networks, close down those that had been compromised and arrest double agents. They were to increase efforts to recruit and train agents with access to foreigners, who were to be kept under constant surveillance: 'follow targets relentlessly, walk in foreigners' footsteps'. Abakumov closed the message with, 'It is imperative to reach such a situation in which not a single foreigner could have free and unobserved access to any corner of the USSR.'[119] This included areas occupied by Soviet troops.

Sovietising Eastern Europe

As Soviet forces re-occupied the Baltic republics and flowed into Eastern Europe in the wake of the receding German army, Soviet state security moved with them to establish Soviet rule and eliminate opposition. Like several of the defectors in the World War II-era group, such as Granovskiy and Mondich, Early Cold War defectors discussed Soviet operations in Eastern European countries that often included thousands of investigations and mass arrests. Soviet intelligence actively sought to neutralise anti-Soviet elements among refugee populations, including assassinations of resistance leaders. Granovskiy and Mondich both discussed Soviet state security activities in post-war Czechoslovakia; Petrov and Pečiulionis added information about Estonia and Lithuania; and Baklanov, Goldfarb, and Pečiulionis provided information about activities in Poland.

In 1939, Petrov received an order from Moscow to contact his agents in the League of Nations Secretariat, in foreign delegations, and among Swiss journalists and to feed them material intended to create unfavourable opinions about Finland and the Baltic states. The order from Moscow did not explain the reasons, but it soon became clear that the Soviet Union would move militarily against Finland and politically against the Baltic states.[120] He described his participation in a meeting in Moscow June 1940 where Vladimir Georgiyevich Dekanozov, Andrey Yanuaryevich Vyshinskiy, and Andrey Aleksandrovich Zhdanov met to plan the annexation of the Baltic republics. The purported reason for the move was to defend the north-west frontier from the incursions of capitalist forces into the Soviet Union only a short while after Soviet leaders had claimed that 'chatter about the Sovietisation of the Baltic States benefits only the enemies of the Soviet Union'.[121]

Petrov claimed to have travelled with Zhdanov to Tallinn, where he witnessed Zhdanov's interaction with Karl Säre, a leader of the small Estonian Communist Party, and Johannes Vares, the socialist Estonian poet whom Zhdanov chose as the prime minister of occupied Estonia. He referred to Säre and Vares as 'the first Quislings'. In meetings Petrov described as if he were present, Zhdanov pushed Säre to persuade Estonian communists to accept

Soviet dominance, despite Säre's protestations that it would not be easy. After this meeting, Zhdanov gave Petrov a list of names of Estonian Communist Party members that the NKVD should eliminate.

Petrov also witnessed a meeting with Johannes Vares at which Zhdanov promised increased Soviet trade with Estonia once it allowed the presence of Soviet troops. Vares agreed to form a new government that would be cooperative with the Soviet Union where Estonian businessmen would benefit from Soviet business. Petrov noted that the exchange with Vares seemed contrary to everything he had been taught: that capitalists wanted only to destroy the Soviet Union, not cooperate with it. But Petrov then witnessed that, just two months later, those same compliant capitalists were loaded onto cattle cars and shipped as prisoners to the Soviet far north to cut trees.

Petrov was on the scene at Narva, Estonia, in June 1940 when the order arrived for Estonian forces to allow Soviet troops into the country. He referred to this incident as the 'assassination of a nation'. He witnessed pro-Russian demonstrations, manned by Russian peasants imported from areas of Russia bordering Estonia, beggars hired for the occasion, and prisoners released from prison specifically to participate in the demonstrations. He also saw Estonian demonstrators surrounding the Soviet embassy in Tallinn protesting Soviet control. The following year, when Petrov was in Estonia after the Germans had invaded the Soviet Union, he encountered a series of roughly dug graves, which he learned were filled with the bodies of Estonians killed for resisting Soviet authority in 1940. Petrov was awarded the Order of the Red Banner along with other NKVD officers for 'welcoming the Baltic countries into the fraternal family of the Soviet republics'.[122]

Pečiulionis's first assignment after completing MGB training was as a prison guard in a political prison in Katowice, Poland. But the MGB recognised his language ability and in late 1947 assigned him to travel clandestinely to a US-sponsored refugee camp in Germany and establish himself as a Lithuanian DP. He was to portray himself as a member of a purportedly powerful anti-Soviet group that was fighting for Lithuania's freedom, and gain the trust of Lithuanian resistance leaders. After receiving DP documents, he was to collect information about prominent Lithuanians in the camp, create disturbances and start fights among refugees. He was ordered to prepare to assassinate prominent anti-Soviet Lithuanian leaders General Stasys Raštikis and Colonel Andrusaitis.[123]

Soviet intelligence activities in Poland were initially directed at identifying and purging Nazi sympathisers, but transitioned to strengthening Polish communists and establishing Soviet rule. Near the end of the war, Baklanov's unit collected the names of Poles who collaborated with the Germans for future counterintelligence operational use, as well as the names of local Polish civic leaders and political figures for the occupation of Poland.[124] Goldfarb's unit also moved into Poland and supported Polish anti-Nazi partisans and participated in the arrests of thousands of Poles.[125] Goldfarb and Samusev both discussed similar operations in the Soviet zone of Germany.

State Security Services' Management of Wismut AG

Two defectors in this group, Salimanov and Grishin, revealed information about Soviet state security involvement in a huge mining venture in Germany named Wismut AG. The Soviet government established Wismut in June 1946 after German scientists found uranium in several mines in eastern Germany and placed it under state security management for several reasons. First, Stalin trusted Beriya, who ran the state security apparatus. Second, the Soviet Union wanted to keep its urgent need for uranium to build an atomic weapon a secret and state security organisations were experienced at operating clandestinely. And third, state security officers were efficient at running large-scale infrastructure and industrial projects using another strategic resource – forced labour. Salimanov and Grishin revealed first-hand insights into a new application of forced labour using non-Soviet workers outside the Soviet Union.

Grishin's position in Wismut is not clear from his writings, but he was likely in a personnel management position based upon the details in his monograph about the history and administration of

Wismut, which he likely wrote under a pseudonym. He noted that Wismut management was dominated by MGB officers and that a special 'Operational Group of the MGB', composed of twelve members, was attached to the company.[126] The employment of the MGB in the Wismut management allowed for the operation to take advantage of the MGB's expertise in clandestinity to hide it from the outside world. Secrecy extended to all aspects of the operation. According to Grishin, all correspondence concerning the work of the company was classified secret, all employees were required to sign an oath of secrecy, and it was forbidden for workers to utter the word 'uranium'.[127]

Salimanov was the Deputy Chief of Wismut and Chief of the Logistics Directorate until his defection in May 1950.[128] He was responsible for procuring goods and equipment for the mine in the western zones of Germany and Austria and arranging for them to be shipped to Berlin via special rail shipments that passed through the zonal border without inspection, and then to Wismut.[129] He procured large amounts of materials clandestinely to avoid Allied knowledge and export restrictions, such as coal, radio tubes, high-voltage condensers, and vehicles,[130] 100 prefabricated wooden barracks from a Vienna-based company,[131] 25 tons of copper tubing,[132] and fuel and oxygen breathing apparatuses for mining operations. His defection furnished some of the first peeks behind the hidden Soviet atomic programme, and he provided unparalleled information about the programme in general, about numerous personnel working in it, and about Wismut specifically that confirmed or corrected much of what US and British intelligence already knew.[133] He also filled gaps in British and US knowledge about Soviet intelligence headquarters and officers, which informed counterespionage operations.[134]

Secrecy was sometimes a detriment, however. Grishin reported about a massive accident that occurred in 1949 when a stock of explosives inadvertently exploded above a mineshaft, causing a landslide that killed seventy employees and injured over one hundred others.[135] The MGB could not hide the accident because it shook towns in a radius of several miles. But an MGB security unit cordoned off an extensive area affected by the blast and contacted local town officials to warn them against allowing information to leak out about the incident. The absence of reliable facts led to wild press speculation that thousands of miners had died.[136]

Conclusion

The Early Cold War group of defectors was the least well known of all defector groups. They broke with the Soviet Union at a time when the United States and Great Britain began to recognise defectors' intelligence value, but while the Western powers were still developing their policies of exploiting defectors for propaganda purposes. Their average age was the lowest of any group of defectors, indicating that most had short careers as intelligence and state security personnel. But they represented some of the best sources of information available about the opaque Soviet Union. Their detailed insights into the Soviet Union's mistrust and hostile attitude towards the Allies laid the groundwork for a transition from wartime ally to Cold War adversary. With only a few exceptions, the Allies protected these insights in tightly controlled classified channels that provided the public little view into the development of this adversarial relationship.

Most were initially hired as linguists – which the Soviet Union desperately needed in its newly occupied satellites – and, similar to World War II-era defectors, they were often recruited despite having tainted pasts, including collaboration with Germany during the war. But as the MGB settled into a post-war routine, it realised its hiring errors, leading to recall notices for many Soviet personnel in Eastern Europe. That, combined with a common feeling that the Soviet Union was turning its state security apparatus against the Soviet people themselves, prompted defections.

A brief break separated the Early Cold War defectors from the next group, which consisted of those who defected in the purge that followed Stalin's death. As relations further deteriorated between the Allies and the Soviet Union, the Allies were less concerned about publicising defections and, unlike the Early Cold War group, several defectors in the next group became prominent names in the East–West rivalry.

Notes

1. For details about the development of defector policies in the United Kingdom and United States from repatriation to acceptance, see Kevin Riehle, 'Early Cold War Evolution of British and US Defector Policy and Practice', *Cold War History*, vol. 19 (2019), no. 3, 343–61.

2. All of these cooperated to some degree with US or British intelligence and were then resettled under pseudonyms. Their existence was kept closely held for their own security initially. The author has submitted a FOIA request requesting their release.

3. 'A. I. Romanov' (aka Boris Ivanovich Baklanov), *Nights Are Longest There: SMERSH from the Inside* (London: Hutchinson, 1972); and *The Nights Are Longest There: A Memoir of the Soviet Security Services* (Boston: Little, Brown, 1972). The other two are 'A. A. Petrov', 'Les souvenirs d'un agent Soviétique' ('The Memoirs of a Soviet Agent'), *La Tribune de Genève*, published serially from 14 December 1949 to 12 January 1950; and Nikolay Grishin, *Soviet Operation of Uranium Mines in Eastern Germany*, Mimeographed Series Number 11 (New York: Research Program on the USSR, 1952). Grishin's monograph was later reprinted as 'The Saxony Uranium Mining Operation' ('VISMUT'), in Robert Slusser and Vasili Yershov et al. (eds), *Soviet Economic Policy in Postwar Germany: A Collection of Papers by Former Soviet Officials* (New York: Research Program on the USSR, 1953), 127–55.

4. Vadim Ivanovich Shelaputin is interviewee number 144. The name of interviewee number 525 is not publicly available.

5. Brook-Shepherd, *The Storm Birds*, 67.

6. Prokhorov, *What is the Cost of Betraying One's Homeland?*, 186–91.

7. Nigel West, *Historical Dictionary of International Intelligence* (Lanham, MD: Rowman & Littlefield, 2015), 95–6. Tokayev's defection was in 1947, not 1946.

8. Brook-Shepherd, *The Storm Birds*, 80.

9. Gurzhiev was a thirty-five-year old operational officer when he defected, and Genrikh was thirty-two years old, making it possible but not certain that they were majors or higher. Grishin's rank is unknown, but he is described as a 'high-ranking officer'; see Grishin, *Soviet Operation of Uranium Mines in Eastern Germany*, title page.

10. CIA Chief of Station, Karlsruhe, Germany, 'Transmittal of Report on Berlin Operations Base', 8 April 1948, 20, CIA Historical Review Program, <https://www.cia.gov/library/center-for-the-study-of-int elligence/csi-publications/books-and-monographs/on-the-front-lines-of-the-cold-war-documents-on-the-intelligence-war-in-ber lin-1946-to-1961/1-2.pdf> (last accessed 13 March 2020). Durand refers to Granovskiy by his CIA codename, SAILOR.

11. 'Reorganization of the RIS in Germany', 11 September 1947, reproduced in Donald Steury (ed.), *On the Front Lines of the Cold War: Documents on the Intelligence War in Berlin, 1946 to 1961* (Washington, DC: Center for the Study of Intelligence, 1999), 119–22.

12. German: Goldfarb, Kravchenko, Petrov, Mikheyev, Genrikh, Ryabenko, Harvard 525, and KGB Wanted List number 21; Hungarian: Denisov, Takacs, and Sharandak; Czech: Shelaputin; Lithuanian: Pečiulionis.

13. 'The Memoirs of a Soviet Agent', *La Tribune de Genève*, 11 January 1950.

14. 7970th CIC Group memo, 'Interrogation of Soviet MGB Civilian Deserter from Oschersleben', 26 November 1948, 3, NARA, RG 319, Entry 134B, Box 830, Vorontzov.

15. Columbia University Rare Book and Manuscript Library, Research Program on the USSR, 'NKVD', box 2.

16. JIC, 'Study of Defectors from the USSR', 31–2.

17. HPSSS, Schedule A, vol. 27, Case 525, type A4, 22.

18. JIC, 'Study of Defectors from the USSR', 29–30.

19. Ibid. 33–4.

20. 'KGB Wanted List', Entry number 307.

21. 'The Memoirs of a Soviet Agent', *La Tribune de Genève*, 5 January 1950.

22. 'The Memoirs of a Soviet Agent', *La Tribune de Genève*, 6 January 1950.

23. JIC, 'Study of Defectors from the USSR', 29–30.

24. Letter from Robert Murphy, US Political Advisor for Germany, to Jacob Beam, US Department of State, 19 October 1948, NARA, RG 59, Central Decimal Files 1945–1949, Box 6651, File 861.2226/10-1948.

25. JIC, 'Study of Defectors from the USSR', 33–4.

26. 7970th CIC Group memo, 'MGB Interpreter – Progress Report no. 1, 20 September 1948, NARA, RG 319, Entry 134B, Box 830, Vorontzov.

27. High Commission for Occupied Germany (HICOG) Frankfurt, 'Soviet Defector Interrogation Report (Sponge no. 5)', 11 February 1950, 10, NARA, RG 59, Central Decimal File 1950–1954, Box 3800, 761.00/2-650.

28. Rafael Ilych Goldfarb, 'Перечень и Описание Наиболее Характерных Следственных Дел на Лиц, Арестованными Органами Советской Контрразведки ГСОВ в Германии за Период с 1946–1949 годы') ('List and Description of the More Characteristic Investigations into People Arrested by Soviet Counterintelligence Organs in the GSOF in Germany for the period from 1946 to 1949'), 16–21, NARA, RG 319, Entry 134B, Box 236, Goldfarb, part 2.

29. Rafael Ilych Goldfarb, 'Автобиография' ('Autobiography'), 1 August 1949, 4–5, NARA, RG 319, Entry 134B, Box 236.

30. HPSSS, Schedule A, vol. 11, Case 144, 12–13.

31. HPSSS, Schedule A, vol. 11, Case 144, 56; HPSSS, Schedule B, vol. 21, Case 144, 9.

32. HPSSS, Schedule A, vol. 11, Case 144, 42–3.

33. Ibid. 24–5.

34. Ibid. 10, 13.

35. 'The Memoirs of a Soviet Agent', *La Tribune de Genève*, 16 December 1949.

36. 'The Memoirs of a Soviet Agent', *La Tribune de Genève*, 23 December 1949.

37. 'The Memoirs of a Soviet Agent', *La Tribune de Genève*, 3 January 1950.

38. 'Testimony of Eastern European Political Refugees of the Necessity of Fleeing Because of Intolerable Conditions Under Communism', US State Department, Division of Research for the Soviet Union and Eastern Europe, 19 February 1953, NARA, RG 59, Entry A1 5498, Box 28, Motivations, Case 7.

39. Romanov, *Nights Are Longest There*, 239–41.

40. 'The Memoirs of a Soviet Agent', *La Tribune de Genève*, 7 January 1950.

41. 'The Memoirs of a Soviet Agent', *La Tribune de Genève*, 9 January 1950.

42. Romanov, *Nights Are Longest There*, 173.

43. 'KGB Wanted List', Entry number 153.

44. HICOG Frankfurt, 'Soviet Defector Interrogation Report (Sponge no. 5)', 12, NARA, RG 59, Central Decimal File 1950–1954, 761.00/2-650.

45. HPSSS, Schedule A, vol. 27, Case 525, type A4, 7.
46. Romanov, *Nights Are Longest There*, 223–4.
47. HPSSS, Schedule A, vol. 27, Case 525, type A4, 8.
48. HPSSS, Schedule A, vol. 11, Case 144, 24–5.
49. '*Обуржуазиться*' in Russian.
50. A. B. V., 'Сеть НКВД во Франции' ('NKVD Network in France'), *За свободу* (*For Freedom*) [New York], no. 18 (1947), 108. A draft copy of this article is in HIA, David J. Dallin Miscellaneous Papers.
51. Romanov, *Nights Are Longest There*, 155, 201.
52. Stephen Dorril, *MI6: Inside the Covert World of Her Majesty's Secret Intelligence Service* (New York: Simon and Schuster, 2002), 148–9.
53. JIC, 'Study of Defectors from the USSR', 29–30.
54. Ibid. 33–4. An abbreviated version of Sharandak's story is also contained in FBI, *Soviet Defectors: A Study of Past Defections from Official Soviet Establishments outside the USSR*, 46–7.
55. Goldfarb, 'List and Description of the More Characteristic Investigations', 16–21.
56. 7970th CIC Group memo, 'MGB Interpreter – Progress Report no. 1', 20 September 1948, NARA, RG 319, Entry 134B, Box 830, Vorontzov.
57. Goldfarb, 'Autobiography'.
58. Michael S. Goodman, *Spying on the Nuclear Bear: Anglo-American Intelligence and the Soviet Bomb* (Palo Alto: Stanford University Press, 2007), 139.
59. O. S. Smyslov, *Генерал Абакумов. Палач или жертва?* (*General Abakumov: Executioner or Victim*) (Moscow: Veche, 2012 published online at <https://www.e-reading.club/chapter.php/1015673/54/Smyslov_-_General_Abakumov._Palach_ili_zhertva.html> (last accessed 13 March 2020).
60. 'Постановление СНК СССР No 1326/301 об организации Советской военной администрации по управлению советской зоной оккупации в Германии' ('Directive of the SNK SSSR No 1326/301 on the Organisation of the Soviet Military Administration to Administer the Soviet Occupation Zone in Germany'), 6 July 1945, in Yan Foytzik, Andrey V. Doronin, Tatyana Viktorovna Tsarevskaya-Dyakina (managing eds), *Советская военная администрация в Германии, 1945–1949. Справочник* (*Soviet Military Administration in Germany. 1945–1949. A Handbook*) (Moscow: ROSSPEN, 2009), 969–70.

61. 'Приказ No 0060 Главноначальствующего Советской военной администрации – Главнокомандующего группой Советских оккупационных войск в Германии о ликвидации органов СВАГ' ('Order Number 0060 of the Supreme Commander of the Soviet Military Administration – Supreme Commander of the Group Soviet Occupation Forces in Germany on the liquidation of the SVAG'), 17 November 1949, in Foytzik, Doronin, and Tsarevskaya-Dyakina, *Soviet Military Administration in Germany. 1945–1949*, 992.

62. Richard W. Cutler, *Counterspy: Memoirs of a Counterintelligence Officer in World War II and the Cold War* (Washington, DC: Brassey's, 2004), 103–4.

63. HPSSS, Schedule A, vol. 27, Case 525, type A4, 6.

64. 'Докладная Записка Начальника Главного Политуправления Советской Армии И. В. Шикина Секретарю ЦК ВКП(б) А. А. Кузнецову об Исчезновении Оперуполномоченного Ростокского Окружного Отдела МГБ Земли Бранденбург Капитана В. К. Гуржиева' ('Report of the Chief of the Political Directorate of the Soviet Army I. V. Shikin to Secretary of the CC All-Union Communist Party (b) A. A. Kuznetsov about the Disappearance of V. K. Gurzhiev, Operational Officer of the Rostock Regional Section of the MGB of Brandenburg State'), in Nikita V. Petrov and Yan Foytzik (eds), *Аппарат НКВД-МГБ в Германии. 1945–1953: Документы* (*The NKVD-MGB Apparatus in Germany 1945–1953: Documents*) (Moscow: International 'Democracy' Foundation, 2009), 418.

65. CIA Information Report, 'Wismut AG: Personnel and Procurement of Supplies', 27 March 1950 (CIA CREST). CIA Information Report, 'Recent Developments in USIA', 14 November 1949 (CIA CREST).

66. HQ 7707 European Command Intelligence Center interrogation report, 'Methods of Investigation', 17 February 1949, NARA, RG 319, Entry 134A, Box 29, Soviet and Satellite Document Project, folder 1 of 2.

67. 'KGB Wanted List', Entry numbers 55 and 278.

68. Grishin, *Soviet Operation of Uranium Mines in Eastern Germany*.

69. 7970th CIC Group, S/R Hersfeld, Region III memo, 3 September 1948, NARA, RG 319. Entry 134B, Box 600, Peciulionis.

70. See, for example, Grishin, *Soviet Operation of Uranium Mines in Eastern Germany*, 11; or 7970th CIC Group memo, 'MGB

Interpreter – Progress Report no. 4', 30 September 1948, NARA, RG 319, Entry 134B, Box 830, Vorontzov.

71. JIC/1033/48, 3 June 1948, TNA, CAB 176/18.

72. Letter from Alan Lang-Brown, TCS chief, to Chairman of the JS/TIC, 6 September 1949, TNA, DEFE 40/26.

73. Kevin Conley Ruffner, *Eagle and Swastika: CIA and Nazi War Criminals and Collaborators* (draft working paper) (Washington, DC: CIA History Staff, 2003), Chapter 13, 1.

74. 7970th CIC Group memo, 'MGB Interpreter – Progress Report no. 1', 20 September 1948, NARA, RG 319, Entry 134B, Box 830, Vorontzov.

75. CIC interrogation report, 7 September 1948, NARA, RG 319, Entry 134A, Box 107, Soviet Army Counterintelligence Directorate, vol. 1. The CIC interrogated him in British custody.

76. Romanov, *Nights Are Longest There*, 241–5.

77. JIC, 'Study of Defectors from the USSR', 29–30.

78. Ibid. 31–2.

79. 'The Memoirs of a Soviet Agent', *La Tribune de Genève*, 12 Janaury 1950.

80. JIC, 'Study of Defectors from the USSR', 33–4.

81. HICOG Frankfurt, 'Soviet Defector Interrogation Report (Sponge no. 5)', 13, NARA, RG 59, Central Decimal File 1950–1954, 761.00/2.650.

82. Romanov, *Nights Are Longest There*, 160–1.

83. Translated letter from Vorontsov to CIC Frankfurt, 20 May 1951, NARA, RG 319, Entry 134B, Box 830, Vorontzov.

84. 'The Memoirs of a Soviet Agent', *La Tribune de Genève*, 7 January 1950.

85. Romanov, *Nights Are Longest There*, 57–8.

86. Ibid. 171.

87. 'The Memoirs of a Soviet Agent', *La Tribune de Genève*, 25 December 1949.

88. 'The Memoirs of a Soviet Agent', *La Tribune de Genève*, 22 December 1949.

89. HPSSS, Schedule A, vol. 11, Case 144, 14–15.

90. 'KGB Wanted List', Entry number 73. See also Prokhorov, who asserts that this attempt occurred in 1953; *What is the Cost of Betraying One's Homeland?*, 189–90. Karavashkin dates it in 1949, which is less likely; see *Who Betrayed Russia*, 613–14.

91. 'The Memoirs of a Soviet Agent', *La Tribune de Genève*, 18 December 1949.

92. 'The Memoirs of a Soviet Agent', *La Tribune de Genève*, 4 January 1950.
93. Romanov, *Nights Are Longest There*, 53.
94. Ibid. 89–94.
95. Ibid. 95–9.
96. Goldfarb, 'Autobiography', 10–11.
97. 7970th CIC Group memo, 'MGB Interpreter – Progress Report no. 4', 30 September 1948, NARA, RG 319, Entry 134B, Box 830, Vorontzov.
98. Goldfarb, 'List and Description of the More Characteristic Investigations', 1–2.
99. Ibid. 27–31.
100. 7970th CIC Group memo, 'MGB Interpreter – Progress Report no. 3', 24 September 1948, NARA, RG 319, Entry 134B, Box 830, Vorontzov.
101. Headquarters, Sub-Region Kassel, Counterintelligence Corps Region III memo, 8 March 1948, NARA, RG 319. Entry 134B, Box 600, Peciulionis.
102. 'The Memoirs of a Soviet Agent', *La Tribune de Genève*, 14 December 1949.
103. 'The Memoirs of a Soviet Agent', *La Tribune de Genève*, 25 December 1949.
104. 'The Memoirs of a Soviet Agent', *La Tribune de Genève*, 22 December 1949.
105. Romanov, *Nights Are Longest There*, 120.
106. HQ 7707 European Command Intelligence Center interrogation report, 'Secret Intelligence (MGB) Schools', 8 February 1949, NARA, RG 319, Entry 134A, Box 29, Soviet and Satellite Document Project, folder 1 of 2, Report of Investigation of Georgi Ivanovitch Samuseff (variant Samousev) (aka Franz Ulrich).
107. Headquarters, Sub-Region Kassel, Counterintelligence Corps Region III memo, 8 March 1948, NARA, RG 319. Entry 134B, Box 600, Peciulionis.
108. Romanov, *Nights Are Longest There*, 144.
109. Ibid. 158.
110. Ibid. 195–6.
111. 7970th CIC Group memo, 'MGB Interpreter – Progress Report no. 14', 2 November 1948, NARA, RG 319, Entry 134B, Box 830, Vorontzov.
112. 7970th CIC Group memo, 'MGB Interpreter – Progress Report

no. 4', 30 September 1948, NARA, RG 319, Entry 134B, Box 830, Vorontzov.

113. HQ 7707 European Command Intelligence Center interrogation report, 'MGB Recruiting and Handling of Informant Nets in Soviet and Western Zones of Germany', 17 February 1949, NARA, RG 319, Entry 134A, Box 29, Soviet and Satellite Document Project, folder 1 of 2, Report of Investigation of Georgi Ivanovitch Samuseff (variant Samousev) (aka Franz Ulrich).

114. 7970th CIC Group memo, 'MGB Interpreter – Progress Report no. 3', 24 September 1948, NARA, RG 319, Entry 134B, Box 830, Vorontzov.

115. Goldfarb, 'List and Description of the More Characteristic Investigations', 3–9, 10–15, 26.

116. JIC, 'Study of Defectors from the USSR', 33–4.

117. David Dallin Notes, 19, Columbia University, Rare Book and Manuscript Library, Research Program on the USSR Manuscripts 1950–1955, Box 2; HPSSS, Schedule A, vol. 11, Case 144, 13.

118. HICOG Frankfurt, 'Soviet Defector Interrogation Report (Sponge no. 5)', 21 , NARA, RG 59, Central Decimal File 1950–1954, 761.00/2.650.

119. Rafael Ilych Goldfarb, 'Приказ Министра государственной безопасности Союза ССР' ('Order of the Minister of State Security of the Union of SSR'), NARA, RG 319, Entry 134A, Box 107.

120. 'The Memoirs of a Soviet Agent', *La Tribune de Genève*, 27 December 1949.

121. 'The Memoirs of a Soviet Agent', *La Tribune de Genève*, 29 December 1949.

122. 'The Memoirs of a Soviet Agent', *La Tribune de Genève*, 2 January 1950.

123. Headquarters, Sub-Region Kassel, Counterintelligence Corps Region III memo, 8 March 1948, NARA, RG 319. Entry 134B, Box 600, Peciulionis.

124. Romanov, *Nights Are Longest There*, 95–9.

125. Goldfarb, 'Autobiography', 8.

126. Grishin, *Soviet Operation of Uranium Mines in Eastern Germany*, 2.

127. Ibid. 1, 13–14.

128. Georgiy G. Andreyev, 'Списки Советских Специалистов, Работавших в САО «ВИСМУТ» 1945–1953, Часть III' ('Lists of Soviet Specialists Working at SAO 'VISMUT' 1945–1953, Part III'), 415. This list part of *Уран и люди. История СГАО*

«ВИСМУТ» в двух томах (*Uranium and People: The History of SGAO 'VISMUT' in Two Volumes*) (Moscow: Spets-Adress Publishers, 2012).

129. CIA Information Report, 'Procurement of Equipment for Wismut AG', 29 December 1949 (CIA CREST).

130. CIA Information Report, 'Wismut AG', 9 January 1950 (CIA CREST).

131. CIA Information Report, 'Purchase of Wooden Barracks by SMV for Shipment of Saxony Uranium Mines', 29 March 1950 (CIA CREST).

132. CIA Information Report, 'Wismut AG: Personnel and Procurement of Supplies', 27 March 1950 (CIA CREST).

133. Henry S. Lowenhaupt, 'On the Soviet Nuclear Scent', *Studies in Intelligence*, vol. 11 (1967), no. 4, 20; Henry S. Lowenhaupt, 'Chasing Bitterfeld Calcium', *Studies in Intelligence*, vol. 17 (1973), no. 2, 27.

134. Harry Rositzke, *The CIA's Secret Operations: Espionage, Counterespionage, and Covert Action* (Boulder, CO: Westview Press, 1977), 141.

135. Grishin, *Soviet Operation of Uranium Mines in Eastern Germany*, 9–10.

136. 'Uranium Mine Fire Toll Put at 3700', *Seattle Daily Chronicle*, 5 December 1949.

5   Post-Stalin Purge Defectors, 1953–1954

The Post-Stalin Purge group represents a surge of defectors – twelve in a seventeen-month period – some of which were the most widely publicised cases of the twentieth century. The defectors in this group broke with the Soviet Union after Stalin's death in March 1953, and equally significantly, six of them defected after Beriya's execution in December 1953. Beriya's arrest in June sent shock waves through the Soviet state security establishment and brought back memories of the 1930s, when purges followed the series of transitions from one state security chief to another. Beriya's arrest and later execution, along with the disappearances of Beriya's supporters, left officers jittery. The typically ominous occasion of a recall to Moscow caused panic, prompting some officers to escape rather than face an anticipated purge. This group ends with the stabilisation of the post-Beriya Soviet state security establishment and the passing of the purge threat.

By 1953, Britain and the United States had institutionalised their processes for handling and exploiting defectors, and both countries' national security leaders recognised defectors as a valuable asset. For example, a quick succession of four defectors in January–February 1954 was a topic of discussion at a US National Security Council (NSC) meeting on 17 February 1954. The four, who were referred to as 'Beriya men', included one in Tokyo, who effectively wrecked the Soviet apparatus in Japan; another who led to the exposure of the MVD network in Norway; and two in Vienna – a lieutenant colonel and a civilian.[1] The defector in Tokyo was a clear reference to Rastvorov and the defector in Norway was Pavlov, who, although he had defected six months earlier, had more recently come into US custody. The

Table 5.1 Post-Stalin Purge Defectors, 1953–1954

Name	Best Known Alias	Service	Became Intel Officer	Date of Defection	Location of Defection	Receiving Country
Grigoriy Stepanovich Burlutskiy		MVD	1940	7 June 1953	Afghanistan	United States
Unknown	KGB Wanted List 27	GRU		July 1953	Turkey	Turkey
Grigoriy Fedorovich Pavlov		MVD	1951	18 August 1953	Norway	Norway, United States
Yevgeniy Vladimirovich Brik	David Semyonovich Soboloff	MVD	1949	November 1953	Canada	Canada
Yuriy Aleksandrovich Rastvorov	Martin F. Simons	Razvedupr MVD	1941	24 January 1954	Japan	United States
Peter Sergeyevich Deryabin	Theodore Orel	MVD	1944	15 February 1954	Austria	United States
Nikolai Yevgenyevich Khokhlov	Josef Hofbauer	MVD	1941	18 February 1954	West Germany	United States
Mikhail Ivanovich Grigoryev		MVD		27 February 1954	Germany	United Kingdom
Afanasiy Mikhailovich Shorokhov	Vladimir Mikhailovich Petrov	MVD	1933	3 April 1954	Australia	Australia
Evdokiya Alekseyevna Kartseva	Evdokiya Alekseyevna Petrova	MVD	1933	19 April 1954	Australia	Australia
Lars Edvin Lindström	Lars Edvin Lövtorp	MVD	1953	22 July 1954	Sweden	Sweden
Bronius Antanovich Stankaitis	August Kiesel	KGB	1954	1 November 1954	Germany	??

NSC meeting occurred only two days after Deryabin's defection in Vienna, and although he was a major, not a lieutenant colonel, that reference was certainly to him. The civilian in Vienna was likely Anatoliy Ignatiyevich Skachkov, a non-intelligence officer whose defection Deryabin was investigating when he decided to defect himself. The NSC meeting was a prominent venue for discussing specific defectors.

However, the Post-Stalin Purge group was a brief anomaly in an otherwise waning flow of Soviet defectors, similar to the plummet in the number of defectors that occurred after 1930, and for equivalent reasons. Whereas a US study found that 110 Soviet individuals – forty-six officers, fifty-one enlisted soldiers, and thirteen civilians – had defected to the US and British zones of Germany in 1947, 1948 saw a slowing of the flow to only fifty-four in the first three quarters of the year.[2] In September 1950, the US Department of Defense assessed, 'Shortly after World War II, the number of persons coming west was great. The flow of defectors, line-crossers, escapees, refugees is now a mere trickle.'[3] The flow reduced even further during the 1950s to the point that between 1951 and 1958, a total of only forty-four Soviets had defected – eleven officers and thirty-three enlisted soldiers. The decrease was due to a combination of Soviet measures designed to block and deter defections, reminiscent of the measures adopted in 1930: strict border controls, careful personnel selection, frequent troop rotations, severe limitations on off-duty activities, restricted fuel allowances for aircraft, and drastic penalties imposed upon those who changed their minds or were caught.[4] Like in 1937, however, a cataclysmic series of events – Stalin's death and Beriya's arrest – pushed intelligence officers to the point of balancing the risk of escaping against the fear of remaining in their positions.

Personal Backgrounds

Of the twelve individuals in this group, four (Rastvorov, Deryabin, Shorokhov, and Kartseva) defected while serving in Soviet diplomatic missions; and two (Burlutskiy and Pavlov) defected from inside the Soviet Union. Their specialties included foreign intelligence, counterintelligence, cipher operations, and border guards. Deryabin's career also included a stint as a counterintelligence officer in the Guard Directorate, which was responsible for personal security of senior Soviet leaders. One, Mikhail Grigoryev, was posted to a Soviet military unit in Berlin. The remaining five (KGB Wanted List number 27, Brik, Lindström, Khokhlov, and Stankaitis) defected while abroad as illegals, and their missions included clandestinely handling recruited sources, establishing stay-behind espionage and sabotage networks, and directing assassination operations. Within all three of those categories, Post-Stalin Purge defectors showed a departure from the World War II and Early Cold War groups, in that their average age was thirty-six years old. The age profile of Post-Stalin Purge group defectors was more similar to *Yezhovshchina*-era defectors, the only group whose average age was higher. This was an indicator of the times: senior officers were more afraid of becoming purge targets because of their personal associations with ousted MVD leaders, which made them guilty by association. This led more senior officers, both during the *Yezhovshchina* era and then following Stalin's death, to consider defection.

Not surprisingly, World War II played a significant factor in the lives of nearly all of the defectors in this group except Grigoryev. Deryabin was drafted in October 1939 and saw action around Stalingrad, Brik and Rastvorov were both drafted the following month, and Lindström and Pavlov were drafted soon after the German invasion. Khokhlov never enlisted because of his eyesight, but he was recruited into the NKGB for covert operations, served behind German lines, and was decorated for his accomplishments. Shorokhov had served in the Soviet Navy in the decade before the war; however, he and his wife Kartseva experienced the dangers of war not as military members, but when a German submarine sank the ship in which they were travelling to their assignment in Sweden in 1943, and they were rescued at sea.[5] They eventually arrived in Sweden and served the rest of the war under diplomatic cover. Burlutskiy graduated from Border Guard officer's school in 1940, and his service during the war included participating in forced resettlement operations in the North Caucasus. Stankaitis had served in a Lithuanian police unit during the war that supported Germany. KGB Wanted List number 27 and Grigoryev were the only members of this group for whom no wartime service is known. KGB Wanted List number 27 reportedly lived in Greece during the war and immigrated to the Soviet Union in 1947. Grigoryev was too young to have served in the war.

Despite their shared wartime experience, defectors in this group were a mix of long-time intelligence operatives and illegals who were inexperienced in intelligence matters. Six became Soviet intelligence officers before or during the war and ranged in rank from captain to colonel when they defected. Others were recruited for their ability to operate unnoticed as illegals in a foreign environment. Khokhlov was able to pass as a German both in appearance and in his German language proficiency. Brik had lived in the United States as a child, giving him native English ability, and he was recruited as an illegal in 1949. KGB Wanted List number 27 was ethnically Armenian, born in Turkey, and immigrated to Greece as a child, and then to Soviet Armenia in 1947.[6] Lindström spoke Swedish natively as a member of a Swedish immigrant community in Estonia, and the NKVD/MGB approached him three times to recruit him as an agent: in 1941, 1946, and finally in 1953 when he accepted the offer. Stankaitis was Lithuanian and had emigrated to Germany before he was located, recruited, and sent back to the Soviet Union for training in 1954. Pavlov was an anomaly in this group, having been recruited into the MGB in 1951 probably involuntarily after his sister was arrested and sentenced to a twenty-five-year prison term.[7] Grigoryev's recruitment date is not known, but was likely in the early 1950s.

Party membership, normally considered a sign of increased dedication, did not necessarily prevent officers from defecting. Pavlov joined the Communist Party less than three weeks before his defection.[8] Burlutskiy joined the Party only a few months before the ethnic resettlement operations that dampened his enthusiasm for his MVD duties.[9] Kartseva joined the Communist Party in 1950, not long before she left for her assignment in Australia. Her Party membership was delayed for over a decade because she fell into suspicion during the *Yezhovshchina* in 1937.[10] The Australian Security Intelligence Organisation

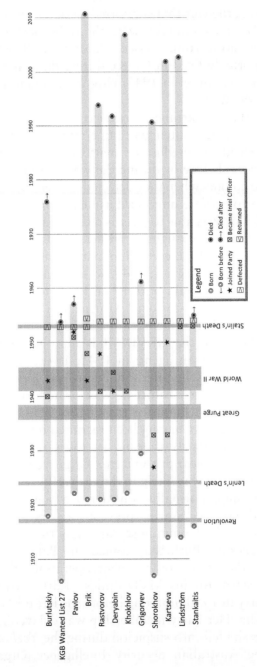

Figure 5.1 Lives of Post-Stalin Purge Defectors, 1953–1954

(ASIO) assessed that, despite Shorokhov's and Kartseva's party membership, the 'resentment at the hypocrisy, insecurity, and ruthlessness of life under the Soviet system ... weakened any feeling of loyalty which they may have had to the machine which they served'.[11] By the time these individuals defected, becoming a Party member was a requirement for career advancement, but did not inoculate them from cynicism and low levels of commitment. In most cases, the backgrounds of these defectors would indicate loyal, or at least acquiescent, Soviet citizens. But events in 1953 altered the playing field for Soviet officials, prompting a new wave of defections.

Motivations

Post-Stalin Purge defectors exhibited a mix of motivations, ranging from disenchantment with the Soviet system as a whole to more specific fear prompted by Stalin's death and Beriya's arrest and execution, personal animosities with co-workers, and disagreements with the tasks they were assigned. But overall, duty in a Soviet intelligence and state security service, with all of the perquisites and accesses that it afforded, did not shelter officers from forces that drove them away from the Soviet Union. Privilege came with a price: the closer to the inner circle an individual approached, the more vulnerable he was in a leadership change. The constant insecurity that reigned during Stalin's tenure was accentuated when post-Stalin leaders jockeyed for prominence, pulling their vassals with them. Beriya's arrest and execution was particularly shocking to MVD officers because many of them had hitched their careers to him rather than to the other pretenders to Stalin's throne.

Ideology was also a factor in some defector cases; however, the amount of influence that dissonance with communism ideology had on defectors' decisions was a matter of debate in the West, depending on one's definition of 'ideology'. A CIA officer who had handled post-war defectors asserted that ideological disagreement with communism was seldom a motivation for Soviet defectors. He wrote, 'Defectors have usually rationalized their defections as stemming from ideological convictions, but in numerous cases this seems to have occurred *after* defection . . . Few of the defections to date can be attributed unequivocally and primarily to pure ideological motivation.' However, he continued, 'political ideology on the theoretical level . . . should nevertheless be listed as a factor strongly influencing a relatively small number of defectors'.[12]

The CIA officer implied that Soviet defectors themselves recognised the difference between communism as an ideology and Soviet governing institutions, and the greater number of defectors expressed dissatisfaction with the system rather than with communism. The author listed three broad types of defector complaints with the Soviet system:

- Threats to personal security: Recognition of the injustice, oppression, lack of present security, accompanied by fear as a primary means of control and an ever-present aura of suspicion in the Soviet Union.
- Dissatisfaction with Soviet life: Inability to plan for the future, lack of material comforts and conveniences, interference in and lack of respect for personal relations and lives, and monotony in Soviet life.
- Systemic falsehoods: Falseness and hiding the truth, unfulfilled promises, and corruption among the Soviet elite.

The officer added other proximate personal motivations that many defectors exhibited:

- Fear of demotion or punishment.
- Recognition of the contrast between life in the West and life in the Soviet Union.
- Attachment to an acquaintance met abroad.
- Dissatisfaction with one's job and demoralisation.[13]

While this CIA officer differentiated between complaints about the system and disagreements with 'ideology', others at the time did not draw that distinction. A 1955 CIA debriefing report indicated that Deryabin defected 'for a combination of ideological and personal reasons'.[14] Deryabin described his ideological reasons in his public writings: although he was a loyal Party member early in his career, he became disenchanted with Soviet leaders' attitudes towards the Soviet people, fuelled by his exposure to the venal private lives of the Soviet elite during his tenure in the Guard Directorate. In addition to ideology, he also had several personal reasons for defecting, including a failing marriage and a feeling of being overworked and underappreciated. He may have also been the victim of denunciations resulting from jealousy: Brook-Shepherd claims that during Deryabin's time in the Austria–Germany Section at MGB Headquarters, a female assistant denounced him for anti-Stalinist statements – consisting of sharing gossip about Stalin's son, Vasiliy – after Deryabin refused her advances.[15] He weathered the ensuing investigation, probably to a great extent because of his senior connections in the MVD, and was even posted abroad, which was clear evidence that the MVD did not take the denunciation seriously. But the incident heightened his dissatisfaction with his work and increased his motivation to seek an escape.

ASIO assessed that a mix of fear, ideology, and an attraction to Western prosperity drove Shorokhov and Kartseva to defect.[16] Their motivation included discontent in their position at the embassy and fear of what could happen if their internal enemies denounced them. Problems at the embassy began soon after they arrived in Australia, and Shorokhov described his situation as being 'persecuted and hounded' by the Soviet ambassador.[17] Shorokhov's independence as MGB *rezident* drew enmity from the ambassador and the Party chairman and created a 'tangled skein of intrigue against them'.[18] The treatment became increasingly petty and Kartseva at times responded with a sharp tongue. In June 1952, Shorokhov received instructions from Moscow to reprimand her for a 'lack of tact in her dealings with fellow workers in the Embassy, including the Ambassador'.[19] Before Kartseva left Canberra on the eve of her defection, a member of the embassy staff predicted that she would be condemned to a prison camp or worse, and she feared for her fate if she were to return to the Soviet Union.[20]

Shorokhov's and Kartseva's motivation also included an element of ideological disenchantment. Both began as true believers, but both had experiences that left them embittered towards the Party and the Soviet elite. Kartseva had endured almost five years of shunning because of her relationship with a man who was arrested as an 'enemy of the people' in 1937.[21] Then, her only child died because of the inefficiency of the Soviet medical system.[22] Yet, she was less cynical than Shorokhov, who complained about how collectivisation led to the destruction of the peasantry, including his own family; how denunciations ruined many lives; the injustice and brutality of Stalin's purges, to which he had direct visibility as a cipher clerk; the growing elite class that showed no interest in the country's mass poverty; and the contrast between official propaganda and reality, compounded by the disparity between life inside and outside the Soviet Union.[23]

Rastvorov also had experience with the purge. He fell under suspicion for the *Yezhovshchina*-era arrest of his father, which was partially based on Rastvorov's grandfather's arrest in 1929 as a kulak. Rastvorov's father had joined the Bolshevik Party in 1919 and served as a military commissar and did nothing to assist his father out of fear of being branded a counterrevolutionary. But his 'kulak' ancestry caught up with him, and his 'social origins' led to his suspension from the Party for a short period in 1936.[24] He was reinstated after an NKVD investigation and eventually retired as a colonel after World War II. However, these same family ties later affected Rastvorov, whose first assignment to Japan suddenly ended when he was recalled to the Soviet Union in December 1946 to face allegations of disloyalty. He was summoned to a board of inquiry because he had failed to mention his father's expulsion from the Party in 1936, even though his father was fully exonerated. Rastvorov underwent what he called a three-month 'humiliating investigation', but he was then reinstated in his position in the MGB Japan Section. The incident left Rastvorov with sour feelings about the Soviet system.[25]

Several defectors expressed distaste with the missions they were ordered to perform, leading to their desire to break from state security employment. Burlutskiy's disenchantment began with his involvement in the forced resettlement of Karachay, Kalmyk, Chechen, Ingush, and Crimean Tatar ethnic groups in 1943 and

1944, about which he provided the first clear evidence to the West. Burlutskiy joined the Communist Party during the summer of 1943, and he described himself as a 'fanatical, 100% devoted communist'. However, he began to consider defection after the Chechen–Ingush resettlement operation in January 1944, even though he received a wristwatch as a reward that was inscribed, 'For the successful accomplishment of a mission of the NKVD, USSR, 1944.'[26] Rastvorov was also involved in the Chechen–Ingush resettlement operation, although he did not experience the same degree of disenchantment from it.[27]

After the resettlement operations, Burlutskiy's border guard unit was transferred to Lithuania to conduct counterinsurgency operations, which led Burlutskiy to write, 'MVD troops are in fact no different from any other troops in the Soviet army except that by decree of the government our principal enemy is not a foreign army but our own countrymen.'[28] This sentiment later prompted Burlutskiy to defect.

Khokhlov began his career as a dedicated sabotage operator, even serving as the model for the protagonist in a Soviet post-war movie about Soviet NKVD officers operating behind German lines.[29] However, his disenchantment began when he lived as an illegal in Romania, where his legend included posing as an anti-communist. To maintain that legend he listened to BBC and Voice of America, through which he began to see the effects of communism on the Romanian state. He wrote, 'During my four years in Bucharest, I saw the deadly origins of a new communist state and was finally revolted. There I watched the progressive wrecking of a free country at the hands of my own leaders.' He gained a reputation for being uncooperative when he returned from Romania in 1949 and requested to resign from the MGB. Naum Isaakovich Eitingon, Lieutenant General Pavel Anatolyevich Sudoplatov's deputy in the NKGB covert action unit, sharply rebuked him, saying, 'You know perfectly well that nobody leaves the intelligence service just like that. We've spent time and money on you, we've fussed over you, and now you talk about leaving just when you're getting useful. It's out of the question.'[30] Sudoplatov later remembered Khokhlov primarily for his 'snivelling'.[31]

Khokhlov's experience in Romania sowed the seeds of doubt in the Soviet system that led to his eventual defection. But Stalin's death in March 1953 and the uncertainty it created compounded them. In late 1952, the MGB began preparations for Khokhlov's wife and child to join him in Germany so they could subsequently be assigned together as illegals in Switzerland. The operation was repeatedly delayed, but when Stalin died, the MGB cancelled it altogether, and his wife never joined him.[32] Khokhlov subsequently made several additional attempts to resign from Soviet state security.

Beriya exploited the uncertainty that followed Stalin's death and used his control over the powerful security services to build his own power. The resulting backlash after Beriya's arrest and execution had a forceful impact on MVD officers' sense of personal security, particularly Shorokhov, Rastvorov, and probably Pavlov. Although Shorokhov had made up his mind to remain in Australia as early as 1952,[33] his ultimate decision to defect came after Beriya's arrest, when the Soviet ambassador and the embassy Party chief denounced him for supposedly forming a 'Beriya group' in the embassy to undermine the authority of the Party.[34] Such an accusation could spell disaster for a Soviet official. Rastvorov wrote of his reaction to Beriya's arrest: 'My own life was profoundly influenced by the Beriya crisis. My slowly-ripening decision to leave the Soviet mission and to break with the Communist regime and system was hastened by the purge of Beriya, portending as it did dismissals and trials of many high officials.'[35] The upheaval in Moscow led Rastvorov to make overt statements to American and British acquaintances about his unhappiness with his job and with the Soviet Union in general, and as early as September 1953, both US and British intelligence initiated operations to induce his defection.[36] Pavlov's motivations are not as clear, but are probably related both to the way he was brought into the MVD – under coercion after his sister's arrest – and to Beriya's downfall. Pavlov defected less than two months after Beriya's arrest, and he noted that the event induced a state of 'semi-panic' in his MVD office.[37]

Similar to previous groups, the Post-Stalin Purge group includes several individuals whose linguistic abilities both attracted Soviet intelligence recruitment attention, and later formed the basis for their defection. Lindström and KGB Wanted List number 27 defected at least in part because of their ethnic and linguistic affinity outside the Soviet Union. Their defections reinforced the risks involved with recruiting individuals as illegals without complete vetting. KGB Wanted List number 27 was born in Turkey and, after he had immigrated to Soviet Armenia, was dispatched back to Turkey as an illegal. Turkish police arrested him, and he revealed his intelligence mission to them. Lindström's home came under Soviet control in 1940 when Soviet troops occupied Estonia, where his family lived in a Swedish immigrant community. He was never a devoted Soviet citizen, but after his 1946 refusal to cooperate with the MGB, he realised that his career was suffering, and in 1952 he was threatened with dismissal from his job. He finally complied in May 1953, but in spite of signing a written agreement to not talk about his operations, he recounted the whole story to his wife and brother.[38] He was always reluctant in his missions, and finally, while on a mission in Sweden, he approached his family members there for assistance in requesting political asylum.[39] Similarly, Stankaitis was recruited as an illegal likely under duress due to his World War II past. He was dispatched to Germany, but quickly abandoned his intelligence mission.

Although Brik had some characteristics that suited him well as an illegal, he also had habits that diminished his effectiveness: he drank heavily, entertained himself with prostitutes, and broke routine security rules. He did not initially intend to defect, and his motive for turning himself over to Canadian authorities was less than noble: he became entangled in an affair with a married Canadian woman to whom he admitted his status, and she convinced him to do it. He operated as a Canadian double agent for over a year and a half until RCMP Constable James Douglas Finley Morrison compromised him. He returned to the Soviet Union on what he thought was a routine training trip and was arrested as soon as he arrived. He served fifteen years in prison and later returned to Canada in 1992.[40]

The combination of these factors – painful reminiscences of the purge, disenchantment with state security missions, fear following

Stalin's death and Beriya's subsequent downfall, and ethnic affinity outside the Soviet Union – resulted in severe losses of sensitive Soviet information.

Receiving Countries

The personal backgrounds of defectors in this group weighed more heavily in determining the receiving country than in any other group. The receiving countries in the Post-Stalin Purge group were more varied than the World War II-era group, when Germany was the primary destination, and the Early Cold War group, when defectors invariably landed in either British or US custody. To the contrary, only half of the defectors in the Post-Stalin Purge group made their way to US custody. Of those, only three – Rastvorov, Deryabin, and Khokhlov – immigrated to the United States. The other two – Burlutskiy and Pavlov – probably remained in Germany. None ended up in Great Britain. The remaining five stayed in the countries where they defected: Shorokhov and Kartseva lived the rest of their lives in Australia. Brik surrendered himself in Canada and would have remained there had he not been lured back to the Soviet Union. The United States and Great Britain may not even have been aware of the defections of KGB Wanted List number 27 and Lindström, because the receiving countries, Turkey and Sweden respectively, granted them residency.

The variance in destinations and the de-emphasis of the United States and Great Britain as recipient countries were partially the result of Soviet intelligence organisations choosing operatives specifically for their ability to melt into the societies where they operated. That does not mean that the United States and Great Britain were never again the recipients of defectors. As the Cold War progressed, numerous defectors made their way to the United States and a smaller number to Great Britain. The diversity was more an indicator of the importance that the Soviet Union placed on illegals in the late 1940s and early 1950s and the troubles that the illegals programme was experiencing.

Operational Priorities

The operational priorities of Post-Stalin Purge defectors showed a continuation from post-war Soviet intelligence: the defeated powers, Germany and Japan, continued to be targets of intelligence operations themselves and as venues for targeting post-war adversaries of the 'Anglo-American bloc'. But as the war receded into the past, Soviet intelligence broadened its reach and began to solidify a security perimeter around the Soviet Union that employed the newly established communist powers of Eastern Europe. Soviet intelligence delegated responsibility for some low-level collection to its satellite services, allowing it to diversify its presence and targets for both intelligence and counterintelligence purposes. This was further facilitated by the operational concept that most distinguished Post-Stalin Purge defectors from their predecessors: the expansion of the illegals programme.

Supporting Illegal Operations

During World War II, the Soviet Union heavily employed the practice of sending officers and agents behind German lines under false identities for espionage and sabotage missions. Although the concept was not new – the VChK had employed illegals from early in Soviet history – the volume significantly increased during the war. World War II-era defectors Yesenina, Dubkov, and Kopatskiy (see Chapter 3), and Early Cold War-era defectors Granovskiy and Pečiulionis (see Chapter 4) each provided insights into the selection and training for these wartime deep cover assignments.

The practice of dispatching illegals did not end with the war. Sudoplatov, who had commanded the wartime illegals programme, wanted to continue it and retain the personnel, like Khokhlov, who already had wartime training and experience and use them in a cadre of illegals who could operate on the territory of the 'future enemy states'.[41] Illegals had some advantages: their separation from the Soviet government meant they would not automatically be expelled along with a Soviet diplomatic representation if a new war broke out. Khokhlov explained Sudoplatov's rationale for post-war illegals:

In the next war, which could begin unexpectedly, we may have to expand our partisan activities. In that event, we might put you in charge of a partisan detachment. At any rate, you should be useful in the countries we're turning into people's democracies, such as Rumania, or possibly in Western Europe. We may leave you in deep cover for several months or maybe several years. Meanwhile, you will learn the ways of the West.[42]

This encapsulated Sudoplatov's realisation that illegals required more than just wartime training and linguistic ability to be successful. They needed knowledge of the differences between routine life in the West and the Soviet Union, like ordering food at a restaurant, paying bus fare, wearing clothing, etc. This was not a new problem: Poretskiy assigned Hede Massing the mission of teaching Soviet personnel to fit into Western society in the mid-1930s (see Chapter 2).[43] Sudoplatov began cautiously. Khokhlov reported that MGB Special Bureau Number One first sent operatives to Eastern European countries, including Romania, Poland, Hungary, and Czechoslovakia, where their initial mission was simply to obtain experience in a non-Soviet environment. This began even before the war ended: Khokhlov started his assignment to Romania in April 1945, the same month as Granovskiy's assignment to Czechoslovakia (see Chapter 3). According to Mitrokhin, by 1949, forty-nine illegals were in training.[44]

Khokhlov indicated that the illegals programme expanded to Austria and East Germany by 1951. It spread outside Europe as well. Brik, for example, arrived in Canada in November 1951 and travelled around Canada for much of his first year, visiting cities where his cover namesake, David Semyonovich Soboloff, had lived so that he could talk credibly about his past. His eventual mission was to legalise himself in Canada and then to immigrate to the United States, where he would assume the role as assistant to another Soviet illegal, William Fisher/Rudolph Abel, who had arrived in New York City in 1948. Brik later passed information about his selection, training, and documentation as an illegal to Canadian counterintelligence.

Lindström was sent on two missions to Norway in 1953 and 1954 simply to observe Norwegians in their daily life, while they travelled on buses or ferries and ate in restaurants, the cost of transport fares, and how foreigners were treated on public transport and whether their documents were checked as they travelled. Lindström's supervisor told him he would receive training in skills that purposefully made use of his Swedish language capabilities that would be particularly valuable in the event of another war. During his first trip he was to familiarise himself with the towns he transited, specifically Hammerfest and Narvik, enough that the next time he visited them he could feel 'at home'. Lindström's second trip took him back to Narvik via Finland and Sweden, where he was supposed to gather information about local companies, public works, and public institutions. He defected during this second mission.[45]

Over time, as illegals established their new identities, they progressed from simply learning about foreign cultures, to creating stay-behind networks for future sabotage operations, to conducting active sabotage and assassination missions. By early 1951, Khokhlov's status as an illegal had progressed to the next level. He received an assignment to travel through Austria, Germany, France, and Denmark using an Austrian identity and passport. The initial purpose of the mission was to obtain a genuine Austrian passport and test it at European borders.[46] Sudoplatov told him that visiting Denmark was especially important, since Denmark might become a Soviet bridgehead to Western Europe in the event of another war. Sudoplatov recalled that Khokhlov travelled to Western Europe not once but several times, and one of the intended purposes of the travel was to become acquainted with a ballerina who performed at the Paris Opera, and who was known to associate with American and NATO officers. Sudoplatov claimed that Khokhlov successfully established a network of intelligence sources and stay-behind sabotage agents to be used if war broke out.[47]

Khokhlov indicated that in about 1951 or 1952, Sudoplatov's illegals section was renamed the Ninth Section for Terror and Diversion and its mission expanded from emplacing stay-behind agents to actively organising sabotage, assassination, and propaganda operations.[48] Deryabin similarly described the section as continuing its wartime role to conduct assassinations and terrorist operations behind enemy lines.[49] In February 1952, Sudoplatov contacted Khokhlov with another 'important job'. He was to travel to Paris, where he would make contact with an old Soviet agent, and through him meet and assassinate a Russian émigré who was 'causing trouble'. Khokhlov resisted and refused the job, adding to his uncooperative reputation. It was later revealed that the 'troublesome' Russian émigré was Alexander Fedorovich Kerensky, chairman of the provisional Russian government in 1917.[50]

At about the same time, Moscow began actively planning to develop an infrastructure for a future illegal *rezidentura* in Australia as well. A number of the items Shorokhov was tasked to acquire were directly related to plans for sending illegals to Australia: the papers necessary for legal entry into and exit from Australia, information about Australian naturalisation and divorce laws, blank passports, blank driver's licence forms, blank checks on the Rural Bank or any other bank, and the documents needed in Australia to exempt a man from military service.[51] When a source gave Shorokhov immigration forms in 1951, Moscow responded, 'These application forms are very important for Moscow to know how people can migrate to Australia.'[52] Once in Australia, illegals would use this knowledge to legalise themselves and seek employment in targeted organisations.[53]

Although Shorokhov denied having worked directly with any Soviet illegals operating in Australia,[54] he was aware of one individual who was designated to become the first illegal *rezident* in Australia: Vintses (variant Vincene) Vintsesovich Divišek (code name PECHEK), who had arrived in Australia in 1949 under refugee cover. Divišek had been a Soviet agent during World War II operating in Czechoslovakia. Moscow gave him instructions similar to the instructions that Granovskiy received: he was tasked to set up a business, preferably a restaurant, assimilate, and prepare for future intelligence missions.[55] However, Divišek surrendered himself to the Australian government soon after arriving and claimed that he never had any intention of fulfilling the instructions, but that he had only accepted the assignment to Australia because he had family there and he planned to settle.[56]

Deryabin similarly claimed to have never worked directly with illegals, but he did provide information about the MGB Headquarters Illegals Section, which he indicated had two subsections, one for training illegals for service abroad and the other for documenting and dispatching illegals.[57] He also had some knowledge of illegal *rezidenturas* in Germany, which consisted of German nationals recruited and organised into three- to six-person cells directed to collect intelligence on Allied installations in Germany and West German government institutions – similar to the sources Khokhlov was tasked to recruit during his tour of duty in Germany in 1952.[58] Deryabin cited the case of an illegal agent codenamed CHEKH who had access to government circles in Bonn and was handled by an MVD case officer in Vienna.[59]

The illegals who defected during the Post-Stalin Purge period were only the tip of an iceberg. Many others completed their missions and their identities were unknown to the West until years later: for example, Fisher/Abel and Morris and Lona Cohen were activated in the United States in 1948; Iosif Romualdovich Grigulevich in Rome in 1949; and Africa de las Heras in Montevideo in 1951.

Post-Stalin Purge defectors' information about the Soviet illegals programme revealed the reality of Soviet fears about the world. The post-war retention of the illegals programme was a direct extension of the Soviet Union's belief that another war with capitalist countries would begin soon. The expansion of the illegals programme in the late 1940s and early 1950s indicated the Soviet Union's sense of urgency to establish a long-term intelligence and sabotage presence in capitalist countries, separate from official establishments, that could remain in place during an imminent war. This same fear also prompted a strengthening of internal security measures to prevent the capitalist countries from doing the same in reverse.

Internal Security and Counterintelligence

Deryabin quoted what he called a familiar saying that summarised the evolving emphasis of Soviet state security: 'In the *Yezhovshchina*, the god of state security sat in the political section. During the period of collectivisation god sat in the economic section. During the war god was in intelligence, after the war in counterintelligence.'[60]

However, as World War II defectors reported, the emphasis on counterintelligence was not unique to the post-war period (see Chapter 3). Burlutskiy's experiences in forced resettlement operations were particularly illustrative. During the fall of 1942, German forces advanced into the North Caucasus, and the peoples of the region found themselves under German control until the summer of 1943. They had previously chafed under Russian rule for many years, and after German forces retreated and Soviet forces reoccupied the region, Stalin claimed entire ethnic groups posed a threat because they collaborated with German occupiers. When Burlutskiy's unit surrounded the population of a Chechen town on 23 February 1944, after they had gathered on the pretext of celebrating Red Army Day, an intelligence officer stood to give a speech:

> For its treacherous attitude . . . the entire population of the Checheno-Ingushskaya ASSR is to be resettled to remote regions of the Soviet Union. Any resistance is senseless. The village is surrounded and arms will be used without warning. You will proceed now in an orderly way to the northern exit of the marketplace, passing between two lines of soldiers placed there and disposing of all weapons you have on your persons before you reach the formation of soldiers. Whoever tries to conceal arms will be shot on the spot.[61]

Whether Stalin's indictment was valid is a matter of debate even today, but he used the claim as a pretext for deploying state security troops to punish Caucasus peoples.

Burlutskiy later wrote that wartime collaboration with, or even association with, Germans continued to be a state security threat throughout Burlutskiy's time as an NKVD/MVD officer. Threatening behaviour divided into two broad categories: active or tacit support to Germans during the war; and other anti-Soviet behaviour, which included showing hostility to the Soviet regime or Communist Party or refusing to cooperate with Soviet military or state security forces.[62] Lindström experienced the latter and found that his employment opportunities were reduced when he failed to cooperate.[63]

Burlutskiy joined with Vyacheslav Artemyev (see Chapter 3) to co-author an article for the Research Program on the USSR describing the mission and activities of Soviet state security organs:

> Inside the country, their task is to unmask and liquidate the active politically-oriented elements of the populations and their organisations and to prevent espionage and other subversive activities on the territory of the USSR. Yet another task is to unmask and render innocuous those elements, which, without being active, are politically unreliable and thus represent a potential threat to the Soviet regime and Communism.[64]

Pavlov's information echoed this description, including counterintelligence operations in the Murmansk Oblast and intelligence operations extending into northern Norway and Finland. These activities showed strong suspicion of foreigners working in the Soviet Union that drove Soviet counterintelligence operations, as well as a Soviet priority for recruiting low-level sources who could provide on-the-ground perspectives on Norwegian – and thus NATO – military preparations for war against the Soviet Union.[65]

Deryabin indicated that the curriculum at the NKVD counterintelligence school focused on re-establishing Party control over the Soviet Union at the end of the war and relabelling wartime allies as enemies. State security resources were directed towards eliminating all associations or affinities outside the Soviet Union, and Soviet soldiers who had been held in German POW camps and Soviet citizens taken to Germany as forced labourers were all suspect, especially anyone affiliated with Vlasov's army. Deryabin cited a series of examples of Soviet citizens being coerced into becoming agents because they had some blemish on their background – a parent was exiled as a kulak in the 1930s, a brother worked for the German police during the war, or a young girl's father had been a German POW.[66]

In 1946, Deryabin was assigned as chief of the surveillance group in the Barnaul MGB Office.[67] Surveillance targets often came from among ethnic groups resettled during the war, which in Deryabin's region included Poles, Volga Germans, Lithuanians,

Latvians, and Estonians. Deryabin estimated that at any time, 1,000 of the two million people in the Altai Krai were the subjects of state security investigations.[68] In December 1946, the Barnaul MGB office produced a detailed report of religious activity in the Altai Krai, including Orthodox and Baptist followers and Old Believers, leading to the arrests of sixteen religious leaders for allegedly harbouring a Soviet army deserter during the war.[69]

Two of the defectors in this group – Deryabin and Shorokhov – also served in Soviet embassies as Line SK (*советская колония*; Soviet colony) officers, who were the manifestation of Soviet internal security and counterintelligence abroad.[70] While the West was generally aware that Soviet state security monitored its official citizens abroad – numerous reports, including from defectors like Kozhevnikov, Arutyunov, and Gouzenko, had discussed embassy-based security officers – Shorokhov's and Deryabin's descriptions of the duties of Line SK officers were the most detailed to date. They reinforced the views articulated by Early Cold War defectors that the post-war Soviet enemy had transitioned from Germany into a combination of encircling capitalist powers and the Soviet people themselves. Soviet citizens posted to capitalist countries were a dangerous combination in the eyes of Soviet decision-makers.

Both Deryabin and Shorokhov described the sources that they recruited in the course of the Line SK work. By the time Shorokhov left Sweden in 1948 he had recruited thirteen sources among the Soviet colony who reported on other Soviet personnel. Deryabin also had numerous agents who monitored the activities of fellow Soviet employees, especially GRU officers posted in Vienna. The MVD *rezident* in Vienna reportedly instructed Deryabin, 'You must always keep your eye on any GRU personnel.'[71] This matches the experience of GRU officer Shelaputin, who was posted as a GRU officer to Vienna five years before Deryabin arrived (see Chapter 4).

Both Shorokhov and Deryabin were responsible for preventing, and if necessary responding to, defections of Soviet personnel. Shorokhov was already familiar with defection before his assignment to Sweden. He had decrypted cables from NKVD representatives in Spain during the civil war, and he noted a particularly 'dramatic cable' from Paris in July 1938 that described the defection of the NKVD *rezident* in Spain – Feldbin (Chapter 2). The cable also communicated Feldbin's threat to reveal Soviet intelligence agents and operations if any harm came to him.[72] In Sweden, Shorokhov's duties included keeping track of Soviet sailors during their port calls and ensuring they did not defect. If they did defect, Shorokhov investigated the incident and met the defector through consular channels to attempt to persuade him to return to the Soviet Union. This was the case with a sailor named Vladimir Semenchenko, who failed to return to his Soviet ship that was ported in Göteborg and requested asylum in June 1947. Sweden granted Semenchenko's request, despite Shorokhov's efforts to convince Swedish authorities that he was a criminal, as mandated from Moscow.[73] Shorokhov would almost certainly also have been aware of Granovskiy, who defected in Sweden from a Soviet ship in September 1946 (see Chapter 3). Strangely, however, neither Shorokhov's writings nor his Swedish Security Police file mentions Granovskiy.

Deryabin's job similarly included investigating disloyalty, and in extreme cases, defections of Soviet employees. In that capacity, Deryabin received a phone call at 5:00 a.m. on 14 February 1954 with a report that a Soviet official, Anatoliy Ignatiyevich Skachkov, had disappeared. The previous evening, Skachkov had come home drunk, packed a suitcase, and bluntly told his wife that he was leaving for the Americans. Skachkov's frightened wife contacted the embassy security officer, which led to Deryabin being assigned to the incident. After investigating for over twenty-four hours and finding little evidence of Skachkov's fate, even being instructed, 'don't dig too deep',[74] Deryabin began wondering whether Skachkov's 'defection' was actually staged to dispatch him as a double agent to US intelligence. However, at the same time, Deryabin asked himself 'what was it like to leave behind the Soviet state and all it stood for?'[75] This thought was compounded by an argument with his wife, who questioned him about why he had been out so late, to which he reportedly responded, 'Maybe I'll never come back.'[76] On 15 February 1954, Deryabin followed that thought and walked into the American Military Command Headquarters in Vienna and requested political asylum.[77]

Accompanying the emphasis on monitoring Soviet citizens was pressure to penetrate foreign counterintelligence services to identify and neutralise threats against those Soviet citizens. On 27 September 1952, Shorokhov received a circular from the MGB headquarters department dealing with US intelligence activities to all *rezidenturas* in democratic countries instructing them to penetrate counterintelligence services. Shorokhov subsequently received a similar instruction specifying Australian, Canadian, British and New Zealand counterintelligence activities.[78] The *rezidentura* received another circular in January 1954 instructing MVD offices to acquire ciphers of countries in the 'Anglo-American Bloc', meaning the United States, Great Britain, France, Australia, and Canada.[79] The purpose for penetrating a foreign counterintelligence service was to learn the contents of the security files on each Soviet diplomat stationed in the country and to uncover security service operations directed against the Soviet Union.[80]

Shorokhov's sources provided information about the targets of Australian counterintelligence surveillance operations,[81] among whom were Kartseva and a Miss Kozlova, who worked for the Soviet embassy commercial attaché.[82] Another MGB source, Rex Chiplin (code name CHARLIE), a communist journalist, also reported ASIO's interest in Kartseva and Kozlova.[83] Rastvorov's sources in Japan provided counterintelligence-related information, including about the Japanese government's handling of an espionage case in 1952 involving Masao Mitsuhashi and Wataru Kaji. Mitsuhashi had been recruited as a Soviet agent while being held as a POW in the Soviet Union; however, he became a US double agent when he returned to Japan and provided US-controlled information by radio to his Soviet handlers.[84] Higurashi Nobunori also used his association with the Metropolitan Police Board to provide the Soviet Union with information about Rastvorov's contacts with US airman John Byington, which Rastvorov assessed was highly valuable.[85]

Penetrations of foreign counterintelligence services gave Soviet intelligence direct knowledge of the threats that Soviet citizens and operations faced abroad. Soviet state security perceived these threats as especially severe in capitalist countries, but they also existed in the 'people's democracies' of Eastern Europe, where occupying Soviet forces continued to encounter opposition.

Sovietising Eastern Europe

Continuing the line of operations noted in Chapter 4, defectors in the Post-Stalin Purge group provided further information about efforts to Sovietise Eastern European countries. Khokhlov and Granovskiy followed nearly identical paths as illegals operating in Eastern Europe after the war. Both were trained for operations behind German lines during the war. Both claimed to have met personally with Sudoplatov, who told them they might be assigned abroad for a long time. Both began as *seksoty* and received training in clandestine tradecraft in 1942–3. Both were in their early twenties – both were born in 1922 – when they were assigned as illegals to Eastern Europe to establish partisan networks in preparation for a future war.[86] Both their missions included developing source networks inside Eastern European governments to identify and eliminate opposition to Soviet dominance.

Deryabin identified the Seventh Section, known as the Advisors' Section, as the element that managed MVD activities in Soviet satellites, with the exception of East Germany. This section supervised a team of MVD officers who operated in each Soviet satellite, including a chief advisor and advisors for intelligence and counterintelligence, police matters, and military counterintelligence.[87] Burlutskiy encountered these forces when he considered defecting for the first time in July 1944, and he realised that the Polish border guards through which he would have to pass included NKVD personnel wearing Polish uniforms. He changed his mind then out of fear that they might recognise him if they encountered him.[88]

Shorokhov provided insights into the China-based workings of the Advisors' Section, which posted officers in non-official cover positions throughout China as liaison officers with local Chinese state security offices. These officers collected information about the Chinese People's Government, members of parliament, and administration officials, and used the data to vet potential Chinese officials for government positions. The Advisors' Section also ran unilateral operations to recruit or entice Russian émigrés back to the Soviet Union. Operations like these were tools in the overall Soviet mission of Sovietising China, along with Eastern Europe.

Émigrés and Repatriation

Directly related to Soviet internal security concerns were operations to pursue émigrés and encourage repatriation. As noted in previous chapters, the Soviet Union actively sought to lure Soviet expatriates back to the Soviet Union, and as émigrés began to resettle beyond Germany and Austria, Soviet efforts to identify them followed, along with operations to assassinate particularly troublesome émigrés. Several defectors in this group were involved in these operations.

Shorokhov revealed that the Canberra *rezidentura* received instructions from Moscow to recruit multiple individuals to provide information about the Russian émigré community in Australia, either to identify pro-Soviet émigrés as potential repatriation cases or anti-Soviet émigrés for kidnapping or assassination. Shorokhov's diplomatic cover assignment gave him plausible reasons to visit the Russian Social Club in Sydney and the Australia Russia Society in Melbourne, both places where Russian and other Eastern European émigrés gathered.[89] Shorokhov's cover also included serving as the representative for the All-Union Society for Cultural Contacts with Foreign Countries (*Всесоюзное Общество Культурных Связей с Заграницей*; VOKS) in Australia, which sponsored screenings of Russian-language films that attracted an émigré audience.

Khokhlov's interaction with émigrés was more sinister, as he was tasked not to entice them back to the Soviet Union, but rather to assassinate them. As noted above, Kerensky was his first target in 1952. Khokhlov's subsequent assignment to Germany in April 1952 exposed him for the first time to the anti-Soviet émigré group NTS and its publishing arm, Possev. NTS literature claimed that anti-Soviet forces had penetrated the seemingly impenetrable Soviet Union and were working to overthrow the Soviet system, and the MGB viewed the NTS as a critical threat that had the potential to organise underground cells inside Soviet territory.

The realisation gave Khokhlov hope that he could ally with them and fight the system that he had grown to dislike. In October 1953, Khokhlov received his final assignment: to assassinate NTS leader Georgiy Sergeyevich Okolovich. The mission was a priority for the Soviet government, as the MGB had tried twice previously to kidnap Okolovich and would spare no expense to have him eliminated.[90] But rather than execute the mission, Khokhlov appealed to Okolovich for help and never returned to the Soviet Union.

Khokhlov's defection and revelations about émigré assassinations had a temporary dampening effect on active anti-émigré operations, although the Soviet government continued to perceive émigrés, non-returnees, and defectors as equivalent national security threats throughout the rest of Soviet history. The 'KGB Wanted List' was designed to give KGB *rezidenturas* lead information to identify and locate Soviet citizens who had escaped Soviet control and neutralise them by luring them back to the Soviet Union, recruiting them as sources, or targeting them for assassination. Rastvorov and Deryabin reported that as of the mid-1950s, the MGB considered assassinating or kidnapping any of its own officers that defected or considered defection to prevent the loss of state secrets.[91] Another Soviet assassin, Bogdan Nikolayevich Stashinskiy, defected seven years after Khokhlov. Like Khokhlov, Stashinskiy had been sent abroad to assassinate Ukrainian nationalist leaders. His defection and public trial caused further embarrassment and again pushed the Soviet Union to weigh the costs and benefits of assassinating émigrés and defectors. But such operations were never completely abandoned.

United States

Wherever Post-Stalin Purge defectors operated, their missions invariably included collecting information about the 'Anglo-American bloc'. The Soviet Union showed interest particularly in Allied relations with countries of Soviet concern, like Japan and Germany, including Western military forces and intelligence activities in those countries. Allied nuclear plans and developments were also of great interest to the Soviet Union, and the

MGB tasked sources in various places to report whatever they could find on the topic, although their reporting varied in value.

Post-Stalin Purge defectors re-emphasised that the Soviet Union directed its intelligence resources against the United States and Great Britain even while they were wartime allies against Germany, and several defectors noted that Soviet state security officer training included a US focus during the war. Rastvorov reported being involved in a deception operation targeting the United States in 1942, when American politician Wendell Willkie travelled to the Soviet Union as Roosevelt's envoy at the invitation of the Soviet government to tour Soviet farms. The operation resembled a Potemkin village created to present an image of the Soviet Union as prosperous.[92] In August 1944, Rastvorov attended clandestine operations training, where students were divided into two cohorts: one training for operations against the 'main target', the United States; and the other focused on the second-tier targets, Germany, Japan, China, and Italy.[93] Burlutskiy also noted that the priority language taught in MVD Border Guard training was English, with fewer students taking German or French.[94] Burlutskiy's operational intelligence training focused primarily on US intelligence as the target, followed by British intelligence.[95]

Soviet intelligence concentration against the Allies intensified after the war. According to Rastvorov, Soviet perceptions of the United States began to worsen during his first tour in Japan in 1946, resulting in increased suspicion of even benign acts by American servicemen. Rastvorov cited an example of an American officer giving baby formula to a Soviet representative whose wife had recently given birth. Another Soviet officer claimed that the Americans were trying to bribe the recipient and demanded that he be sent home.[96] Much of the efforts of the Tokyo *rezidentura* were directed against US information during Rastvorov's assignment. Not long after arriving in Tokyo in July 1950, Rastvorov joined the Tokyo Lawn Tennis Club, a gathering place for diplomats and wealthy foreigners, with the goal of contacting and targeting Americans for recruitment and to 'pick up loose talk'.[97] He developed friendships with Americans and British servicemen and submitted several names to Moscow for intelligence development. But none of the leads progressed very far, and his involvement at the tennis club did more to expose him to Western influences than to facilitate recruitments.

Rastvorov provided actionable information about Soviet targeting of US service members who it believed were vulnerable to a Soviet approach and could provide classified US military and diplomatic information, leading to several US counterintelligence investigations. These included Ernest J. Lissner, a CIC officer stationed in Japan who initially approached Rastvorov's predecessor in Tokyo in 1947 and offered US classified information.[98] The Tokyo *rezidentura* also received instructions from Moscow in 1952 to recruit Major Rose Esther Ennis, a Russian language teacher in the US Far Eastern Command G2. Her Russian heritage and family members still living in the Soviet Union brought her to the MGB's attention.[99] In April 1953, John Byington, a US Air Force military policeman stationed in Japan, walked into the Soviet mission in Tokyo and offered to sell US military information. Rastvorov became his handler, and Byington's arrest in May 1953 and the ensuing investigation gave US Air Force counterintelligence its first indications that Rastvorov was an intelligence officer.[100]

Rastvorov also identified at least four Japanese officials with access to classified information whom the Tokyo *rezidentura* handled as agents, three of which, Shoji Hiroshi, Shii Masaji, and Higurashi Nobunori, were among over half a million Japanese military members, mostly members of the Kwantung Army in Manchuria, interned by the Soviet Union after the war. The NKGB/MGB viewed POWs as a source pool, screened them, and gave them ideological training in preparation for repatriating them to Japan as recruited sources. Rastvorov had been posted to Khabarovsk from January to August 1948 to participate in interrogations and recruitments of interned Japanese personnel.[101]

Shii was a Japanese intelligence officer whom the MVD had used as an interpreter in a POW camp because of his Russian language proficiency. He was repatriated to Japan in November 1948 with instructions to await further contact by Soviet intelligence and avoid any contact with the Japanese Communist Party.[102] In February 1949, the US Far Eastern Command G2 hired Shii to debrief other repatriated Japanese officers and perform intelligence analysis, and he soon began informing Rastvorov about US intelligence interest in mapping Soviet cities for possible future military targeting.[103] In 1952 and 1953, Rastvorov tasked Shii to report on the Korean conflict, the future plans of US forces in Korea, and US plans for deploying atomic weapons and delivery capabilities to Japan. Shii responded with information he claimed to have gleaned from newspapers, including a report about US atomic weapons in Okinawa and plans for placing atomic artillery in Hokkaido and South Korea. He also claimed to have intentionally exaggerated US atomic strength to give the Soviet Union grounds for demanding that the United States remove its forces from Japan. Rastvorov also asked Shii for information about three named US military intelligence officers, but Shii did not know them and could offer no information.[104]

The Soviet Union attempted to recruit similar agents in Germany to penetrate US institutions for both intelligence and sabotage purposes. When Khokhlov reported for duty at the Group of Soviet Forces in Germany in April 1952, his assignment was to recruit agents among the German population for eventual infiltration into West Germany with instructions to sabotage West German and US forces, rail yards, and military installations in the event of war. He worked with German Communist Party members to identify and vet potential agents, particularly among returning POWs and refugees, and claimed that his team recruited about twenty agents during his time there and dispatched them to Germany and Denmark, with plans to send others to the Netherlands.[105]

The Broader 'Anglo-American Bloc'

The Soviet Union defined the 'Anglo-American bloc' to include the United States, Great Britain, Australia, Canada, and to a lesser extent, France. Shorokhov's and Kartseva's operations in Australia gave them a detailed picture of Soviet intelligence collection priorities that reflected requirements against other members of the 'Anglo-American bloc'. Shorokhov's operational targets in Australia fell into several major categories: penetrating the Australian Department of External Affairs (DEA) and other countries' diplomatic organisations, collecting intelligence about Allied political movements and plans, and penetrating Australian and other security services to ascertain foreign counterintelligence activities directed against Soviet personnel. Shorokhov identified over thirty individuals in Australia whom Soviet intelligence had highlighted as potential targets to penetrate these institutions, although the Canberra *rezidentura* had little success recruiting most of them.

When Shorokhov and Kartseva arrived in Australia, Moscow lamented that it lacked even basic information about Australian government institutions and leaders. In August 1951, Kartseva and a fellow MGB officer were assigned to compile a series of foundational reports, using both secret and open-source materials, concerning Australian government and political leaders, including the prime minister, minister for foreign affairs, minister for defence, and others.[106] In January 1952, MGB headquarters complained that it had received no response to this tasking and requested an update, indicating the Centre's urgency.[107]

According to Shorokhov, one of the primary institutions about which the Soviet Union sought intelligence was a country's foreign policy establishment, aligning with Feldbin's 'diplomatic intelligence' mission (see Chapter 2). Correspondingly, the sources that Soviet *rezidenturas* were tasked to recruit were often either staff employees of such a department, particularly those with access to secret information, or associates of such personnel.[108] In pursuit of that priority, many of the people that Shorokhov targeted for intelligence recruitment were inside or associated with the DEA or in an equivalent third-country organisation represented in Australia, such as the embassies of France, Indonesia, and Israel.

The Canberra *rezidentura* also received instructions in 1953 to collect information about atomic tests in Australia and the people who were involved in them. According to Kartseva, the Canberra *rezidentura* used the special top secret code word ENORMAZ to refer to 'anything connected with materials used for manufacture of atomic bombs'.[109] Kartseva remembered seeing ENORMAZ for the first time in a message to Canberra fifteen days after an atomic test, probably referring to the British nuclear test conducted in the Australian desert in October 1953.[110] Kartseva indicated that the *rezidentura*'s only source for this information was newspapers.[111] Nevertheless, the enquiry to Canberra identified Soviet interest as a high-priority topic.

Shorokhov's most explosive revelation involved second-hand information about Soviet intelligence activities not in Australia, but in Great Britain. Another MGB officer, Fillip Vasilyevich Kislitsyn, recounted to Shorokhov his role in preparing a plan to exfiltrate Guy Burgess and Donald Maclean from the UK to the USSR in 1951. Kislitsyn was a cipher clerk in London during Burgess and Maclean's active espionage period, and he photographed and prepared their information for transmission to Moscow.[112] He told Shorokhov about their recruitment as students in the 1930s, and that they became crucial agents who supplied a large volume of classified British information. Shorokhov's revelations about Burgess and Maclean attracted intense press attention because it explained the 'missing diplomats' stories and offered the first public confirmation of their long-time espionage careers.[113]

Some potential recruits in capitalist countries were already ideologically inclined towards the Soviet Union, and ideological persuasion yielded the majority of Soviet intelligence recruits in both Australia and Canada. Shorokhov reported exploiting anti-Allied sentiments to pursue sources.[114] In his overt role as a consular officer, he met a young man in September 1951 who wanted to travel to the Soviet Union, join the Soviet Army, and 'go to Korea and kill Yanks and bloody Australians'. Shorokhov praised the young man and told him, 'You are a good Soviet citizen already.'[115] In July 1952, Shorokhov took over the handling of Rose-Marie Ollier (code name OLGA), a Second Secretary at the French Embassy in Canberra. Moscow instructed Shorokhov to use an ideological approach to recruit her, telling her that she could give considerable service to the cause of peace by providing information about the 'machinations of the British, American, French, and Australian ruling circles directed against the Soviet Union and the countries of the People's Democracies'.[116] Unfortunately for Shorokhov, Ollier never became a profitable source.

Canada was similarly a venue for Soviet collection, including similar targets. After Brik had legalised himself, he was made the illegal *rezident* in Canada in charge of five agents. Four were primarily operational support agents who managed safe houses and live letterboxes. The fifth agent, codenamed LIND, was an Irish–Canadian communist who worked for the Canadian aircraft company A. V. Roe and passed Brik photographs of plans for the advanced fighter aircraft Avro CF-105.[117] Brik informed the RCMP of this collection tasking, and the RCMP instructed him to purposefully develop LIND's photos out of focus to minimise their value to the Soviets.[118]

Japan and Germany

Operations worldwide, wherever they occurred, placed collection of information about the 'Anglo-American bloc' as the top priority. However, that did not preclude collecting intelligence about other countries, particularly Japan and Germany, which continued to be collection targets in their own right in relation to their rearmament and integration into Western alliances, in addition to being venues for observing the 'Anglo-American bloc' itself. Shorokhov wrote about his work in the Special Cipher Section during the *Yezhovshchina*, where he processed communications between NKVD offices and headquarters, including frequent cables that reported suspects' confessions to being British, German, or Japanese spies.[119]

As noted in previous chapters, Japan had been a target of Soviet concern since the 1920s. Shorokhov, Kartseva, and Rastvorov provided additional insights into Soviet intelligence collection of Japanese politics, foreign affairs, and especially post-war rearmament separate from the US presence. Kartseva's initial assignment as a code clerk focused specifically on Japan, and by 1942 she had reached the rank of captain of state security specialising in decrypting Japanese communications.[120] Both Rastvorov and Shorokhov cited examples of the NKVD targeting Japanese officials stationed in Moscow, although with different results. Rastvorov told of the NKVD introducing a Kyodo News Agency correspondent in Moscow in 1945 to a young Russian woman, who soon claimed to be pregnant with the correspondent's baby. The NKVD used the prospect of a scandal to persuade the correspondent to become a Soviet agent.[121] Shorokhov's case ended differently: the MGB dangled a girl for a Japanese diplomat, and he took the bait. The MGB photographed the couple in an intimate situation and confronted him with the photos. However, in this instance, the Japanese diplomat responded that he was authorised by Japanese law to have intimate relations with women while he was abroad and was unfazed by MGB threats to publish the photos. Shorokhov cited this case as the reason why the MGB needed to learn the laws of the countries they were targeting to allow operations to proceed smoothly.[122]

Because he was a career Japan targets officer, Rastvorov was naturally the most fruitful source among Post-Stalin Purge defectors about Soviet intelligence activities in Japan. In addition to information about US forces, Rastvorov tasked Japanese sources like Shii to provide information about Japanese policies, often appealing to their anti-American sentiments. From November 1953 until March 1954, Shii worked for the Japanese Foreign Ministry, where he analysed information about China, Taiwan, and Korea, and he reported to Rastvorov that he, along with many employees in the Foreign Office, wanted the Japanese government to invest in social development instead of remilitarisation and resume normal relations with China.[123]

According to Rastvorov, Soviet intelligence spotted another Japanese source, Takamore Shigeru, in his job as a Russian interpreter in December 1950 and recruited him to provide Japanese economic information, Foreign Office documents and reference materials, Japanese opinions of Russia, and information about US economic policy in Japan. His handlers also requested a copy of the Japanese Foreign Ministry's communications codes, but Takamore did not have access to them.[124] The Soviet Union expected that Japan would expel Soviet government representatives after the 1951 Japan–US Security Treaty, thereby reducing the Soviet intelligence presence. In anticipation of that, they gave Takamore instructions for communicating with the Soviet Union via radio, trained him to encode and decode messages, and gave him money to buy a radio and a camera with which to make microphotographs.[125] Takamore received some test radio messages, although he complained that they were difficult to understand.[126] However, at about the same time, to the Soviets' relief, another source, Higurashi, reported about Japan's decision not to expel members of the Soviet Mission even though the Japanese government did not recognise it as a diplomatic representation.[127] Takamore similarly provided a Foreign Office policy document that described a Japanese policy to allow Soviet and other vessels flagged by communist countries into Japanese ports after the Security Treaty.[128] Takamore's handlers never activated the radio communications method, but continued to meet him in person until Rastvorov's defection.

While the Soviet Union's post-war intelligence collection in Japan was directed primarily at Japanese reconstruction and relations with the United States, operations in Germany were initially concentrated more on counterintelligence, likely forming the core of Deryabin's saying about the 'god' of state security after the war. Deryabin and Khokhlov were European specialists focusing much of their attention on Germany, and they provided insights into Soviet priorities there during and after the war. Khokhlov's wartime missions were directed almost exclusively at Germany because of his ability to pass as a German. Early in the war, he was summoned to an NKVD office and recruited into an NKVD-sponsored theatre performing group that would stay behind in Moscow and conduct anti-German sabotage if the Germans overran the city. By autumn of 1941, it appeared that Moscow would survive the German advances and the theatre group was never called into action. Khokhlov's later assignments included a year behind German lines conducting espionage, sabotage, and assassination missions during the war, a posting in Germany as a case officer recruiting German sources, and his final assignment to assassinate an NTS activist in Germany.

Deryabin's time in foreign intelligence was focused almost entirely on Germany. From his perspective in the Austria–Germany section, Deryabin claimed that Soviet state security concentrated its efforts in Germany, and that his section was the second largest in the Second Chief Directorate after only the American Section. However, despite the Soviet Union's role in a victory over Nazi Germany, Deryabin noted that the Soviet government perceived a series of defeats at the end of the 1940s and early 1950s. They included the Berlin Airlift in 1948, the formation of NATO in

1949, and American military operations against Soviet-sponsored forces in Korea in 1950. The Soviet Union used its intelligence capability in Germany to counter those perceived setbacks.[129]

Deryabin reported that the activities of the Austria–Germany section were heavily dominated by the pursuit of anti-Soviet Germans, echoing reports from Early Cold War defectors. MGB Minister Abakumov directed an operation to recruit ex-Nazis as sources in 1947, and the MGB interrogated Nazi POWs into the early 1950s.[130] As late as 1952, the section continued to investigate the German Operation ZEPPELIN (see Chapter 3). The section was responsible for counterintelligence operations against the Gehlen Organization, the US-sponsored West German intelligence service led by former Nazi intelligence officer Richard Gehlen.[131] While Deryabin was working in Moscow, he was also involved in planning the July 1952 kidnapping of a German lawyer, Dr Walter Linse, who worked for the Association of Free Jurists, a powerful anti-communist organisation in Germany. For several years after Linse's disappearance, the Soviet government denied any knowledge of his whereabouts, and Deryabin's reporting was the first indication of Soviet involvement coming from inside the Soviet system.[132]

Other Countries

In addition to these primary countries, several others, particularly along the Soviet perimeter, also attracted Soviet intelligence interest, according to the Post-Stalin Purge defectors. The Soviet Union viewed these countries, including Norway, Sweden, Finland, Turkey, Iran, and Afghanistan, as potential entry points for foreign intelligence and influence and escape points for dissatisfied Soviet citizens. The targeting was partially directed at the 'Anglo-American' presence within these countries. But Soviet intelligence also sought to penetrate these countries themselves along with their Moscow-based representations for intelligence, counterintelligence, and influence purposes. Seven defectors in this group – Burlutskiy, Kartseva, Lindström, Pavlov, Rastvorov, Shorokhov, and KGB Wanted List number 27 – had experience working in or against periphery countries.

Soviet intelligence work in periphery countries was a mix of intelligence, counterintelligence, and liaison with communist activities as an extension of Soviet influence. Kartseva, for example, reported that the NKVD Special Department where she worked in June 1934 was responsible for decrypting the codes used by foreign diplomatic missions in Moscow, including Chinese, Romanian, Turkish, and Scandinavian, as well as British, American, and Japanese.[133] When Shorokhov was assigned as a Line SK officer in Stockholm in 1942, most of his duties focused on scrutinising Soviet personnel residing in or visiting Sweden, but also serving as a liaison with the Swedish Communist Party. His intelligence affiliation was compromised early in his tour in Sweden. SIS identified him as an intelligence officer as early as 1945.[134] He came under Swedish counterintelligence scrutiny before August 1945,[135] and by May 1946, the Swedish security police had compelling grounds to suspect that he was an NKVD officer.[136] In April 1947, Swedish surveillance observed him contacting Swedish communists and conducting surveillance detection en route to agent meetings,[137] using the false names Johan Johansson and Jakob Pettersson while operating in Sweden.[138]

Kartseva accompanied Shorokhov to Sweden, initially assigned to clerical duties in the embassy. But after several years in Sweden, she was given her first chance to recruit an agent. Her target was a young Swedish woman, whom she referred to as Maria, who worked as a secretary in the Swedish Ministry of Foreign Affairs. Kartseva told Maria that the Soviet Union needed to know the content of secret agreements between capitalist countries and their negotiation strategies with the Soviet Union. Kartseva indicated that Sweden and the Soviet Union were at that time negotiating a treaty, and she asked Maria to obtain copies of the Swedish plans. Maria firmly refused, and Kartseva's first recruitment attempt collapsed.[139] Kartseva's next assignment was to handle a Swedish communist who was already an active NKVD agent, with whom she had more success.[140]

As a Finnish linguist, Pavlov's mission was also directed at Scandinavian countries, primarily for counterintelligence purposes. His first assignment was to translate the results of meetings with a Finnish agent who reported on the activities of Finns living near Murmansk. He was later assigned to conduct surveillance on a person of Finnish descent who had emigrated from the United States. In 1952, he monitored the workers at the joint Soviet–Finnish–Norwegian Boris Gleb hydroelectric project along the Pazvik (Paz) River, which flows through all three countries and formed the border between Norway and the Soviet Union. He made contacts with Finnish workers and became aware of several Norwegians who were working as MGB double agents against the Norwegian security service.[141] For a short period, Pavlov worked as a clerk in the agent registry and had access to a card catalogue of intelligence agents that the MGB dispatched into Norway and Finland during and after the war to report about military outposts in far northern Norway, iron ore output, and local government leaders.

Lindström went on two low-level missions into Norway to collect foundational information about Norwegian people, society, and government. His supervisors discussed the possibility of Lindström making contact with a Norwegian army captain whose mother lived in Narvik. However, Lindström's supervisors dismissed the idea, claiming that he was too green to make contact with a military officer. They agreed instead that he would contact dockworkers to obtain information about the Narvik port, which they explained had been a valuable asset during World War II.[142]

As Akhmedov described in his debriefings (see Chapter 3), Turkey was another periphery country that attracted Soviet intelligence interest, both as a platform for launching operations against priority targets and as a target of its own. Khokhlov's first planned mission in 1942 was to infiltrate Turkey posing as a German refugee, get himself arrested by Turkish authorities, and request repatriation to Germany, where he would make contact with Soviet agents and begin his assignment behind German lines. Little is known about KGB Wanted List number 27, except that the Transcaucasus Military District dispatched him to Turkey on a clandestine mission in July 1953, likely as a GRU illegal. His specific targets are unavailable, but he was arrested before he could fulfil his mission.[143]

Conclusion

Post-Stalin Purge defectors broke with the Soviet Union at a time when anti-Soviet sentiment was running high in the West. In 1950, the US Department of Defense proposed a policy for active efforts to entice defectors. It recommended that the US government

> weld the Russian and Satellite defectors already in Western Germany into a strong, unified organization to spearhead the appeal to their countrymen to leave their native land today . . . Announce to the world in dramatic fashion . . . the launching of an International Liberation Policy, which would have as its program the solid assurance to all those who voluntarily come from under Communist domination three guarantees: life, freedom, and settlement.[144]

The appeal would have several goals, including spreading confusion within the Soviet Union and satellite countries and weakening the confidence of Communist Party members.

The British government similarly sought to encourage defectors, assessing that 'defectors, particularly Russian defectors, are a first-class source of intelligence on the Soviet Union and are likely to remain so within the foreseeable future. It is therefore more desirable that defection should be encouraged and defectors fully exploited to our own advantage.'[145]

The waning flow of defectors in the early 1950s provided few opportunities to achieve these goals. However, Stalin's death and the power struggle that followed ignited a brief rush of intelligence officer defectors whose stories could be exploited. Like 1930, 1954 became another year of the defector. SIS assessed in May 1954 that recent defections had caused 'extreme anxiety of the Soviet authorities to win back the allegiance of Soviet defectors, and to take all possible steps to prevent others from taking the same course'. SIS noted increased Soviet threat perceptions in 1954, and special countermeasures were announced at a meeting of Soviet officials in Paris after Shorokhov's defection.[146] Even political cartoons lampooned Soviet anxiety over its diplomats (see Figure 5.2).[147] For a brief time, it appeared that defections were causing the confusion and doubt that US policy had sought.

Figure 5.2 Political Cartoon: 'After the Petrov Affair'

The publicity given to defectors in the West accentuated these effects. This contrasted with the quiet handling of defectors in the 1940s (see Chapter 4), and it further fed anti-Soviet sentiment that had grown to a fever pitch in the early 1950s. The espionage trials that resulted from Pavlov's revelations, for example, spurred intense media reaction. An article published in June 1954 suggested, 'The Finnmark trials will surely disturb the complacency of pro-Russian sympathisers in the north and elsewhere in Norway.'[148] Despite Soviet denials and counterclaims, defectors had an adverse impact on the Soviet Union's ability to operate around the world.

Notes

1. Memorandum for Director of Central Intelligence, 'Notes on NSC Meeting – 17 February 1954' (CIA CREST). Names have been redacted from the declassified document.
2. US Political Advisor for Germany memo, 19 October 1948, with enclosure 'Russian Deserters', NARA, RG 59, Central Decimal Files 1945–1949, Box 6651, 861.2226/10-1948. These numbers include many more than just intelligence officers.
3. Memo for the Secretary of Defense, 'Policy on Defectors, 26 September 1950, NARA, RG 59, Entry A1 1583D, Box 117.
4. Lt Col David L. Jones, 'Communist Defection', *Military Review*, March 1966, 22–3.
5. Vladimir and Evdokiya Petrov, *Empire of Fear* (London: André Deutsch, 1956), 157–70.
6. 'KGB Wanted List', Entry number 27.
7. Dmitriy Anatolyevich Yermolayev, 'Охота на Ведмь по-Норвежски' ('Witch Hunt Norwegian Style'), part two of three-part series, 'Тайная Битва Спецслужб' ('Secret Battle of Special Services'), *Мурманский Вестник* (*Murmansk Chronicle*), 16 June 2005, published online at <https://www.mvestnik.ru/our-home/pid200506162116l> (last accessed 2 April 2020).
8. Gunnar Haarstad, *I Hemmelig Tjeneste: Etterretning og overvåking i krig og fred* (*In Secret Service: Intelligence and Surveillance in War and Peace*) (Oslo: Aschehoug, 1988), 135.
9. Charles W. Thayer, 'MVD Man's Declaration of Independence', *Life*, 72–3.
10. Petrov and Petrov, *Empire of Fear*, 138–9.
11. 'Defection of Vladimir Mikhailovich Petrov @ Proletarski, and Evdokia Alexeevna Petrova @ Kartseva', undated but probably November 1954, NAA, A6283, folder 15, item 4104676, 135.
12. CIA memo, 'Inducement of Soviet Defectors', 4 May 1954 (CIA FOIA site). Emphasis in the original. The author's name is redacted.
13. Ibid.
14. CIA Report, 'Economic Enterprises of the MVD', 13 July 1955, NARA, RG 319, Entry 134A, Box 138.
15. Brook-Shepherd, *The Storm Birds*, 101–2.
16. 'Defection of Vladimir Mikhailovich Petrov @ Proletarski, and Evdokia Alexeevna Petrova @ Kartseva', 132–54.
17. 'The Year 1953', 12 May 1954, NAA, A6283, folder 1, item

4104669, 127; duplicate in NAA, A6283, folder 14, item 4104675, 30; extract from ASIO source report, 22 February 1952, NAA, A6117, folder 7, item 12037437, serial 84.

18. 'Defection of Vladimir Mikhailovich Petrov @ Proletarski, and Evdokia Alexeevna Petrova @ Kartseva', 136.

19. MGB telegram to Canberra, 6 June 1952, NAA, A6283, folder 1, item 4104669, 11.

20. 'Copy of Statement in the Handwriting of Mrs Petrov Setting Out the Reasons for Her Departure', 7 May 1954, NAA, A6283, folder 14, item 4104675, 55–6; duplicated at 112–23; 'Exhibit 63', NAA, A6283, folder 14, item 4104675, 58.

21. Petrov and Petrov, *Empire of Fear*, 142–7.

22. Ibid. 155.

23. 'Defection of Vladimir Mikhailovich Petrov @ Proletarski, and Evdokia Alexeevna Petrova @ Kartseva', 135.

24. G2, US Forces Far East report, 'RASTVOROV, Yurii Alexandrovitch', 25 March 1954, NARA, RG 319, Entry A1 314B, Box 627. The same story was later published in Yuri Rastvorov, 'Goodby to Red Terror', *Life*, 13 December 1954, 52.

25. 441st CIC Detachment Report of Investigation, 'RASTVOROV, Yuriy A.', 2 February 1954, NARA, RG 319, Entry A1 314B, Box 627.

26. Thayer, 'MVD Man's Declaration of Independence', 72–3.

27. G2, US Forces Far East report, 'RASTVOROV, Yurii Alexandrovitch', 25 March 1954, NARA, RG 319, Entry A1 314B, Box 627.

28. Thayer, 'MVD Man's Declaration of Independence', 70.

29. The 1947 movie was titled Подвиг разведчика (*Exploits of an Intelligence Officer*). It was released in the United States under the title *Secret Agent*, see Internet Movie Database, <http://www.imdb.com/title/tt0039716/> (last accessed 13 March 2020).

30. Nikolai E. Khokhlov, 'I Would Not Murder for the Soviets', *Saturday Evening Post*, 27 November 1954, 72.

31. Mary-Kay Wilmers, *The Eitingons: A Twentieth Century Story* (New York: Verso Books, 2012), 415.

32. Khokhlov, 'I Would Not Murder for the Soviets', 4 December 1954, 141.

33. 'The Year 1953', 12 May 1954, NAA, A6283, folder 1, item 4104669, 127.

34. Petrov and Petrov, *Empire of Fear*, 251–2.

35. Yuri A. Rastvorov, 'Beria's Plot', 21–2, undated typescript, HIA,

Boris Nicolaevsky Collection, Box 295, folder 21 (microfilm reel 255).

36. 441st CIC Detachment memo to G2, US Far Eastern Forces, 15 September 1953, NARA, RG 319, Entry A1 314B, Box 627; Brook-Shepherd, *The Storm Birds*, 75–7.

37. CIA Report, '1. MVD Administration Data; 2. Miscellaneous Data on Resistance and on Military Installations', 18 August 1954 (CIA CREST).

38. Swedish State Police debriefing report, 13 August 1954, SUK Hemliga Archivet, F4, Volume 11.

39. Swedish State Police debriefing report, 18 August 1954, SUK Hemliga Archivet, F4, Volume 11.

40. Donald G. Mahar, *Shattered Illusions: KGB Cold War Espionage in Canada* (Lanham, MD: Rowman & Littlefield, 2016).

41. Khokhlov, *The Right to Conscience*, 122–3. See also SIS memo, 8 May 1954, enclosing Khokhlov debriefing report, 'Organisation of the 9th Otdel', TNA, KV 5/107, serial 86.

42. Khokhlov, 'I Would Not Murder for the Soviets', 27 November 1954, 72.

43. *Personal History of Hede Massing*, 15–17, HIA, Hede Massing Papers, Box 1, Folder 1.

44. Andrew and Mitrokhin, *The Sword and the Shield*, 146.

45. Swedish State Police debriefing report, 16 August 1954, SUK Hemliga Archivet, F4, Volume 11.

46. 'Questions Put to Khokhlov and His Answers Thereto', 13 May 1954, TNA, KV 5/107, serial 87a.

47. Sudoplatov, *Special Operations*, 188.

48. Khokhlov debriefing report, 'Organisation of the 9th Otdel'.

49. Deryabin debriefing Report, 'Organisation of the MVD USSR', undated but from March 1954, 6, TNA, KV 5/107, serial 75a; Deriabin and Gibney, *The Secret World*, 187.

50. Wilmers, *The Eitingons: A Twentieth Century Story*, 416.

51. Extract from ASIO source report, 12 and 21 July 1952 and 21 October 1952, NAA, A6117, folder 7, item 12037437, serial 148, 150, and 215; extract ASIO from source report, 13 March and 1 April 1953, NAA, A6117, folder 8, item 12077929, serials 100, 118.

52. Statement by Petrova, 8 September 1954, NAA, A6283, folder 14, item 4104675, 218.

53. ASIO memo, 7 May 1954, NAA, A6283, folder 1, item 4104669, 71; duplicate in NAA, A6283, folder 14, item 4104675, 18.

54. 'Liaison Between the Soviet and Chinese State Security Services', 29 March 1955, NAA, A6283, folder 9, item 4199156, 54.
55. Statement by Petrov, 12 August 1954, NAA, A6283, folder 14, item 4104675, 238–49; Statement by Petrov, 18 October 1954, NAA, A6283, folder 15, item 4104676, 104.
56. M. G. L. Dunn, *Royal Commission on Espionage, 1954–1955*, PhD thesis for the University of Adelaide, 1979, 208–15.
57. Deryabin debriefing report, 'Organisation of the MVD USSR', 8.
58. Khokhlov, 'I Would Not Murder for the Soviets', 4 December 1954, 140.
59. Deryabin Report no. 7, 'Establishment of Illegal Residentura in Western Germany', 6 May 1954, TNA, KV 5/107, serial 93a.
60. Deriabin and Gibney, *The Secret World*, 63.
61. CIA Report, 'Resettlement of Population of Checheno-Ingushskaya ASSR', 26 February 1954 (CIA CREST).
62. V. P. Artemiev and G. S. Burlutsky, 'Internal Activities of the Soviet Organs of State Security After World War II', in Wolin and Slusser (eds), *The Soviet Secret Police*, 323.
63. Swedish State Police debriefing report, 11 August 1954, SUK Hemliga Archivet, F4, Volume 11.
64. Vyacheslav P. Artem'yev and Grigori S. Burlutski, 'Postwar Organization and Activities of Soviet State Security Organs', undated typescript, 1, Columbia University Rare Book and Manuscript Library, Research Program on the USSR, box 8.
65. Yermolayev, 'Witch Hunt Norwegian Style'.
66. Deriabin and Gibney, *The Secret World*, 77–8.
67. Ibid. 81.
68. Ibid. 85.
69. US Congress. Senate. Judiciary Committee. *Communist Controls on Religious Activity*, 86th Congress, First Session (Washington, DC: Government Printing Office, 1959). See also Deriabin and Gibney, *The Secret World*, 86–7. Rastvorov also testified before the US Senate and discussed state security control over religious affairs; see US Congress. Senate. Judiciary Committee. *Scope of Soviet Activity in the United States*, 84th Congress, Second Session (Washington, DC: Government Printing Office, 1956), part 13, 780–2.
70. Deryabin debriefing report, 'Security of Soviet Personnel and Installations, Vienna', 25 March 1954, TNA KV 5/107, serial 78a.
71. Deriabin and Gibney, *The Secret World*, 244.
72. Petrov and Petrov, *Empire of Fear*, 57–8.

73. State Police memo 30 June 1947, Säkerhetspolisen, P5279, löp. nr. 2, 40–1; Petrov and Petrov, *Empire of Fear*, 199–200.
74. Brook-Shepherd, *The Storm Birds*, 107.
75. Peter Deriabin and Frank Gibney, 'Red Agent's Vivid Tale of Terror', *Life*, 23 March 1959, 111–26. Deryabin places the date at 13 February in Deriabin and Gibney, *The Secret World*, 262–3. US Embassy Vienna telegram, 15 February 1954, confirms the 14 February date, although his approach probably occurred in the early hours of the morning; NARA, RG 59, Central Decimal File, 761.00/2-1654. On Skachkov's defection, TNA, KV 5/83, serial 98a.
76. Brook-Shepherd, *The Storm Birds*, 107.
77. US Embassy Berlin cable, 16 February 1954, NARA, RG 59, Box 3798, 761.00/2-1654.
78. ASIO memo, 12 April 1954, NAA, A6283, folder 1, item 4104669, 92.
79. 'The Year 1953', 12 May 1954, NAA, A6283, folder 1, item 4104669, 123–4.
80. 'Soviet State Security Service Foreign Intelligence Operational Techniques ("Legal" Residency System)', 18 May 1955, NAA, A6283, folder 1, item 4104669, 133.
81. Excerpt from ASIO report, NAA, A6283, folder 14, item 4104675, 76.
82. Statement of Petrova, 24 August 1954, NAA, A6283, folder 14, item 4104675, 192.
83. Excerpt from ASIO debriefing transcript, NAA, A6283, folder 14, item 4104675, 76.
84. 'Jap Says He's a Spy for both US and Russia', *Chicago Tribune*, 17 December 1952.
85. CIC investigative report, 'HIGURASHI Nobinuri', 4 November 1954, NARA, RG 319, Entry A1 314B, Box 289.
86. Curriculum vitae attached to Khokhlov letter to the UK Secretary of State for Foreign Affairs, 13 December 1954, TNA, FO 371/111756.
87. Deryabin debriefing report, 'Organisation of the MVD USSR', 8.
88. Thayer, 'MVD Man's Declaration of Independence', 76.
89. Extract from ASIO source report, 29 August 1951, NAA, A6117, folder 7, item 12037437, serial 15. 'Meer Israilevitch Neplokh', 15 June 1955, NAA, A6283, folder, item 4199158, 38–9.; ASIO Investigative memo, 11 February 1952, NAA, A6117, folder 7,

item 12037437, serial 70; Nikolay Vasilyevich Yalinichev, in June 1952, see ASIO investigative memo, 6 September 1954, NAA, A6283, folder 11, item 4199158, 7; Major Prokopenko in January 1953, see 'Interview with V. Petrov by [redacted] on Monday, 24th May, 1954: Re Lisenko and Major Prokopenko, New Zealand Personalities', NAA, A6283, folder 1, item 4104669, 72.

90. US Army G-2 memo and attached Kukowitsch debriefing report, 29 Mach 1954, NARA, RG 319, Entry A1 314B, Box 443, Kukowitch file; Khokhlov, 'I Would Not Murder for the Soviets', *Saturday Evening Post*, 11 December 1954, 126.

91. 'Soviet Use of Assassination and Kidnapping', *Studies in Intelligence*, vol. 9, no. 3 (Fall 1965), 1–10.

92. Yuri Rastvorov, 'Red Fraud and Intrigue in the Far East', *Life*, 6 December 1954, 178, 180.

93. 441st CIC Detachment Report of Investigation, 'RASTVOROV, Yuriy A.', 2 February 1954, NARA, RG 319, Entry A1 314B, Box 627. He did not specifically mention the United Kingdom as a target.

94. V. P. Artemiev and G. S. Burlutskiy, 'Personnel, Conditions of Service and Training in the Border Troops', in Wolin and Slusser (eds), *The Soviet Secret Police*, 306.

95. Ibid. 317.

96. Rastvorov, 'Red Fraud and Intrigue in the Far East', 190.

97. US Navy memo, 'Yuri Alessandrovich Rastovoro', 2 February 1954, NARA, RG 329, Entry A1 314B, box 628.

98. Rastvorov, 'Goodby to Red Terror', 50.

99. 441st CIC Detachment Investigative Summary, 'ENNIS, Rose Esther', 13 March 1945, NARA RG 319, Entry A1 314B, Box 627.

100. 441st CIC Detachment Agent report, 'BYINGTON, John M.', 3 June 1953, NARA RG 319, Entry A1 314B, Box 627; 441st CIC Detachment Agent reports, 28 April 1954 and 4 May 1954, NARA RG 319, Entry A1 314B, Box 716.

101. 441st CIC Detachment Report of Investigation, 'RASTVOROV, Yuriy A.', 6 March 1954, NARA, RG 319, Entry A1 314B, Box 627.

102. Copy of SHII Masaji investigative file from 1950 is in NARA, RG 319, Entry A1 314B, Box 627.

103. 441st CIC Detachment investigative summary, 5 May 1954, NARA, RG 319, Entry A1 314B, Box 716.

104. 441st CIC Detachment Agent report, 12 May 1954, NARA, RG 319, Entry A1 314B, Box 716.

105. Khokhlov, 'I Would Not Murder for the Soviets', 4 December 1954, 140.

106. MGB telegram to Canberra, 6 June 1952, NAA, A6283, folder 1, item 4104669, 18–19.

107. MGB telegram to Canberra, 2 January 1952, NAA, A6283, folder 1, item 4104669, 7; MGB telegram, 2 January 1952, NAA, A6283, folder 14, item 4104675, 1, 3; Statement of Petrov, 8 December 1954, NAA, A6283, folder 16, item 4104677, 87–8.

108. 'Soviet State Security Service Foreign Intelligence Operational Techniques ("Legal" Residency System)', 18 May 1955, NAA, A6283, folder 1, item 4104669, 129–49.

109. 'Operation Cabin 12', 11 April 1954, NAA, A6283, folder 14, item 4104675, 15.

110. ASIO memo, 12 May 1954, NAA, A6283, folder 1, item 4104669, 99; duplicate in NAA, A6283, folder 14, item 4104675, 34. The US VENONA decryption program had identified the code word ENORMOZ by the late 1940s as referring to the US Manhattan Project. Kartseva remembered the same code word as describing the equivalent programme in Australia.

111. 'Memorandum for Counsel', 9 May 1954, NAA, A6283, folder number 14, item 4104675, 24.

112. ASIO memo, 13 April 1954, NAA, A6283, folder 1, item 4104669, 94; 'Questions Raised by Mr Richards about Burgess and Maclean', 6 April 1954, NAA, A6283, folder 1, item 4104669, 33; ASIO memo, 13 April 1954, NAA, A6283, folder 1, item 4104669, 93–4. See also SIS telegrams from Canberra to London, 7 and 9 April 1954, TNA, KV 2/3440, serials 74a and 85a.

113. See, for example, Percy Hoskins, 'Maclean: Petrov Tells: The Full Story of Vanished Diplomats Sent to Britain', *Daily Express* (London), 28 April 1954.

114. Extract from ASIO source report, 29 August 1951, NAA, A6117, folder 7, item 12037437, serial 15. 'Meer Israilevitch Neplokh', 15 June 1955, NAA, A6283, folder 11, item 4199158, 38–9.

115. Extract from ASIO source report, 12 November 1951, NAA, A6117, folder 7, item 12037437, serial 41.

116. 'Translation and Interpretation of Document E.12.', 6 June 1952, NAA, A6283, folder 1, item 4104669, 12–13.

117. Andrew and Mitrokhin, *The Sword and the Shield*, 167.

118. Mahar, *Shattered Illusions*, 86.

119. Petrov and Petrov, *Empire of Fear*, 75.

120. 'Mrs Petrov's Statement Concerning Her Past Intelligence History',

15 May 1954, NAA, A6283, folder 14, item 4104675, 37–41; also in TNA, KV 5/107, serial 96a; an extract also in TNA, KV 5/83, serial 99a.

121. Rastvorov, 'Red Fraud and Intrigue in the Far East', 182.
122. ASIO memo, 14 April 1954, NAA, A6283, folder 1, item 4104669, 96.
123. 441st CIC Detachment Agent report, 12 May 1954, NARA, RG 319, Entry A1 314B, Box 716.
124. CIC investigative report, 'TAKAMORE Shigeru', 7 January 1955, NARA, RG 319, Entry A1 314B, Box 716, Takamore file.
125. CIC investigative report, 'TAKAMORE Shigeru', 11 January 1955.
126. CIC investigative report, 'TAKAMORE Shigeru', 18 December 1954 and 31 January 1955.
127. CIC investigative report, 'HIGURASHI Nobinuri', 10 November 1954.
128. CIC investigative report, 'TAKAMORE Shigeru', 7 January 1955.
129. Deriabin and Gibney, *The Secret World*, 188.
130. CIA Memo, 'Debriefing of Peter Deryabin Concerning Operation ZEPPELIN', 6 February 1964 (CIA FOIA site).
131. CIA Memorandum for the Record, 'Heinrich MUELLER, last Chief of the Gestapo, Viktor ABAKUMOV, et al', 18 November 1971 (CIA FOIA site).
132. Deriabin and Gibney, *The Secret World*, 189–92.
133. 'Mrs Petrov's Statement Concerning Her Past Intelligence History', enclosure to UK High Commissioner to Canberra memo, 7 June 1954, TNA, KV 5/107, serial 96a.
134. SIS report on Activities of Soviet Legation in Stockholm, 8 May 1946, TNA, KV 2/3439, serial 1a; Report on Vladimir Mikhailovich Petrov, 9 November 1950, TNA, KV 2/3439, serial 4a; SIS telegram to SLO Australia, 8 November 1950, TNA, KV 2/3429, serial 3a, 4a.
135. Surveillance report, 29 August 1945, Swedish National Archives, Säkerhetspolisen, P5279, löp. nr. 1, 1.
136. Security Police memo, 4 May 1946, Säkerhetspolisen, P5279, löp. nr. 2, 7.
137. Security Police memo, 22 April 1947, Säkerhetspolisen, P5279, löp. nr. 2.
138. Security Police memo, 'Report of visits to Göteborg on 21/4 1947 6:35 – 22/4 1947 22:40 by Russia legation member Vladimir

Petrov, born 15/2 1907', 23 April 1947, Säkerhetspolisen, P5279, löp. nr. 2, 31–7.

139. Petrov and Petrov, *Empire of Fear*, 176–83.

140. Ibid. 183–5.

141. Yermolayev, 'Шпионскими Тропами – По Нашей Земле' ('Via Spy Trails on Our Soil'), part one of three-part series, 'Тайная Битва Спецслужб' ('Secret Battle of Special Services'), *Мурманский Вестник* (*Murmansk Chronicle*), 15 June 2005, published online at <http://www.mvestnik.ru/shwpgn.asp?pid=200506152109> (last accessed 13 March 2020).

142. Swedish State Police debriefing report, 18 August 1954, SUK Hemliga Archivet, F4, Volume 11, 1 5.

143. 'KGB Wanted List', Entry number 27.

144. Memo for the Secretary of Defense, 'Policy on Defectors', 26 September 1950, NARA, RG 59, Entry A1 1583D, Box 117.

145. JIC report, JIC (49)107, 21 February 1950, TNA, CAB 301/136.

146. 'Effects of Recent Soviet Defections and Desertions', TNA, KV 5/107, serial 89a.

147. Political cartoon from the French magazine *Verité*, reprinted in *The Washington Post*, 1 June 1954, 15.

148. 'Intrigue in the Arctic: Revelations in Spy Trial', *The Times*, 1 June 1954.

Conclusion

This book has compiled all available information from and about Soviet intelligence and security service defectors up to the purge that followed Stalin's death. It has used the revelations and personal backgrounds of one-hundred officers with access to Soviet intelligence information to explore the insights that defectors provided into Stalin's closed political system. These officers represented political, S&T, and military intelligence; covert action and assassinations; border guards; internal security; political investigations; forced-labour camp administration; and finance specialisations. Their aggregate information spanning these fields and time provides valuable insights into Soviet national security decision-making. The result is a detailed picture of threat perceptions and national security priorities from the Bolshevik revolution to 1954.

Several major themes thread through each of the five groups of defectors, and these themes reflect the priorities and focus of Soviet intelligence and state security, and thus Soviet national security, throughout this period. First, the motivations that led intelligence officers to defect provide insights into the anxieties and pressures that state security officers were feeling. Second, the vetting standards that intelligence and state security organisations applied to recruiting and hiring employees are an indicator of stability and crisis within the system. And finally, the threats that the Soviet intelligence and state security system was tasked to counter show evolving priorities of the Soviet national security system overall. This conclusion chapter analyses those three themes that cut across all of the five chronological groups.

Evolution of Motivations

Motivations for defection changed over time among the five groups described in this study. In modern literature, the motivation to commit espionage is often described in terms of the acronym MICE – money, ideology, compromise, and ego.[1] Although these four factors were often present in the defectors described herein, other fundamental factors drove them to break with the Soviet Union. These factors and their evolution over time are a reflection of the environment within the Soviet national security establishment at the time, and thus provide some insights into that environment.

The motivation for defecting among members of the first group of defectors from 1924 to 1930 was often based on dissatisfaction with the people that the new Bolshevik regime was attracting. Defectors described their associates as being coarse, vulgar, and sycophantic; they described hypocrites who claimed to believe in Marxism–Leninism, but who still enjoyed the luxuries of the capitalist world. Among those who never joined the party, and who were thus more inclined to see its faults, this was not surprising. Sipelgas, for example, wrote of Soviet officials spending time in expensive nightclubs with beautiful women on their arms. He wrote: 'What if I sent a photo to the Moscow "Pravda" and showed the hoodwinked proletariat how the military representative of the Workers and Peasant Army "lives and works".'[2] Sobolev described how чистки ('cleansings') gradually stripped the party of sincere members and replaced them with 'enviers, loafers, and grabbers, the party is more and more filled with people very low in moral terms . . . who came to the party just for the "rank"'.[3] Stefens complained that the OGPU attracted losers and dropouts into its ranks, and their behaviour reflected the unrefined nature of the recruits. Women were especially vulnerable to supervisors' whims: Stefens related a situation where one of his supervisors, a gloomy, brutal man, would walk through the office, point to a female clerk, and say, 'You are coming to my place today.' Kiselev, who conducted operations inside a prison camp, describes OGPU personnel as brutal and having no interest in prisoners' welfare, even taking joy at making them suffer, but also attempting to hide evidence of their brutality from the outside world.[4]

Karpov, who probably served as a finance specialist, also described a lack of accountability within the OGPU, which led to substantial financial irregularities among intelligence officers. The lack of accountability originated when the Bolshevik regime authorised the Red Army to 'requisition' private property for Army use due to a scarcity of funds available to pay troops during the Civil War. The Red Army turned the stolen property into cash by selling it abroad, creating a thriving but illegal business. The OPGU was eventually forced to confront this problem, causing significant discontent among the troops who benefited from it.[5] Some of these descriptions could be influenced by the anti-Bolshevik sentiment among the Russian émigrés in Paris at the time. However, the consistency of the stories is notable.

More significant among the early defectors were those who began their careers as Bolshevik loyalists, but who lost their faith in the system before 1930 due to the same dislike of their fellow Bolsheviks. Dzevaltovskiy called his associates venal and self-centred.[6] Dumbadze claims that the first cracks in his idealistic view of Bolshevism began to form while he was participating in ChK interrogations and summary executions.[7] In Tbilisi and Poti he described the extreme behaviour of some OGPU officers and Party officials, who created further doubts in his mind about the justness of the Bolshevik system. Dumbadze noted an OGPU executioner named Shulman, who used cocaine to dull his senses while fulfilling his deadly assignments.[8] Arutyunov discussed the love triangles, embezzlement, and laziness that typified Soviet life abroad. He especially highlighted extramarital affairs, describing animosity and intrigue surrounding the few women assigned abroad, which often led to recalls to Moscow for inappropriate behaviour.[9] In each of these cases, officers who had joined the Bolshevik party as young, enthusiastic devotees became disenchanted enough to defect, partially motivated by the intolerable behaviour of their fellow Bolsheviks.

Among *Yezhovshchina*-era defectors, the motivation was different. They survived the early Bolshevik years without losing their enthusiasm; in some cases they may have been among the people that early defectors found distasteful. The decision to defect among the *Yezhovshchina*-era defectors was driven by two fundamental factors: a feeling of betrayal of the Leninist ideals they had fought to establish, and a fear for their lives.

As noted in Chapter 2, Poretskiy, Ginsberg, Graff, and Helfand all publicly expressed the view that Stalin had abandoned true Marxism–Leninism and taken a path of opportunism and authoritarianism that replaced ideology with Stalin. Graff, Ginsberg, and Helfand had been early Bolsheviks, joining the Party before 1920. When they defected, they did not shed their Marxist–Leninist beliefs immediately, but they contrasted a purist interpretation of their world philosophy with Stalin's and found Stalin's lacking.

Fear of execution was also prominent among the members of this group, most of whom were senior officials in their organisation and thus were close to other senior officials who had fallen victim to the purge. Feldbin claimed that doubts about his service to the Soviet Union began as early as 1936, when he gained a first-hand view of Stalin's pursuit of old Bolsheviks. But in July 1937, Feldbin's cousin, Zinoviy Borisovich Katsnelson, who was a senior NKVD officer with the rank commissar of state security second rank and Feldbin's mentor during his early career, was arrested. He was executed in March 1938.[10] Simultaneous with Katsnelson's arrest, Feldbin received a cable from Moscow warning him that the NKVD had learned of a plot to kidnap Feldbin in Spain. NKVD headquarters informed him that ten bodyguards from Moscow would be coming to Spain to protect his life. Feldbin, already frightened by his cousin's and many other colleagues' arrests, suspected that the bodyguards themselves were the real plot against his life, and cabled back informing Moscow that he already had a bodyguard made up of Spanish communists. But he decided to reinforce his security detail with a dozen 'tough' German communists whom he felt he could trust more than local Spanish guards or an NVKD-supplied security detail.[11] Then in June 1938, Feldbin received a message summoning him to a meeting on board a Soviet ship in port at Antwerp, Belgium. He was convinced that the invitation was a trap, and he decided that his time had come to escape. He began to travel to France as if he would continue to Belgium, collected his wife and daughter, who were already staying in France away from the war zone, boarded a ship for Canada, and arrived on 21 July 1938.[12]

Lyushkov was a senior NKVD officer, and nearly all of his peers had been purged by the time he defected. He supervised purge operations himself, such as 'ethnic operations' through which over 135,000 Korean residents from the Soviet Far East were forcibly resettled to Kazakhstan and Uzbekistan, and 25,000 Chinese residents were resettled to Xinjiang beginning in December 1937.[13] Lyushkov never vocalised doubts in the system while he was in it, even being elected to the Supreme Soviet in December 1937.[14] He was carrying a Supreme Soviet identification card when he surrendered to Japanese forces.[15] But in spring 1938, he received a dreaded message informing him of an impending transfer to Moscow; he fully understood the implications.[16]

Helfand felt a circle begin to tighten around him after the Molotov–Ribbentrop Pact. He had gained an anti-German reputation in Rome, and the German government attempted as early as April to persuade Molotov to recall him to remove what they saw as an obstacle to Italian–Soviet, and hence Italian–German relations. The Soviet government eventually came to Germany's side and sent Helfand a recall notice in June 1940.[17] He defected instead. His wife Sonia later wrote that his flight was motivated by fear that his recall was a preface to being purged, as was the case with many of his associates.[18]

Different extreme circumstances beget different motivations for World War II Era defectors, although in some cases they expressed anti-Stalinism similarly to *Yezhovshchina*-era defectors. Most of the World War II-era defectors were captured on the battlefield and held in German prisoner-of-war camps. They realised that their chance of surviving the brutal conditions in the camps was greatly improved if they contributed their knowledge and skills to the German cause. It was not necessarily the case, however, that their act of collaboration with Hitler's Germany meant they had adopted Nazism. Most of them viewed themselves not as pro-Nazi, but anti-Stalin, although in contrast to the *Yezhovshchina*-era defectors, several expressed not Marxism–Leninism, but pre-Leninist socialism as their ideology. Less is known of those in the World War II-era group who defected after the defeat of

Germany, but a sense of antipathy towards the Stalinist regime was still visible in defectors like Granovskiy, Gouzenko, Mondich, and Volkov. Interestingly, Pines expressed views about the Soviet officials with whom he worked that sounded much like the complaints made by pre-1931 defectors – he viewed his colleagues as being lazy and more concerned about accumulating Western goods than fighting Nazis.[19]

Early Cold War defectors, from 1947 to 1951, expressed yet another reason for anti-Stalinism, which was a clear indicator of state security priorities after the war. In line with Deryabin's saying that the 'god of state security' was in counterintelligence after the war, several Early Cold War defectors noted a shift from fighting a Nazi enemy, which they viewed as honourable, to fighting the Soviet people themselves, which they did not. Defectors noted that the Soviet leadership was concerned about shielding the Soviet population, especially state security officers, from the West's relative economic prosperity and political influences. Their efforts were spent investigating Soviet soldiers who were fraternising with German women and allegations that Soviet soldiers were considering defection. Suspicion of Soviet citizens led several defectors to question the direction Soviet state security took after Germany's defeat and to complain that the Soviet government viewed its own people as the enemy, despite the sacrifices they had made during the war. This was articulated most clearly by KGB Wanted List number 278, who claimed that the MGB was not concerned with combatting espionage but instead with 'persecuting the people who spoke the truth',[20] and Baklanov, who contrasted the mission of a wartime chekist and a peacetime chekist. He felt that forcing Soviet citizens to repatriate and dooming them to Soviet prison camps was more than he could stand.[21] Several of the defectors in this group fell victim to that internal security emphasis. Rebrov, Vorontsov, Goldfarb, Harvard 525, and possibly Salimanov were at risk of being arrested themselves in the more intense counterintelligence environment of the late 1940s.

Finally, the Post-Stalin Purge group of 1953 and 1954 experienced a return of the fear that had driven *Yezhovshchina*-era defectors to leave. Association with Beriya's network of MVD officers darkened future prospects for Burlutskiy, Rastvorov,

Shorokhov, and Kartseva. Shorokhov was directly threatened when the ambassador in Canberra accused him of forming a 'Beriya group' in the embassy to undermine the authority of the Party.[22] Rastvorov stated, 'My own life was profoundly influenced by the Beriya crisis.'[23] Pavlov, although he was more junior than others in this group, noted a state of 'semi-panic' in his MVD office after Beriya's arrest.[24]

Another motivation may have also prevailed in the Post-Stalin Purge group related to the increased use of illegals, particularly those with native foreign language and cultural proficiency, like Brik, Lindström, and KGB Wanted List number 27. Their ability to melt into their background did not inoculate them from the lures of the outside world, and in fact likely even increased their draw.

In each of these time periods, other personal factors contributed to defectors' decisions to break with the Soviet Union. Many of them had suffered assaults on their egos or were undergoing personal crises like failing marriages, the death of family members, transgressions of rules, and others. As a CIA officer noted in 1954, many defectors exhibited proximate personal motivations like fear of demotion or punishment, recognition of the contrast between life in the West and life in the Soviet Union, attachment to an acquaintance met abroad, or dissatisfaction with one's job and demoralisation.[25] These proximate issues added fuel to the above trends to persuade defectors that life outside the Soviet Union would be safer and more comfortable than remaining.

Fluctuating Vetting Standards

The lives and revelations of Soviet intelligence officer defectors provide insights into Soviet hiring and vetting practices for sensitive state security positions, which fluctuated widely from very tight to very loose. These fluctuations in turn reflected periods of stability and crisis in the Soviet system. Initially, after the Bolsheviks seized power, individuals hired for Soviet state security positions had varied backgrounds, ranging from ardent Bolsheviks and Socialist Revolutionaries, to former tsarist officials and even anti-Bolsheviks who were vulnerable to coercion. The majority of the individuals in the first two chronologic groups joined a Soviet intelligence and security organisation during Lenin's lifetime, and their diversity reflected the Bolsheviks' urgent need for people to stabilise the Bolshevik hold on Russia, regardless of their background. This also begat the institution known as political commissars, many of whom were selected from among young zealots like Dzevaltovskiy, Arutyunov, and Dumbadze, whose job was to prevent non-Bolsheviks in the military and government from turning against their new masters.

In the decade between Lenin's death in 1924 and the assassination of Sergey Mironovich Kirov in 1934, the NKVD, Razvedupr, and their predecessor organisations recruited new officers either from among *seksoty* or by patronage. This was especially true after the Soviet Union enacted stronger measures to prevent defection in 1929. Former tsarist officials were gradually culled from the ranks of Soviet government organisations through a series of mini-purges and replaced with more strictly vetted personnel for whom an already trusted employee could vouch. A few indispensable tsarist-era specialists who conformed to the Bolshevik line remained, among whom was Sobolev. But new officers fit the stricter criteria. Among these were Volodarskiy, who probably worked as a co-opted Soviet specialist in Great Britain before he was recruited into the NKVD; and Shorokhov and Kartseva, who were recommended by other state security officers.

According to Zhigunov, Kirov's assassination precipitated renewed purges of less loyal individuals, including many who had been active during Lenin's lifetime, leading eventually to the *Yezhovshchina*. NKVD recruitment from that time drew primarily from the Komsomol and Party organisations, which identified promising young students and professionals and drafted them for NKVD duty, from which there was no refusal.[26] This accompanied a stiffening of vetting procedures for state security positions that disqualified anyone with a 'kulak' or tsarist family history. Zhigunov, Yesenina, Petrov, and KGB Wanted List number 367 were probably among this select group of young recruits.

The *Yezhovshchina* and the crisis it created briefly interrupted this period of stricter standards, temporarily forcing the NKVD to lower the bar to replace thousands of employees who had been arrested and executed. Anokhin indicated that when he joined the NKVD in 1937, the screening criteria for new NKVD trainees were less strict and previously unacceptable individuals were hired – Anokhin himself benefited from this brief lax period because the NKVD did not thoroughly investigate his personal history.[27] Denisov was similarly fortunate, having been recruited into the NKVD despite his father's arrests. He claimed that new recruits during this time fell into three broad categories:

- Party fanatics who were blindly obedient and willing to do anything, even commit violent NKVD acts, to further the interests of the Party;
- Careerists who used the NKVD to advance their own personal situations, even with the realisation that NKVD acts were not in the interests of the Russian people; these people realised that they could not turn back from the NKVD to become regular citizens, because they had become hated chekists;
- Psychologically abnormal, sadistic people, and people who were too stupid to survive in any other job but want to escape their low social status.[28]

It is unclear in which of these groups Denisov counted himself. Both Chikalov and Lyushkov noted that Stalin replaced purged leaders with young, green officers who were fiercely loyal to Stalin and owed their careers to him.[29] However, recruits with questionable backgrounds were also among the thousands of individuals who were hired into the NKVD at this time.

A renewed tightening of vetting standards followed Beriya's ascent to chief of the NKVD in 1938. He ordered another purge and directed the recruitment of competent officers exclusively from Party ranks, many of whom were technical specialists with university degrees. But Beriya's brief strictness again waned when hundreds of thousands of Soviet soldiers, intelligence officers, and state security personnel were killed or captured on the battlefield in the first few months of World War II in the Soviet Union. This led to more mass recruitments, which, compounded by the hasty relocation of the NKVD's investigative records from Moscow to Sverdlovsk during the summer of 1941, when Moscow was under threat of capture, prevented thorough background investigations. Emergency investigations granted clearances to many individuals with tainted family backgrounds, like Goldfarb and Granovskiy, and allowed the re-employment of others who had been arrested during the *Yezhovshchina*, like Bessonov, Artemyev, and Chikalov.

Crisis hiring accelerated as Soviet forces occupied territories abandoned by a retreating Germany. The NKVD during this time especially sought linguists, many of whom had backgrounds, including collaboration with anti-Soviet forces during the war, that would typically land them in a forced labour camp rather than in a position with sensitive security access. Peciulionis, Mondich, Vorontsov, KGB Wanted List numbers 75, 107, 304, and possibly an NKVD officer who defected in November 1945 known to the OSS as 'Vladimir',[30] benefited from chaos in MGB files that allowed them to hide their anti-Soviet backgrounds and serve as interpreters at the end of the war.

This wartime hiring is clearly manifested in the average ages of intelligence officer defectors in each of the five periods in this study. Overall, the average age of intelligence officer defectors is about thirty-three years old. However, from the latter part of World War II to the late 1940s, the average age of defectors was only about twenty-six. The World War II period is divided into two segments in Figure 6.1 to show this age difference.

As the dust settled in the Soviet Union after the war, the MGB began to restore order to its records and to integrate Gestapo files captured in Germany that identified thousands of wartime German collaborators. According to Goldfarb, this allowed the MGB to revisit the background investigations of Soviet officers in the Group of Soviet Forces in Germany in late 1948 and early 1949, leading to a special purge and recall of a number of officers.[31] This included Goldfarb himself, as well as Vorontsov and possibly KGB Wanted List number 55.

Many of the younger recruits had strong linguistic skills, either because they had been born in places where non-Russian languages were predominant, or because they had been in German prison camps during the war (see Chapter 3). Linguistic skills

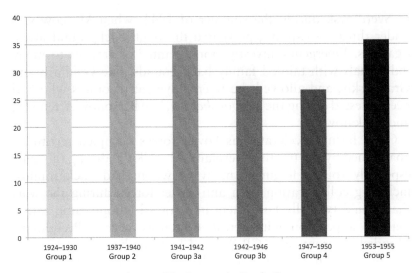

Figure 6.1 Average Ages of Defectors in Each Group

continued to be a vulnerability for Soviet intelligence services long after the war, and later defectors like Yevgeniy Yevgenyevich Runge, Reino Häyhänen, and Karlo Tuomi were initially recruited for their language proficiency and their ability to operate freely in a foreign environment.

The fluctuation of vetting standards for sensitive intelligence and state security positions and the types of people those organisations recruited were indicators of the pressure that the Soviet leadership was experiencing at the moment. The graver the sense of crisis and urgency to increase numbers, the lower the standards. When stability returned, new purges often ensued that removed undesirables who had slipped in during the crisis. The periods of laxity likely reflected the overall emphasis that the Soviet system placed on quantity over quality in relation to meeting centrally dictated goals and targets, even to the detriment of security.

Soviet Threat Calculations and the Development of the 'Main Enemy' Concept

A theme that threads through all five groups in this study is the concept of threat perceptions, reflected in testimony about the threats against which the Soviet system applied its intelligence and state security capabilities. This was manifested through the material that defectors revealed as well as through the countries to which they chose to surrender themselves. These factors combined provide an excellent window into the evolution of Soviet national security thinking. Defectors also provide greater nuance on the question of Soviet threat calculus than has often appeared in published literature.

Herbert Romerstein and Stanislav Levchenko – a Soviet intelligence officer defector – begin their 1989 book *The KGB against the 'Main Enemy'* with the premise, 'The Soviet Intelligence Service has always considered the United States its ultimate *glavnyy vrag* (the main enemy).'[32] Oleg Gordievsky narrows the time scope somewhat, and claims in his 1990 book that the United States became the 'main enemy' at the end of the World War II.[33] However, although the label 'main enemy' clearly applied to the United States when Levchenko defected in 1979 and Gordievsky defected in 1985, none of the defectors in this study used the phrase 'main enemy'. Instead, they provided a more nuanced perspective on Soviet priorities and national security threat perceptions over the history of the Soviet Union, showing an evolution of what eventually came to be the 'main enemy'.

Russian author Sergey Chertoprud assessed that before World War II there was no clear concept of the 'main enemy', but that Soviet intelligence prioritised operations against any country that represented a military threat.[34] Defector revelations over the first two decades of the Soviet Union support this assessment. Defector information showed that the Soviets' perception of threats evolved from White military forces during the civil war, to Russian émigré organisations abroad, to the foreign governments that the Soviet Union perceived as sponsoring them. The choice of France as the destination of most defectors in the early period reflected the threat that Soviet state security perceived from the prominent anti-Soviet émigré groups that were headquartered there. Many of these early defectors surrendered not to a country, but to an anti-Soviet émigré cause, and no single country in the 1920s was the equivalent of the later concept of the 'main enemy' that drew the bulk of Soviet intelligence and national security attention.

Eventually, threat perceptions settled on Great Britain, which presented the most potent threat to Soviet influence in Europe and Asia in the 1930s. Six of the eight *Yezhovshchina*-era defectors ran operations in and against Great Britain. According to Ginzberg, from 1935, Stalin considered the Soviet Union to be at war with Great Britain, and Stalin directed both the NKVD and Razvedupr to prepare for war.[35] Germany and France followed Britain in the Soviet's threat calculation to varying degrees, either because they were technological competitors, because they continued to be safe havens for anti-Soviet émigré groups, or because they were the bastions of anti-Soviet propaganda, although, as noted earlier, operations against Germany were suspended for a brief time in 1936–7 while the Soviet Union was deliberating on negotiations with Germany. Contrary to Romerstein's and Levchenko's assertion, defectors' revelations indicated that the United States factored little in Soviet intelligence priorities in the 1920s and early 1930s, except as a source of false travel documents and a target of clandestine influence operations directed towards obtaining diplomatic recognition.

Soviet intelligence officers' attention was distracted in the mid- to late 1930s by the *Yezhovshchina*, during which purged officials were often accused of espionage on behalf of Germany, Great Britain, Japan, or Poland. The United States rose marginally in Soviet intelligence interest in the 1930s primarily because of its technological advances. However, the United States began to number among anti-Soviet forces in the late 1930s, and Shorokhov described the Soviet effort in China in the late 1930s as a 'dramatic purge', condemning to death any British, American, and other anti-Soviet elements.[36] However, *Yezhovshchina*-era defectors' choice of the United States as a destination was probably more an indicator that they viewed the United States as a benign and safe location, rather than an enemy that could use their information against the Soviet Union, at least until Ginsburg's death in 1941 – this was evidenced by the fact the US government did not thoroughly debrief Poretskiy, Graff was initially hired only as a Russian translator, and Feldbin provided no information to the US government until 1953.

Soviet priorities quickly turned to Germany after 22 June 1941, the first time any country truly earned the label 'main enemy' in the Soviet calculation. Soviet intelligence attention and counter-intelligence resources aligned with military campaigns to slow the advances of German troops into Soviet territory and eventually roll them back. But Germany did not last long as the exclusive 'main enemy'. Soviet intelligence organisations turned their attention to collecting US, British, and other allies' information beginning as early as 1943. Soviet successes on the battlefield, combined with suspicions of Western intentions, prompted a partial redirection of Soviet intelligence resources towards the wartime allies. These suspicions were at least partially driven by Marxist–Leninist dogma that viewed the capitalist world as an eternal enemy, even if it was necessary to enter into a temporary alliance with one capitalist bloc to fight another. The NKVD established its first full-time *rezidenturas* in Canada and Australia in 1943. Baklanov noted that the NKGB foreign intelligence directorate also 'discovered' America on a large scale for the first time in about 1943 and had dispatched numerous agents to collect intelligence about the United States.[37]

During the war and in the early post-war years, the Soviet Union began to define that capitalist world as the 'Anglo-American bloc', in which the United States and Great Britain played the joint leading role, with France, Canada, and Australia being secondary. A number of defectors from the mid- to late 1940s cited the Soviet Union's merging of the United States and Great Britain into a single threat. Grishin referenced a visit in 1948 to Wismut by a visitor from Moscow who connected uranium mining with the Soviet competition against the United States and Great Britain: 'The more ore we turn over to the Soviet Union, the stronger our "defensive capacities" will become and the easier it will be for our diplomats to deal with the Anglo-American imperialists.'[38] Goldfarb reported that during the summer of 1948,

MGB headquarters transmitted a message to all Soviet state security offices inside the Soviet Union and in military units, including in Soviet occupation forces in Germany, censuring counterintelligence officers for their lack of vigilance in pursuing and neutralising foreign intelligence threats.[39] Foreign intelligence services of the 'imperialist' powers, it said, particularly American and British, actively used embassy officials and journalists for intelligence purposes. The message ordered Soviet counterintelligence officers to relook all of their agent networks. Abakumov closed the message with, 'It is imperative to reach such a situation in which not a single foreigner could have free and unobserved access to any corner of the USSR.'[40] Vorontsov reported that, in the absence of more accurate information, the MGB suspected many individuals of being 'Anglo-American' agents without further specificity. He mentioned the investigation of an individual named Grimpe who fled to the western zones of Germany and was received by American or British intelligence in the West; Vorontsov did not know which.[41] According to defector revelations, the United States and Great Britain shared a joint position in the Soviet Union's threat calculation in the 1940s, rather than either of them being a unitary 'main enemy'.

This converges with other materials that have become available since the dissolution of the Soviet Union. Soviet foreign policy experts placed blame on the 'Anglo-American bloc' for starting the Cold War, claiming conversely that Soviet policies had created 'democratic regimes . . . which maintain relations with the Soviet Union on the basis of friendship and mutual aid agreements'.[42] Similarly, a training manual for Soviet KGB officers published in 1977 followed the theme of a combined capitalist bloc in which the United States and Great Britain shared the leading role in 'conducting a policy of "cold war"', and tasks assigned to Soviet state security organs were directed equally against the United States and Great Britain.[43]

The intensification of intelligence activities directed against the Soviet Union's wartime allies implied a less peace-loving Soviet intent. A Soviet 'cold war' mindset already existed even before war in Europe was over, and grew in the first year after the war. The statements of at least six defectors, who independently noted hearing about the coming war with capitalism, underlined this perception. As early as 1942, Akhmedov's supervisor told him that the World War II alliance would only last until the defeat of Germany and that the Soviet Union would eventually fight the British and Americans.[44] Deryabin indicated that his counterintelligence training in 1944 focused on Germany, followed closely by Great Britain, France, and the United States, and Deryabin quoted his instructor as saying, 'Remember that your allies today are your enemies tomorrow.'[45] Mondich recalled his commander congratulating his SMERSH unit on the successful defeat of the Nazis, followed by a warning that for Soviet counterintelligence, the war was not over.[46] Baklanov similarly wrote about the mood in the NKVD at the end of the war, when his unit commander told the troops that, while for some the war was over, for chekists it was not.[47] Gouzenko claimed that the Soviet Union was preparing for World War III even before World War II ended.[48] And Pečiulionis's NKVD training in 1946 included similar predictions that the Soviet Union would soon be at war with Great Britain and the United States.[49]

Granovskiy's training as an illegal in 1943 included reading books about espionage in the West to prepare him for his ultimate target: Western Europe or the United States. Granovskiy quotes Sudoplatov as saying, 'You have an interesting duty to perform, Captain Granovskiy, as soon as we can be sure that you can be trusted. You may be sent abroad to remain there for years, maybe all your life, as a permanent agent of the People's Commissariat of State Security. You will have the chance to win great honors.'[50] Correspondingly, when Granovskiy was assigned to Czechoslovakia in early 1945, he began preparations for a long-term mission to penetrate Czech society, and from there to become a 'refugee' and eventually immigrate to the United States.[51]

Over the five years following the war, the United States gradually grew in importance as a threat, overshadowing Great Britain in the 'Anglo-American bloc'. Rastvorov perceived growing antipathy towards the United States during his first tour in Japan in 1946, resulting in increased suspicion of Americans.[52] This corresponds with other events occurring at the same time, including a telegram from the Soviet ambassador to the United States, Nikolay

Vasilyevich Novikov. Novikov wrote in September 1946, 'US foreign policy has been characterised in the post-war period by a desire for world domination.' He contrasted that to Great Britain, which he indicated had been dealt strong blows from the war and faced enormous economic and political difficulties.[53] Russian historian Vladimir Pechatnov assessed that Novikov's views reflected the overall sentiments in the Soviet foreign policy establishment, and that high-ranking officials who did not share this black-and-white picture of the world lost influence.[54] Chertoprud accredited this change to the looming threat of nuclear war, in which the United States held the upper hand.[55] Novikov's telegram analysed the situation similarly, as did Baklanov, who wrote that America's possession of an atomic weapon caused a great deal of Soviet concern and was the topic of propaganda spread throughout Soviet forces.[56]

The phrase 'main enemy' began to appear in relation to the United States specifically in about 1950. Chertoprud assessed that the Committee of Information (*Комитет Информации*; KI) concluded in February 1950 to 'consider intelligence against the USA to be among the most important missions of all operational directorates'. Then, in March 1951, all *rezidenturas* were ordered to prioritise collection against the United States as the 'main enemy' and to review all agent networks to identify opportunities to penetrate US targets. This included a reinvigoration of illegal *rezidenturas* directed against the United States in response to the increasingly hostile counterintelligence environment there.[57]

Chertoprud's assertions align with defectors' revelations. By the time Shorokhov, Kartseva, and Rastvorov defected, US targets weighed heavily in their operations. When Rastvorov arrived in Japan in July 1950, recruiting American sources and Japanese sources with access to US information was a priority for the Tokyo *rezidentura*. As soon as he arrived in Japan Rastvorov was directed to target Americans for recruitment or elicitation of 'loose talk'.[58] The Tokyo *rezidentura* was instructed in fall 1951 to recontact an American who had offered classified information three years earlier but who had been dropped because he had demanded too much money. The specific requirement was to procure a copy of the US–Japan peace treaty.[59] The 27 September

1952 circular that Shorokhov received from Moscow detailing requirements for collecting information about foreign intelligence and counterintelligence services similarly emphasised the United States.[60] Additionally, the choice of the United States as the recipient country for the majority of defectors after the war indicated the new prominence that the United States held in Soviet threat perceptions.

From the opposite direction, the CIA began using the concept of a Soviet 'main enemy' at least as early as 1952 to persuade non-communist allies to maintain their vigilance against Soviet propaganda. A CIA summary of the 19th Party Congress, which took place from 5 to 14 October 1952, indicated that the Congress singled out the United States as the 'main enemy' and the primary target of the united front of world communist parties. The Congress reportedly concluded that Party propaganda was to emphasise the leading role that the United States played in the capitalist world, which according to the CIA was 'aimed, obviously, at arousing hatred for the US and suspicions of US intentions towards its allies'. The CIA instructed its stations around the world to share the summary with liaison services to warn them, 'the Communist order of the day is to split the Western Alliance. Friendly western services should be brought into line to stave off the attack.'[61] Thus, by 1952, the 'main enemy' concept was of propaganda value for both sides of the Cold War ideological conflict.

There were some topics about which Soviet intelligence officer defectors were not the best sources. These included Soviet recruitment of agents with access to US political information before World War II. Gouzenko provided ambiguous leads about a penetration of the US diplomatic establishment, but other non-intelligence officer defectors like Elizabeth Bentley and Whittaker Chambers were more knowledgeable. However, even these other sources provided information that was consistent with the revelations of defectors in this study. The topics about which the Soviet Union sought intelligence in the United States, according to these sources, aligned with the priorities identified by intelligence officers: science and technology information and intelligence about US policy towards the Soviet Union's primary targets, Great Britain and Germany.

In the broad sense, Soviet intelligence officer defectors gave unique insights into the closed Soviet decision-making system regarding the threats it faced, both internal and external, at a time when few other sources were available. They showed the evolving and growing priorities and reach of Soviet intelligence, beginning with the security of the new regime and broadening to manipulation of international partners and adversaries. They showed the initial Bolshevik emphasis on spreading revolution throughout the world, along with the challenges of executing that vision. They showed a gradual shift from internationalism to nationalism under Stalin, to the chagrin of Leninist purists, who fell victim to Stalin's power concentrating purges. They reported the shifting balance and interaction between internal and external threat perceptions, and the heavy focus on monitoring and mitigating suspected threats from among Soviet people themselves. Their information identified priority foreign adversaries, including Great Britain, France, and Germany, with Japan also factoring in before and during World War II, and the United States rising above the rest after the war. They made it clear that the Soviet Union planned for war against the capitalist powers even before Germany was defeated in World War II. In the final analysis, Soviet intelligence officer defectors' elite accesses to insider information were valuable in understanding the evolution of Soviet national security thinking.

Notes

1. David L. Charney and John A. Irvin, 'The Psychology of Espionage', *The Intelligencer*, vol. 22, no. 1 (Spring 2016), 71–7.
2. 'Notes of a Razvedupr Agent', 11 March 1930, 4.
3. A. Sobolev, 'Записки Невозвращенца' ('Notes of a Non-Returnee'), *Vozrozhdenie*, 17 May 1930, 2.
4. Kiselev, 'Death Camps', *Rul*, 4 October 1931.
5. *The Organisation of the GPU*, 6–8.
6. 'Развал Изнутри: Большевик Дзевалтовский Бежал из Советской России' ('Crumbling From Within: Bolshevik Dzevaltovskiy Escaped from Soviet Russia'), *Возрождение* (*Vozrozhdenie*), 14 November 1925, 1. 'Вечерние Известия' ('Evening News'), *Последние Новости* (*Latest News*), 14 November 1925, 1.

7. Ibid. 50–2.
8. Ibid. 60–4. See also (Igor Simbirtsev, *ВЧК в ленинской России. 1917–1922: В зареве революции* (*VChK in Lenin's Russia, 1917–1922: In the Glow of the Revolution*) (Moscow: Tsentropoligraf, 2008), which describes possibly the same Shulman, who eventually went insane.
9. See, for example, Agabekov, *The ChK at Work*, 72–3.
10. Petrov and Skorkin, *Who Led the NKVD 1934–1941*.
11. FBI Summary of Orlov's information provided to MI5 in Washington, dated 26 October 1953, 5, TNA, KV 2/2878, serial 9a.
12. Ibid.
13. Coox, 'The Lesser of Two Hells', Part I, 155–6.
14. US military attaché in Moscow, USSR, dispatch, 'Comments on Statements of Fugitive Generals', dated 1 August 1938, NARA, RG 165, Correspondence of the Military Intelligence Division Relating to General, Political, Economic, and Military Conditions in Russia and Soviet Union 1918–1941, MID number 2037-1997/9, microform series M-1443, roll 17.
15. Coox, 'The Lesser of Two Hells', Part I, 147.
16. Ibid. 159.
17. Weinberg, *Germany and the Soviet Union*, 92–6.
18. Biography of Helfand's wife titled 'Sonia Moore: A Dedicated Life In Art', The Bennett TheatreLab and Conservatory, available at <https://www.bennetttheatrelab.com/history#biographies> (last accessed 13 March 2020). Sonia died in 1995 at the age of ninety-three.
19. Pines's interrogation, US Forces Austria, Project SYMPHONY, file number LVX 231, dated 9 May 1946 (CIA FOIA cite).
20. 'Testimony of Eastern European Political Refugees of the Necessity of Fleeing Because of Intolerable Conditions Under Communism', US State Department, Division of Research for the Soviet Union and Eastern Europe, 19 February 1953, NARA, RG 59, Entry A1 5498, Box 28, Motivations, Case 7.
21. Romanov, *Nights Are Longest There*, 239–41.
22. Petrov and Petrov, *Empire of Fear*, 251–2.
23. Yuri A. Rastvorov, 'Beria's Plot', 21–2, undated typescript, HIA, Boris Nicolaevsky Collection, Box 295, folder 21 (microfilm reel 255).
24. CIA Report, '1. MVD Administration Data; 2. Miscellaneous Data on Resistance and on Military Installations', 18 August 1954 (CIA CREST).

25. CIA memo, 'Inducement of Soviet Defectors', 4 May 1954 (CIA FOIA site). The author's name is redacted.

26. Zhigunov, 'NKVD-VChK-OGPU-NKVD-NKBG-NKVD', 64–5.

27. HPSSS, Schedule B, vol. 1, Case 147, 4–5.

28. HPSSS, Schedule B, vol. 3, Case 105, 41–2.

29. Almazov, 'The Red Terror'; 'Interrogation of Liushkov G. S. November 1938', 6.

30. Cutler, *Counterspy*, xv–xxi, 100–3.

31. Rafael Ilych Goldfarb, 'Структура Советской Военной Контрразведки' ('Structure of Soviet Military Counterintelligence'), dated 19 December 1949, NARA, RG 319, Entry 134B, Box 236. An English translation of this document is HQ 66th CIC Det Memo, 'Counter Intelligence Directorate, Ministry of State Security, GOFG', R-M62-49, dated 17 February 1950, in NARA, RG 319, Entry 134A, Box 107.

32. Herbert Romerstein and Stanislav Levchenko, *The KGB Against the 'Main Enemy': How the Soviet Intelligence Service Operates against the United States* (Lexington, MA: Lexington Books, 1989), ix.

33. Andrew and Gordievsky, *KGB: The Inside Story*, 367.

34. Sergey Vadimovich Chertoprud, *Научно-техническая разведка от Ленина до Горбачева* (*Scientific and Technical Intelligence from Lenin to Gorbachev*) (Moscow: OLMA Media Group, 2002), 280.

35. MI5 Krivitsky Debriefing Notes, 3 and 10 February 1940, TNA, KV 2/804, serials 28a and 42a; MI5 Krivitsky Debriefing Notes, 2 February 1940, TNA, KV 2/804, serial 25a.

36. Petrov and Petrov, *Empire of Fear*, 59–66.

37. Romanov, *Nights Are Longest There*, 120.

38. Grishin, *Soviet Operation of Uranium Mines in Eastern Germany*, 11.

39. HICOG Frankfurt, 'Soviet Defector Interrogation Report (Sponge no. 5)', 21, NARA, RG 59, Central Decimal File 1950–1954, 761.00/2.650.

40. 'Directive from the Minister of State Security of the Union of SSR', translated in Headquarters 66th CIC Detachment debriefing report R-M57-49, 17 November 1949, NARA, RG 319, Entry 134B, Box 236, Goldfarb Volume 1.

41. 7970th CIC Group memo, 'MGB Interpreter – Progress Reports' nos 4 and 14, dated 30 September 2 and November 1948 respectively, NARA, RG 319, Entry 134B, Box 830, Vorontzov.

42. Telegram from Nikolai Novikov, Soviet Ambassador to the US,

to the Soviet Leadership, 27 September 1946, History and Public Policy Program Digital Archive, AVP SSSR, f. 06. op. 8, 45, 759, published in *Mezhdunarodnaya Zhizn* #11 (1990), 148–54.

43. Viktor Mikhailovich Chebrikov (managing ed.), *История Советских органов государственной безопасности: учебник* (*History of Soviet Organs of State Security: A Manual*) (Moscow: The Dzerzhinsky Higher Red Banner KGB School, 1977), 446–7, 454.

44. Akhmedov, *In and Out of Stalin's GRU*, 160.

45. Deriabin and Gibney, *The Secret World*, 63–6.

46. Sinevirsky, *SMERSH*, 144.

47. Romanov, *Nights Are Longest There*, 144.

48. SIS telegram, Ottawa to London, number 419, dated 22 March 1946; TNA, KV 2/1421, serial 157a.

49. Headquarters, Sub-Region Kassel, Counterintelligence Corps Region III memo, 8 March 1948, NARA, RG 319. Entry 134B, Box 600, Peciulionis.

50. Granovskiy, *I Was an NKVD Agent*, 143–4. See Chapter 5 for additional discussion of Sudoplatov's post-war plans.

51. Ibid. 200.

52. Rastvorov, 'Red Fraud and Intrigue in the Far East', 190.

53. Novikov telegram, 27 September 1946 (see n42 above).

54. Vladimir O. Pechatnov, 'The Soviet Union and the World', in Melvyn P. Leffler and Odd Arne Westad (eds), *The Cambridge History of the Cold War: Volume 1, Origins* (Cambridge: Cambridge University Press, 2012), 101.

55. Chertoprud, *Scientific and Technical Intelligence*, 280–1.

56. Romanov, *Nights Are Longest There*, 195–6.

57. Chertoprud, *Scientific and Technical Intelligence*, 280–1.

58. US Navy memo, 'Yuri Alessandrovich Rastovoro', 2 February 1954, NARA, RG 329, Entry A1 314B, box 628.

59. Rastvorov, 'Goodby to Red Terror', 50.

60. ASIO memo, 12 April 1954, NAA, A6283, folder 1, item 4104669, 92. A copy of the Moscow to Canberra telegram, 27 September 1952, is in TNA, KV 2/3477, Document A, A10.

61. CIA, Memo for All Stations Concerned, undated but late 1952 (CIA CREST).

Appendix A: Organisational Changes in Soviet Intelligence and State Security, 1918–1954

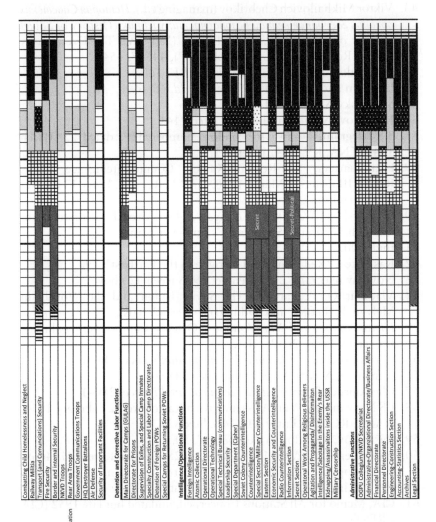

OGPU

GUGB/NKVD

NKVD

NKGB

SMERSH

MGB

Committee of Information

MVD

Combatting Child Homelessness and Neglect
Railway Militia
Transport (and Communications) Security
Fire Security
Border and internal Security
NKVD Troops
Rear Area Troops
Government Communications Troops
HQ Destroyer Battalions
Air Defense
Security of Important Facilities

Detention and Corrective Labor Functions
Main Directorate for Camps (GULAG)
Directorate for Prisons
Supervision of Exiles, and Special Camp Inmates
Specialty Construction and Labor Camp Directorates
Detention of Foreign POWs
Special Camps for Returning Soviet POWs

Intelligence/Operasional Functions
Foreign Intelligence
Atomic Collection
Operational Directorate
Operational Technology
Special Technical Bureau (communications)
Leadership Security
Special Department (Cipher)
Soviet Colony Counterintelligence
Counterintelligence
Special Section/Military Counterintelligence
Eastern Section
Economic Security and Counterintelligence
Radio Counterintelligence
Information Section
Secret Section
Operatonal Work Among Religious Believers
Agitation and Propaganda/ Disinformaiton
Intelligence/Sabotage in the Enemy's Rear
Kidnapping/Assassinaitons inside the USSR
Military Censorship

Administrative Functions
OGPU Collegium/NKVD Secretariat
Administrative-Organziational Directorate/Business Affairs
Financial Directorate
Personnel Directorate
Engineering-Construction Section
Accounting-Statistics Section
Archives
Legal Section

286

Bibliography

Works by Intelligence Officer Defectors (Including Post-1954)

'Les souvenirs d'un agent Soviétique' ('Memories of a Soviet Agent'), *La Tribune de Genève*, published serially from 14 December 1949 to 12 January 1950. (A. A. Petrov)

'Нравы и Работа ГПУ: Из Рассказов Секретного Сотрудника Чрезвычайки' ('Mores and Work of the GPU: From the Tales of a Cheka Secret Collaborator'), *Vozrozhdenie*, published serially from 11 September to 6 October 1926. (Stefens, aka Ivan Vasilyevich Gavrilchenko)

Agabekov, Georgiy Sergeyevich, *Г.П.У. Записки чекиста* (*GPU: Notes of a Chekist*) (Berlin: Strela, 1930).

Agabekov, Georgiy Sergeyevich, *ЧК за работой* (*The Cheka at Work*) (Berlin: Strela, 1931).

Agabekov, Georgiy Sergeyevich, *OGPU: The Russian Secret Terror*, trans. Henry W. Bunn (New York: Brentano's, 1931; Westport, CT: Hyperion Press, 1975).

Agranyants, Oleg, *Enemy of the people. Treacherous document. In the name of truth: 3 Plays* (London: Overseas Publications Interchange, 1989).

Agranyants, Oleg, *Что делать?, или деленинизация нашего общества – главная задача дня* (*What to Do?, or the Deleninisation of our Society – the Primary Task of the Day*) (London: Overseas Publications Interchange, 1989).

Akhmedov, Ismail Gusseynovich, *In and Out of Stalin's GRU: A Tatar's Escape from Red Army Intelligence* (Frederick, MD: University Publications of America, 1984).

Akhmedov, Ismail Gusseynovich and Pentti Lehtinen, *Stalinin GRU: puna-armeijan tiedustelu-upseerin muistelmia vallankumouksen, sodan ja rauhan päiviltä* (*Stalin's GRU: Red Army Intelligence Officer's Memoir of Revolution, War and Peace*) (Helsinki: Aleakirja, 1988).

Almazov, A. F. (pseudonym of Chikalov), *Грозная Лубянка* (*Terrible Lubyanka*), undated manuscript and typescript, Hoover Institution Archives, Boris Nicolaevsky Collection; Box 233, Folder 4 (microfilm reel 199).

Almazov, A. F. (pseudonym of Chikalov), *Система Следствия в МГБ* (*The Investigation System in the MGB*), undated manuscript and typescript, Hoover Institution Archives, Boris Nicolaevsky Collection; Box 233, Folder 5 (microfilm reel 199).

Almazov, A. F. (pseudonym of Chikalov), *Голубок* (*Golubok*), undated manuscript and typescript, Hoover Institution Archives, Boris Nicolaevsky Collection; Box 233, Folder 6 (microfilm reel 199).

Almazov, A. F. (pseudonym of Chikalov), *На Службе в Советской Разведке* (*In the Service of Soviet Intelligence*), undated manuscript and typescript, Hoover Institution Archives, Boris Nicolaevsky Collection; Box 233, Folder 7 (microfilm reel 199).

Andersen, Jakob and Oleg Gordievsky, *De røde spioner: KGB's operationer i Danmark fra Stalin til Jeltsin, fra Stauning til Nyrup* (*The Red Spies: KGB Operations in Denmark from Stalin to Yeltsin, from Stauning to Nyrup*) (Copenhagen: Høst & Søn, 2002).

Andrew, Christopher and Oleg Gordievsky, *KGB: The Inside Story of its Foreign Operations from Lenin to Gorbachev* (New York: HarperCollins Publishers, 1990).

Andrew, Christopher and Oleg Gordievsky, *Instructions from the Centre: Top Secret Files from the KGB's Foreign Operations, 1975–85* (London: Hodder & Stoughton, 1991).

Andrew, Christopher and Oleg Gordievsky, *More 'Instructions from the Centre': Top Secret Files on KGB Global Operations, 1975–1985* (London; Portland, OR: Frank Cass, 1992).

Andrew, Christopher and Oleg Gordievsky, *Comrade Kryuchkov's Instructions: Top Secret Files on KGB Foreign Operations, 1975–1985* (Stanford, CA: Stanford University Press, 1993).

Andrew, Christopher and Vasili Mitrokhin, *The Sword and the Shield: The Mitrokhin Archive and the Secret History of the KGB* (New York: Basic Books, 1999).

Andrew, Christopher and Vasili Mitrokhin, *The Mitrokhin Archive: The KGB in Europe and the West* (London: Allen Lane/Penguin Press, 1999).

Andrew, Christopher and Vasili Mitrokhin, *The World Was Going Our*

Way: The KGB and the Battle for the Third World (New York: Basic Books, 2005).

Andrew, Christopher and Vasili Mitrokhin, *The Mitrokhin Archive II: The KGB and the World* (London: Penguin, 2006).

Artemyev, Vyacheslav Pavlovich, *Деятельность Органов Государственной Безопасности в Советском Союзе* (*Activity of the Organs of State Security in the Soviet Union*), typescript dated 1950 in Bavaria, Columbia University Rare Book and Manuscript Library, Research Program on the USSR, Box 7.

Artemyev, Vyacheslav Pavlovich, *Исправительно-Трудовые Лагеря МВД СССР* (*Corrective Labour Camps of the USSR MVD*), typescript dated 1953 in Germany, Columbia University Rare Book and Manuscript Library, Research Program on the USSR, Box 7.

Artemyev, Vyacheslav Pavlovich, *Охрана Государственных Границ Союза Советских Социалистических Республик* (*Protection of State Borders of the Union of Soviet Socialist Republics*), typescript dated December 1950 in Bavaria, with handwritten revisions dated January 1955, Columbia University Rare Book and Manuscript Library, Research Program on the USSR, Box 7.

Artemyev, Vyacheslav Pavlovich, *Особые Отделы Советской Армии* (*Special Sections of the Soviet Army*), typescript dated January 1952 in Bavaria, with handwritten revisions dated October 1953, Columbia University Rare Book and Manuscript Library, Research Program on the USSR, Box 7.

Artemyev, Vyacheslav Pavlovich, *Вооруженные Силы МВД СССР* (*Military Forces of the USSR MVD*), typescript dated January 1951 in Bavaria, with handwritten revisions dated March 1955, Columbia University Rare Book and Manuscript Library, Research Program on the USSR, Box 8.

Artemyev, Vyacheslav Pavlovich, *Political Controls in the Soviet Army*, undated typescript, Columbia University Rare Book and Manuscript Library, Research Program on the USSR, Box 58.

Artemyev, Vyacheslav Pavlovich, *Военная Наука и Подготовка Кадров Советской Армии* (*Military Science and the Preparation of Soviet Military Cadres*), undated typescript, Hoover Institution Archives, Boris Nicolaevsky Collection, Box 233, Folder 10 (microfilm reel 199).

Artemyev, Vyacheslav Pavlovich, *Мобилизационная Работа Штаба Военного Округа в СССР* (*Mobilisation Work of a Military District Headquarters in the USSR*), undated typescript, Hoover Institution Archives, Boris Nicolaevsky Collection, Box 233, Folder 11 (microfilm reel 199).

Artemyev, Vyacheslav Pavlovich, *Фронтовики* (*Frontline Soldiers*), type-script dated April 1952 in Bavaria, Hoover Institution Archives, Boris Nicolaevsky Collection, Box 233, Folder 12 (microfilm reel 199).

Artemyev, Vyacheslav Pavlovich, *Особый Карательный Взвод* (*Special Disciplinary Detachment*), typescript dated January 1952 in Bavaria, Hoover Institution Archives, Boris Nicolaevsky Collection, Box 233, Folder 13 (microfilm reel 199).

Artemyev, Vyacheslav Pavlovich, *Медведь* (*Medved*), typescript dated September 1951 in Bavaria, Hoover Institution Archives, Boris Nicolaevsky Collection, Box 233, Folder 14 (microfilm reel 199).

Artemyev, Vyacheslav Pavlovich, *Майор Дои Сан* (*Major Doi San*), undated typescript, Hoover Institution Archives, Boris Nicolaevsky Collection, Box 233, Folder 15 (microfilm reel 199).

Artemyev, Vyacheslav Pavlovich, six fragments from a draft book on General Vlasov, undated typescript, Hoover Institution Archives, Boris Nicolaevsky Collection, Box 233, Folder 16 (microfilm reel 199).

- *Белая Рабыня* (*White Slave*)
- *Советский Пленный* (*Soviet Prisoner*)
- *Протест Генерала Буняченко* (*General Bunyachenko's Protest*),
- *Первые Столкновения с Немцами* (*First Conflicts with the Germans*)
- *Советские Пропагандисты* (*Soviet Propagandists*)
- *Участь Власовцев* (*The Vlasovites' Fate*)

Artemyev, Vyacheslav Pavlovich, *Selection and Training of Soviet Personnel for Trade Missions Abroad and the Soviet Trade Mission in Iran: Two Brief Studies* (New York: Research Program on the USSR, 1954).

Artemyev, Vyacheslav Pavlovich, *Режим и охрана исправительно-трудовых лагерей МВД* (*Regime and Security of MVD Corrective Labour Camps*) (Munich: Institute for the Study of the USSR, 1956).

Artemyev, Vyacheslav Pavlovich, *Living Conditions and Policing of MVD Corrective Labour Camps* (Munich: Institute for the Study of the USSR, 1956).

Artemyev, Vyacheslav Pavlovich, *Первая дивизия РОА. Материалы к истории освободительного движения народов России (1941–1945)* (*First Division of the ROA: Historical Materials of the Liberation Movement of the Peoples of Russia (1941–1945)*) (London, ON: Publisher of the Union for the Struggle for the Liberation of the Peoples of Russia, 1974).

Artemyev, Vyacheslav Pavlovich, 'Manning the Iron Curtain', *Bulletin of the Institute for the Study of the USSR*, vol. 9 (July 1962), pp. 14–21.

Artemyev, Vyacheslav Pavlovich, 'Crime and Punishment in the Soviet Armed Forces', *Military Review*, vol. 42, no. 11 (November 1962), pp. 68–74.

Artemyev, Vyacheslav Pavlovich, 'OKR: State Security in the Soviet Armed Forces', *Military Review*, vol. 43, no. 9 (September 1963), pp. 21–31.

Artemyev, Vyacheslav Pavlovich, 'The Communist Party and the Soviet Armed Forces', *Military Review*, vol. 44, no. 2 (February 1964), pp. 29–37.

Artemyev, Vyacheslav Pavlovich, 'Party Political Work in the Soviet Armed Forces', *Military Review*, vol. 44, no. 3 (March 1964), pp. 62–8.

Artemyev, Vyacheslav Pavlovich, 'Soviet Military Penal Units', *Military Review*, vol. 48, no. 4 (April 1964), pp. 90–6.

Artemyev, Vyacheslav Pavlovich, 'Soviet Military Educational Institutions', *Military Review*, vol. 46, no. 1 (January 1966), pp. 11–14.

Artemyev, Vyacheslav Pavlovich, 'Soviet Mobilization Doctrine', *Military Review*, vol. 46, no. 6 (June 1966), pp. 63–9.

Artemyev, Vyacheslav Pavlovich, 'Soviet Volunteers in the German Army', *Military Review*, vol. 47, no. 11 (November 1967), pp. 56–64.

Artemyev, Vyacheslav Pavlovich, 'Officer Courts of Honor in the Soviet Armed Forces', *Military Review*, vol. 48, no. 11 (November 1968), pp. 53–8.

Artemyev, Vyacheslav Pavlovich, 'Coercion and Fear in the Soviet Armed Forces', *Military Review*, vol. 49, no. 11 (November 1969), pp. 51–5.

Artemyev, Vyacheslav Pavlovich and Grigoriy Sergeyevich Burlutskiy, *Кадры, прохождение службы и подготовка пограничных войск МВД СССР* (*Personnel, Conditions of Service and Training of the Border Troops*), Columbia University Rare Book and Manuscript Library, Research Program on the USSR, Box 8.

Artemyev, Vyacheslav Pavlovich and Grigoriy Sergeyevich Burlutskiy, *Пограничные военноучебные заведения* (*Military Training Institutions of the MVD Border Troops*), Columbia University Rare Book and Manuscript Library, Research Program on the USSR, Box 8.

Artemyev, Vyacheslav Pavlovich and Grigoriy Sergeyevich Burlutskiy, *Послевоенная организация и деятельность советских органов государственной безопасности* (*Post-war Organisation and Activities of Soviet Organs of State Security*), Columbia University Rare Book and Manuscript Library, Research Program on the USSR, Box 8.

Artemyev, Vyacheslav Pavlovich and Grigoriy Sergeyevich Burlutskiy, *Послевоенные сведения о генералитете госбезопасности СССР, 1945–1955 (Post-war Information about the General Corps of USSR State Security, 1945–1955)*, Columbia University Rare Book and Manuscript Library, Research Program on the USSR, Box 8.

Artemyev, Vyacheslav Pavlovich and Grigoriy Sergeyevich Burlutskiy, *Activities of the State Security Organs Within the USSR – Operational State Security Measures Inside the Country*, undated typescript, Columbia University Rare Book and Manuscript Library, Research Program on the USSR.

Artemyev, Vyacheslav Pavlovich and Grigoriy Sergeyevich Burlutskiy, 'Structure and Condition of the Soviet Organs of State Security after World War II', in Simon Wolin and Robert M. Slusser (eds), *The Soviet Secret Police* (New York: Praeger, 1957), pp. 152–78.

Artemyev, Vyacheslav Pavlovich and Grigoriy Sergeyevich Burlutskiy, 'Personnel, Conditions of Service and Training in the Border Troops', in Simon Wolin and Robert M. Slusser (eds), *The Soviet Secret Police* (New York: Praeger, 1957), pp. 280–321.

Artemyev, Vyacheslav Pavlovich and Grigoriy Sergeyevich Burlutskiy, 'Internal Activities of the Soviet Organs of State Security after World War II', in Simon Wolin and Robert M. Slusser (eds), *The Soviet Secret Police* (New York: Praeger, 1957), pp. 322–37.

Artemyev, Vyacheslav Pavlovich and Grigoriy Sergeyevich Burlutskiy, 'Postwar Activities of the Soviet Organs of State Security in Western Europe', in Simon Wolin and Robert M. Slusser (eds), *The Soviet Secret Police* (New York: Praeger, 1957), pp. 338–54.

Barmin, Aleksandr Grigoryevich (pseudonym of Graff), 'Stalin a Betrayer Ex-Envoy Asserts', *New York Times*, 23 December 1937, pp. 1, 11.

Barmin, Aleksandr Grigoryevich (pseudonym of Graff), 'Russian Disunity is Laid to Stalin', *New York Times*, 25 December 1937, p. 6.

Barmin, Aleksandr Grigoryevich (pseudonym of Graff), '2 Executions Held a Sop to Cossacks: Ex-Envoy Says Stalin Makes Peace Offering to Returning Exiles in Policy Shift', *New York Times*, 26 December 1937, p. 12.

Barmin, Aleksandr Grigoryevich (pseudonym of Graff), 'Bukharin Believed Already Executed: Old Bolshevik Who Called Stalin "Genghis Khan" Refused to "Confess," Ex-Envoy Says', *New York Times*, 29 December 1937, p. 5.

Barmin, Aleksandr Grigoryevich (pseudonym of Graff), *Memoirs of a*

Soviet Diplomat: Twenty Years in the Service of the USSR (London: Lovat Dickson, 1938; Westport, CT: Hyperion Press, 1973).

Barmin, Aleksandr Grigoryevich (pseudonym of Graff), *A Russian View of the Moscow Trials: Significance of Trotsky Trial; Time Fights on the Side of Democracy; Editorials from the New York Times* (New York: Carnegie Endowment for International Peace, Division of Intercourse and Education, 1938).

Barmin, Aleksandr Grigoryevich (pseudonym of Graff), *Vingt Ans Au Service de l'U.R.S.S.: Souvenirs d'un Diplomate Soviétique* (*Twenty Years in the Service of the USSR: Memories of a Soviet Diplomat*) (Paris: Albin Michel, 1939).

Barmin, Aleksandr Grigoryevich (pseudonym of Graff), 'The New Communist Conspiracy', *Reader's Digest*, vol. 45, October 1944, pp. 27–33.

Barmin, Aleksandr Grigoryevich (pseudonym of Graff), 'New Defender for Yenan', *New Leader*, vol. 28, 7 April 1945, pp. 10, 14.

Barmin, Aleksandr Grigoryevich (pseudonym of Graff), *One Who Survived: The Life Story of a Russian under the Soviets* (New York: G. P. Putnam's Sons, 1945; Read Books, 2007; Kessinger Publishing, 2010).

Barmin, Aleksandr Grigoryevich (pseudonym of Graff), *Двадцать Лет в Разведке* (*Twenty Years in Intelligence*) (Moscow: Algoritm, 2014) (Russian translation of *Memoirs of a Soviet Diplomat*).

Benar, Leonard Frantsovich (pseudonym of Drugov), 'Нации в Плену' ('Nations in Prison'), 20 March 1930, National Archives of Finland, State Police (Valpo I) files, Box 102, Folder 11033.

Brazhnev, Aleksandr (pseudonym of Anokhin), *Записки Чекиста* (*Notes of the Chekist*) (Typescript in Hoover Institution Archives, Boris Nicolaevsky Collection, Box 294, Folder 11 (microfilm reel 253)).

Brazhnev, Aleksandr (pseudonym of Anokhin), Школа Опричников (*Oprichniki School*) (Kiev: Diokor, 2004).

Denisov, Vadim Andreyevich, *Комплекс Советской Тайной Работы за Рубежами СССР* (*The Complex of Soviet Clandestine Work Outside the Borders of the USSR*), typed chart, Hoover Institution Archive, Alexander Dallin Papers, Box 71, Folder K, Aparat II.

Denisov, Vadim Andreyevich, *Внешний Оперативный Центр ИНУ НКВД Западноевропейского Отдела в Антверпене, Белгия* (*INU NKVD Foreign Operational Center of the Western Department in Antwerp, Belgium*, handwritten chart, Hoover Institution Archive, Alexander Dallin Papers, Box 71, Folder K, Aparat II.

Denisov, Vadim Andreyevich, *Mass Persecutions by the NKVD in*

1932–1938, Hoover Institution Archive, Alexander Dallin Papers, Box 71, Folder K, Aparat II.

Denisov, Vadim Andreyevich, *Замечания к Рукописи по НКВД* (*Notes to the Manuscript on the NKVD*), Hoover Institution Archive, Alexander Dallin Papers, Box 71, Folder K, Aparat II. Another version is also contained in Hoover Institution Archive, Boris Nicolaevsky Collection, Box 293, Folder 12 (microfilm reel 253).

Denisov, Vadim Andreyevich, *Советская Тайная Работа Вне СССР* (*Soviet Secret Work Outside the USSR*), Hoover Institution Archive, Alexander Dallin Papers, Box 71, Folder K, Aparat II. Another version of the same paper is also contained in Hoover Institution Archive, Boris Nicolaevsky Collection, Box 293, Folder 10 (microfilm reel 253).

Denisov, Vadim Andreyevich, *Первый Специальный Отдел МГБ СССР* (*First Special Section of the USSR MGB*), Hoover Institution Archive, Boris Nicolaevsky Collection, Box 293, Folder 9 (microfilm reel 253).

Denisov, Vadim Andreyevich, *14-я Погранзастава* (*The 14th Border Guard Post*), handwritten manuscript, Hoover Institution Archive, Boris Nicolaevsky Collection, Box 411, Folder 20 (microfilm reel 298).

Denisov, Vadim Andreyevich, *История Владимира Ивановича Волкова в Документах* (*History of Vladimir Ivanovich Volkov in Documents*), Hoover Institution Archive, Boris Nicolaevsky Collection, Box 411, Folder 21 (microfilm reel 298).

Denisov, Vadim Andreyevich, *На Лесозаготовках в Архангельской Области* (*At the Lumber Works in the Archangel Oblast*), Hoover Institution Archive, Boris Nicolaevsky Collection, Box 411, Folder 22 (microfilm reel 298).

Denisov, Vadim Andreyevich, *Политическая Работа в Советской Армии* (*Political Work in the Soviet Army*), Hoover Institution Archive, Boris Nicolaevsky Collection, Box 411, Folder 24 (microfilm reel 298).

Denisov, Vadim Andreyevich, *Экономическое Управление ГУГБ НКВД СССР, Сокращение ЭКУ НКВД* (*The Economic Directorate of the GUGB NKVD USSR, abbreviation EKU NKVD*), Hoover Institution Archive, Boris Nicolaevsky Collection, Box 293, Folder 5 (microfilm reel 252).

Denisov, Vadim Andreyevich, *Использование Моряков Советского Торгового Флота в Целях Разведки* (*The Use of Soviet Merchant Fleet Sailors for Intelligence Purposes*), Hoover Institution Archive, Boris Nicolaevsky Collection, Box 293, Folder 6 (microfilm reel 252).

Denisov, Vadim Andreyevich, *Организация, Методы, и Техника*

Следствия в Органах Госбезопасности СССР (*Organisation, Methods, and Technology of Investigations in the USSR Organs of State Security*), Hoover Institution Archive, Boris Nicolaevsky Collection, Box 293, Folder 7 (microfilm reel 252).

Denisov, Vadim Andreyevich, *Организация Госбезопасности в Советских Вооруженных Силах* (*The Organisation of State Security in the Soviet Armed Forces*), handwritten manuscript, Hoover Institution Archive, Boris Nicolaevsky Collection, Box 293, Folder 8 (microfilm reel 252).

Denisov, Vadim Andreyevich, *Тихоокеанский Военно-морской Флот Советского Союза* (*The Pacific Fleet of the Soviet Union*), Hoover Institution Archive, Boris Nicolaevsky Collection, Box 293, Folder 8 (microfilm reel 252).

Denisov, Vadim Andreyevich, 'Массовые акции КРУ и СПУ НКВД' ('Mass Operations of the NKVD KRU and SPU'), *Народная правда* (*Narodnaya Pravda*), September 1950, nos 9–10, pp. 29–30.

Deryabin, Peter Sergeyevich, *Watchdogs of Terror: Russian Bodyguards from the Tsars to the Commissars* (New Rochelle, NY: Arlington House, 1972) (Frederick, MD: University Publications of America, 1984).

Deryabin, Peter Sergeyevich, and Frank Gibney, 'Red Agent's Vivid Tale of Terror', *Life*, 23 March 1959, pp. 110–12, 114, 116, 119–20.

Deryabin, Peter Sergeyevich, and Frank Gibney, 'Kremlin Intrigue and Debauchery', *Life*, 30 March 1959, pp. 80–5, 87–8, 90.

Deryabin, Peter Sergeyevich, and Frank Gibney, *The Secret World* (New York: Doubleday, 1959).

Deryabin, Peter Sergeyevich, with Tennent H. Bagley, *KGB, Masters of the Soviet Union* (New York: Hippocrene Books, 1990).

Deryabin, Peter Sergeyevich, with Jerrold L. Schecter, *The Spy Who Saved the World: How a Soviet Colonel Changed the Course of the Cold War* (New York: Scribners, 1992).

Deryabin, Peter Sergeyevich, with Joseph Culver Evans, *Inside Stalin's Kremlin: An Eyewitness Account of Brutality, Duplicity, and Intrigue* (Washington, DC: Brassey's Publications, 1998).

Drugov, Fedor Pavlovich, 'С Дзержинским в ВЧК: Исповедь раскаявшегося чекиста' ('With Dzerzhinsky in the VChK: The Confession of a Repentant Chekist'), *Иллюстрированная Россия* (*Illustrated Russia*), 31 January 1931, pp. 1–2, 4–5; 7 February 1931, pp. 6, 8–9; 14 February 1931, pp. 4, 6; 21 February 1931, pp. 8–9; 28 February 1931, pp. 10–11.

Drugov, Fedor Pavlovich, 'Анархисты в русской революции: Октябрьские дни в Смольном' ('Anarchists in the Russian Revolution: The October Days in Smolniy'), *Пробуждение* (*Awakening*), 1932, nos 23–7.

Dumbadze, Yevgeniy Vasilyevich, *На службе Чека и Коминтерна. Личные воспоминания* (*In the Service of the Cheka and Comintern: Personal Reminiscences*) (Paris: Mishen, 1930), typescript draft in Hoover Institution Archives, Boris Nicolaevsky Collection, Box 294, Folder 18 (microfilm reel 254).

Dumbadze, Yevgeniy Vasilyevich, *Дело Агабекова-Арутюнова* (*The Agabekov-Arutyunov Affair*), typescript in the Hoover Institution Archives, Boris Nicolaevsky Collection, Box 294, Folders 21 and 22 (microfilm reel 254).

Dumbadze, Yevgeniy Vasilyevich, *Способ приготовления секретных агентов ГПУ для экспорта, непатентованное изобретение бывшего резидента ОГПУ Агабекова* (*The Method of Preparing GPU Secret Agents for Export: The Unpatented Invention of Former OGPU Rezident Agabekov*), 1933 typescript in the Hoover Institution Archives, Boris Nicolaevsky Collection, Box 294, Folder 22 (microfilm reel 254).

Dzhirkvelov, Ilya, 'How the KGB Operates: Answers From a KGB Defector', *Intelligence Report* (Standing Committee on Law and National Security, American Bar Association) vol. 3, July 1981, pp. 3–6.

Dzhirkvelov, Ilya, *Secret Servant: My Life with the KGB and the Soviet Elite* (London: Collins, 1987; New York: Harper & Row, 1988; New York: Touchstone, 1989).

Ege, Ismail (pseudonym of Akhmedov), 'The Drive for Final Victory', in US Congress. House. Committee on Un-American Activities, *The Great Pretense: A Symposium on Anti-Stalinism and the 20th Congress of the Soviet Communist Party*, 84th Congress, Second Session (Washington, DC: Government Printing Office, 1956), pp. 63–6.

Gai, Boris Aleksandrovich, *Perechen' spetsial'nykh chekistskikh terminov k rukopisi 'NKVD SSSR'* (*List of Special Terms to the Manuscript 'USSR NKVD'*) (Research Program on the USSR).

Golitsyn, Anatoliy Mikhailovich, *New Lies for Old: The Communist Strategy of Deception and Disinformation* (New York: Dodd, Mead & Co., 1984; London: Bodley Head, 1984).

Golitsyn, Anatoliy Mikhailovich, *The Perestroika Deception: Memoranda to the Central Intelligence Agency* (London and New York: Edward Harle, 1995).

Gordievsky, Oleg Antonovich, *Next Stop Execution: The Autobiography of Oleg Gordievsky* (London: Macmillan, 1995).

Gouzenko, Igor Sergeyevich, 'I Was Inside Stalin's Spy Ring', *Cosmopolitan*, February 1947, pp. 23–5, 162–70.

Gouzenko, Igor Sergeyevich, *The Iron Curtain* (New York: E. P. Dutton, 1948; Toronto: Dent, 1948).

Gouzenko, Igor Sergeyevich, *This Was My Choice* (London: Eyre & Spottiswoode, 1948; 2nd ed. Montreal: Palm, 1968).

Gouzenko, Igor Sergeyevich, *The Fall of a Titan* (novel) (New York: W. W. Norton, 1954).

Granovskiy, Anatoliy Mikhailovich, 'Eu Fui Espião de Stalin' ('I Was Stalin's Spy'), *A Noite* [São Paolo, Brazil], published serially from 30 December 1948 to 10 May 1949.

Granovskiy, Anatoliy Mikhailovich, *All Pity Choked: The Memoirs of a Soviet Agent* (London: Kimber, 1955).

Granovskiy, Anatoliy Mikhailovich, *I Was an NKVD Agent: A Top Soviet Spy Tells His Story* (New York: Devin-Adair, 1962).

Grishin, Nikolay, *Soviet Operation of Uranium Mines in Eastern Germany*, Mimeographed Series Number 11 (New York: Research Program on the USSR, 1952). This monograph was later reprinted as 'The Saxony Uranium Mining Operation ('VISMUT'), in Robert Slusser et al., *Soviet Economic Policy in Postwar Germany: A Collection of Papers by Former Soviet Officials* (New York: Research Program on the USSR, 1953), pp. 127–55.

Helfand, L. B., *Командный Состав Транспорта СССР* (Command Staff of USSR Transportation) (Moscow: TransPechat NKPS, 1924).

Kalugin, Oleg Danilovich, *The First Directorate: My 32 Years in Intelligence and Espionage against the West* (New York: St Martin's Press, 1994).

Kalugin, Oleg Danilovich, *Прощай Лубянка! (XX Век Глазами Очевидцев)* (*Farewell Lubyanka: The 20th Century through the Eyes of Witnesses*) (Moscow: Olimp, 1995).

Kalugin, Oleg Danilovich, *Spymaster: My 32 Years in Intelligence and Espionage against the West* (New York: Basic Books, 2009).

Karpov, Peter Mikhailovich, *Организация ГПУ* (*The Organisation of the GPU*), undated typescript, Hoover Institution Archive, Boris Nicolaevsky Collection, Box 217, Folder 6 (microfilm reel 187).

Kiselev-Gromov, Nikolay Ignatyevich, *Борьба с Бандитами на Кубани?* (*Fight against Bandits in Kuban?*), Hoover Institution Archive, Boris Nicolaevsky Collection, Box 182, Folder 27 (microfilm reel 155).

Kiselev-Gromov, Nikolay Ignatyevich, 'Лагери Смерти' ('Death Camps'), *Руль* (*The Helm*) [Berlin, Germany], published serially between 13 September and 4 October 1931.

Kiselev-Gromov, Nikolay Ignatyevich, *Лагери Смерти в СССР: Великая братская могила жертв коммунистического террора* (*Death Camps in the USSR: The Great Grave of Honor for Victims of Communist Terror*) (Shanghai: N. P. Malinovskiy, 1936).

Khokhlov, Nikolay, as told to Milton Lehman, 'I Would Not Murder for the Soviets', *Saturday Evening Post*, published serially between 20 November and 11 December 1954.

Khokhlov, Nikolay Yevgenyevich, 'Interview with Former Soviet Spy Nikolai E. Khokhlov: Executioners' Shots Reveal New Struggle Inside Kremlin', *US News and World Report*, 21 January 1955, pp. 42–7.

Khokhlov, Nikolay Yevgenyevich, 'Mit Mordauftrag aus Moskau' ('With a Murder Order from Moscow'), *Die Weltwoche* (Zürich), published serially from 21 January to 11 March 1955.

Khokhlov, Nikolay Yevgenyevich, 'Interview with Nikolai E. Khokhlov, former Soviet Intelligence Officer: Revolt in Soviet Russia Starting', *US News and World Report*, 30 March 1956, pp. 26–35.

Khokhlov, Nikolay Yevgenyevich, *Право на Совесть* (*The Right to Conscience*) (Frankfurt am Main: Possev, 1957).

Khokhlov, Nikolay Yevgenyevich, *In the Name of Conscience: The Testament of a Soviet Secret Agent* (New York: David McKay, 1959; London: Muller, 1960).

Krivitsky, Walter Germanovich (pseudonym of Ginzberg), 'Stalin's Hand in Spain', *Saturday Evening Post*, 15 April 1939, pp. 5–7, 115–22.

Krivitsky, Walter Germanovich (pseudonym of Ginzberg), 'Why Stalin Shot His Generals', *Saturday Evening Post*, 22 April 1939, pp. 16–17, 71–4, 76–7.

Krivitsky, Walter Germanovich (pseudonym of Ginzberg), 'Stalin Appeases Hitler', *Saturday Evening Post*, 29 April 1939, pp. 12–13, 84–9.

Krivitsky, Walter Germanovich (pseudonym of Ginzberg), 'Why Did They Confess', *Saturday Evening Post*, 17 June 1939, pp. 5–6, 96–8, 100–1.

Krivitsky, Walter Germanovich (pseudonym of Ginzberg), 'My Flight from Stalin', *Saturday Evening Post*, 5 August 1939, pp. 7, 73–4, 76–80.

Krivitsky, Walter Germanovich (pseudonym of Ginzberg), 'When Stalin Counterfeited Dollars', *Saturday Evening Post*, 30 September 1939, pp. 8–9, 80–4.

Krivitsky, Walter Germanovich (pseudonym of Ginzberg), 'The Great Red Father', *Saturday Evening Post*, 4 November 1939, pp. 12–13, 66–8, 62–75.

Krivitsky, Walter Germanovich (pseudonym of Ginzberg), 'The Red Army: Auxiliary of Germany's Military Might', *Saturday Evening Post*, 1 June 1940, pp. 9–10, 91–4, 96.

Krivitsky, Walter Germanovich (pseudonym of Ginzberg), *In Stalin's Secret Service: An Expose of Russia's Secret Policies by the Former Chief of the Soviet Intelligence in Western Europe* (New York: Harper and Brothers, 1939; Frederick, MD: University Press of America, 1985, 1995).

Krivitsky, Walter Germanovich (pseudonym of Ginzberg), *I Was Stalin's Agent* (London: Hamish Hamilton, 1939; New York: Faulkner Books, 1992).

Krivitsky, Walter Germanovich (pseudonym of Ginzberg), *In Stalin's Secret Service: Memoirs of the First Soviet Master Spy to Defect* (New York: Enigma, 2000).

Krivitsky, Walter Germanovich (pseudonym of Ginzberg), *MI5 Debriefing & Other Documents on Soviet Intelligence*, trans. Garn Kern (Riverside, CA: Xenos, 2004).

Kuzichkin, Vladimir Anatolyevich, 'Crime, Corruption Rampant in Russia', *Sunday Telegraph*, 2 February 1982.

Kuzichkin, Vladimir Anatolyevich, *Inside the KGB: Myth and Reality* (London: André Deutsch, 1990).

Kuzichkin, Vladimir Anatolyevich, *Inside the KGB: My Life in Soviet Espionage*, trans. Thomas B. Beattie (New York: Pantheon, 1990; New York: Ivy Books, 1992).

Levchenko, Stanislav Aleksandrovich, *On the Wrong Side: My Life in the KGB* (Washington, DC: Permagon-Brassey's, 1988).

Levchenko, Stanislav Aleksandrovich, *The KGB Against the 'Main Enemy': How the Soviet Intelligence Service Operates against the United States* (Lexington, MA: Lexington Books, 1989).

Lunev, Stanislav, *Through the Eyes of the Enemy: Russia's Highest Ranking Military Defector Reveals Why Russia Is More Dangerous Than Ever* (New York: Regnery, 1998).

Lyushkov, Genrikh, 'Почему я бросил Советскую Россию' ('Why I Quit Soviet Russia'), in brochure titled *Почему бегут из СССР?* (*Why Are They Running from the USSR?*) (Shanghai: Vega, 1939).

Mitrokhin, Vasili, *KGB Lexicon: The Soviet Intelligence Officer's Handbook* (London; Portland, OR: Frank Cass, 2002).

Mitrokhin, Vasili, *'Chekisms': A KGB Anthology* (London: Yurasov Press, 2008).

M., Sh. G., 'По Тюрьмам Кавказа' ('On the Prisons of the Caucasus'), *Vozrozhdenie*, published serially on 1, 5, 8, and 11 June 1932.

Myagkov, Alexey Alexeyevich, *Inside the KGB: An Expose by an Officer of the Third Directorate* (New Rochelle, NY: Arlington House, 1977; Richmond, UK: Foreign Affairs Publishing, 1976; New York: Ballantine, 1981).

Myagkov, Alexey Alexeyevich, *KGB Intern: Enthüllungen eines Offiziers der III Hauptabteilung* (*Inside the KGB: Revelations of an Officer of the III Chief Directorate*) (Stuttgart: Seewald Verlag, 1976).

Myagkov, Alexey Alexeyevich, 'Confessions of a KGB Officer', *Soviet Analyst*, vol. 6, 13 January 1977, pp. 5–7.

Myagkov, Alexey Alexeyevich, 'The Role of the KGB in World Affairs', *Foreign Affairs Research Institute*, April 1977, p. 6.

N., L. (probably a pseudonym of Feldbin), 'Суд и Жизнь: Дело Госторга' ('The Court and Life: The Gostorg Case'), *Еженедельник Советской Юстиции* (*Soviet Jurisprudence Weekly*), 26 April 1923, pp. 370–2.

Nikolayev, L. (pseudonym of Feldbin), 'Суд и Жизнь: "Судебные Деятели"' ('The Court and Life: "Judicial Officials"'), *Еженедельник Советской Юстиции* (*Soviet Jurisprudence Weekly*), 19 April 1923, p. 349.

Nikolayev, L. (pseudonym of Feldbin), 'Суд и Жизнь: "Следователь" Гернуши' ('The Court and Life: "Investigator" Gernushi'), *Еженедельник Советской Юстиции* (*Soviet Jurisprudence Weekly*), 17 May 1923, p. 444.

Olshanskiy, Aleskandr (pseudonym of Sipelgas), *Записки Агента Разведупра* (*Notes of a Rezvedupra Agent*), *Vozrozhdenie*, published serially from 4 March to 3 May 1930, subsequently published in book form (Paris: Mishen, 1930; Moscow: Detektiv-Press, 2010).

Olshanskiy, Aleskandr (pseudonym of Sipelgas), *En Sovjetspion i Helsingfors* (Helsingfors: Söderström & Co., 1931).

Orlov, Alexander Mikhailovich (pseudonym of Feldbin), 'Ghastly Secrets of Stalin's Powers', *Life*, 6 April 1953, pp. 111–12, 115–23.

Orlov, Alexander Mikhailovich (pseudonym of Feldbin), 'Stalin's Secrets: Inside Story of How the Trials Were Rigged', *Life*, 13 April 1953, pp. 160–1, 164–6, 168, 170, 173–4, 177–8.

Orlov, Alexander Mikhailovich (pseudonym of Feldbin), 'Stalin's Secrets: Treachery to His Friends, Cruelty to Their Children', *Life*, 20 April 1953, pp. 142–4, 145, 148, 150, 153–4, 156, 159.

Orlov, Alexander Mikhailovich (pseudonym of Feldbin), 'Stalin's Secret: The Man Himself', *Life*, 27 April 1953, pp. 145–6, 148–52, 157–8.

Orlov, Alexander Mikhailovich (pseudonym of Feldbin), 'The Beria I Knew', *Life*, 20 July 1953, pp. 33–6.

Orlov, Alexander Mikhailovich (pseudonym of Feldbin), *The Secret History of Stalin's Crimes* (New York: Random House, 1953).

Orlov, Alexander Mikhailovich (pseudonym of Feldbin), 'The Sensational Secret Behind the Damnation of Stalin', *Life*, 23 Apr 1956, pp. 34–8, 43–5.

Orlov, Alexander Mikhailovich (pseudonym of Feldbin), 'The Theory and Practice of Soviet Intelligence', *Studies in Intelligence,* vol. 7, no. 2 (Spring 1963), pp. 45–65.

Orlov, Alexander Mikhailovich (pseudonym of Feldbin), *Handbook of Intelligence and Guerrilla Warfare* (Ann Arbor: University of Michigan Press, 1963).

Orlov, Alexander Mikhailovich (pseudonym of Feldbin), 'How Stalin Relieved Spain of $600,000,000', *Reader's Digest*, November 1966, pp. 37–50.

Orlov, Alexander Mikhailovich (pseudonym of Feldbin), *The March of Time: Reminiscences* (London: St Ermin's, 2004).

Ovchinnikov, Ivan Vasilyevich, *Исповѣдь Кулацкого Сына* (*Confession of a Kulak's Son*) (Moscow: Desnitsa, 2000).

Petrov, Vladimir (pseudonym of Shorokhov), 'Mystery of Missing Diplomats Solved: First Story of How Maclean and Burgess Fled to Moscow with British-American Secrets', *US News and World Report*, 23 September 1955, pp. 21–5.

Petrov, Vladimir Mikhailovich (pseudonym of Shorokhov) and Evdokia Alekseyevna Petrova (pseudonym of Kartseva), 'The Petrovs' Own Story', *The Sun* (Sydney), published serially from 17 September to 7 October 1955.

Petrov, Vladimir Mikhailovich (pseudonym of Shorokhov) and Evdokia Alekseyevna Petrova (pseudonym of Kartseva), 'The Petrovs' Own Story', *Sydney Morning Herald*, published serially from 17 September to 13 October 1955.

Petrov, Vladimir Mikhailovich (pseudonym of Shorokhov) and Evdokia Alekseyevna Petrova (pseudonym of Kartseva), *Empire of Fear* (New York: Praeger, 1956; London: André Deutsch, 1956).

Pik, Eugene (pseudonym of Kozhevnikov), *China in the Grip of the Reds* (Shanghai: North China News, 1927).

Rastvorov, Yuriy Aleksandrovich, 'How Red Titans Fought for Supreme Power', in *Life*, 29 November 1954.

Rastvorov, Yuriy Aleksandrovich, 'Red Fraud and Intrigue in the Far East', in *Life*, 6 December 1954.

Rastvorov, Yuriy Aleksandrovich, 'Goodby to Red Terror', in *Life*, 13 December 1954.

Rastvorov, Yuriy Aleksandrovich, 'Newest Trick of the Kremlin', in US Congress. House. Committee on Un-American Activities, *The Great Pretense: A Symposium on Anti-Stalinism and the 20th Congress of the Soviet Communist Party*, 84th Congress, Second Session (Washington, DC: Government Printing Office, 1956), pp. 69–70.

Rastvorov, Yuriy Aleksandrovich, 'What I Did as a Spy in Japan', *Yomiuri Japan News*, published serially from 23 to 27 July 1956.

Repin, Aleksandr Fedorovich (pseudonym of Chikalov), Repin's autobiography and outline of biographical essays; Repin was a deputy chief of Belorussian OGPU-NKVD), 1947–1949 (Hoover Institution Archive, Boris I. Nicolaevsky Collection, 1801–1982; Box 497, Folder 35).

Romanov, A. I. (pseudonym of Baklanov), *Nights Are Longest There: SMERSH from the Inside* (London: Hutchinson, 1972).

Romanov, A. I. (pseudonym of Baklanov), *The Nights Are Longest There: A Memoir of the Soviet Security Services* (Boston: Little, Brown, 1972).

Sakharov, Alexander, 'The Problems and Prospects of Arms Control: A View from the Soviet Side of the Table', 9 October 1984, lecture at the University of California, Santa Barbara, Arts and Lectures Records (Box 33, Folder 17), <http://pdf.oac.cdlib.org/pdf/ucsb/spcoll/uarch16_arts_lectures.pdf> (last accessed 13 March 2020).

Sakharov, Alexander, *Human values have to save the world: Alexander Sakharov speaks about US–Soviet Relations* (San Francisco: Fine Line Productions, 1985).

Sheymov, Viktor Ivanovich, *Tower of Secrets: A Real Life Spy Thriller* (Annapolis, MD: Naval Institute Press, 1993; New York: HarperSpotlight, 1994).

Sheymov, Viktor Ivanovich, *Tiebreaker: Tower of Secrets II* (Cyber Books Publishing, 2013).

Sigl, Rupert, *In the Claws of the KGB: Memoirs of a Double Agent* (Philadelphia: Dorrance and Co., 1978).

Sinevirsky, Nicola (pseudonym of Mondich), *СМЕРШ: Год в Стане Врага* (*SMERSH: A Year in the Enemy's Camp*) (Limburg an der Lahn, Germany: Possev, 1948; Frankfurt am Main: Possev, 1984).

Sinevirsky, Nicola (pseudonym of Mondich), *SMERSH* (New York: Henry Holt and Co., 1950).

Sobolev, Aleksandr Aleksandrovich, *Красный Флот в Гражданской Войне 1918–1920 гг.* (*The Red Fleet in the Civil War, 1918–1920*) (Leningrad: Publishing Section of the Navy Department, 1924).

Sobolev, Aleksandr Aleksandrovich, 'Мой ответ коммунистам' ('My Answer to the Communists'), *Vozrozhdenie*, 9 May 1930, p. 2.

Sobolev, Aleksandr Aleksandrovich, 'Мой разрыв с советской властью' ('My Break with the Soviet Union'), *Vozrozhdenie,* 9 May 1930, pp. 3, 5.

Sobolev, Aleksandr Aleksandrovich, 'Записки Невозвращенца' ('Notes of a Non-Returnee'), *Vozrozhdenie*, 17 May 1930, p. 2.

Suvorov, Viktor (pseudonym of Rezun), *The Liberators: My Life in the Soviet Army* (New York and London: Norton, 1981).

Suvorov, Viktor (pseudonym of Rezun), *Inside the Soviet Army* (New York: Macmillan, 1982).

Suvorov, Viktor (pseudonym of Rezun), *Inside Soviet Military Intelligence* (New York: MacMillan, 1984).

Suvorov, Viktor (pseudonym of Rezun), *Soviet Military Intelligence* (London: Hamish Hamilton, 1984).

Suvorov, Viktor (pseudonym of Rezun), *Aquarium: The Career and Defection of a Soviet Military Spy* (Hamish Hamilton, 1985).

Suvorov, Viktor (pseudonym of Rezun), *Inside the Aquarium: The Making of a Top Soviet Spy* (New York: Stein & Day, 1986).

Suvorov, Viktor (pseudonym of Rezun), *Spetsnaz: The Story behind the Soviet SAS* (London: Hamish Hamilton, 1987).

Suvorov, Viktor (pseudonym of Rezun), *Spetsnaz: The Inside Story of the Soviet Special Forces* (New York and London: Norton, 1988).

Suvorov, Viktor (pseudonym of Rezun), *Ice-breaker: Who Started the Second World War?* (London: Hamish Hamilton, 1990).

Suvorov, Viktor (pseudonym of Rezun), *Ледокол: кто начал Вторую мировую войну* (*Ice-breaker: Who Started the Second World War*) (Moscow: Novoe Vremya, 1993).

Suvorov, Viktor (pseudonym of Rezun), *День 'М': Когда началась Вторая мировая война?* (*'M' Day: When Did the Second World War Start?*) (Moscow: Vse Dlya Vas, 1994).

Suvorov, Viktor (pseudonym of Rezun), *Контроль: Роман* (*Control: A Novel*) (Moscow: AST, 1994).

Suvorov, Viktor (pseudonym of Rezun), *Ледокол; День 'М'* (*Ice-breaker: 'M' Day*) (Moscow: AST, 1994).

Suvorov, Viktor (pseudonym of Rezun), *Последняя Республика: Почему Советский Союз Проиграл Вторую Мировую Войну* (*The Last Republic: Why the Soviet Union Lost the Second World War*) (Moscow: AST, 1995).

Suvorov, Viktor (pseudonym of Rezun), *Выбор* (*The Choice*) (Moscow: AST, 1997).

Suvorov, Viktor (pseudonym of Rezun), *Очищение* (*Cleansing*) (Moscow: AST, 1998).

Suvorov, Viktor (pseudonym of Rezun), *Самоубийство: зачем Гитлер напал на Советский Союз?* (*Suicide: Why Did Hitler Attack the Soviet Union?*) (Moscow: AST, 2000).

Suvorov, Viktor (pseudonym of Rezun), *Золотой Эшелон* (*Golden Echelon*) (Moscow: Gudial-Press, 2000).

Suvorov, Viktor (pseudonym of Rezun), *Тень победы* (*The Shadow of Victory*) (Donetsk: Stalker, 2003).

Suvorov, Viktor (pseudonym of Rezun), *Беру свои слова обратно* (*I Take Back My Words*) (Donetsk: Stalker, 2005).

Suvorov, Viktor (pseudonym of Rezun), *The Chief Culprit: Stalin's Grand Design to Start World War II* (Annapolis, MD: Naval Institute Press, 2008).

Suvorov, Viktor (pseudonym of Rezun), *Змееед* (*Snake Eater*) (Moscow: Dobraya Kniga, 2012).

Suvorov, Viktor et al., *Союз звезды со свастикой: Встречная агрессия* (*The Union of the Star with the Swastika: Counter Aggression*) (Moscow: Yauza-Press, 2012).

Tuomi, Kaarlo R., *Isanmaattoman Tarina: Amerikansuomalaisen Vakoojan Muistelmat* (*Stateless Story: Finnish American Spy Memoirs*) (Porvoo, Helsinki, Juvo: Söderström, 1984).

Tuomi, Kaarlo R., 'Karelian Fever: A Personal Memoir', in Michael Karni (ed.), *The Best of Finnish Americana* (New Brighton, MN: Penfield, 1994).

Tuomi, Kaarlo R., *Spy Lost: Caught Between the KGB and the FBI* (New York: Enigma Books, 2013).

United States Congress. House. Special Committee on Un-American Activities, *Investigation of Un-American Propaganda Activities in the United States*, vol. 9 (Washington, DC: Government Printing Office, 1939), pp. 5719–42. (Krivitsky)

United States Congress. House. Special Committee on Un-American Activities, *Investigation of Communist Activities in the Los Angeles, California, Area*, 84th Congress, Second Session (Washington, DC: Government Printing Office, 1956). (Khokhlov)

United States Congress. House. Special Committee on Un-American Activities, *The Kremlin's Espionage and Terror Organisations* (Washington, DC: Government Printing Office, 1959). (Deryabin)

United States Congress. Senate. Committee on the Judiciary, *Interlocking Subversion in Government Departments* (Washington, DC: Government Printing Office, 1953). (Akhmedov)

United States Congress. Senate. Committee on the Judiciary, *Testimony of Former Russian Code Clerk Relating to the Internal Security of the United States* (Washington, DC: Government Printing Office, 1955). (Gouzenko)

United States Congress. Senate. Committee on the Judiciary, *Testimony of Alexander Orlov*, 84th Congress, First Session (Washington, DC: Government Printing Office, 1955).

United States Congress. Senate. Committee on the Judiciary, *Scope of Soviet Activity in the United States*, 84th Congress, Second Session (Washington, DC: Government Printing Office, 1956). Part 1, pp. 1–23; Part 13, pp. 778–813. (Rastvorov)

United States Congress. Senate. Committee on the Judiciary, *Scope of Soviet Activity in the United States*, 84th Congress, Second Session, part 3 (Washington, DC: Government Printing Office, 1956), pp. 57–75. (Akhmedov)

United States Congress. Senate. Committee on the Judiciary, *Scope of Soviet Activity in the United States*, 84th Congress, Second Session (Washington, DC: Government Printing Office, 1956). (Graff)

United States Congress. Senate. Committee on the Judiciary, *Scope of Soviet Activity in the United States*, 85th Congress, First Session, Part 50 (Washington, DC: Government Printing Office, 1957). (Orlov)

United States Congress. Senate. Committee on the Judiciary, *Communist Controls on Religious Activity*, 86th Congress, First Session (Washington, DC: Government Printing Office, 1959). (Deryabin)

United States Congress. Senate. Committee on the Judiciary, *Murder International Inc.: Murder and Kidnapping as an Instrument of Soviet Policy*, 89th Congress, First Session (Washington, DC: Government Printing Office, 1965).

United States Congress. Senate. Committee on the Judiciary, *Testimony of Colonel Yevgeny Runge*, 91st Congress, Second Session (Washington, DC: Government Printing Office, 1970).

United States Congress. Senate. Committee on the Judiciary, *The Legacy of Alexander Orlov,* 93rd Congress, First Session (Washington, DC: Government Printing Office, 1973).

United States Congress. Senate. Committee on the Judiciary. Subcommittee to Investigate the Administration of the Internal Security and Other Internal Security Laws, *Activities of Soviet Secret Service*, 83th Congress, Second Session (Washington, DC: Government Printing Office, 1954). (Khokhlov)

United States Congress. Senate. Committee on the Judiciary. Subcommittee to Investigate the Administration of the Internal Security and Other

Internal Security Laws, *Testimony of Frances G. Knight*, 92nd Congress, Second Session (Washington, DC: Government Printing Office, 1972). (Gouzenko)

Government Assessments Regarding Defectors

Central Intelligence Agency, *Biography of Yevgeniy Yevgen'yevich Runge*, 8 January 1968 (received via FOIPA).

Commonwealth of Australia, *Report of the Royal Commission on Espionage* (Sydney: Australian Government publication, 1955).

Federal Bureau of Investigation, *Soviet Intelligence Communications*, September 1952 (available through CIA CREST).

Federal Bureau of Investigation, *Soviet Defectors: A Study of Past Defections from Official Soviet Establishments outside the USSR* (Washington, DC: Federal Bureau of Investigation, 1955) (available at <https://archive.org>).

Joint Intelligence Committee, *A Study of Defectors from the USSR*, August 1948 (TNA, FO 1093/551).

Kellock-Taschereau Commission, *Report of the Royal Commission Appointed under Order in Council P.C. 411 of February 5, 1946 to Investigate the Facts Relating to and the Circumstances Surrounding the Communication by Public Officials and Other Persons in Positions of Trust of Secret and Confidential Information to Agents of a Foreign Power* (Ottawa: Privy Council, 1946).

US Director of Central Intelligence, Directive 14/1, 'Establishment of Interagency Defector Committee', 17 July 1950.

US Congress. House. Committee on Un-American Activities. *The Shameful Years: Thirty Years of Soviet Espionage in the United States*, 82nd Congress, 2nd Session (Washington, DC: Government Printing Office, 1952).

US Congress. Senate. Committee on Governmental Affairs. Permanent Subcommittee on Investigations, *Federal Government's Handling of Soviet and Communist Bloc Defectors*, 100th Congress, First Session, 8, 9, and 21 October 1987 (Washington, DC: US Government Printing Office, 1988).

US National Security Council, National Security Council Intelligence Directive 13, 'Exploitation of Soviet and Satellite Defectors Outside the United States', 19 January 1950 [S/S–NSC (Miscellaneous) Files: Lot 66 D 95.].

US National Security Council, National Security Council Intelligence

Directive 14, 'Exploitation of Defectors and Other Citizens within the United States', 3 March 1950 [S/S–NSC (Miscellaneous) Files: Lot 66 D 95.].

Works about Defector Cases

'Russian Diplomat Quits and Scores Soviet; Says He Will Be Slain, Pleads for Others', *New York Times*, 4 December 1937, p. 1. (Graff)

Agrell, Wilhelm, *Fru Petrovas sko: en rysk spiontragedi i 50-talets Australien* (*Mrs Petrova's Shoe: A Russian Spy Tragedy in 50s Australia*) (Stockholm: Bokförlaget Atlantis, 2014).

Aleksandrov, Kirill Mikhailovich, *Офицерский Корпус Армии Генерал-Лейтенанта Ал. Власова, 1944–1945* (*Officer Corps of the Army of General Lieutenant Vlasov, 1944–1945*) (St Petersburg: Русско-Балтийский информационный центр, «БЛИЦ», 2001).

Aleksandrov, Kirill Mikhailovich, *Армия Генерала Власова 1944–1945* (*General Vlasov's Army 1944–1945*) (Moscow: Yauza EKSMO, 2006).

Aleksandrov, Kirill Mikhailovich, *Генералитет и Офицерские Кадры Вооруженных Формирований Комитета Освобождения Народов России 1943–1946 гг.* (*General and Officer Corps of the Armed Formations of the Committee for the Liberation of the Peoples of Russia 1943–1946*) (Dissertation written for the Russian Academy of Sciences, St Petersburg History Institute, 2015).

Ali, Tariq, 'The Spymaster's Son', *The Guardian*, 19 February 1999. (Poretskiy)

Anders, Karl (pseudonym of Hendrik van Bergh), *Murder to Order* (London: Ampersand, 1965). (Stashinskiy)

Andryukhin, Vadim, 'Судьба резидента' ('The Fate of the Rezident'), *Zemlya Nizhegorodskaya*, 14 May 2012, <https://zem-nn.ru/?p=3556> (Gai/Morozov).

Barron, John, 'Inheritor: A Tale of KGB Espionage in America', *Reader's Digest*, March 1982, pp. 193+. (Herrmann)

Barron, John, 'The Spy Who Knew Too Much', *Reader's Digest*, June 1983, pp. 124–30, 207–18, 222–30. (Levchenko)

Belenkin, Boris, *Pasynki Revoliutsii: Savinkov, Opperput i dr.* (*Stepchildren of the Revolution: Savinkov, Opperput, and Others*) (Moscow: Yauza, EKSMO, 2005).

Bialoguski, Michael, 'I Got Petrov', *The Sun* (Sydney), published serially from 2 to 17 June 1955.

Bialoguski, Michael, 'How I Weaned Petrov from Communism', *Saturday Evening Post*, published serially from 6 August to 10 September 1955.

Bialoguski, Michael, *The Case of Colonel Petrov* (New York: McGraw Hill, 1955).

Black, J. L. and Martin Rudner (eds), *The Gouzenko Affair: Canada and the Beginnings of Cold War Counter-Espionage* (Newcastle, ON: Penumbra Press, 2006).

Bothwell, Robert and J. L. Granatstein (eds), *The Gouzenko Transcripts: The Evidence presented to the Kellock-Taschereau Royal Commission of 1946* (Ottawa: Breakthrough Publishing Co., 1982).

Brook-Shepherd, Gordon, *Storm Petrels* (New York: Harcourt Brace Jovanovich, 1977).

Brook-Shepherd, Gordon, *The Storm Birds: Soviet Post-War Defectors* (New York: Weidenfeld & Nicolson, 1989).

Carr, Barbara, *Loginov Spy in the Sun: The Story of Yuriy Loginov* (Cape Town: Howard Timmins, 1969).

Chuev, Sergey Gennadiyevich, Проклятые Солдаты. Предатели на Стороне III Рейха (*Cursed Soldiers: Traitors on the Side of the Third Reich*) (Moscow: EKSMO, 2004).

Coox, Alvin D., 'L'Affaire Lyushkov: Anatomy of a Defector', *Soviet Studies*, vol. 19 (January 1968), pp. 405–20.

Coox, Alvin D., 'An Intelligence Case Study: The Lesser of Two Hells: NKVD G. S. Lyushkov's Defection to Japan, 1938–1945, Part I', *The Journal of Slavic Military Studies*, vol. 11, no. 3 (1998), pp. 145–86.

Coox, Alvin D., 'An Intelligence Case Study: The Lesser of Two Hells: NKVD G. S. Lyushkov's Defection to Japan, 1938–1945, Part II', *The Journal of Slavic Military Studies*, vol. 11, no. 4 (1998), pp. 72–110.

Costello, John and Oleg Tsarev, *Deadly Illusions: The KGB Orlov Dossier Reveals Stalin's Master Spy* (New York: Crown Publishers, 1993).

Early, Pete, *Comrade J: The Untold Secrets of Russia's Master Spy in America after the End of the Cold War* (New York: Putnam's, 2008). (Tretyakov)

Edele, Mark, *Stalin's Defectors: How Red Army Soldiers Became Hitler's Collaborators, 1941–1945* (Oxford: Oxford University Press, 2017).

Ennis, Jerry D., 'Anatoli Golitsyn: Long-time CIA Agent?', *Intelligence and National Security*, vol. 21, no. 1 (February 2006), pp. 26–45.

Ennis, Jerry D., 'What Did Angleton Say about Golitsyn?', *Intelligence and National Security*, vol. 22, no. 6 (December 2007), pp. 905–9.

Eunson, Robert, 'How We Nabbed Russia's No. 1 Spy', *Saturday Evening Post*, 25 September 1954, pp. 27, 141–2. (Rastvorov)

Gazur, Edward, *Secret Assignment: The FBI's KGB General* (London: St Ermin's Press, 2001).

Gazur, Edward, *Alexander Orlov: the FBI's KGB General* (New York: Carroll & Graf, 2002).

Genis, Vladimir Leonidovich, 'Невозвращенцы 1920-х- начала 1930-х годов' ('Nonreturners in the 1920s and Early 1930s'), *Вопросы Истории* (*Questions of History*), 2000, no. 1, pp. 46–63, published online at <http://historystudies.org/2012/07/genis-v-l-nevozvrashhency-1920-x-nachala-1930-x-godov/> (last accessed 13 March 2020).

Gruntman, Mike, *Enemy Amongst Trojans: A Soviet Spy at USC* (Los Angeles: Figueroa Press, 2010).

Haarstad, Gunnar, *I Hemmelig Tjeneste: Etterretning og overvåking i krig og fred* (*In Secret Service: Intelligence and Surveillance in War and Peace*) (Oslo: Aschehoug, 1988).

Hellman, Ben, 'Писатель Алекцандр Сипельгас, он же разведчик А. Смирнов. Русско-финско-эстонская загадка' ('Author Alexander Sipelgas, also known as Intelligence Officer A. Smirnov: Russo-Finno-Estonian Riddle') in *Встречи и столкновения: Статьи по русской литературе* (*Meetings and Clashes: Articles on Russian Literature*), Slavica Helsingiensia 36 (Helsinki: Helsinki University Press, 2008), pp. 199–231.

Heuer, Richards J., 'Nosenko: Five Paths to Judgment', *Studies in Intelligence,* vol. 31, no. 3 (Fall 1987), pp. 71–101. Reprinted in H. Bradford Westerfield (ed.), *Inside CIA's Private World: Declassified Articles from the Agency's Internal Journal, 1955–1992* (New Haven: Yale University Press, 1995), pp. 379–414.

Hinchley, Vernon, *The Defectors* (London: Harrap, 1967).

Hyde, Earl M., Jr., 'Still Perplexed about Krivitsky', *International Journal of Intelligence and Counterintelligence* 16, no. 3 (Fall 2003), pp. 428–41.

Karavashkin, Vitaliy Vasilyevich, *Кто Предал Россию* (*Who Betrayed Russia*) (Moscow: AST, 2008).

Katkov, George, *The Khokhlov Case*, St Anthony's Papers on Soviet Affairs (Oxford: St Anthony's College, 1954). (A copy is in TNA, FO 371/109322.)

Kern, Gary, *A Death in Washington: Walter G. Krivitsky and the Stalin Terror* (New York: Enigma Books, 2004).

Kern, Gary, *Walter G. Krivitsky: MI5 Debriefing & Other Documents on Soviet Intelligence* (Riverside, CA: Xenos, 2004).

Kern, Gary, *The Kravchenko Case: One Man's War on Stalin* (New York: Enigma Books, 2007).

Kessler, Ronald, *Escape from the CIA: How the CIA Won and Lost the Most Important KGB Spy Ever to Defect to the US* (New York: Pocket Books, 1991).

Knight, Amy, *How the Cold War Began: The Igor Gouzenko Affair and the Hunt for Soviet Spies* (New York: Carroll & Graf, 2005).

Krasnov, Vladislav, *Soviet Defectors: The KGB Wanted List* (Stanford, CA: Hoover Institution Press, 1985).

Maffei, Ricardo, 'Il "Caso Helfand": La Defezione nel 1940 del Diplomatico Sovietico a Roma nei Documenti Americani' ('The "Helfand Case": The Defection in 1940 of a Soviet Diplomat to Rome from American Documents'), *Nuova Storia Contemporanea*, vol. 18, no. 5 (September–October 2014), pp. 49–74.

Mahar, Donald G., *Shattered Illusions: KGB Cold War Espionage in Canada* (Lanham, MD: Rowman & Littlefield, 2016). (Brik)

Manne, Robert, *The Petrov Affair: Politics and Espionage* (Sydney: Pergamon, 1987).

Melville, Frank, 'The Soviets: Coups and Killings in Kabul: A KGB Defector Tells How Afghanistan Became Brezhnev's Viet Nam', *Time*, 22 November 1982, pp. 33–4. (Interview with Kuzichkin)

Nishino, Tatsukichi, 謎の亡命者リュシコフ (*Nazo no bōmeisha Ryushikofu; The Mysterious Exile Lyushkov*) (Tokyo: Sanichi Shobo, 1979).

Orloff, Vladimir, *Underworld and Soviet* (New York: The Dial Press, 1931). (Karpov)

Poretsky, Elizabeth, *Our Own People: A Memoir of Ignace Reiss and His Friends* (London: Oxford University Press, 1969).

Prokhorov, Dmitriy Petrovich, *Сколько стоит продать Родину?* (*What is the Cost of Betraying One's Homeland?*) (Moscow: Olma-Press, 2005).

Prokhorov, Dmitriy Petrovich and Oleg Lemekhov, *Перебежчики Заочно Расстреляны* (*Defectors Executed in Absentia*) (Moscow: Veche, 2001).

Quinlan, Kevin, *The Secret War between the Wars: MI5 in the 1920s and 1930s* (London: Boydell & Brewer Ltd, 2014). (Krivitsky, Helfand)

Raschhofer, Hermann, *Political Assassination: The Legal Background of the Oberlander and Stashinsky Cases* (Tubingen: F. Schlichtenmayer, 1964).

Reiss, Elsa, 'Ignace Reiss: In Memoriam', *New International*, vol. 4, no. 9 (September 1938), pp. 276–8, available at <https://www.marxists.org/> (last accessed 2 April 2020). An original German version signed

'Elsa R.' is held in the Hoover Institution Archives, Boris Nicolaevsky Collection, Box 375, Folder 54 (microfilm reel Trotsky 41).

Rondeau, John, 'Book Review of *The Soviet Secret Police*, by Simon Wolin and Robert Slusser', *Studies in Intelligence*, vol. 2, Winter 1958, pp. 123–9. (Artemyev, Burlutskiy)

Sawatsky, John, *For Services Rendered: Leslie James Bennett and the RCMP Security Service* (New York: Doubleday, 1983).

Shalett, Sidney, 'How the Russians Spied on Their Allies', *Saturday Evening Post*, 25 January 1947, pp. 19, 85–8; 1 February 1947, pp. 24, 78–9. (Gouzenko)

Thayer, Charles W., 'MVD Man's Declaration of Independence', *Life*, 5 July 1954, pp. 69–80. (Burlutskiy)

Thwaites, Michael, *Truth Will Out: ASIO and the Petrovs* (Sydney: Collins, 1980).

Trotsky, Leon, 'En Septembre 1937 Ignace REISS tombait les balles de la Guépéou' ('In September 1937 Ignace Reiss Fell to the GPU's Bullets', *La Lutte Ouvrier* (*The Worker's Struggle*), 21 October 1938.

US Congress. Senate. Judiciary Committee. *Scope of Soviet Activity in the United States*, 84th Congress, Second Session, part 27 (Washington, DC: Government Printing Office, 1956), pp. 1519–20. (Isaac Don Levine testimony about Krivitsky)

Verkhturov, Dmitriy, *Виктор Суворов врет! Потопить «Ледокол»* (*Viktor Suvorov Lies: Sinking 'The Icebreaker'*) (Moscow: LitRes, 2014).

Volodarsky, Boris, *The Orlov KGB File: The Most Successful Espionage Deception of All Time* (New York: Enigma Books, 2009).

Volodarsky, Boris, *Stalin's Agent: The Life and Death of Alexander Orlov* (Oxford: Oxford University Press, 2014).

Wise, David, 'K.G.B. Defector Gundarev, It's Cold Coming Out', *New York Times Magazine*, 17 September 1989.

Wise, David, 'The Spy Who Wouldn't Die', *Gentlemen's Quarterly (GQ)*, July 1998, pp. 148–55, 183–6. (Bokhan)

West, Nigel, 'Cold War Intelligence Defectors', in Loch K. Johnson (ed.), *Handbook of Intelligence Studies* (London: Routledge, 2006), pp. 229–36.

Yermolayev, Dmitriy Anatolyevich, 'Тайная Битва Спецслужб' ('Secret Battle of Special Services'), *Мурманский Вестник* (*Murmansk Chronicle*), three-part series, 15–17 June 2005.

Works about Soviet Intelligence, Mentioning Defectors

Abramov, Vadim, *Евреи в КГБ: Палачи и Жертвы* (*Jews in the KGB: Executioners and Victims*) (Moscow: Yauza EKSMO, 2005).

Barron, John, *KGB: The Secret Work of Soviet Agents* (New York: Reader's Digest Press, 1974).

Barron, John, *KGB Today: The Hidden Hand* (New York: Reader's Digest Press, 1983).

Bergman, Jay, 'The Memoirs of Soviet Defectors: Are They a Reliable Source about the Soviet Union?', *Canadian Slavonic Papers/Revue Canadienne des Slavistes*, vol. 31, no. 1 (March 1989), pp. 1–24.

Bernikow, Louise, *Abel* (New York: Trident Press, 1970).

Birstein, Vadim, *SMERSH: Stalin's Secret Weapon; Soviet Military Counterintelligence in World War II* (London: Biteback Publishing, 2011).

Bones, Stian, *I oppdemmingspolitikkens grenseland: Nord-Norge i den kalde krigen 1947–70* (*The Frontier of the Containment Policy: Northern Norway in the Cold War 1947–70*) (Dissertation written for University of Tromso, 2007). (Pavlov)

Brackman, Roman, *The Secret File of Joseph Stalin: A Hidden Life* (London; New York: Routledge, 2004). (Orlov, Krivitsky, Lyushkov, Reiss)

Brzezinski, Zbigniew (ed.), *Political Controls in the Soviet Army. A study based on reports by former Soviet officers* (New York: Research Program on the USSR, 1954). (Artemyev)

Cookridge, E. H., *Soviet Spy Net* (London: Frederick Muller, 1955).

Corson, William R., Robert T. Crowley, *The New KGB: Engine of Soviet Power* (New York: W. Morrow, 1985).

Dallin, David J., *Soviet Espionage* (New Haven: Yale University Press, 1955).

Damaskin, Igor Anatolyevich, *100 великих разведчиков* (*100 Great Intelligence Officers*) (Moscow: Veche, 2001).

Degtaryev, Klim and Aleksandr Ivanovich Kolpakidi, *Внешняя разведка CCCP* (*Foreign Intelligence of the USSR*) (Moscow: EKSMO, 2009).

Drozdov, Yuriy Ivanovich, *Записки Начальника Негальной Разведки* (*Notes of a Supervisor of Illegal Intelligence*) (Moscow: Olma-Press, 2000).

Evancevich, Michael, 'Defector Possibilities: Past, Present, Future', *Military Intelligence*, vol. 8, no. 4 (1982), pp. 25–6.

Foytzik, Yan, Andrey V. Doronin, and Tatyana Viktorovna Tsarevskaya-

Dyakina (managing eds), *Советская военная администрация в Германии, 1945–1949. Справочник* (*Soviet Military Administration in Germany. 1945–1949: A Handbook*) (Moscow: ROSSPEN, 2009).

Garthoff, Raymond L., *Soviet Leaders and Intelligence: Assessing the American Adversary during the Cold War* (Washington, DC: Georgetown University Press, 2015).

Haynes, John Earl and Harvey Klehr, *Venona: Decoding Soviet Espionage in America* (New Haven: Yale University Press, 1999).

Hirsch, Richard, *The Soviet Spies: A Story of Russian Espionage in North America* (New York: Duell, Sloane and Pearce, 1947).

Hollander, Paul, *Political Will and Personal Belief: The Decline and Fall of Soviet Communism* (New Haven: Yale University Press, 1999).

Knight, Amy, *The KGB* (Winchester, MA: Allen and Unwin, 1988).

Kochik, Valeriy Yakovlevich, *Разведчики и резиденты ГРУ: За пределами Отчизны* (*GRU Intelligence Officers and Rezidents: Beyond the Motherland*) (Moscow: Yauza, 2004).

Kolpakidi, Aleksandr Ivanovich and Dmitriy Petrovich Prokhorov, *Империя ГРУ* (*Empire of the GRU*) (Moscow: Olma-Press, 1999).

Lamphere, Robert J. and Tom Schachtman, *The FBI-KGB War: A Special Agent's Story* (New York: Random House, 1986).

Leggett, George, *The Cheka: Lenin's Political Police* (New York: Oxford University Press, 1987).

Leonard, Raymond W., 'Studying the Kremlin's Secret Soldiers: A Historiographical Essay on the GRU, 1918–1945', *The Journal of Military History*, vol. 56, no. 3 (July 1992), pp. 403–22.

Leonard, Raymond W., *Secret Soldiers of the Revolution: Soviet Military Intelligence 1918–1933* (Westport, CT: Greenwood Publishing Co., 1999).

Lurye, Vyacheslav Mikhailovich and Valeriy Yakovlevich Kochik, *ГРУ: Дела и Люди* (*GRU: Cases and People*) (Moscow: Olma-Press, 2002).

Marbes, Wilhelm, 'Psychology of Treason', *Studies in Intelligence* vol. 30, no. 2 (Summer 1986): 1–11. Reprinted in H. Bradford Westerfield (ed.), *Inside CIA's Private World: Declassified Articles from the Agency's Internal Journal, 1955–1992* (New Haven: Yale University Press, 1995), pp. 70–82.

Newman, Robert P., *Owen Lattimore and the 'Loss' of China* (Berkeley: University of California Press, 1992). (Graff)

Nikolskiy, Vitaliy Aleksandrovich, *ГРУ в годы Великой Отечественной войны* (*GRU during the Great Patriotic War*) (Moscow: Yauza EKSMO, 2005).

Parrish, Michael, *Soviet Security and Intelligence Organisations, 1917–1990: A Biographical Dictionary and Review of Literature in English* (Santa Barbara, CA: ABC-CLIO, 1992).

Parrish, Michael, *The Lesser Terror: Soviet State Security, 1939–1953* (Westport, CT: Greenwood Publishing Group, 1996).

Petrov, Nikita V. and K. V. Skorkin, *Кто Руководил НКВД 1934–1941* (*Who Led the NKVD 1934–1941*) (Moscow: International Memorial Society, 1999), published online at <http://www.memo.ru/history/nkvd/kto/> (last accessed 13 March 2020).

Petrov, Nikita V. and Yan Foytzik (eds), *Аппарат НКВД-МГБ в Германии. 1945–1953: Документы* (*The NKVD-MGB Apparatus in Germany 1945–1953: Documents*) (Moscow: International 'Democracy' Foundation, 2009).

Philby, Harold Adrian Russell, *My Secret War* (New York: Grove Press, 1968).

Pincher, Chapman, *Too Secret Too Long* (London: Sidgwick & Jackson, 1984).

Polgar, Tom, 'Defection and Redefection', *International Journal of Intelligence and Counterintelligence*, vol. 1, no. 2 (Summer 1986), pp. 29–42.

Pringle, Robert W., *Historical Dictionary of Russian and Soviet Intelligence* (Lanham, MD: Scarecrow Press, 2006).

Pryanishnikov, Boris, *Незримая Паутина: ВЧК – ОГПУ – НКВД Против Белой Эмиграции* (*Invisible Web: VChK-OGPU-NKVD against the White Emigration*) (St Petersburg: Chas Pik, 1993).

Ra'anan, Uri, *Inside the Apparat: Perspectives on the Soviet System from Former Functionaries* (Lexington, MA: Lexington Books, 1990).

Rafalko, Frank J. (ed.), *CI Reader: American Revolution into the New Millennium* (Washington, DC: Office of the National Counterintelligence Executive, 2004).

Rositzke, Harry, *The KGB* (Garden City, NY: Doubleday, 1984).

Schulte, Jörg, Olga Tabachnikova, and Peter Wagstaff, *The Russian Jewish Diaspora and European Culture, 1917–1937* (Leiden: BRILL, 2012). (Dumbadze, Agabekov)

Smyslov, Oleg Sergeyevich, *Генерал Абакумов. Палач или жертва?* (*General Abakumov: Executioner or Victim?*) (Moscow: Veche, 2012). (Salimanov)

Sokolov, Aleksandr, *'Суперкрот' TsRU v KGB* (*'Supermole': The CIA in the KGB*) (Moscow: Almanakh 'Vympel', 1999).

Sudoplatov, Pavel, *Special Tasks: The Memoirs of an Unwanted Witness, a Soviet Spymaster* (Boston: Little, Brown, 1994).

Sullivan, Brian R., 'Soviet Penetration of the Italian Intelligence Services in the 1930s', in Tomaso Vialardi di Sandigliano and Virgilio Ilari (eds), *The History of Espionage: Italian Military Intelligence, Electronic Intelligence, Chinese Intelligence* (Biella, Italy: Associazione Europea degli Amici degli Archivi Storici, 2005), pp. 83–104. (Helfand).

Volodarsky, Boris, *The KGB's Poison Factory* (Minneapolis, MN: Zenith Press, 2010).

Volodarsky, Boris, *Soviet Intelligence Services in the Spanish Civil War, 1936–1939* (Dissertation written for the London School of Economics, 2010).

Walton, Calder, *British Intelligence and Threats to National Security* (Dissertation written for Cambridge University, 2006).

West, Nigel, *MASK: MI5's Penetration of the Communist Party of Great Britain* (London; New York: Routledge, 2007), pp. 31–5. (Bazhanov, Agabekov, and Krivitsky)

Whaley, Barton, *Soviet Clandestine Communication Nets: Notes for a History of the Structures of the Intelligence Services of the USSR* (Cambridge, MA: Center for International Studies, Massachusetts Institute of Technology, September 1969).

Wolton, Thierry, *The KGB in France* (Charlottesville, VA: US Army Foreign Science and Technology Center, 1987).

Works about Western Intelligence, Mentioning Defectors

'Soviet Use of Assassination and Kidnapping', *Studies in Intelligence*, vol. 19, Fall 1975, pp. 1–10.

Andrew, Christopher, 'The Evolution of Australian Intelligence', *Studies in Intelligence*, vol. 32, Fall 1988, pp. 67–97.

Ankerbrand, John, 'What to Do with Defectors', *Studies in Intelligence*, vol. 5, Fall 1961, pp. 33–43.

Ashley, Clarence, *CIA Spymaster* (Gretna, LA: Pelican Press, 2004).

Bagley, Tennant H., *Spy Wars: Moles, Mysteries, and Deadly Games* (New Haven: Yale University Press, 2008).

Bearden, Milton and James Risen, *The Main Enemy: The Inside Story of the CIA's Final Showdown with the KGB* (New York: Random House, 2003).

Brabourne, Martin L., 'More on the Recruitment of Soviets', *Studies in Intelligence*, vol. 9, Winter 1965, pp. 39–60.

Chester, Eric Thomas, *Covert Network: Progressives, the International Rescue Committee, and the CIA* (New York: M. E. Sharpe, 1995).

Cummings, Richard H., *Cold War Radio: The Dangerous History of American Broadcasting in Europe* (Jefferson, NC: MacFarland and Co, 2009).

Debevoise, John, 'Soviet Defector Motivation', *Studies in Intelligence*, vol. 2, Fall 1958, pp. 33–42.

Dulles, Allen, *The Craft of Intelligence* (Westport, CT: Greenwood Press, 1963), pp. 134–44.

Farndon, Stanley B., 'Interrogation of Defectors', *Studies in Intelligence*, vol. 4, Summer 1960, pp. 9–30.

Fischer, Benjamin B., 'Spy Dust and Ghost Surveillance: How the KGB Spooked the CIA and Hid Aldrich Ames in Plain Sight', *International Journal of Intelligence and CounterIntelligence*, vol. 24, no. 2 (2011), pp. 268–306.

Goodman, Michael S., *Spying on the Nuclear Bear: Anglo-American Intelligence and the Soviet Bomb* (Stanford, CA: Stanford University Press, 2007).

Granatstein, J. L. and David Stafford, *Spy Wars: Espionage and Canada from Gouzenko to Glasnost* (Toronto: Key Porter Books, 1990).

Halpern, Samuel and Hayden Peake, 'Did Angleton Jail Nosenko?', *International Journal of Intelligence and CounterIntelligence*, vol. 3, no. 4 (1989), pp. 451–64.

Hart, John Limond, *CIA's Russians* (Annapolis, MD: Naval Institute Press, 2003).

Jeffery, Keith, *MI6: The History of the Secret Intelligence Service 1909–1949* (London: Bloomsbury, 2010).

Jeffreys-Jones, Rhodri and David Stafford (eds), *American-British-Canadian Intelligence Relations, 1939–2000* (Portland, OR: Frank Cass, 2000). (Gouzenko)

Jenks, John, *British Propaganda and News Media in the Cold War* (Edinburgh: Edinburgh University Press, 2006).

Jones, David L., 'Communist Defection: Its Impact on East-West Relations', *Military Review*, vol. 46, no. 3 (1966), pp. 20–8.

Kessler, Ronald, *Moscow Station: How the KGB Penetrated the American Embassy* (New York: Charles Scribner, 1989).

Lyubimov, Mikhail P., 'Perspective on Spying: Here's a Red Herring to Chew On: A former KGB colonel ties into a package the spectacular 1985 un-defection of Vitaly Yurchenko and the Aldrich Ames case', *Los Angeles Times*, 7 March 1994.

Martin, David, *Wilderness of Mirrors* (New York: Harper and Row, 1980).

Mikheyev, Dmitry, 'Defectors' Problems in the West', *Studies in Intelligence*, vol. 32, Spring 1988, pp. 67–74.

Murphy, David E., Sergei A. Kondrashev, George Bailey, *Battleground Berlin: CIA vs. KGB in the Cold War* (New Haven: Yale University Press, 1999).

Pincher, Chapman, *Treachery: Betrayals, Blunders and Cover-ups: Six Decades of Espionage* (London: Mainstream Publishing, 2011).

Richelson, Jeffrey T., *A Century of Spies: Intelligence in the Twentieth Century* (New York: Oxford University Press, 1995).

Riehle, Kevin, 'Early Cold War Evolution of British and US Defector Policy and Practice', *Cold War History*, vol. 19 (2019), no. 3, 343–61.

Riste, Olav, *The Norwegian Intelligence Service, 1915–1970* (London: Frank Cass, 1999). (Pavlov)

Rositzke, Harry, *The CIA's Secret Operations: Espionage, Counterespionage, and Covert Action* (Boulder, CO: Westview Press, 1977).

Ruffner, Kevin Conley, *Eagle and Swastika: CIA and Nazi War Criminals and Collaborators* (Draft working paper) (Washington, DC: CIA History Staff, 2003).

Schellenberg, Walter, *The Labyrinth: Memoirs of Walter Schellenberg, Hitler's chief of Counterintelligence* (Boulder, CO: Da Capo Press, 2000).

Smith, Michael, *MI6: The Real James Bonds 1909–1939* (London: Dialogue, 2010)

Steury, Donald (ed.), *On the Front Lines of the Cold War: Documents on the Intelligence War in Berlin, 1946 to 1961* (Washington, DC: Center for the Study of Intelligence, 1999).

Thurlow, Richard, 'Soviet Spies and British Counter-Intelligence in the 1930s: Espionage in the Woolwich Arsenal and the Foreign Office Communications Department', *Intelligence and National Security*, vol. 19, no. 4 (Winter 2004), pp. 610–31.

Trento, Joseph J., *The Secret History of the CIA* (New York: Carroll & Graf Publishers Inc., 2005).

Trimble, Delmege, 'Defector Disposal (US)', *Studies in Intelligence*, vol. 2, Fall 1958, pp. 43–54.

Twiddy, Andrew J., 'Recruiting Soviet Officials', *Studies in Intelligence*, vol. 8, Winter 1964, pp. 1–15.

West, Nigel, *Games of Intelligence* (New York: Crown Publishers, 1989).

West, Nigel, *Historical Dictionary of British Intelligence* (Lanham, MD: Scarecrow Press, 2007).

West, Nigel, *Historical Dictionary of Cold War Counterintelligence* (Lanham, MD: Scarecrow Press, 2007).

Wise, David, *Molehunt: The Secret Search for Traitors That Shattered the CIA* (New York: Random House, 1992).

Whitaker, Reg, Gregory S. Kealey, and Andrew Parnaby, *Secret Service: Political Policing in Canada From the Fenians to Fortress America* (Toronto: University of Toronto Press, 2012).

Wright, Peter, *Spycatcher: The Candid Autobiography of a Senior Intelligence Officer* (New York: Viking Penguin, 1987).

Archival Repositories: Governments

Australia
National Archives of Australia

Canada
National Archives of Canada

Finland
Kansallisarkisto (National Archives of Finland)

Latvia
Latvijas Nacionālā bibliotēka (Latvian National Library)
Digital Library (<http://www.periodika.lv>)

Russia
Государственная Публичная Историческая Библиотека России (State Public Historical Library of Russia) (<http://elib.shpl.ru/ru/nodes/9347-elektronnaya-biblioteka-gpib>)
Aleksandr N. Yakovlev Archive (<http://www.alexanderyakovlev.org>)

Sweden
Riksarkivet (Swedish National Archives)

United Kingdom
The National Archives

United States
National Archives and Records Administration
Federal Bureau of Investigation, The Vault

Central Intelligence Agency, Freedom of Information Act Electronic
   Reading Room
New York Public Library, Archives and Manuscripts
David Dallin Papers

Archival Repositories: Universities

Columbia University, Rare Book and Manuscript Library
Research Program on the USSR Manuscripts, 1950–1955
David J. Dallin, Manuscripts 1847–1952
Sergei L'vovich Voitsekhovskii Papers, 1945–1977

Georgetown University, Special Collections Research Center
Alexander Orlov Papers
Robert L. Morris Collection

Harvard University
Harvard Project on the Soviet Social System: <https://library.harvard.
   edu/collections/hpsss/index.html>

Hoover Institution Archives, Stanford University
Alexander Dallin Papers
Andrei Terent'evich Bel'chenko Papers, 1898–1962
Boris I. Nikolaevsky Collection, 1801–1982
David J. Dallin Miscellaneous Papers
Hede Massing Papers
Nikolay Evgenyevich Khokhlov Papers
Soviet Communist Party and Soviet State Microfilm Collection, 1903–
   1992: Russian State Archives of Social and Political History (Rossiiskii
   gosudarstvennyi arkhiv sotsialno-politicheskoi istorii; RGASPI)
Vladislav Krasnov Writings

Princeton University Library
Historical Newspapers Collection

University of Notre Dame, Hesburgh Libraries
Richard J. O'Melia Collection

Index

Abakumov, Viktor Semenovich, 200, 250, 278
Abel, Rudolf *see* Fisher, William August
Aberdeen Proving Grounds, 140
Abraham Lincoln Battalion, 87
Abryutin, Yevgeniy Viktorovich, 103, 109, 120, 122, 175
Adams, Eric, 137
Akhmedov, Islam Guseynovich, 61, 101, 104, 109–11, 114, 119, 122, 124–8, 130, 136, 138–40, 143, 153–4, 193, 252, 279
All-Russian Cooperative Society (ARCOS), 32, 57, 63–4
All-Russian Extraordinary Commission for Combating Counter-Revolution, Profiteering and Corruption (VChK), 11, 15, 17–18, 27–9, 45, 118, 229, 287
All-Union Society for Cultural Contacts with Foreign Countries (Всесоюзное Общество Культурных Связей с Заграницей; VOKS), 240
Amtorg Trading Company, 34, 57, 82–3, 140
Andrusaitis, Colonel, 203
Anokhin, Aleksandr Vladimirovich, 101, 104, 107, 109–10, 115, 121–2, 124–6, 137, 146–7
Arabadzhev, Gasan Artemovich, 102, 105, 109
Artemyev, Vyacheslav Pavlovich, 102, 106, 108–10, 117, 121–2, 137, 151, 155, 235
Arutyunov, Georgiy Sergeyevich, 12–13, 15, 20, 23, 25–32, 35, 56, 87, 139, 236, 266, 271
Association of Free Jurists, 250
Australian Security Intelligence Organisation (ASIO), 219, 223, 238
A. V. Roe Corporation, 247
Avro CF-105 (aircraft), 247

Babich, Tony *see* Mercader, Ramón
Baklanov, Boris Ivanovich, 171–3, 178, 182–4, 188–91, 193–4, 197–8, 201, 203, 269, 277, 279–80
Baksa, Laszlo *see* Sharandak, Vasiliy Mikhailovich
Bank Sass and Martini, 77
Barmin, Aleksandr Grigoryevich *see* Graff, Aleksandr Grigoryevich
Basmachis, 28–30
Basov, Sergey, 84
Bavaria, Bolshevik Republic of, 68
Bayerskiy, Vladimir Gelyarovich, 117
Bazhanov, Boris Georgiyevich, 31
Bazikov, (FNU), 155
Bekker, Rafael Ilych, 101, 109, 121, 133–4
Belkin, Naum Markovich, 67
Bentley, Elizabeth, 85, 165 124n, 281
Beriya, Lavrentiy Pavlovich, 5, 8, 118, 147, 191, 203, 215, 217, 221, 226–8, 269–70, 272
Berlin Operations Base (BOB), 174
Berzin, Jan Karlovich, 23, 73, 86
Besedovskiy, Grigoriy Zinovyevich, 18, 31
Bessonov, Ivan Georgiyevich, 101, 105–7, 109, 111, 116–17, 121, 150, 273
Biddle, Francis, 54
Blagodatov, Aleksey Vasilyevich, 135, 137
Bobrishchev, Ardalyon Aleksandrovich, 19, 22
Bondarev, Nikolay Ivanovich, 172, 178, 181, 188
Borah, William, 34
Boris Gleb hydroelectric project, 252
Borovoy, Mikhail, 81–2
Bottai, Giuseppe, 79
Boyer, Raymond, 140
Brandes, Mary (pseudonym), 81
Brandes, Willy *see* Borovoy, Mikhail
Brazhnev, Aleksandr Glebovich *see* Anokhin, Aleksandr Vladimirovich
Brik, Yevgeniy Vladimirovich, 216, 218–20, 227–8, 230, 246, 270
British Broadcasting Corporation (BBC), 192, 225
Brodnikov, Viktor Viktorovich, 117

Bukovina, 126, 157
Burgess, Guy, 61–2, 246
Burlutskiy, Grigoriy Stepanovich, 216–20,
   224–5, 228, 234–5, 239, 242, 250, 269
Burtsev, Vladimir Lvovich, 87
Byington, John, 238, 243

Carpathian Ruthenia, 142, 147–8
Carr, Sam, 145, 157
Central Intelligence Agency (CIA), 55, 122–3,
   132, 174, 186, 189, 221–2, 270, 281
Chamberlain, Austen, 32
Chamberlain, Neville, 196
Chambers, Whittaker, 165 124n, 281
Chaplygina, Nina Ilinichna, 101, 109
Chechen-Ingush resettlement, 224–5, 234
Chernykh, Aleksey Sergeyevich, 22
Chetniks (Serbian), 149
Chikalov, Aleksandr Fedorovich, 102, 106,
   108–10, 112, 114, 121–3, 130–33, 145,
   150, 154, 272–3
Chiplin, Rex (code name CHARLIE), 238
Chivin (aka Smith), 46, 50, 53–4, 56, 80–1
Churchill, Winston, 59, 191
Ciano, Galeazzo, 79
Cohen, Lona, 233
Cohen, Morris, 87, 233
collectivisation, 110, 133, 224, 233
Colloredo-Mansfeld, Count, 148
Columbia University, 122, 188, 197
Committee for the Liberation of the Peoples
   of Russia (Комитет Освобождения
   Народов России; KONR), 108, 115,
   117–19, 132, 134, 182
Committee of Imperial Defence (CID), 59
Committee of Information (Комитет
   Информации; KI), 280, 286
Communist International (Comintern), 11,
   18, 30, 35, 52, 57, 67–70, 73, 75, 80
Communist Party
   Canada, 138, 139
   Czechoslovakia, 148
   Estonia, 201
   Germany, 68, 195, 244, 268
   Great Britain, 61
   Japan, 243
   Sweden, 251
   USA (CPUSA), 80, 83
Continental Affairs Research Institute, 152
Counterintelligence Corps (CIC), US Army,
   123, 132, 174, 189–92, 200, 243
Counterintelligence Directorate (Управление
   Контрразведки; UKR), 174, 181, 185
Crimean Tatars resettlement, 224

Dallin, Alexander, 122
Dallin, David, 121–2

de las Heras, Africa, 233
decomposition work, 62, 88
Defector Reception Center, 122
Dekanozov, Vladimir Georgiyevich, 127,
   201
denazification, 193, 195
Denisov, Mikhail Filipovich, 172, 176, 178,
   185, 189
Denisov, Vadim Andreyevich, 101, 109–10,
   112–13, 121–2, 124, 127, 130, 133,
   140, 152, 156, 272
Department of External Affairs (DEA)
   (Australia), 244
Deryabin, Petr Sergeyevich, 216–18, 220,
   222–3, 228, 231–3, 235–7, 239, 241,
   249–50, 269, 279
Deutsch, Arnold, 61, 74
Directorate of Northern Special Purpose
   Camps (Управление Северных Лагарей
   Особого Назначения; USLON), 28
Divišek, Vintses (variant Vincene), 232
Dobříš Castle, 148
Doi Akio, 151
Dorn, Joseph, 76–7
Dovydenko, Kiril Vasilyevich, 101, 109
Drugov, Fedor Pavlovich, 12, 14–15, 17,
   25–8
Dubkov, Viktor Aleksandrovich, 102, 105,
   109, 119, 175, 229
Dulles, Allen, 54
Dumbadze, Yevgeniy Vasilyevich, 12–13, 15,
   18–19, 25, 27–8, 35, 266, 271
Dümmler, Miss, 22
Durand, Dana, 174
Dzerzhinsky, Feliks Edmundovich, 11, 17
Dzevaltovskiy, Ignatiy Leonovich, 12–13, 15,
   19, 25, 27, 29–31, 266, 271

Eingorn (variant Einhorn), Abram Osipovich,
   80–1
Eitingon, Naum Isakovich, 225
ELLI (code name), 138
Ennis, Ruth Esther, 243
ENORMAZ (code word), 245
Evdokimov (FNU), 20

Far Eastern Republic, 19, 31
Federal Bureau of Investigation (FBI), 57,
   76–7, 82, 84–7, 142
Feldbin, Leyba Lazarevich, 46–7, 49–51,
   53–5, 57–62, 64–5, 67, 70, 73–82,
   85–8, 91, 237, 245, 267, 277
Feldman, Armand Labis see Volodarskiy,
   Iosif Volfovich
Fisher, William August, 57, 230, 233
Fomenko, Vladimir Dmitriyevich, 102,
   109

Franco, Francisco, 73–5
Franklin, Zalmond David, 87
Frinovskiy, Mikhail Petrovich, 111

Gallacher, William, 61
Gehlen Organization, 250
Gehlen, Richard, 250
Genrikh, Isaak Moiseyevich, 172, 174, 178, 183
Gerson, Harold, 157
Gestapo, 125, 131, 135, 154, 195, 273
Ginzberg, Samuel Gershovich, 3, 46–7, 49–50, 52–62, 65, 67–78, 80–4, 86–8, 125, 180, 276
Glasser, Abraham, 86
Goldfarb, Rafael Ilych, 172, 175, 178–80, 183, 185–7, 190, 193–5, 199–201, 203, 269, 273, 277
Goldin, William see Feldbin, Leyba Lazarevich
Golitsyn, Anatoliy Mikhailovich, 123
Golos, Jacob, 80–1, 86
Golubok, Vladislav Iosifovich, 145
Goold-Verschoyle, Brian (code name FRIEND), 76
Gordievsky, Oleg Antonovich, 275
Gorshkov, Mikhail Vasiliyevich, 103, 105, 109, 121, 173
Gottwald, Klement, 149
Gouzenko, Igor Sergeyevich, 81–2, 102–4, 109, 113–14, 120, 128, 129, 131, 137–44, 150–52, 157, 173, 175, 236, 269, 279, 281
Grachev, Ivan Matveyevich, 101, 108, 109, 116, 121, 132
Graff, Aleksandr Grigoryevich, 46–7, 50, 52–6, 66, 68–9, 72, 74–5, 78, 83, 87–8, 267, 277
Granovskiy, Anatoliy Mikhailovich, 103–4, 109–10, 114, 120, 129–31, 133–4, 141–2, 147–9, 173–4, 201, 229–30, 232, 237, 239, 269, 273, 279
Gregory, Victor see Shelaputin, Vadim Ivanovich
Grigoryev, Ivan Matveyevich, 172, 174, 178, 186, 188
Grigoryev, Mikhail Ivanovich, 216, 218–20
Grigulevich, Iosif Romualdovich, 233
Grimpe, (FNU), 199, 278
Grishin, Nikolay, 172, 174, 178, 188, 203–4, 277
Groves, Leslie R., 141
GRU (Main Intelligence Directorate of the General Staff; Glavnoe Razvedyvatelnoe Upravlenie), 81–2, 127, 129, 131, 137–9, 143–5, 150, 152, 156–7, 175–6, 180, 184, 193, 200, 236, 252

Gurzhiev, Boris Kupriyanovich, 172, 174, 178, 187, 206 9n

Harnack, Arvid, 67
Harvard 525, 172, 175, 178, 183–4, 187–8, 269
Harvard Project on the Soviet Social System (HPSSS), 121
Häyhänen, Reino, 274
Helfand, Lev Borisovich, 46–50, 52–4, 56–8, 68, 79, 85, 139, 267–8
Hendler, Mikhail, 12, 15, 25–6, 30, 34–5, 53
Hess, Rudolf, 136
Higurashi Nobunori, 238, 243, 249
Himmler, Heinrich, 195
Hiss, Alger, 142
Hitler, Adolf, 47, 66, 72–3, 75, 100, 104, 116, 118–19, 125, 193, 196, 198, 268
Hollis, Roger, 138
honorary weapon award, 65, 150
Hovanesyan, Artush Sergeyevich, 7

IG Farbenindustrie, 66
illegals (intelligence officer cover), 6, 21, 25, 29–30, 49, 57–8, 60–1, 65, 67, 78, 81–2, 84, 128, 138, 152, 218–19, 226–7, 228–33, 239, 270
Ingush resettlement see Chechen-Ingush resettlement
International Brigade, 73, 75–6, 82, 86–7
International Relations Department (Отделение Международных Связей; OMS), 11
International Section (Иностранный отдел; INO), 29–31, 47, 51, 59, 72, 88

Johansson, Johan see Shorokhov, Afanasiy Mikhailovich
Junkers aircraft, 65

Kaji, Wataru, 238
Kalmyk resettlement, 224
Kalugin, Mikhail Alekseyevich, 101, 109, 112, 133
Karachay resettlement, 224
Karpov, Petr Mikhailovich, 11, 12, 14–15, 17–18, 21–2, 25, 27–8, 31, 33–5, 266
Kartseva, Yevdokiya Alekseyevna, 216–20, 223, 228, 238, 244–5, 247, 250–51, 270–71, 280
Kashtanov, Petr Vasilyevich, 101, 105, 108, 109, 118, 121–2
Katsnelson, Zinoviy Borisovich, 267
Katz, Joseph, 85
Kepp, Viktor see Prasolov, Yuriy Alekseyevich

Kerensky, Aleksandr Fedorovich, 14, 232, 240
KGB Wanted List number 21, 172, 178, 189
KGB Wanted List number 27, 216, 218–20, 227, 228, 250, 252, 270
KGB Wanted List number 55 *see* Grigoryev, Ivan Matveyevich
KGB Wanted List number 75, 103, 109, 120, 175, 273
KGB Wanted List number 81 *see* Grigoryev, Ivan Matveyevich
KGB Wanted List number 107*see* Abryutin, Yevgeniy Viktorovich
KGB Wanted List number 153 *see* Genrikh, Isaak Moiseyevich
KGB Wanted List number 278 *see* Bondarev, Nikolay Ivanovich
KGB Wanted List number 304 *see* Roze, Petr Berngardovich
KGB Wanted List number 307 *see* Ryabenko, Aleksandr Ivanovich
KGB Wanted List number 338 *see* Kirsanov, Aleksandr Stepanovich
KGB Wanted List number 367 *see* Marchenkov, Nikolay Ivanovich
Khokhlov, Nikolay Yevgenyevich, 216, 218–20, 225, 228–32, 239, 240, 241, 244, 249, 252
King, John Herbert, 58
Kirov, Sergey Mironovich, 271
Kirsanov, Aleksandr Stepanovich, 103, 109, 157
Kiselev (variant Kiselev-Gromov), Nikolay Ignatyevich, 12, 15, 17, 26–8, 35, 265
Kiselev, Vasiliy Grigoryevich, 101, 105, 109
Kislitsyn, Fillip Vasilyevich, 246
Komsomol, 15, 271
Kopatskiy, Aleksandr Grigoryevich, 102, 109, 122–3, 130–32, 229
Korean conflict, 244, 246, 250
Korniyevskiy, Vasiliy Pavlovich, 172, 173, 178, 188
Kovalchuk, Nikolay Kuzmich, 199
Kozhevnikov, Yevgeniy Mikhailovich, 12–13, 15, 21–2, 24–7, 30–2, 236
Kozlova, Miss, 238
Krajowa, Armija, 194
Kramish, Dr Arnold, 186
Krasnov, Vladislav Georgiyevich, 7–8
Kravchenko, Aleksandr Stepanovich, 172, 174–5, 177–8, 187, 189
Kravchenko, Viktor Andreyevich, 120
Krestinskiy, Nikolay Nikolayevich, 134
Krieger, Dr Arnold, 144, 152
Kristoffy, Jozsef, 126
Krivitsky, Walter Germanovich *see* Ginzberg, Samuel Gershovich

Krupp (German company), 64–5
Kulagin, Vladimir Vasilyevich, 103, 109, 190
Kulikov, Colonel, 149
Kurayev, Aleksandr Petrovich, 101, 109
Kurdistan, 153
Kutepov, Aleksandr Pavlovich, 29, 49, 88
Kwantung Army, 243
Kyodo News Agency, 247

Labour Union of Russian Solidarists (Народно-Трудовой Союз Русских Солидаристов; NTS), 148
Lapin, Nikolay Fedorovich, 101, 109, 121
League of Nations, 58, 196–7, 201
Lenin, Vladimir Ilych, 11, 45, 51–2, 68, 75, 108, 126, 271
Lester, Seán, 197
Levitsky, Maurice, 21
LIND (code name), 247
Lindström, Lars Edvin, 216, 218–20, 227–8, 230–31, 234, 250, 252, 270
Line SK, 236, 251
Linse, Dr Walter, 250
Lissner, Ernest J., 243
Little Entente, 33
Litvin, Zalman Volfovich, 82, 145, 152, 157
Lyalin, Oleg Adolfovich, 173
Lyushkov, Genrikh Samoilovich, 46, 47, 49–50, 53, 56, 65, 71, 78, 152, 268, 272

Ma Zhongying, 150
McGill University, 140
Maclean, Donald, 59–60, 85, 246
main enemy, 9, 56, 127, 134, 275–81
Main Information Department of the Polish Army (*Główny Zarząd Informacji Wojska Polskiego*), 149
Maly, Theodore Stephanovich, 58–9, 74, 81
Marchenkov, Nikolay Ivanovich, 172, 178, 187
Marcovitch, Aaron, 81
Massing, Hede, 86, 230
Melkishev, Pavel Petrovich, 139
Mercader, Ramón, 82
MI5 (British Security Service), 32, 57–60, 63–4, 73–4, 105, 138
Mikhailov, Pavel Petrovich *see* Melkishev, Pavel Petrovich
Mikheyev, Aleksandr Nikolayevich, 172, 175–6, 178–9, 185–6, 189–90, 195, 199, 269, 273, 278
Miller, Eduard, 12, 14–15, 23, 25–6, 35
Miller, Yevgeniy-Ludvig Karlovich, 30, 88
Milshteyn, Mikhail Abramovich, 156–7
Ministry of State Security (MGB), 2, 105, 121, 177, 179, 181–8, 190, 195–6,

198–200, 202–5, 219, 223–5, 227, 230, 232, 235, 236–8, 240–41, 243, 245, 246, 248, 251–2, 269, 273, 278, 288
Mitskevich, Colonel, 30
Mitsuhashi Masao, 238
MOLIERE (code name) *see* Melkishev, Pavel Petrovich
Molotov, Vyacheslav Mikhailovich, 52, 268
Molotov-Ribbentrop Pact, 52, 72–3, 124–5, 145–6, 193, 268
Mondich, Mikhail Dmitriyevich, 102, 109, 114, 122, 134, 143, 147–8, 175, 198, 201, 269, 273, 279
Moore, Leon *see* Helfand, Lev Borisovich
Morozov, Boris Alekseyevich, 102–4, 109–10, 115, 122
Morrison, James Douglas Finley, 227
Munich Accords, 79
Mussolini, Benito, 73, 78, 79
MVD (Ministry of Internal Affairs), 120, 176, 183, 198, 215, 218–19, 221, 223, 225–6, 233–4, 236, 238–9, 242–3, 269–70

Nachumsiedlung, 127
National Research Council (NRC), 140
National Security Council (NSC), 215, 217
NATO (North Atlantic Treaty Organization), 231, 235, 249
Nesterovich, Vladimir Stepanovich, 12–13, 15, 18–19, 25, 28–32, 49
Night of the Long Knives, 47, 72
Nikitin, Ivan, 12–13, 15, 20, 26, 28, 105
Nikolayev, Georgiy Petrovich *see* Akhmedov, Izmail Guseynovich
Nikolayev, Lev L. *see* Feldbin, Leyba Lazarevich
Nikolayevskiy, Boris Ivanovich, 122, 132
Norris, George, 34
Novikov, Nikolay Vasilyevich, 280
Nunn May, Alan, 129, 141

Office of Strategic Services (OSS), 54, 87, 273
OGPU (Unified State Political Directorate), 13, 16–17, 19–27, 29–33, 35, 37, 45, 47, 49, 56–8, 61, 63, 67, 70, 72, 76–7, 79–83, 87–8, 118, 145, 265–6, 287
Okhrana, 17, 28, 35
Okolovich, Georgiy Sergeyevich, 241
Oldham, Ernest Holloway, 58
Ollier, Rose-Marie (code name OLGA), 246
Operation Barbarossa, 100, 126, 128, 136
Operation HAGBERRY, 132
Operation RUSTY, 123
Operation ZEPPELIN, 107, 250
Oppenheimer, Robert, 141
Order of the Red Banner, 78, 202

Orlov, Aleksandr Mikhailovich *see* Feldbin, Leyba Lazarevich
Orlov, Igor Grigoryevich *see* Kopatskiy, Aleksandr Grigoryevich
Orlov, Vladimir Grigoryevich, 25, 34
Orlov, Vladimir Mitrofanovich, 59
Osintorf Brigade *see* Russian National People's Army
Ovakimyan, Gaik Badalovich, 82–4

Pasha, Enver, 29
Pavlov, Grigoriy Feodorovich, 215–20, 226, 228, 235, 250–51, 254, 270
Pečiulionis, Simas, 172, 176, 178, 188, 195, 198, 201–2, 229, 273, 279
People's Commissariat of Internal Affairs (NKVD), 2, 37, 45–7, 53, 58–61, 64, 73–6, 82–8, 105, 108, 111–12, 114, 118, 124, 126–8, 131, 134–5, 137, 142–3, 145–9, 151–4, 157, 174–7, 179–80, 185–6, 193–4, 196–7, 201–2, 219, 224–5, 234–6, 239, 247, 249–51, 267–8, 271–3, 276–7, 279, 287
People's Commissariat of State Security (NKGB), 129, 131, 135, 142, 147–9, 197, 218, 225, 243, 277, 287
Perlin, Sergey Naumovich, 103, 109, 149
Petrov, A. A. (pseudonym), 171–3, 175, 177–8, 180–82, 184, 187, 190–93, 196–7, 201–2
Petrov, Vladimir Mikhailovich *see* Shorokhov, Afanasiy Mikhailovich
Petrova, Yevdokiya Alekseyevna *see* Kartseva, Yevdokiya Alekseyevna
Pettersson, Jakob *see* Shorokhov, Afanasiy Mikhailovich
Philby, Harold A. R. 'Kim', 59, 61, 71, 73–4, 85, 105, 119–20, 138
Pieck, Henri Christiaan, 58, 74
Pines, Michael, 102, 109, 114, 130, 135, 137, 149, 269
Ploieşti oil fields (Romania), 126
Political Centre for the Struggle with Bolshevism (Политический центр борьбы с большевизмом; PTsB), 107
Pollitt, Harry, 61
Polyakova, Mariya Iosifovna, 138
Poretskiy, Natan Markovich, 46, 49–50, 52–3, 58–9, 65–6, 68–9, 73–4, 76, 87, 230, 267, 277
Potapov, Nikolay *see* Anokhin, Aleksandr Vladimirovich
Potsdam Declaration (1945), 144
Povarov, Konstantin Fedorovich, 101, 104, 109, 115, 131, 131, 133
Prasolov, Yuriy Alekseyevich, 21, 24

Rachkova, Margarita, 142
Radek, Karl Berngardovich, 69, 71
Radio Liberty, 122, 192
Raštikis, General Stasys, 203
Rastvorov, Yuriy Aleksandrovich, 150, 173, 215–18, 220, 224, 226, 228, 238, 241–4, 247–8, 250, 269–70, 279–80
Razvedupr (Intelligence Directorate of the Red Army Staff; Разведывательное Управление), 11, 18, 22–3, 29–30, 35, 45, 49, 56, 60–2, 65, 67–9, 73–5, 77, 80–4, 86, 88, 124–5, 127–8, 138–40, 152–4, 271, 276
RCMP (Royal Canadian Mounted Police), 82, 85, 227, 246
RDX (explosive), 140
Rebrov, [Aleksandr Nikolayevich?], 172, 178, 186, 187, 269
Red Orchestra see Rote Kapella
REDCAP, 189
Regensburg, Germany Intelligence School, 122
Reich Main Security Office (Reichssicherheitshauptamt; RSHA), 107
Reilly, Sidney, 32
Reiss, Ignatiy (Ignace) Stanislavovich see Poretskiy, Natan Markovich
Research Program on the USSR, 122, 155, 188, 235
Reval, Estonia, Bolshevik uprising, 30
Rola-Żymierski, Michał, 149
Romanov, A. I. see Baklanov, Boris Ivanovich
Roosevelt, Franklin Delano, 191, 196, 242
Rose, Fred, 81, 137, 139
Rosenberg, Simon A., 84
Rote Drei ('Red Three'), 138
Rote Kapella ('Red Orchestra'), 67
Round the World Trading Company, 82–3
Roze, Petr Berngardovich, 103, 109, 173, 175
Rubens, Adolph Arnold (code name EWALD), 81
Runge, Yevgeniy Yevgenyevich, 274
Russian All-Military Union (Русский Обще–Воинский Союз, ROVS), 87–8
Russian National People's Army (Русская Национальная Народная Армия; RNNA), 107, 115–16, 119
Russian Oil Products, 63
Russo-Finnish War, 111–12
Ryabenko, Aleksandr Ivanovich, 172, 177, 178, 187
Ryabtsev, Georgiy Petrovich, 102, 105, 109, 121

Sabatini, Amadeo, 87

St Nedelya Church, Sofia, Bulgaria, 18, 30
Salimanov, Georgiy Vasilyevich, 172–3, 178, 186–7, 193, 203–4, 269
Samusev, Georgiy Ivanovich, 172, 178, 188, 195, 197, 199, 203
San Francisco United Nations Conference, 143
Saracoğlu, Sukru, 154
Säre, Karl, 201
Schellenberg, Walter, 107
Scotland Yard, 57, 63
Second Bureau of the French General Staff, 88
Secret Intelligence Service (SIS), 22, 61–2, 66, 107, 121, 137–9, 186, 188, 200, 251, 253
Sedashov, Yuriy Ivanovich, 102, 109
Semenchenko, Vladimir, 237
Semenova, Viktoriya Grigoryevna, 122
Shanghai Municipal Police, 21–2, 32
Sharandak, Vasiliy Mikhailovich, 172, 176, 178–9, 185, 190, 200
Shelaputin, Vadim Ivanovich, 172–3, 178, 180, 184, 188, 192, 200, 236
Shell-Mex Oil Company, 63
Shii Masaji, 243–4, 248
Shoji Hiroshi, 243
Shorokhov, Afanasiy Mikhailovich, 216–21, 223, 226, 228, 232, 235–40, 244–7, 250–51, 253, 270–71, 276, 280–81
Shturm de Shtrem, Vitold, 29, 49
Shulman (FNU), 19, 266
Sidorovich, Michael, 87
Sipelgas, Aleksandr Yanovich, 12, 15, 18–19, 22, 25, 27–30, 33, 35, 265
Sivtsov, Nikolay Vasilyevich, 102, 109
Skachkov, Anatoliy Ignatiyevich, 217, 237
Skripkin, Vladimir Aleksandrovich, 61, 102–4, 109–10, 120, 173
Slutskiy, Abram Aronovich, 47, 59, 72
SMERSH, 105, 133–5, 148, 174–5, 181–2, 191, 194–5, 198, 279, 286
Smith, Durnford, 140
Sobolev, Aleksandr Aleksandrovich, 12, 14–15, 20, 23–5, 28, 35, 265, 271
Soboloff, David Semyonovich see Brik, Yevgeniy Vladimirovich
Socialist Revolutionaries (SRs), 13–14, 17, 28, 270
Soviet Planning Committee (GOSPLAN), 66
Sovietisation, 145–50, 171, 193, 195, 201, 238–9
Soyuzneft, 63
Spanish Civil War, 67, 73–6, 82, 86, 137
special sections (особые отделы; OO), 133, 151
Spychalski, Marian, 150

Stalin, Iosif Vissarionovich
  and Lenin's revolutionary ideal, 51–3, 70,
    73, 75, 267, 282
  and prisoners of war, 106
  counterfeiting US dollars, 76–7
  death and effects, 5, 54, 205, 215, 217–18,
    221, 226–8, 253
  defectors' desire to remove, 100, 107–8,
    115–18, 157
  industrialisation, 83–4
  reaction to defectors, 37
  relationship with Germany, 64, 66, 71–3,
    88, 193
  relationship with Italy, 78–9
  relationship with Japan, 67, 78
  relationship with Security Services, 3,
    58–9, 61, 65, 127, 136, 203
  relationship with UK, 56, 62, 138, 276
  relationship with World War II allies,
    135–6, 140, 196
  reported assassination plot, 133
  role in purges, 49, 76, 147, 224, 234, 272
  Russian nationalism under, 47
Stalin, Vasiliy Iosifovich, 223
Stankaitis, Bronius Antanovich, 216, 218–20,
  227
Stark, Adolph, 81
Stashinskiy, Bogdan Nikolayevich, 241
Stefens, 12, 15, 20, 25, 27–8, 265
Stein, Miguel (Mikhail) see Hendler, Mikhail
Stettinius, Edward, 142
Strategic Services Unit (SSU), 186–7
Streater, Isabel, 23, 26
Sudoplatov, Pavel Anatolyevich, 225,
  229–31, 239, 279

Takacs, Veronika Feodorovna, 172, 176–8,
  185, 189
Takamore Shigeru, 248
Treaty of Versailles, 69, 72
Trikoz, Aleksandr Yakovlevich, 102, 109
Trilisser documents, 31
Triple Entente (aka Big Entente), 33
Trotsky, Lev, 82, 193
Trotskyists, 49, 76, 78, 193
Tukhachevskiy, Mikhail Nikolayevich, 71,
  78, 111, 133
Tuomi, Kaarlo, 274

Ukhto-Pechorsk prison camps, 112
unknown, aka 'Vasiliy Petrovich' (1929), 12,
  15, 21, 22, 24–5
unknown, aka 'Vladimir' (1945), 102, 109
unknown defector (August 1926), 12–13, 28

Vainio, Khelge Eynarovich, 102, 105, 109
Vakhromeyev (FNU), 37
Vares, Johannes, 201–2
Vartanyan, Artak Armenakovich,
  140
Vinogradov, Sergey Aleksandrovich, 154
Vlasov, Andrey Andreyevich, 108, 117–19,
  134, 235
Voice of America, 54, 225
Voland, Professor, 200
Volkov, Konstantin Dmitriyevich, 61, 104,
  109, 114, 120, 138, 153, 173, 269
Volodarsky, Iosif Volfovich, 46, 50, 52–5,
  63, 81–6, 271
von Papen, Franz, 154
von Rintelen, Franz, 141
Vorontsov, Aleksandr Nikolayevich see
  Mikheyev, Aleksandr Nikolayevich
Voroshilov, Kliment Yefremovich, 59
Vyshinskiy, Andrey Yanuaryevich, 201

Weinstein, Marcus, 83
Weisband, William, 87
Werewolves (former Nazi cells), 195
Wieck, Lieselotte, 185
Wilgress, Dana, 137
Willkie, Wendell, 242
Willsher, Kathleen, 137
Wismut AG, 203–4, 277
Witczak, Ignacy Samuel see Litvin, Zalman
  Volfovich
Woikin, Emma, 149
World Tourists (American company), 80

Yagoda, Genrikh Grigoryevich, 47, 118
Yalta Agreements, 100, 182, 189, 191
Yalta Conference, 142
Yarkho, Colonel, 185
Yesenina, Lidiya Pavlovna, 102, 107, 109,
  113, 121, 124, 128–9, 146, 229, 271
Yezhov, Nikolay Ivanovich, 3, 45, 47, 51,
  53, 59, 64, 72, 74, 85, 111, 124

Zabotin, Nikolay Ivanovich, 150
Zasansky, (FNU), 150
Zhdanov, Andrey Aleksandrovich, 201–2
Zhiveinov, Nikolay (code name MARTIN),
  143
Zhigunov, Aleksandr Yakovlevich, 101,
  109–10, 115, 118, 121, 124–7, 133–4,
  137, 154, 193, 271
Zinovyev, Grigoriy Yevseyevich, 69

Printed and bound by CPI Group (UK) Ltd, Croydon, CR0 4YY

15/11/2024

01789278-0006